Asian Religions in British Columbia

Asian Religions and Society Series

Also in the series:

Pilgrims, Patrons, and Place: Localizing Sanctity in Asian Religions
Edited by Phyllis Granoff and Koichi Shinohara

Images in Asian Religions: Texts and Contexts
Edited by Phyllis Granoff and Koichi Shinohara

Gandhāran Buddhism: Archaeology, Art, and Texts
Edited by Kurt Behrendt and Pia Brancaccio

Japan's Modern Prophet: Uchimura Kanzô, 1861-1930
John F. Howes

American Missionaries, Christian Oyatoi, *and Japan, 1859-73*
Hamish Ion

Reforming Japan: The Woman's Christian Temperance Union in the Meiji Period
Elizabeth Dorn Lublin

Edited by Larry DeVries, Don Baker,
and Dan Overmyer

Asian RELIGIONS IN BRITISH COLUMBIA

UBCPress · Vancouver · Toronto

© UBC Press 2010

All rights reserved. No part of this publication may be reproduced, stored in a retrieval system, or transmitted, in any form or by any means, without prior written permission of the publisher, or, in Canada, in the case of photocopying or other reprographic copying, a licence from Access Copyright (Canadian Copyright Licensing Agency), www.accesscopyright.ca.

21 20 19 18 17 16 15 14 13 12 11 10   5 4 3 2 1

Printed in Canada -on FSC-certified ancient-forest-free paper (100% post-consumer recycled) that is processed chlorine- and acid-free.

Library and Archives Canada Cataloguing in Publication

Asian religions in British Columbia / edited by Larry DeVries, Don Baker, and Dan Overmyer.

(Asian religions and society, ISSN 1705-4761)
Includes bibliographical references and index.
ISBN 978-0-7748-1662-5 (bound); ISBN 978-0-7748-1663-2 (pbk.)

1. Asians – British Columbia – Religion. 2. British Columbia – Religion. I. DeVries, Larry, 1942- II. Baker, Don III. Overmyer, Daniel L., 1935- IV. Series: Asian religions and society series

BL2530.C3A85 2010   200'.89950711   C2010-900109-5

e-book ISBNs: 978-0-7748-1664-9 (pdf); 978-0-7748-5942-4 (epub)

Canada

UBC Press gratefully acknowledges the financial support for our publishing program of the Government of Canada through the Book Publishing Industry Development Program (BPIDP), and of the Canada Council for the Arts, and the British Columbia Arts Council.

UBC Press also gratefully acknowledges the support of the Institute of Asian Research at the University of British Columbia and the Universal Buddhist Temple.

Printed and bound in Canada by Friesens
Set in Adobe Garamond by Artegraphica Design Co. Ltd.
Copy editor: Frank Chow
Proofreader: Dianne Tiefensee

UBC Press
The University of British Columbia
2029 West Mall
Vancouver, BC V6T 1Z2
604-822-5959 / Fax: 604-822-6083
www.ubcpress.ca

Contents

Illustrations / vii

Preface / ix

Introduction / 1
Don Baker and Larry DeVries

Part 1: Traditions from South Asia

1 Hindu and Other South Asian Religious Groups / 17
  Larry DeVries

2 The Making of Sikh Space: The Role of the Gurdwara / 43
  Kamala Elizabeth Nayar

3 Religion, Ethnicity, and the Double Diaspora of Asian Muslims / 64
  Derryl N. MacLean

4 Zoroastrians in British Columbia / 85
  Rastin Mehri

Part 2: Traditions from Southeast Asia

5 Thai and Lao Buddhism / 107
  James Placzek and Ian G. Baird

6 Sri Lankan and Myanmar Buddhism / 124
  Bandu Madanayake

7 Vietnamese Buddhist Organizations / 141
   Cam Van Thi Phan (Thích nữ Trí Khả)

PART 3: TRADITIONS FROM EAST AND CENTRAL ASIA

8 Korean Religiosity in Comparative Perspective / 163
   Don Baker

9 Tibetan Religions / 184
   Marc des Jardins

10 Traditional and Changing Japanese Religions / 212
   Michael Newton

11 Christianity as a Chinese Belief / 233
   Li Yu

12 Chinese Religions / 249
   Paul Crowe

   Concluding Comments / 275
   Dan Overmyer

   Suggested Readings / 281

   Contributors / 286

   Index / 290

Illustrations

1.1 The Temple of Divine Light in Kootenay Bay / 22

1.2 The Victoria Hindu Parishad / 28

1.3 Interior of the South Okanagan Hindu Temple in Summerland / 31

3.1 The Ismaili Jamatkhana and Centre in Burnaby / 78

4.1 Plaque donated by the Zoroastrian Society of British Columbia to the people of British Columbia in 1971 / 86

4.2 A worshipper at the Dar-e Mehr (Court of Mithra) in Burnaby / 98

7.1 Interior of the Chân Nguyên Temple in Surrey / 147

7.2 The Vạn Hạnh Temple in Victoria / 150

8.1 The Vancouver Korean Presbyterian Church on Vancouver's West Side / 167

8.2 A Lutheran church in New Westminster that provides space for two Korean congregations / 169

8.3 Seogwangsa, a Korean Buddhist temple in Langley / 176

Preface

Our book is about a place, written by a group of people of that place, for the people of the place. The contributors to this book share not only the common thread of scholarship but also the experience of living and working here. Scholars of the Asian religions of British Columbia, their varied backgrounds reflect the diversity of the province. The editors extend our deepest gratitude to this dedicated and professional group of men and women for their hard work and keen ideas.

Our companions have been the people of British Columbia who, before the beginning of the province to the present moment, have come together to celebrate, to discuss, to share the traditions (and innovations) of the religions discussed in the book. During our research, these British Columbians have often been our hosts, our informants, our fellow citizens, and our friends. Many have literally fed us, and all have given us intellectual and sometimes spiritual sustenance. Some individuals are credited in chapter notes, but many who do not appear in these chapters have added to our understanding. To all of them, individuals and families, leaders and folk, wise elders and bouncing kids, we extend our heartfelt gratitude.

Our book would not have been possible without initial funding from the Institute of Asian Research at the University of British Columbia. The Institute also matched some modest contributions from Simon Fraser University and Langara College. Throughout the writing process, we have benefited from the wise counsel of Emily Andrew, senior editor at UBC Press. The Universal Buddhist Temple (世界佛教會) in Vancouver provided funding as well to cover publication expenses, with the intent of making a contribution to the understanding of our multicultural society (not, of course, as an endorsement of the multitude of practices described in this book).

Regarding the representation of the many languages found in this book, where there is a choice of methods, we have been guided by practicality and readability. We have often simplified words by omitting diacritics, but only when we believe that philologists will understand and that others won't mind. Where we have found it desirable to retain more complex styles of representation, we hope that the accuracy of the record offsets any inconvenience to the non-specialist. Citations of sources, diverse in kind, have likewise been made with simplicity and practicality in mind.

Asian Religions in British Columbia

Introduction
Don Baker and Larry DeVries

The three co-editors of this volume have spent most of our professional careers studying Asian religions in Asia. When travelling around the southwest corner of the British Columbia mainland, however, we could not help but note that much of the religious activity that we have studied overseas has become increasingly visible right here in the province. Indeed, over the last three decades, the Vancouver metropolitan area has been transformed into a truly multicultural community.

This will be obvious to anyone who looks to the west while driving through the city of Richmond on Highway 99. Along No. 5 Road, running parallel to the highway and called by some the "highway to heaven," are a number of religious schools and houses of worship that serve many of Vancouver's ethnic groups with roots in Asia: a gurdwara for the Sikh community, the Ram Krishna Mandir Vedic Cultural Society for Hindus, the Az-Zahraa Islamic Centre for Shia Muslims (the Jami'a Mosque, for Sunni Muslims, is nearby, just off No. 5 Road), the Ling Yen Mountain Temple for Chinese Buddhists, and the Richmond Chinese Evangelical Free Church. The Fujian Evangelical Church, with a predominantly Filipino Chinese congregation, sits close to No. 5 Road, around the corner from the Vedic Cultural Society.

Evidence of the Asian impact on British Columbia is no less visible elsewhere in the Lower Mainland. Sikh and Buddhist temples, mosques, and Chinese, Japanese, and Korean churches are found all over the southwest corner of the province. Asian restaurants abound. Both the new Chinatown along No. 3 Road in Richmond and the old Chinatown in downtown Vancouver are famous for the quality and variety of their cuisine. When British Columbians want a taste of India, they head for Main Street in Vancouver. And North Road, running between Burnaby and Coquitlam, has grown during the last decade into a magnet for those who love spicy Korean food.

We mention food because it is one of the two features of immigrants' home culture that are most resistant to change. The other, of course, is religion. By the third generation, hyphenated Canadians are usually no longer fluent in the language of their forebears, and family dynamics tend to become Canadianized over time, but cuisine and religion survive. In fact, they often go together, since after Sunday services many houses of worship offer their congregations food in the style of their countries of origin. Such communal meals serve to affirm the ethnic solidarity of those who partake, or to commit the group to the beliefs, values, and practices of the ethno-religious community identified with a particular type of food.

The persistence of both cuisine and religion is not unique to communities with roots in Asia; for example, Italians, Greeks, and, more recently, Africans have contributed to the religious and culinary landscape of British Columbia. In this book, however, we focus on Asian Canadian communities, for several reasons. In the percentage of its population with roots in Asia, not only is the Greater Vancouver area one of the most Asian metropolitan areas in continental North America but British Columbia itself leads the nation (along with Ontario) in the multicultural character of its citizens. Moreover, the province has some of the oldest substantial Asian communities outside Asia. For example, Victoria has the oldest Chinatown in Canada, second in North America only to that of San Francisco.

According to the 2006 census, out of a total population of a little over 4 million in British Columbia, there were 432,435 Chinese (plus 10,565 who identify themselves as Taiwanese), 274,205 South Asians (including 7,975 Pakistanis, 4,150 Sri Lankans, and 570 Nepalis), 94,250 Filipinos, 51,860 Koreans, 41,585 Japanese, and 30,835 Vietnamese, plus Cambodians, Laotians, Indonesians, Malaysians, Mongolians, and Tibetans.[1] The vast majority of this Asian Canadian population lives in the Greater Vancouver metropolitan area. Vancouver is almost 30 percent Chinese, Richmond 43.6 percent (making Richmond the most Chinese mid-sized city in North America). Surrey is over 27 percent South Asian and around 5 percent Chinese; Burnaby, on the other hand, is 30 percent Chinese and 8 percent South Asian. Coquitlam, to round out the list of cities in the Vancouver metropolitan area with large Asian populations, is 17 percent Chinese, as well as 5 percent Korean and 3.6 percent South Asian. The many East Asians, South Asians, and Filipinos and other Southeast Asians living in Richmond make up 60 percent of the population, making it a majority Asian city. Burnaby was 49 percent Asian in the 2006 census, but immigration trends suggest that it has passed the 50 percent mark by now. Vancouver was not far behind at 46 percent Asian.[2]

Parallel to this, Asian religious groups have also burgeoned, with the greatest growth by far being seen in the Lower Mainland. A list maintained by Larry

DeVries shows about 250 Asian religious groups in British Columbia, of which nearly two-thirds are in Vancouver or vicinity. Most of the nearly 40 groups in the BC Interior are either Sikh, reflecting their early presence in the resource industries, or Buddhist, for diverse reasons such as the relocation of Japanese Canadians during the Second World War as well as the diffusion of especially Zen and Tibetan Buddhism among Euro-Canadians. Another 40 or so Asian religious groups are located on Vancouver Island as well as the smaller islands and the Sunshine Coast. Here also, Buddhist and Sikh groups are in the majority, but, unlike in the Interior, there are more of the former than the latter. There is hardly an area of the province without an Asian religious presence; even the British Properties in West Vancouver, established as an ethnic bastion, has recently become host to a Buddhist group, while the region of Kelowna, one of the province's least ethnically diverse cities, is home to a temple established by Buddhist nuns from Taiwan as well as to the Interior's only ethnic Hindu temple.

British Columbia and its Lower Mainland did not look like this forty or even thirty years ago. Canada began changing its immigration laws in the 1960s to eliminate the preference for Europeans that had been so strong previously. In addition, the adoption by the Trudeau government in 1971 of an official policy of multiculturalism made immigrants from Asia feel more welcome here. The result has been a surge of immigrants from all across Asia that has not only widened the range of culinary choices available to British Columbians but also greatly diversified the province's religious landscape.

The transformation of British Columbia by Asians and Asian religions occurred in three major stages. The first wave of Asians came from the United States in 1858, in the form of gold seekers from California who arrived in Victoria by steamer. The 450 men included, according to a journalistic chronicle, "only 60 ... British subjects," in a milieu where "Negroes, Kanakas, Chinese, Jews, Frenchmen, Englishmen, Germans, and other nationalities" were to congregate.[3] Their entry into an essentially British, colonial, class society virtually created by private enterprise (the Hudson's Bay Company) introduced two pertinent and persistent themes in the province's history, namely, extremely rapid growth through immigration and frictions based on class and place of origin.

The resource-extraction export economy boomed, with a peak in immigration in the last decade of the nineteenth and first decade of the twentieth centuries.[4] It was during this period that the "elders" of BC Asian societies were formed – the Chinese, Japanese, and South Asians, largely Punjabis. As a reflection of this, we now find, respectively, the Tanggong Miao, established in Victoria in 1876;[5] the Vancouver Buddhist Church (Jōdo Shinshū), founded in 1905; and the Vancouver Sikh gurdwara, founded in 1908 (a surviving gurdwara from 1911 in Abbotsford was recently designated a national historic site).[6] Adding to religious diversity in the Kootenay region were the Doukhobors, who arrived in 1908, and the Mennonites, who arrived in 1911, with later Mennonites coming from Russia to settle in the Fraser Valley in the 1920s. Ethnic segregation was the rule, perhaps best exemplified by separate camps for Japanese, Chinese, South Asians, and whites in the company towns of various resource industries.[7] In fact, anti-Asian race riots in Vancouver (as well as in Washington state, just over the border) were an important factor leading to Sikh migrations to California's Central Valley.

Despite these multicultural beginnings, British Columbia famously wended its way through the first half of the twentieth century as a "White Man's Province" (the title of one of three books on the topic by University of Victoria professor emerita Patricia Roy). The British majority decreased as the continental European percentage grew, but Asian exclusion resulted in the low point in immigration from Asia in 1961.[8] The mid-1950s to mid-1970s saw rapid development in free enterprise, megaprojects, and parallel unionization[9] with persistent class polarization. Two major universities opened in the mid-1960s, the Swami Radha group was founded in British Columbia in 1957, and the first class in Buddhism was offered at the University of British Columbia in 1964.[10] Although the province removed the ethnic voting barrier in 1947-52, it has generally lagged behind other provinces in social reforms such as women's suffrage and, until 2007, elimination of age discrimination. Racist practices continued in such areas as the British Properties until 1954, while racist labour laws persisted until 1968, long after they had been abolished elsewhere in Canada.[11]

But change was imminent, at least in policy. Although immigration had reflected a preference for Britons and Europeans (especially Northern Europeans), practice changed in 1962 and was replaced with a policy based on skill sets (the point system) in 1967, following a similar US liberalization in 1965. Alan B. Simmons describes the transition as one from "official colonial racism" to "widespread informal racism in civil society."[12] (In Chapter 4, Rastin Mehri shows how this attitude led to a negative reaction in 1985 to a proposed Zoroastrian temple in West Vancouver, just down the street from the British Properties.) A further complexity was added to the social makeup of the province in the 1960s and 1970s by the arrival of an extraordinary number of Vietnam War resisters from the United States, many of whom became Canadian academics, artists, and professionals. This second time period seems to be a time of transition, with rapid change on the ground offset by social conservatism. Here we find the establishment of such diverse groups as the Konkō Church of Vancouver, the Shree Sanatan Dharam Ramayana Mandali of Fiji, and the British Columbia Muslim Association, all in 1966; the Vivekananda Vedanta Society of British Columbia, begun informally in 1967 with connections to Seattle; and the International Society for Krishna Consciousness (ISKON) centre in

British Columbia, formed "in 1969 [when] two of Srila Prabhupada's disciples came up from San Francisco."[13] Both the Zen Centre of Vancouver, established in 1970, and the Dharmasara Satsang Society, established in 1974, also have strong connections to California. The West Coast and Asia thus continued to have an impact on BC society.

The third stage in the arrival of Asian worldviews in British Columbia can aptly be titled after a speech by Prime Minister Brian Mulroney, "Multiculturalism Means Business."[14] A slightly earlier Business Immigration program was reworked in 1984 and extended in 1986 to actively attract immigrant capital in the "business" and "investor" classes. In the period 1978-2001, international immigration to British Columbia rose from a low of 6,836 to a peak of 47,965 in 1996/97. Taking the year 2001 as normative, over three-quarters of these immigrants were most recently established residents (a census category) of Asia. Immigration to the province from overseas in the investor class peaked in the years 1993 and 1994, with 6,867 and 6,292, respectively. The "entrepreneur" class reached levels of 4,072 in 1993, 4,172 in 1994, and 4,231 in 1996.[15] Thus, investment in the province by immigrant Asians rose substantially, especially in the mid-decade before 2000. Since well over 90 percent made their homes in the Vancouver area on arriving in British Columbia, it is not difficult to connect this with the building of the province's largest Buddhist temples in Vancouver suburbs: the Japanese Jōdoshū Tozenji in 1989 in Coquitlam, the Taiwanese/Hong Kong Pure Land Ling Yen Mountain Temple in 1999 in Richmond, and the Korean Chogye Buddhist Seogwangsa in 2001 in Langley.

The highly visible "Asian mall" phenomenon, studied by David Lai, also developed at this time. Such development had begun in the 1980s in the Vancouver suburb of Richmond, leading to forty-nine "Asia-themed" malls in 2000 and spreading also to Burnaby, Surrey, and Port Coquitlam, as well as augmenting Vancouver's Chinatown.[16] In the 1970s and 1980s, a much smaller area of South Vancouver was developed as the "Punjabi Market" (with Punjabi and English street signs),[17] along with a similar area on the border of Surrey and North Delta designated as the "Punjabi Bazaar." Don Baker reports that most Korean stores used to be located along the highly multicultural Kingsway, running from Vancouver's Main Street through Burnaby to New Westminster. Starting with one Korean supermarket in 2000, however, an area along North Road (the border between Burnaby and Coquitlam) has developed until there are strip malls filled with various types of Korean shops, including medical and dental clinics, Korean lawyers' offices, pubs, travel agencies, bakeries, restaurants, coffee shops, video shops, insurance offices, and so on, spread along three blocks, with many Korean shops adjacent to the main area. Korean shopping areas are also found in Vancouver and Port Coquitlam.

Given this growing contribution of communities with roots in Asia to the economic, social, and cultural life of British Columbia, we felt that it is important to learn more about these communities and how they are helping to make the province, in the words of Tourism BC, "the best place on earth." One way to do so is by exploring the role that Asian religious organizations play in British Columbia today. This is the path we have chosen.[18]

By Asian religious organizations we mean both those whose members are predominantly ethnically Asian and those that have mostly "convert" members but have their roots in Asia and maintain strong ties to Asia. Including both types of organizations in our study enables us to discuss both the role of religious organizations in fortifying ethnic solidarity and the ways in which they add new elements to an already diverse religious culture in Canada's Pacific Rim province.

Most of the BC communities surveyed in this volume consist primarily of people with Asian roots who are affiliated with a religious tradition that is a significant part of their ancestral culture. Because the rise in Asian immigration to British Columbia began only relatively recently, many in such communities are first-generation immigrants. For example, most of the Chinese Buddhists introduced by Paul Crowe in Chapter 8, the Sikhs discussed by Kamala Nayar in Chapter 2, and the Muslims introduced by Derryl MacLean in Chapter 3 represent recent Asian contributions to the globalization of BC culture. Such contributions, however, are not the only Asian religious influence on cultural diversification in the province.

In our research, we also found non-Asian converts to Asian religions, such as practitioners of Hinduism who are of European ancestry (discussed by Larry DeVries in Chapter 1) and non-Tibetan members of Tibetan Buddhist organizations (discussed by Marc des Jardins in Chapter 9). There are Asian congregations in traditional Western religious groups too. Don Baker and Li Yu (in Chapters 8 and 11, respectively) found sizable vibrant Christian communities that were predominantly Chinese, Korean, or Filipino, which, in most cases, were as culturally Asian as their Buddhist, Hindu, Zoroastrian, or Sikh counterparts. They, too, are manifestations of religious globalization in our multicultural environment.

Before proceeding further with our discussion of the Asian component of religious and ethnic diversity in British Columbia, we should define the terms "ethnicity" and "religion." Both are often used but almost never defined, mainly because it is difficult to come up with definitions for either term that are specific enough to be meaningful while being general enough to encompass all the phenomena that each is intended to refer to.

We should begin with the term "religion," since the focus of this book is Asian religious communities. Most of the congregations discussed here focus on interaction with God or with gods through prayer and rituals, whereas others focus on stilling the mind through meditation, with little or no reference to a deity. Some of the groups we studied are led by trained, certified clergy, whereas others have no formal clergy at all. How can we justify calling both types of groups "religious"?

DeVries states in Chapter 1 that religion is "a kind of language ... an instrument of expression, communication, and contemplation." Seen as such, religion refers less to beliefs about the supernatural, to ethical codes, or even to rituals per se than it does to the affirmation of shared beliefs and values through regular group activities such as rituals and through declarations of such beliefs and values. In this book, we consider such affirmations to be religious, and those who meet regularly to make such affirmations to be religious communities.

Obviously, not all group expression of shared beliefs is religious. We would not normally consider a group's declaration of its belief that the Vancouver Canucks will win the Stanley Cup to be religious. Nor are all regular group activities religious. Playing golf with the same group of friends every Saturday morning would not normally be considered a religious activity. What sets religious communities apart from other groups is their assumption that they are engaged in activities that rise above everyday, mundane concerns, whether they are interacting with supernatural beings or trying to quiet the normal noise of the mind. Whether they are praying or meditating, they feel that what they are doing is qualitatively different from shopping for groceries, working at a desk, or skiing down the slopes of Whistler Mountain. Moreover, coming together regularly with like-minded individuals in order to engage in communal rituals creates a strong sense of being part of an in-group, almost like an extended family, albeit one united not by blood but by its distinctive beliefs, practices, and values. Many such communities affirm their conviction that their particular group is distinctive and special by applying to it the label "religious." In this book, we accept this self-designation, and we also consider as religious a few communities that, although they may not explicitly refer to themselves as such, nevertheless behave in ways so similar to consciously religious communities that they arguably fall into the same category.

Most, though not all, of the religious communities examined in this book are what might be called "ethno-religious communities." They are communities of people who not only share the same religious beliefs, values, and practices but are also mostly members of a single ethnic group. One of the themes running through most of the chapters is this interplay of religiosity and ethnicity. Thus, we need to explain what we mean by "ethnicity."

We prefer the term "ethnic group" to "race." As physical anthropologists point out, there is so much overlap in biological characteristics within the various communities that share a major region of the world that there is no physical basis for dividing the peoples within East Asia, South Asia, or Southeast Asia into different races. What criteria do we use, therefore, to distinguish one ethnic group from another?

We could base ethnic labels on political identity, on the political entity that people migrated from or where their ancestral home is, and this would enable us to distinguish, for example, Japanese from Chinese, Vietnamese from Thais, and Indians from Pakistanis. It is not always possible to identify an ethnic community with a national community, however. For example, Sri Lankan Buddhists tend to see themselves as ethnically distinct from Sri Lankan Tamils. The Sikh organizations in British Columbia attract Punjabis but few members with roots in the rest of India. Moreover, not all Punjabis in British Columbia are Sikhs. Relying on a narrow political criterion would also make it difficult to differentiate Parsees, discussed in Chapter 4, from other peoples from India.

What about language, then? One feature of most ethno-religious communities is that the preferred language of their religious services is the language of the home country rather than English. In the case of Chinese, however, we find more than one Chinese dialect being used by Chinese ethno-religious communities. Moreover, although Cantonese and Mandarin are usually called dialects, they actually function as different languages in that they are mutually unintelligible. Yet, Chinese, whether they speak Mandarin or Cantonese, consider themselves to be members of the same Chinese community.

Language as a defining criterion also falls short when we discuss ethno-religious communities of the children or grandchildren of immigrants from Asia. Although those in the second generation usually speak and understand some of the language that their parents use, they are often not fluent enough to feel comfortable at a religious service conducted only in that language. Those in the third generation are even less likely to speak the language of their ancestors. Thus, if we use language as a defining criterion of ethnicity, we would have to deny the label "Chinese" to most third-, fourth-, and fifth-generation Chinese Canadians; nor could we call "Japanese" the Pure Land Buddhist temples that are frequented by Japanese Canadians who don't speak Japanese (discussed by Michael Newton in Chapter 10). Relying on language as a criterion for ethno-religious identity would also cause problems when we talk about Filipinos. They are the third largest Asian ethnic community in Canada, after Chinese and South Asian, but English shares national-language status with Filipino in the Philippines and many Filipinos, including the immigrants themselves, feel at home with English. In fact, only one of the many Roman Catholic Masses celebrated for Filipino congregations in the Lower Mainland every month is regularly conducted in Tagalog. The rest are in English.

Despite the difficulty of finding one objective definition of ethnicity that applies to all the ethnic groups discussed in this book, we still use that term simply because many of the religious groups with Asian roots that we studied use ethnic labels to refer to themselves and their organizations. As with the term "religion," we rely heavily on self-identification rather than on any narrow linguistic, political, or physical criteria.

Even with such a flexible understanding of ethnicity, we found that not all the religious communities we studied could be defined in ethnic terms. Thus, we have to distinguish ethnic communities such as those who congregate in Korean and Chinese churches and Vietnamese Buddhist temples from non-ethnic communities such as Tibetan Buddhist groups. They play different roles in society.

Ethnically defined religious organizations have several secular functions besides satisfying the religious needs of their members. First, they provide opportunities for new Canadians to meet regularly with those who speak the same language that they speak, eat the same food that they eat, and have basically the same beliefs and values that they have. Second, they provide a venue for immigrants to reaffirm their ethnic identity in the midst of the cultural and ethnic mosaic that is Canada. In fact, they may even strengthen an ethnic identity that was simply assumed in the mother country but that is highlighted in contrast with other ethnicities in Canada. Third, they give members of immigrant communities an opportunity to attain high-status positions, such as elder in a Korean church, that might be difficult for them to achieve in Canadian society at large. Finally, they provide an avenue for promoting ethnic consciousness in the children and grandchildren of immigrants, through the nature of the religious community, the language used in its services, and the types of events that are celebrated by the community (which often include secular as well as religious holidays from the old country). Ethno-religious communities can be powerful tools for reminding the second and third generations where their ancestral roots lay.

In addition to the mono-ethnic religious communities that comprise most of the groups discussed in this book, there are what can be called multi-ethnic religious communities in British Columbia. For example, the Islamic community, discussed in Chapter 3, is divided more along sectarian than ethnic lines. Those who frequent the Sunni mosques come from a wide range of countries and linguistic communities. There is no specifically Pakistani mosque, for example, and Pakistanis and Arabs may worship side by side with Indonesians or Malaysians. Similarly, Shia mosques attract Muslims from a variety of national and linguistic backgrounds. Islam in British Columbia is mainly Asian, since most active Muslims are of Asian, primarily South Asian, ancestry, but it encompasses many different ethnic Asian groups, speaking different languages at home and considering different nations as their ancestral homelands. It cannot, therefore, be considered a mono-ethnic community.

Nevertheless, the various mosques and Islamic associations in British Columbia have one thing in common with many mono-ethnic organizations. They all reinforce a distinctive identity for their members within mainstream Canadian society. They provide a supportive community for those who want to maintain their specific Asian religious identity. They help Muslims remain Muslims, for example, despite pressures toward conformity in what is still predominantly a Christian society, at least culturally. (Thirty-five percent of British Columbians say they have no religious affiliation; most of the rest say that they are Catholic, Anglican, or Protestant.)[19]

The link between ethnicity and religious affiliation may be tenuous in the case of Muslims, but it is almost totally absent from a few other communities in British Columbia that are centred on religions with roots in Asia. Tibetan Buddhism is one example. There are only about 100 Tibetans living in British Columbia but, according to Marc des Jardins, a third of all Buddhist centres in the province are associated with Tibetan Buddhism. Obviously, most "Tibetan" Buddhists in British Columbia are not Tibetan. Some are Chinese, but many others are of European background. Vietnamese Buddhism has, along with its many temples for Vietnamese practitioners, a Mindfulness Practice Centre that looks to a Vietnamese monk living in France for guidance but that has a predominantly non-Vietnamese membership. The Japanese new Buddhist organization Sōka Gakkai has more non-Japanese than Japanese adherents in British Columbia. Even Hinduism has a non-ethnically South Asian component. DeVries points out in Chapter 1 that the first "Hindu" community in the province was founded by a German Swami! Also, both the Daoist group Fung Loy Kok and the new Chinese religion Falun Gong have attracted many non-Chinese practitioners.

Despite these examples of religious organizations originating in Asia that have attracted many non-Asian members in British Columbia, ethnic, linguistic, and cultural affinity usually overrides shared religious beliefs and values and splits religious communities into ethnic enclaves. Because many Asian religious organizations also serve as cultural organizations, as ways to affirm and promote a specific ethnic identity, they are often composed primarily of members of one ethnic group. We see this even within religions that claim to be world religions rather than national religions. For example, Chapters 8 and 11 show that Asian Christian communities divide along ethnic lines, with Chinese Christians attending churches frequented by other Chinese, Koreans attending churches with mostly Korean congregations, and Filipinos flocking on Sundays to churches where other Filipino Christians gather. We find the same phenomenon with Buddhism, as evidenced by the separate chapters on Chinese, Japanese, Vietnamese, Thai and Laotian, and Sri Lankan and Myanmar Buddhism. There is little indication of a shared Buddhist affiliation drawing together those communities separated by differences in ethnicity. Besides the role of religious communities in affirming a separate and distinct ethnic identity, cultural differences in the roles of religious leaders, in the rituals that they and lay practitioners perform, and in the language used in those rituals keep communities apart even if they share the same general religious affiliation.

Asian religious groups continue to diversify. The year 2000 saw the establishment of three unique Hindu groups in southwestern British Columbia: the Fraser Valley Hindu Society in Abbotsford (a city that is also home to the province's newest university program in South Asian Studies, at the University of the Fraser Valley); Shri Durga Bhameshwari Mandir in Surrey, one of British Columbia's other burgeoning cities and winner of the 2008 Cultural Capital of Canada Award; and Arul Migu Thurkadevi Hindu Society (BC), with its distinctive connections to Hawaii and Sri Lanka. The past decade has also seen the development of multi-ethnic Buddhist groups such as the Shinzanji Heart Mountain Temple in 1999 in Victoria, with unique British Columbia – Japan connections; the Mountain Rain Zen Community on Vancouver's ethnically diverse south Fraser Street in 2002, in association with US groups; and the Sherab Chamma Ling Tibetan Bon Buddhist Centre in 2003 at Courtenay on Vancouver Island, with Canada's first Bön priest.

So, in what sort of place do these Asian religious groups find themselves? When Larry DeVries studied Buddhist groups in 2004, he observed gloomily that in Vancouver they were virtually an exclusively "east side" phenomenon. This fits very neatly with John Porter's demonstration in *The Vertical Mosaic* (1965) that Canada is a class-based society in which non-establishment groups such as immigrants are systematically absorbed and remain at lower levels of social and economic mobility. Even with the addition of the business and investor immigration categories, one can argue that class distinctions persist. We would like to take a different tack, however, and end with a brief reflection on the direction of Asian religious groups in British Columbia.

In Chapter 3, Derryl MacLean detects a growing congruence between realization of the *ummah*, a Muslim term for an ideal society, and the multicultural society developing in the province. In other words, the policies and the social fact of multiculturalism have made possible initiatives to create conditions inherent in the ideals of the religious groups. In Chapter 6, Bandu Madanayake finds that the religious ideals held by the Buddhist groups he studied are quite consistent with generally held Canadian values. In Chapter 8, Don Baker points out the value of ethnic religious groups as a positive social resource in a multicultural society, while cautioning that mere passive tolerance can be fragmenting unless augmented by an active effort to understand and resolve cultural differences and create a "healthy diversity." A few recent examples will suffice to show this kind of healthy diversity in action.

- The Fraser Valley Buddhist Temple (Jōdo Shinshū) officially reopened on 3 October 2004, after the original temple was destroyed by fire in 2002.[20] In the interim, the temple's Japanese-language school was housed first in the Church of Jesus Christ of Latter-day Saints on Blueridge Drive (also neighbour to Abbotsford's newest Sikh gurdwara), then was invited in by the Seventh-day Adventist Church, which saw the opportunity to make "some wonderful new friends."[21]
- The Radha Yoga and Eatery, at the heart of Vancouver's Downtown Eastside is a reincarnation of the original Radha House located in upscale Marine Drive in Burnaby. Since December 2004, the Radha group has brought not only the Shivananda tradition but also organic cuisine and local musicians and artists to a part of town known for its poverty and social problems. In short, Radha Yoga is a good neighbour.
- The Avatamsaka Monastery Meditation Centre (Hoa Nghiêm Temple) was established in the Fraser Valley community of Mission by Venerable Master Thích Nguyên Thảo. Founded in 2000 with many years' worth of donations from its congregation, the temple was put up for sale in early 2005 and the proceeds were donated to the Canadian Red Cross to help the victims of the 26 December 2004 tsunami in Asia.[22]

As noted earlier, ethnic relations in Canada have been guided since 1971 by an official policy of multiculturalism. The policy attempts to create a national community that is inclusive while recognizing linguistic and ethnic differences within Canadian society. This book addresses the question of how well this policy has worked. African Americans have long pointed out that, in the United States, the most segregated hour of the week is 10:00 a.m. on Sunday morning, when most churches have services. Is the same true of Canada? Do Asian religious organizations help people of Asian ethnicity, especially recent immigrants, feel a part of the Canadian national community, as the foregoing examples suggest? Or do they reinforce a division of Canadian society into separate and distinct ethnic communities? If the latter is true, is it a problem that we should worry about, or is it a positive phenomenon that contributes to the multicultural mosaic that we Canadians like to brag about?

The chapters that follow will help answer these questions. They discuss in their own ways the historical backgrounds, social contexts, and manifestations of the religious traditions represented by various communities in British Columbia, and the relationship of these religious communities to Canadian society and multiculturalism. Our goal is not just to describe the diversity of religious life in the province but also to draw attention to what we have in common. Where relevant, the authors discuss significant similarities and differences between the communities surveyed in their chapters and other groups described in this book. The result is a portrait of the mosaic that is British Columbia, in which many diverse cultural and religious elements have come together to form the multicultural society that makes Canada's Pacific province such a comfortable and interesting place in which to live.

NOTES

1. http://www12.statcan.ca/english/census06/data/highlights/ethnic/pages/. Statistics Canada information is used with the permission of Statistics Canada. Users are forbidden to copy the data and redisseminate them, in an original or modified form, for commercial purposes, without permission from Statistics Canada. Information on the availability of the wide range of data from Statistics Canada can be obtained from Statistics Canada's Regional Offices, its World Wide Web site at http://www.statcan.ca, and its toll-free access number, 1-800-263-1136.
2. http://www12.statcan.ca/english/census06/data/profiles/community.
3. Harry Gregson, *A History of Victoria, 1842-1970* (Victoria, BC: Victoria Observer, 1970), 12-13.
4. Immigrant Voices, http://www.canadianhistory.ca/iv/.
5. David Chuenyan Lai, *The Forbidden City within Victoria* (Victoria, BC: Orca Book Publishers, 1991), 60-68. See also Chapter 12.
6. Immigrant Voices, http://www.canadianhistory.ca/iv/. See Chapter 2.
7. Patricia Roy and John Herd Thompson, *British Columbia: Land of Promises* (Toronto: Oxford University Press, 2005), 109. Many well-known incidents of discrimination of this period, such as the "head tax," Asian exclusion in both immigration and labour, the *Komagata Maru* incident, and Japanese internment, are treated in this keenly analytical source.
8. Veronica Strong-Boag, "Society in the Twentieth Century," in *The Pacific Province: A History of British Columbia*, ed. Hugh J.M. Johnston (Vancouver: Douglas and McIntyre, 1996), 277.
9. Jean Barman, *The West beyond the West: A History of British Columbia* (Toronto: University of Toronto Press, 1996), 284.
10. Daniel L. Overmyer, "Glowing Coals: The First Twenty-five Years of the Department of Asian Studies at the University of British Columbia, 1960-1985," *BC Asian Review, UBC 75th Anniversary Issue* 3/4 (1990): 8.
11. Aprodicio A. Laquian, Eleanor R. Laquian, and T.G. McGee, eds., *The Silent Debate: Asian Immigration and Racism in Canada* (Vancouver: Institute of Asian Research, University of British Columbia, 1998), 8.
12. Ibid., 35.
13. Temple brochure.
14. Katharyne Mitchell, *Crossing the Neoliberal Line: Pacific Rim Migration and the Metropolis* (Philadelphia: Temple University Press, 2004), 204.
15. BC STATS and Statistics Canada websites as cited above for years 1978-2001.
16. David Chuenyan Lai, "Chinese: The Changing Geography of the Largest Visible Minority," in *British Columbia, the Pacific Province: Geographical Essays*, ed. Colin J.B. Wood (Victoria, BC: Western Geographical Press, 2001), 147-74.

17 "Harry Lali's Motion Asking for 'Punjabi Market-Langara Station' (RAV) Carries Unanimously," *VoiceOnline.Com*, 6 May 2006, http://www.voiceonline.com/voice/060506.
18 For a complementary approach, see Paul A. Bramadat, and David Seljak, eds., *Religion and Ethnicity in Canada* (Toronto: Pearson Longman, 2005), the plan for which appears to rest on Harold B. Barclay, Harold G. Coward, and Leslie S. Kawamura, eds., *Religion and Ethnicity: Essays* (Waterloo, ON: Wilfrid Laurier University Press, 1978). Both books highlight certain themes, such as gender and generational relations, and complement our focus on the more or less public presence of religious organizations. The Canadian studies, including this book, can be read in the context of what has become an established field of Asian American studies, in which some sociologists of religion have queried ethnicity, transnational movements, immigration, and settlement, and aimed to redress an often-stated lack of religion in such studies. See most recently Richard D. Alba, Albert J. Raboteau, and Josh DeWind, eds. *Immigration and Religion in America: Comparative and Historical Perspectives* (New York: New York University Press, 2009). Synthesis of these and emerging, more global studies remains a desideratum.
19 2001 Census Profile: British Columbia, http://www.bcstats.gov.bc.ca/data/cen01/profiles.
20 *The Light of the Buddha*, newsletter of the Steveston Buddhist Temple, Richmond, BC, September 2004, http://www.sbt.shawbiz.ca.
21 Bill Gerber, "FVAA New Home to Fraser Valley Japanese Language School," British Columbia Adventist Conference, 11 June 2003, http://www.bcalive.ca/artman/publish.
22 This article was widely distributed over the Internet. One source is "Canadian Temple Offers Proceeds to Red Cross," *Peace, Earth and Justice News*, 6 January 2005, http://www.pej.org.

PART I
Traditions from South Asia

Hindu and Other South Asian Religious Groups

Larry DeVries

> *draṣṭum icchāmi te rūpam aiśvaraṃ puruṣottama*
> "I wish to see your Divine Form, O Supreme Person."
> – (*Bhagavadgītā* 11.3)

A group of Indian immigrants, mostly Punjabi and Hindi speakers in the area of Abbotsford, a fast-growing city East of Vancouver in the Fraser Valley, the agricultural breadbasket of Southwestern BC, colloquially referred to as the "bible belt," had been attending the Vishva Hindu Parishad in Burnaby since its founding in 1974. This meant a drive of about an hour each way, often in the evening, to attend services such as Tuesday devotions to Hanuman. As the Abbotsford community grew, so did the desire to have a local Hindu temple. Darshan Sharma relates how things got started one Sunday evening in July 1998, when the core group met at his furniture store. "I said, 'Do you really want to start a temple here?' Then I just took a calendar, like the one over there." Gesturing toward a religious poster on the wall of the temple dining area, he continued: "I washed my hands. I took some *agarbhati* [incense] and prayed. Then I wrote a cheque for $5,000 and said, 'OK, who will do the same?'" Seven cheques were written, and before the evening was over, phone calls had brought in enough funds for a down payment on a temple property. Thus was born the Fraser Valley Hindu Society. In 1999, the group purchased a property adjacent to the Abbotsford airport, which, significantly, became an international airport around this time. Currently the temple serves about 200 families in the Fraser Valley and plans are underway for a new 3,000-square-foot structure.[1]

In these roots can be seen the community nature of the temple. All the work of the temple, other than the religious duties performed by a full-time priest, is done by the members, including bringing in a city water line, refurbishing the former auto body shop on the property to serve as the *mandir* (temple proper), and advertising for a priest. The current priest, Pandit Vasishth, lives with his family in the original house on the property, conducts Monday and Tuesday evening services for Shiva and Hanuman, respectively, as well as Sunday general services, and opens the temple for certain periods every morning and afternoon for devotees. He was trained in Delhi but served most recently in Yuba City, California, and in Edmonton.

The gathering I attended began at 10:30 a.m. on Sunday with *bhajans* (devotional songs) in Hindi, led mostly by a dozen women who accompanied the singing on percussion instruments (two drums, hand cymbals, and so on). About eight or nine men sat separately at first, as was the case at many temples I visited in BC, and two small children circulated between the gender groups. Members arrived continually, sometimes ringing the small bell in the middle of the hall, paying their respects by prostration, with some touching their heads to the floor, others their full bodies, rising with hands in *anjali* (folded prayer gesture), and praying before taking a place on the green-carpeted floor. By 11:30 a.m., there were twenty-one women, ten men, and about ten children.

Throughout the service, members continually arrived or departed, attending to business, especially collecting donations, distributing receipts, keeping a list of the day's donors, and preparing for the communal meal to follow. At 11:30 a.m., the priest offered a prayer to Krishna and a long invocation highlighting the ideas of calming the passions, religious devotion (*bhakti*), and gaining insight (*jnana*). The altar was curtained while offerings were made, then the curtains were withdrawn so that all could view the freshly reverenced images and sing the beautiful hymns accompanying *arati* (devotional offering of lamps). The congregation approached the altar one by one to wave the tray of oil lamps in graceful circles to the images, with the temple bell being rung all the while to heighten the religious awe of the moment. The priest recited verses from the Vedas and Upanishads, along with a recitation of divine names. He then blessed the congregation with a sprinkling of water, and the lamp trays were taken to each devotee to return the light to the individuals, who, after offering a coin, received it with cupped hands and applied it to head, eyes, and body. The canopy of the altar itself proclaimed in Sanskrit the sacred and once-secret Gayatri Mantra of the Rigveda: "Let us think deeply on the radiance to be desired of God Savitr; may he stimulate our minds!" The liquid and fruit offerings were taken by the devotees as *prasada*, literally the "grace" of the deities. This basic pattern of *bhajan*, *puja* (offerings), *arati*, and *prasada*, no doubt familiar to many readers, has remained a stable element of virtually all groups in this study, even when not performed in an established temple.[2]

The Abbotsford temple, a community temple, is a sign of the continued growth of the Hindu population in British Columbia and reflects where recent South Asian immigrants are choosing to live. Over the past two decades, immigrants from India have generally been the immediate relatives of earlier immigrants and have avoided the inflated land values of Vancouver in favour of the adjacent suburbs, especially Surrey (about one-third of new arrivals) and Abbotsford (about 10 percent).[3] Among these, there is a wide range of people from various parts of India and groups forming a secondary diaspora from "intermediate" locales, especially Guyana and Fiji, as well as Tamils from Sri Lanka, Fiji, and Malaysia – what Derryl MacLean refers to as the "double diaspora" (Chapter 3). In addition, there are organizations such as the Vedanta Society, where an extremely well educated and successful group of older immigrants from India are in the majority. The society's founder first set foot on North American soil in Vancouver in 1893 on his way to the World's Parliament of Religions in Chicago, but its closest ties have been to societies formed in California and Seattle as well as in India. There are also groups such as the followers of the Swami Shivananda Radha and Paramahamsa Yogananda, which draw from the general multi-ethnic British Columbia population.

Since the groups discussed in this chapter mainly follow religious traditions that originate in the Indian subcontinent,[4] share (although unequally) a certain set of practices and ideas, and acknowledge (again unequally) a central body of literature, they may be roughly called "Hindu." This study acknowledges, but does not attempt to resolve, the many historical, social, and ideological issues raised by this term. To depict the diversity in these groups, I have chosen for the epigraph a line from the *Bhagavad Gita*, a text central to most of the traditions and often depicted in temple booklets: "I wish to see your Divine Form, O Supreme Person." It is a request for revelation (*darsana*), a prayer for insight, and a major strand in the self-representation of Hindu religious groups in British Columbia and elsewhere.

Like the Daoist and Buddhist traditions discussed in this book, Hindu traditions have arrived in British Columbia in two ways: by diffusion of ideas and practices through an existing population and by immigration. In studying this process with regard to Buddhism, the scholar Martin Baumann reconsidered the implications of a widespread typology of "convert" versus "ethnic," and suggested a shift away from dichotomies of origin (sometimes tinged with race consciousness) toward a focus on religious practice.[5] In an earlier study of Buddhists in British Columbia, I found that practitioners can be quite flexible in crossing boundaries asserted by scholars! A prime example of this is reported by a Vancouver neighbourhood paper in an article about "ethnic" Sikhs attending the Guru Ram Dass Ashram of Vancouver, whose members are sometimes referred to as "White Sikhs." The Punjabi devotees felt the Ram Dass Ashram to be "much more committed to prayer, more committed to the Sikh way, more committed to finding peace in oneself."[6] Here religious practice takes precedence over ethnicity.

Throughout my research, I have found groups, such as those described by Don Baker and others, that have served as sites where new immigrants could establish and ground themselves. I have also noted, however, the phenomenon – described by Kamala Nayar in Chapter 2, by Paul Bramadat elsewhere,[7] and by others – followers of an immigrant tradition, once established, seeking the deeper intellectual and spiritual roots of the tradition. Indeed, Bramadat has found that both religious and ethnic self-identification are "increasingly elastic." In view of all these considerations, I have included a range of groups in this discussion, based simply on the felicitous statement of Vasudha Narayanan that they "speak the Hindu idiom"[8] to express meanings that are always ethnic and cultural or political and national, but also deeply personal.

The Place of "Hinduism" in British Columbia

British Columbia is a province of contrasts, both geographical and social. Remarkably wealthy in natural resources (its economic base), it is also home to Canada's poorest neighbourhood, Vancouver's Downtown Eastside. The stark contrast of mountains and sea is mirrored in social and class dichotomies. The Downtown Eastside is simply the most visible part of a city with a clear "East Side" versus "West Side" split that is evidenced by property values, voting patterns, and so forth. This is not idle observation, for Hindu practice in Vancouver is almost exclusively an "East Side" phenomenon, most precisely following the pattern discovered in a 2004 study of Buddhist groups in British Columbia[9] (a trend recently challenged, however, by the patrons of some Tibetan Buddhist groups, as discussed in Chapter 9). The Vancouver suburbs are also home to most "Hindu" groups, sometimes prominently located, especially if the area is home to a variety of newer religious buildings. Just as often, or perhaps more often, one finds these pockets of beauty in neglected areas betwixt and between – between urban developments, in the Downtown Eastside, or in a decidedly secular industrial park.

The earliest days of Hindu practice in British Columbia are essentially undocumented. An earlier study points to the existence of a South Asian population in the 1880s in Golden.[10] Although the religious focus of this population was a Sikh gurdwara that functioned until 1925, it is unlikely that there were no Hindu practitioners among the mostly Punjabi population. One study indicates that about one-fifth of the Indian immigrant population in Canada at the start of the twentieth century – about 1,000 people – were Hindus.[11] Despite these early dates, the history of Hindu practices in the subsequent half-century remains obscure, or may be summarized in the words of one interviewee in another study who stated that "Hindu, Sikh and Muslim families from India all attended the Gurdwara."[12]

Speaking the Dialect of Universalism

The oldest BC group "speaking the Hindu idiom" provides a counterpoint to the Fraser Valley Hindu Society described above. The Radha House organization was founded in 1957 by the German swami Sylvia Hellman, known as

Swami Shivananda Radha or simply Swami Radha,[13] in a private home in South Burnaby that served as headquarters for Swami Radha and several young male disciples, who typically held outside jobs to support themselves and the group. In 1963, the group moved its headquarters to Yashodhara Ashram in the small community of Kootenay Bay in the BC Interior. Radha House as a cooperative home in Burnaby came to an end several years ago, and its place was taken in 2004 by the experimental Radha Yoga and Eatery in the Downtown Eastside.

Although the Radha group has six centres in British Columbia and others elsewhere in Canada, the United States, and England, the heart of the movement is the Kootenay Bay ashram established at the opposite end of the province from Vancouver. At this "Yoga Retreat and Study Centre," members of the small, permanently resident spiritual community of twelve to fifteen, some initiated in the Radha lineage, offer a variety of courses to guests throughout the year. On the day I visited, a bland vegetarian meal was eaten in silence by seventy to eighty persons, aged perhaps nineteen to senior, at least 80 percent of whom were women. The extensive grounds are traversed by well-kept paths and stairs winding among native pines and fir, grassy openings, apple trees nurtured from the original farm, flower and rock gardens, a stream, and images of religious personages such as the Hindu god Shiva, Guanyin, and the Virgin Mary.

Of course, the refreshing mountain air and sparkling lake are exhilarating, but one is reminded to bring this experience within. This message is intentionally conveyed by the Temple of Divine Light, a large pure white hemispherical structure about sixty feet in diameter (Figure 1.1). Save for a modest wooden altar with a few pictures of the founder, it is completely empty inside, in this respect not unlike the Baha'i temple in Wilmette, Illinois – an enclosed space surrounded by gardens. Here was the architectural realization of the teachings of the Divine Light Society and its "divine light invocation Mantra." The building is often photographed from the outside because of its beauty, but the space inside best conveys the meaning: quiet, still, and empty – a container of light.

Swami Gopalananda (formerly David Forsee) spoke with me afterwards and gave me a copy of his book *Can You Listen to a Woman* (Timeless Books, 1999). Studying, travelling, searching, David's narrative seems emblematic of a significant segment of North American youth in the 1960s and '70s. He describes Swami Radha's method of aesthetic activities (painting, music, dance, writing) as paths toward "the divine," serving as a foil to the rational and ego-centred orientations of school, jobs, or social roles. In the context of the present book, perhaps this is a "youth culture" counterpart to what Don Baker considers for immigrants as "cultural oases."

The Swami Radha group, with its combining of sacred figures and texts from a variety of religious streams, clearly falls in with a tradition beginning in India in the nineteenth century that speaks a universalizing dialect of the "Hindu

FIGURE 1.1 The Temple of Divine Light in Kootenay Bay is a veritable *container* of light. *Photo by Larry DeVries*

idiom." This current in Indian religion grows out of India's encounter with Western influences. Here, universalism may be seen as a form of discourse addressing the "universal element existing in all particular religions."[14]

Other "universalizing" groups (in the Hindu idiom) include the Self-Realization Fellowship and the Vivekananda Vedanta Society of British Columbia. The former was founded in 1935 by a Bengali émigré to the United States, and began in British Columbia in the 1950s as a small meditation group meeting in private homes.[15] There are now roughly half a dozen BC branches. Religious services are conducted every Sunday and also several evenings a week in a rented facility in a mixed commercial-residential area of Vancouver. I attended a Sunday Readings Service with about thirty people in a spacious and quiet room. On the altar were six pictures of the figures central to the tradition, Krishna and Jesus in the centre, flanked by the founder, Yogananda, and his three predecessors in the Kriya Yoga lineage. The service opened with a prayer addressing the altar figures as well as "the saints of all religions," and included readings from the Gospel of Mark, the *Bhagavad Gita,* and Yogananda's *Autobiography of Yogi.* Although the society has a base in (Ranchi) India, the most immediate connection of the BC groups is to a monastic group in Los Angeles and an ashram in Nevada City, California, "Ananda Village."[16] A distinctly West Coast theme emerges in quite a few of the groups studied.

The Vivekananda Vedanta Society of British Columbia also has a West Coast connection in its close relationship to the society in Seattle and in its leader since 1978, Swami Bhaskarananda, who is also president of the Interfaith Council of Seattle.[17] As mentioned earlier, the founder of the Vedanta Society, Swami Vivekananda, passed through Vancouver in 1893 on his way to Chicago. The BC society began in 1967 when early members began driving to Seattle to attend meetings with the Seattle group, which had been established in 1938. A core group of four people met weekly in private homes in Vancouver for meditation and study of texts such as the *Bhagavad Gita* and the writings of Ramakrishna. The Vancouver group now has about eighty members and has contributed at least two monks to the movement. The meeting I attended at an East Vancouver community centre was open to the public on the occasion of Swami Bhaskarananda's visit and had been preceded the day before by a private session. Among the twenty or so members present, there was a remarkable representation of retired professors. Proceedings were conducted before a table set up with portraits of Jesus, Ramakrishna, and the Buddha between two candles, two vases with fresh flowers, and incense burning at the centre.

The Language of the Particular

The Vancouver area is home to a number of small temples patronized by members of specific ethnic communities (largely self-defined in terms of geography and language) or subdivisions of these communities, namely, Punjabi, Fijian, South Indian Fijian, and Sri Lankan. Steven Vertovec has noted similar cases, in which "caste, sectarian and linguistic/regional traditions and communities ... remain more or less intact."[18] In Vancouver, region and language often appear to be the deciding factors.

The oldest in this group is the Shree Sanatan Dharam Ramayan Mandali of Fiji.[19] According to members, the group began in 1966 through a desire to recite the Tulsi Ramayana (a devotional text) from a copy held by one of the members.[20] Meeting in homes at first, members attended the Vishva Hindu Parishad (see below) when it was established in 1974. They soon decided, however, to form a separate worship group where they would "feel more at home," presumably in a more familiar diasporic form of practice.[21] They purchased a church building in 1977 and converted it to serve as a temple in the Commercial Drive neighbourhood, well known and frequented by Vancouverites for its ethnic diversity. They plan to build a new temple on a property on East 41st Avenue.

Services and other activities are all conducted on a volunteer basis, including priestly duties. The altar reflects a pan-Hindu diversity of images, including Krishna, Radha, and Hanuman, with Shiva and Parvati at the centre. I counted more than twenty-five images on the altar. Altar inscriptions are more specific: *Oṃ namaḥ śivāya namaḥ satyaṃ śivaṃ sundaram om hara hara mahādeva* "Om. Obeisance to Shiva. (The Godhead) is Truth, Mild (*śiva*), Beautiful." Worship consists of Monday evening recitations from the Shiva Purana and Tuesday evening recitations of the Ramayana. The Tuesday service I attended began with *puja* (offerings), followed by singing of the Ramayana with harmonium, drum, and other percussion accompaniment, interspersed with homilies both read from a book and delivered extemporaneously in Hindi, and concluding with *arati* and distribution of fruit and sweets on plates as *prasada*. Partway through the singing, six devotees separated to the side for a brief *havan*, the fire offering.

The Then India Sanmarga Ikya Sangam Educational and Cultural Society, formerly the Sangam Educational and Cultural Society of BC (Fijian), is even more specific in its regional origin, consisting of a group of Fijian Hindus of South Indian origin. Its founder, Sevaratnakam Sadhu Kuppuswami, established the society in 1926 in Fiji specifically for the social and educational upliftment of South Indian Fijians, who had arrived a bit later than the North Indians and felt some discrimination from them. A large framed picture of the founder adorns the side of the altar, with an account of his activities celebrating him as a founder of many schools for children in Fiji. The group began with devotions in private homes in 1982 and purchased a former warehouse in north Richmond in 1992. The property overlooks the abandoned tracks of the former inter-urban streetcar line. Interestingly, just down this street on the margins of industry and neighborhood is the location of a group following one of British Columbia's major Tibetan Buddhist leaders (see Chapter 9) – both groups quite literally beneath the notice of the "mainstream" travelling over the Highway 99 bridge overhead, on the main route to the United States.

Religious services, led by three volunteer pandits (priests), are held on Fridays and on Sundays, when there are also Hindi and Bharatanatyam (classical dance) classes for children. The community consists of around 600 families. Most are from Surrey, Richmond, Vancouver, and Burnaby, but some also cross the border from Washington state. The *thaipusam* (a major South Indian annual festival) ceremony I attended took place on a Friday evening. Many families took part, with around twice as many women as men. Prayers were in a mixture of Tamil, Hindi, and Sanskrit from a booklet printed in Roman script. The altar contained *murtis* (images) of virtually all major Hindu deities, plus the South Indian Balaji and Shirdi Sai Baba. Members informed me that images had simply been gathered over time from the homes of devotees. The ceremony concluded with the procession of a portable shrine to Murugan, the focus of the celebration, flanked by his two consorts. As we circled, stopping to break open coconut offerings at the cardinal directions, the drumming, the dancing of some men, the singing of all, and the swaying of the multi-coloured shrine with its deities peering out from layers of raiment and garlands made the air come alive with a sacred vibration. The ceremony concluded with announcements and food.

We continue our journey deeper into the realm of the particular with a visit to Shri Durga Bhameshwari Mandir, also known as Shri Durga Mandir Surrey, founded in 2000 and thus among the newest temples in British Columbia. The location is a small commercial-industrial "park" in Surrey. The temple honours a "living goddess" as she appeared in the Punjabi village of Bham in 1955.[22] Devotees come from all over British Columbia as well as from Seattle. There are Tuesday devotions to Hanuman and *purnima* (full moon) observances, but the main focus is *puja* on Sundays, from 11:00 a.m. to 2:00 p.m., to Durga as the living goddess Bhamesvari. A large framed photo installed in 2003 is the centrepiece of the temple altar and is accompanied by more generic Durga images. The Sunday service I attended began with a meditative playing of the harmonium by Pandit Rajpal Sharma, followed by *bhajan*s sung mainly by the women with especially inspired *dholak* (drum) playing. After *puja*, the altar curtain opened on a tableau lit with a strobe light, and there was recitation of the verses of the *Śrīdurgāsaptaśatī*, in which is mentioned the goddess as "*bhāma*," that is, "light" itself, but also understood by worshippers as "the goddess in Bham." The temple is self-supporting and attended by families; it is a community enterprise.

The fourth group I wish to consider in this section is the Arul Migu Thurkadevi Hindu Society (BC), consisting mainly of Sri Lankan Tamil Hindu practitioners. The society, which meets in a "storefront temple" just over the Vancouver border in South Burnaby, was registered on 1 January 2000 at virtually the same time as the Bhameshwari Mandir in Surrey. The temple occupies a modest location on a commercial thoroughfare. Like the other sites in this group, it generates vibrant religious activity inside, which, in this case, often spills out into the streets in the form of circumambulation of the temple or processions through the neighbourhood. The temple started in 1999 with the installation (*pranasamsthapana*, or "establishing the living presence" in the image) of its principal deity, Durga Devi. There are images of Hanuman and Murugan on either side of the Devi altar. As with temples in India and Sri Lanka, there are also separate shrines to other deities: Nataraja (Shiva in dancing posture) and Parvati, Ayyapan (a Keralan deity), and Bhairava, a "fierce" form of Shiva represented by his trident (*trisula*) alone. As at the above temples, *puja* and *arati* are performed for these deities, but individually rather than at a collective altar. A variety of deities is in worship, but the group identifies closely with the Saiva Siddhanta tradition that originated in Tamil Nadu in the ninth century, so its worship centres on Shiva.

Although this small and lovely temple would appear to be the epitome of the particular, with its regional (Sri Lanka), linguistic (Tamil), and sectarian specificity, it steps beyond itself in a universalizing direction in two ways. First, the roots of the Saiva Siddhanta tradition are universalizing, as are virtually all *bhakti* (devotional) traditions in India. The founders are well known to cut across social boundaries and to critique "orthodox" ritual and thought. In so doing, however, they paradoxically become a sect of those who espouse universal Oneness *in that idiom.*[23] Although the temple is a social paradox, the universalizing language of the "Hindu idiom" is evident in terms of religion.

The temple also transcends its boundaries as a representative of a globalized "Hinduism." In a quiet corner near the main shrine, there is a series of seven small portraits of major figures of the Saiva Siddhanta tradition. These begin with several Nayanars, the founding poet-saints, and culminate with Tamil siddha (non-sectarian "adept") Yogar Swami (d. 1964)[24] and his disciple, the late American swami Shivaya Subramuniyaswami. Subramuniyaswami was born Robert Walter Hansen in Alameda County, California, in 1927.[25] Initiated in Sri Lanka in 1949, he founded the Saiva Siddhanta Yoga Order and Saiva Siddhanta Church in Sri Lanka, and afterwards on the Hawaiian island of Kauai. Among the many international activities of this energetic swami was the establishment in 1979 of the well-known magazine *Hinduism Today,* an issue of which a member of the Durga temple placed in my hands to help explain the religion of the community. When Subramuniyaswami established (in his book *How to Become a Hindu,* published in 2000) the requirement to renounce one's connection to one's present or any other religion, the Saiva Siddhanta Church embarked on a path of sectarianism quite at odds with the kind of universalism that sees itself as an augmentation of any sincere religious belief and practice. Still, the church continues to enrich the religious practice of independently established temples worldwide, including others in British Columbia such as the Sri Ganesh Temple Society of BC, founded in 1999 and established in a home on south Main Street in Vancouver in 2004, and the Sri Murugan Temple on River Road in Richmond. These temples represent a kind of global Hindu ecumenism but retain an underlying sectarian and ethnic (Tamil) specificity.

The Large Temples

Burnaby is best known among local Hindus as home to the oldest and largest Hindu temple in the province, the Vishva Hindu Parishad of British Columbia (renamed the Hindu Cultural Society and Community Centre of BC in 2000).[26]

This and several other larger temples serve the community by combining diverse traditions in the "Hindu idiom" quite consciously under one roof, often in an explicitly pan-Hindu and inclusive way. The Parishad is an international organization based in India, founded by Swami Chinmayananda in 1964. Its work has multiple aspects, but, in general, it has been studied for its conservative Hinduism domestically and its service to "non-resident Indians" internationally. Vertovec gives the network its own category among his three types as "ultimately unitary" and "nationalistic."[27] Since I am not addressing politics in this chapter, being without systematic empirical evidence, I shall concentrate on its pan-Hindu inclusivism.

The uniting feature is evident, for the larger BC temples serving an immigrant community predominantly from India were very intentionally inclusive. Here were: the "Hindu idiom" spoken most deliberately and consciously, the use in teaching of the widely understood language Hindi, reference to major texts such as the *Bhagavad Gita* and the *Tulsi Ramayana,* liturgy drawing on the Vedas and Upanishads, and Indian cultural traditions of music and dance. All these traditions play a role in the lives and spirit of practitioners, sustaining and nurturing them with what they feel to be their own and in which they could take pride of both heart and intellect. It is not historical studies or esoteric etymologies that constitute a religion, nor even the philosophical rigour of its doctrines, attractive though this may be. Rather, it is the religion's ability to come to life in its devotees as a support for everyday life, a solace in sorrow, and a home for expressions of joy.

A Victoria temple is representative of this group of religious societies. The Victoria began in September 1974, meeting in the basement of its now immediate past president, Gurudutt Jhagra. After a year or so, meetings began rotating among members' homes on Sundays. From 1977 to 1993, having outgrown house meetings, the group rented church halls on Saturday evenings because these were occupied on Sundays. Mr. Jhagra described the years of careful packing, unpacking, and repacking of religious pictures (only posters, no *murtis*) and communal items to and from car trunks. On several occasions, the group was asked to leave when church members became aware that a Hindu group was meeting on church property. With manifest happiness and relief, it purchased the old wooden church building of St. Mary's Anglican (now located in a new building a block away) on 17 July 1995. The first *murtis* (sacred images) of Lakshmi and Narayana (Vishnu) were purchased by a donor and arrived from Hyderabad in 1996. Services were conducted by members themselves as before, until the first full-time priest arrived in April 2001. The pandit now travels frequently to serve virtually the entire Vancouver Island area, with temple attendees coming from the Island, the Lower Mainland, and occasionally Seattle,

FIGURE 1.2   The steeple of the former St. Mary's Anglican Church, now Victoria Hindu Parishad, proclaims the sacred sound *Om*. *Photo by Larry DeVries*

Calgary, or even Toronto. Members speak Hindi, Telugu, Punjabi, Gujarati, Bengali, and Tamil, but services are conducted in Hindi. I met at the temple a very aged member whose father had come to Victoria in 1906.

On the day I attended, a continuous, round-the-clock recital of the *Tulsi Ramayana* was just finishing. Having already visited the Shree Mahalakshmi Temple in Vancouver, which was also (barely) recognizable as a former church (as, apparently, is the much larger Hindu Cultural Society and Community Centre in Burnaby), I was surprised to see the steeple intact in Victoria but surmounted with a beautifully calligraphed red *Om* on a white background (Figure 1.2). Since its founding, a variety of *murti*s in both North and South Indian styles have been added to the altar area. Seven or eight people were present when I arrived, but by the time of *bhajan*s there were more than fifty. The service began with a long chant by Mr. Jhagra and proceeded in much the same way as I have already described elsewhere. Realizing his central role in so many years of religious activities, I asked Mr. Jhagra how he had prepared. His immediate and very reverent response was "my *guruji*," Swami Satyamitranand Maharaj, who had visited in 1976 and is now extremely well known as the founder of the Bharat Mata (Mother India) temple in the sacred pilgrimage city of Hardwar.[28] The swami's *satsang* (devotional gathering) and "video presentation" are given one evening a month at the Burnaby temple, illustrating the broad connections within the province.[29]

This temple represents a diverse and broad-minded community, indeed. Announcements included a reference to an upcoming Ahmadiyya World Religion Conference,[30] and members here, as at numerous other temples, shared many recommendations for contacts with diverse religious groups connected with India. An active educational program for children offered Hindi classes, music, and scriptural stories, and dance will be added in the near future. The Victoria Hindu Parishad has come into its own. The group is active, open, and confident. This characterization applies also to other, larger temples such as Lakshmi Narayan Temple, founded in 1990 and established in 1992 in a spacious building in Surrey, and Shree Mahalakshmi Temple, founded in 1990 in Vancouver. I met a Muslim man at one of the larger temples I visited. When I asked about his temple attendance, he simply replied that "many streams lead to one ocean." This widely quoted Hindu tenet appears to express the confidence of a community in control of its own social and spiritual destiny.

Other large metropolitan temples show similar growth. The Ram Krishna Mandir at the Vedic Cultural Society of British Columbia[31] is situated on No. 5 Road in Richmond, just north of a small Sri Lankan Hindu temple, Subramaniya Swamy Temple, in an area where a succession of Buddhist, Sikh, Christian, Muslim, and Jewish houses of worship has inspired the local appellation "Highway to Heaven." Sri Sri Radha Madana-Mohan Temple[32] is located on the International Society for Krishna Consciousness (ISKON) property on Southeast Marine Drive in Burnaby. According to the temple brochure, ISKON was established in British Columbia in 1969 by two disciples from San Francisco. Although it has a distinctly Euro-Canadian clergy, the Krishna temple is extremely popular locally, with an estimated 1,000 mostly Indo-Canadian visitors celebrating *Krisna janmastami* (birthday) in the summer of 2007. The Vishva Hindu Parishad has recently broken ground for a new temple on the immediately adjacent property,[33] showing the continued blending of a tradition that arrived via the United States (the "Hare Krishnas") with the Vishva Hindu Parishad, which came directly from India.[34] It is interesting that these two are located only a few blocks from the original Radha House in Burnaby.

There is one final temple that best fits with the "large temples" in this section because of its pan-Indian ecumenism, even though it is much smaller due to its location. The South Okanagan Hindu Temple in Summerland[35] is the only ethnic Hindu temple in the BC Interior, located about halfway between the temples in the Lower Mainland and Victoria described above and the Radha temple in Kootenay Bay. According to temple vice president Arvinder Mohan, Hindu families began arriving in the Okanagan Valley in 1965 and met with local Sikhs for devotions for quite some time. The small Hindu community, now about fifteen families in Summerland and ten families in adjacent Penticton, founded its own temple with the purchase of a Spanish mission-style church building and the formal installation of the divine images on 25 July 1993. All religious services are conducted by the devotees themselves, for there is no resident pandit. According to Arvinder, this has the advantage of affording them a degree of freedom from the formalism of ritual actions and timing.

The service I attended was indeed relaxed and happy. There were about thirty people, with slightly more women than men, as at other temples, and a number of children and youth, the latter participating fully. Women, men, and young people all took part in *bhajan*s, sung from books. Arvinder then led the group from a photocopied sheet in more formal *bhajan*s, the *arati* hymn (although there was no formal offering of flame), and the invocation of peace. He identified these recitations as having been compiled from Arya Samaj sources (discussed below). The simplicity of the service sheet made it easy for the youth to memorize, and they participated fully in the singing. The group was remarkably diverse for its size, with Punjabi and Gujarati families of three generations, a local Sikh family, and visitors from England, from Assam and Karnataka, India, and from Surrey, British Columbia. A Euro-Canadian woman from neighbouring Kelowna occasionally comes to teach the children.

The main hall contains *murti*s of Radha and Krishna, Shiva, Parvati, Brahma, Ganesha, and Shiva's bull, Nandi (Figure 1.3). In addition to these images, there was much evidence of the work of the devotees themselves, not only in the canopy, lights, and hand-stitched "*om*" (upper left corner of Figure 1.3) but also in the selection of pictures. One object initially escaped my attention as I was preoccupied with recording the expected images – a reindeer, visible on the left of Figure 1.3, which I saw only after the photos were developed. This revelation (confirmed by a temple devotee) drove home the point that this was a Canadian altar, made by Canadians, in Canada. In one of British Columbia's least ethnically diverse areas,[36] the South Okanagan Hindu Temple is at home in a church building strongly reminiscent of the significant Portuguese presence in the Okanagan Valley. The temple is securely established and is an active participant in its community in such ways as student aid in the form of the "Okanagan Hindu Temple and Culture Society Bursary."[37] The "Hindu idiom" is spoken here with a distinctly Canadian accent.

Re-formations New and Old

The large temples account for by far the greatest portion of collective Hindu practice in British Columbia. They are rooted in the religious insights and organizations of recent centuries in India and are closely connected to both the

FIGURE 1.3 The reindeer *murti* (left) joins Krishna, Radha, Brahma, Parvati, and Shiva at the South Okanagan Hindu Temple in Summerland. *Photo by Larry DeVries*

development of that country as a modern nation and its cultural contribution to global society. This presence does not just reproduce classical Hinduism but grows out of a virtual habit of self-examination and reform in the nineteenth and twentieth centuries, and ultimately from practically the earliest ages. Stages in the development of reform and reformulation in Indian religious tradition, really present in all, are salient in several BC groups, such as the Brahma Kumaris, a group headquartered in Rajasthan, India, and the Sant Nirankari Mission, with headquarters today in Delhi. Both were founded around 1930 and are worldwide missions.[38]

Hindu education and practice in British Columbia have been greatly supported by the presence of the Chinmaya Mission Advaita Vedanta Centre since 1972. Swami Chinmayananda, well known as the founder of the Vishva Hindu Parishad in India in 1964 (see above), also established a remarkable pan-India network of centres for religious education that quickly grew into a worldwide organization. Swami Chinmayananda's work, indeed his conversion, was inspired by a visit in 1947 to the Shivananda Ashram in Rishikesh, India, later the site of Swami Radha's initiation (see above). Swami Chinmayananda's visit to Vancouver in 1972 was one of his many tours known as *jnana-yajna* (offerings of insight), at first in India and then throughout the world, which essentially democratized a previously elitist course of study and practice. He delivered three lectures at Simon Fraser University in Burnaby, but more importantly, became the personal guru of his host couple, Mr. and Mrs. Raj Kapahi, who formed the centre of the new group.[39] As with the Vivekananda Vedanta Society, close connections were established with a Seattle group, with teachers travelling to Vancouver on a regular basis. The Vancouver group, the only active one in British Columbia, is small, with a little over a half-dozen students, but clearly presents a rigorous course of textual study. Connections are maintained with groups at four centres in California.

An earlier reform movement stems from 1875, when the Arya Samaj was founded in the Punjab by Swami Dayananda Sarasvati. This reform arose from a radical rejection of image worship and temples, moving toward the religion of the earlier Vedas and Upanishads and the *Bhagavad Gita*. With this came a reinterpretation of the caste system along lines arguably consistent with the earliest texts, as expressive of social function rather than status based on ritual purity. Interpretation of the canon is always allowed in the "Hindu idiom."

The Arya Samaj remains influential in India as well as in the diaspora, as seen earlier. The BC group draws mainly on Fijian Hindus and some diasporic Guyanese.[40] It meets weekly in the small stucco one-storey Fiji Canada Association building in Burnaby, just over the boundary with Vancouver, like the Vishva Hindu Parishad to the north and the Devi temple to the south. The service, which is attended by a dozen or so families of elders, parents, and children, consists entirely of a fire ritual (*havan*) accompanied by mantras (verses and formulas) of the Vedas. Shobha Rae, a priestess of the group, and the other priest wore the garb of North Indian pandits, and all officiants donned a yellow sash on which was printed in Sanskrit the beautiful Gayatri Mantra of the Rigveda: "Let us think deeply on the radiance to be desired of God Savitr; may he stimulate our minds!" The mantra is symbolic of spiritual illumination, but also in this case social liberation, for Swami Dayananda insisted that it be available to all, contrary to its traditional restriction based on caste and gender. The central rite is the *havan* (literally "offering"), in which the fire itself is the divine element, there being no image required. The service concluded with *bhajan*s in Hindi and a reading from a biography of Swami Dayananda in Hindi. A communal meal followed. Shobha, who works as a freedom of information officer for the city of Vancouver, became the first woman priest of the group in British Columbia through an intense course of self-study together with the guidance of Dr. Satish Prakash, director of a *gurkul* (Arya Samaj school) in Queens, New York, and continues her study with annual visits to Queens for mentoring by Dr. Prakash.

Whereas Swami Dayananda was active in the late nineteenth century, the remarkable poet-saint Kabir dates from perhaps the fifteenth century, in Northern India, and is the spiritual focus of the Kabir Cultural Centre (Guru Kabir Association of Canada). The poetry of Kabir, at once mystical and plainspoken, is claimed by both Muslims and Hindus and is also found in the Sikh holy book (*Adi Granth*).[41] They are thus consistent with the first Sikh Guru's teaching that there is "neither Muslim nor Hindu," only a God beyond description (or "without qualities," Sanskrit *nirguṇa*), beyond portrayal as image, but nevertheless accessible to human intuition. Kabir was a mystic who spoke as a devotee.

In British Columbia, the work of Kabir has been brought to life in the Kabir Cultural Centre, especially by its president, Dr. Jagessar Das. The group has met since 1976, in members' homes at first, and acquired its present location in Surrey in 1996.[42] It has remained stable since its beginnings at about fifteen to twenty members, most of whom are of Guyanese heritage, with a few from Fiji or other communities. The location is a modest two-storey suite in an industrial-commercial park, not unlike that of the Bhameshwari Mandir. The worship area is above (with eating and visiting areas below) and is furnished with a large framed portrait of Kabir, below which is an altar with pictures of the two most recent leaders of the group in India, together with flowers, the *Bijak* (a book of Kabir), including Dr. Das's English translations, a lamp, and offerings. The group has services every Sunday, yoga and meditation classes on Monday evenings, *purnima* (full moon) services, and a special service for Kabir (Kabir *chalisa*) on the first Wednesday of each month. It celebrates an annual festival of Kabir's birth as well as the traditional Indian holidays of Holi and Diwali.

Dr. Das was born of parents belonging to the Kabir *panth* (sect) who indentured to Guyana in 1910. As a young man, he attended the University of British Columbia Medical School and read Rabindranath Tagore's translations of Kabir's poetry. "It was the first thing I read in English on Kabir," he says. He typed out a copy of the whole book. In the early 1960s, Dr. Das attended lectures by Swami Shivananda's successor (see above), Swami Chidananda, at the YWCA on Burrard Street in Vancouver. After beginning his medical practice, Dr. Das met weekly with Pandit Gian Chandje Shastri of the Burnaby Vishva Hindu Parishad to read and translate the Hindi verses of Kabir. The assistance of the pandit was necessary since Dr. Das's first language is English, not Hindi. It is also a tribute to the successful outreach of the Vishva Hindu Parishad. In the mid-1980s, Jagdish Shastri, a monk of the Kabir sect from India, stayed in Dr. Das's home for three years, and the two of them pored over Dr. Das's translations, correcting and polishing. Two of three volumes have now been published as *The Bijak of Guru Kabir* (Surrey: Guru Kabir Association of Canada).

A fourth kind of reformulation is rooted in the compendium of yoga compiled by Patanjali in the early centuries of the Common Era. In British Columbia, these teachings are practised by the Dhyan Yoga Meditation Society of Vancouver, headed by Dr. Avinash Anand.[43] The group is not formally active as such, but remains a network of practitioners that spans the globe in a unique way. The society traces its beginnings to a visit in 1981 by Dr. Usharbudh Arya (now internationally known as Swami Veda Bharati),[44] when he delivered lectures in a member's home, and a second visit in April the following year, during which five to six people were initiated. Members practise meditation on Monday nights and *hatha yoga,* the discipline of yogic postures, on Saturdays. Dr. Anand emphasized that the connection between disciple and guru transcends distance and time. Once one is connected to the lineage, which is ultimately traced back to the deity Shiva, "they help you." When I asked Dr. Anand about other religious practices, he related how he had once been a regular temple attendee, maintaining a regular schedule of offerings, but that his yoga practice had gradually taken more time and seemed more in harmony with his personal development. The Dhyan Yoga Meditation Society clearly shares features with such groups as Yashodhara Ashram; both seek a deepening of religious experience on a personal level, beyond the ritual and social, and presumably beyond language or sect.

Jains, Indian Buddhists, and Ravidasis

British Columbia is also home to South Asian immigrant practitioners of Jainism and Buddhism, religions that, although not "orthodox Hindu," share much of its idiom.[45] Jainism dates itself far back in time in India, with a succession of twenty-four enlightened teachers, the latest of whom was Mahavira, an elder contemporary of the Buddha in the sixth century BCE. By contrast, Indian Buddhism was virtually lost around 1200 CE and was revitalized by Dr. B.R. Ambedkar, a lawyer and constitutionalist in the Indian Independence movement who saw Buddhism as a movement for the upliftment of untouchables.[46] Shortly before his death in 1956, Ambedkar led many of low status in the newly independent country in converting to Buddhism.

The local Jain community consists of thirty-five to forty families who meet in homes, particularly on the annual occasions of the birth of Mahavira in spring; Dashalakshana, a ten-day observance of ten principal virtues in summer; and Jain Diwali, celebrating the nirvana of Mahavira in the fall. Unlike Ontario, which has a much larger Jain population (and also more Hindus), British Columbia has no temple or resident monastic. The community belongs mostly to the Svetambara sect, but the earliest members, Ananda K. Jain and Gyan Chand Singhai, who arrived in 1966, are Digambara Jains. An excellent book explaining Jain belief and practice and extending it to the contemporary world has been published by Vastupal Parikh, a former professor at the former Notre Dame University in Nelson, British Columbia.[47]

The Buddhist group known as the Dr. Ambedkar Memorial Association began in 1981, led by Mohan Bangai. Mohan came to Canada as a student and was associated with a practising group of fifteen to twenty families meeting in homes in Victoria, Vancouver and elsewhere in the Lower Mainland, and Quesnel. From this group, the Shri Guru Ravidass Sabha (see below) split off; it still houses a collection of Ambedkar's works and remains dedicated to ameliorating caste-based injustice.[48] After reading an article on Ambedkar's work for the Scheduled Castes (untouchables) in India, Mohan was inspired to further study Ambedkar and his eventual religion of choice, Buddhism. The essential message, he felt, was first one of spiritual development, and this entailed development of an egalitarian society through education. Studies in Buddhism led to an encounter with the Goenka movement and continuing study with local *vipassana* (meditation) groups. S.N. Goenka lectured to a group of 800 at the Shri Guru Ravidass Sabha during his visit to British Columbia in 2002. Both Mohan and his wife, Pam, are practitioners and teachers of *vipassana* because "without meditation Buddhism is not Buddhism." Mohan sees the Buddhism of Ambedkar as contributing to a general social uplift, not only for "oppressed people, but for all people," since it, simply put, "increases good values and decreases bad values." Ambedkar's Buddhism thus fits hand-in-glove with Canadian multiculturalism, defined by Mohan as "extracting universal ideas out of various contributions for the benefit of all." Mohan has also been active with the Indian Buddhist Society of Canada (discussed by Bandu Madanayake in Chapter 6, particularly with respect to the Surrey Buddhist Vihara, with which the Indian Buddhist Society of Canada cooperates).

The Shri Guru Ravidass Sabha, located in Burnaby, is quite closely related to the Indian Buddhists in British Columbia and elsewhere.[49] Established in 1982 for the "primary purpose of propagating the teachings of Shri Guru Ravidass Ji," it acts as both a gurdwara following a Sikh code of conduct (*rehat-maryada*) and a community centre. Annual events celebrate "Shri Guru Ravidassji, Dr. B.R. Ambedkar, Shri Guru Arjan Devji, Shri Guru Nanak Devji, and anniversary of Shri Guru Ravidass Sabha."[50] The worship service follows the Sikh *rehat-maryada*, but the hall contains a large portrait of Guru Ravidas, just to the side of the Guru *Adi Granth*. I was informed that some members removed the portrait but that it was reinstalled after a while. This indicates the dynamic state of the Ravidasi religion, a "creative tension," as one member put it.[51]

The portrait issue as well as the very name of the Sabha designating Ravidas as "guru" point to the dialogue between Sikh identity and Ravidasi identity. The Ravidasi faith, like the Kabir *panth* discussed earlier or the Sikhs, whose sacred text also contains the poems of both, is universalist in its religious message, worshipping the "one true God,"[52] but it is uniquely particularist in at least one area of social practice: caste. The Ravidasi faith centres on Ravidas precisely because he was of the same "untouchable" or *dalit* (oppressed) caste status as the worshippers, the Chamar subcaste. Some scholars explain this adoption by saying that Ravidas "values his own lowly position as a vantage point,"[53] while a worshipper at the Burnaby temple simply says that with a separate temple (from the mainstream Sikh gurdwaras), they "feel more comfortable, not being reminded of low status." Indeed, the temple recently restricted *membership* to those of the caste of Guru Ravidas (although all are invited to *worship*), a decision that was challenged at and upheld by the British Columbia Human Rights Tribunal.[54] The group acts as a focal point for caste uplift and social conscience in general, with activities related to minority issues and non-violence. The temple is a refuge from which to speak most authentically against social inequity in the context of both theological universalism and liberal democracy, an invaluable thread woven into the fabric of Canadian multiculturalism.

Conclusion

South Asian religious groups in British Columbia are, like the province itself, diverse and divided, but also seek in many ways to transcend these divisions.[55] They vary widely from universalizing to highly particularist with regard to practice, focus of worship or spiritual practice, language, or even caste. Their ideas and practices have arrived both with immigration from South Asia or intermediate points and by diffusion through an existing receptive population. The diversity within groups may be ideologically crafted as a unifying factor or it may appear as the spontaneous colloquy of many voices that T.N. Madan calls "folk pluralism."[56]

The gatherings and dispersals represented by group members are reflected in their practices. The multiplicity of trajectories of those gatherings is often noted. Some have remarked on the "twice migrant" path; I have noted above the ripple of ideas that occurs in a variety of ways. Not yet fully studied is the rural-to-urban migration that has been experienced both in the home country and in Canada. Once or several times, migrant folk may congregate in a home, a rented space, or a "temple" that may call itself a community centre, where people can feel at home. Like many of the groups studied in the other chapters, Hindus worship at home as well as in temples. But these new "temples" are in this sense new homes. Having frequently begun in private homes, they are refuges, as Don Baker notes in Chapter 8, shelters in which not only the linguistic but also the religious idiom and much else (including dress and food) are shared. Once secure and collectively engaged, the community may reach out, for example, from Hindu to Sikh, as I found in several groups, or in a "universalist" mode sought by some groups studied in this chapter and in Chapter 12 – in any case, knitting together the fabric of Canadian multicultural society.

These groups of people are interconnected within and outside the province, and are connected with Canadian society as a whole. Most of them are community-based, supported by and serving those in a particular locale. Some groups appear to have a particular affinity with other groups along the West Coast, such as ISKON, the Yogananda group, and the Chinmaya Mission, all with groups in California; and the Vedanta Society and others with groups in Washington state. There are connections to the east as well, with the Sri Murugan Temple drawing priests from Montreal and practitioners of the Arya Samaj making annual journeys to New York. Among social connections, perhaps the most striking is the maintenance of caste affiliation by the Guru Ravidass Sabha. While Vertovec reasonably predicts the effacement of caste essentially on the grounds that as an entire system it does not travel well piecemeal,[57] in the case of the Guru Ravidass Sabha, *dalit* status is foregrounded as a means of raising consciousness and seeking social justice across multiple (not only caste) boundaries. Canadian multiculturalism, while stemming from a liberal egalitarianism, also recognizes distinctiveness and provides the milieu for this work.

Throughout this chapter, I have tried to maintain the focus on religion, although I have sometimes needed to use a synonym. Not only is "religion" a somewhat ignored topic compared with others in the academic realm but the religions discussed in this book are some of the least studied, although they are neighbours and constituents of the very fabric of modern democracies like Canada.[58] Speaking of religion as a kind of language ("the Hindu idiom"), as an instrument of expression, communication, and contemplation, has enabled us to see an immense variety of groups as speakers of "dialects" of the "Hindu idiom" – different dialects, but mutually intelligible. Since these groups are constituents of BC society, they expand the expressive range of and the potential for communication between all residents of the province. New residents find a ready-made home in established groups, and established groups avail themselves of new ideas and practices to enrich their spiritual lives. Charles Taylor identified the lifeblood of a liberal multicultural society as recognition of the dignity of the individual, which "forges identity" and allows one to live in such a society as a whole human being.[59] To take one example, the richness of the religious and social fabric in this province enabled Dr. Das to study Hindi at the Vishva Hindu Parishad and parlay this into a contribution to the development in British Columbia of a religious group that he first knew growing up in Guyana. In another example, newcomers directly from India both find recognition in, and themselves recognize, the religious foundations in the Vedanta Society or ISKON, and flourish within these groups simply because of the power and authenticity of the "Hindu idiom."

Taylor observed that a multiculturalism of respect and recognition can be rather passive and fragmenting. He proposed in addition a "multiculturalism of value." This kind of multiculturalism actively reaches beyond mere "recognition" or a passive "tolerance," actively seeking the value and worth of complex, long-standing, and widely practised human institutions such as religions. The necessity in modern pluralistic democracies of active engagement with others is widely recognized in the contemporary study of religious pluralism.[60] Certainly, South Asian immigrants to British Columbia have valued the religious footholds established not only by other immigrants but also by converts attracted to "the Hindu idiom" because of its relevance to their lives in a modern society – all being elements of the "Divine Form" mentioned in the inscription at the beginning of this chapter.

Notes

1 Information in this section comes from field visits of 29 January and 21 February 2006, and from interviews with Mr. Darshan (Dave) Sharma, president of the temple.
2 Religious activities in many of the traditions studied in this book also take place in homes, places of business, or informal gatherings. Additional information on the practices of ethnic Hindus in Canada can be found in Harold Coward and Sikata Banerjee, "Hindus in Canada: Negotiating Identity in a 'Different' Homeland," in *Religion and Ethnicity in Canada,* ed. Paul A. Bramadat and David Seljak (Toronto: Pearson Longman, 2005), 35, 37. Coward's brief characterization of Hindu congregational religious practice as "Protestant-style" ignores a long-standing practice in South Asian devotional traditions that is described in many sources. Fenggang Yang and Helen Rose Ebaugh, in "Transformations in New Immigrant Religions and Their Global Implications," *American Sociological Review* 66, 2 (2001): 269-88, consider "congregational structure" more systematically under a number of factors. Both studies would benefit from the vivid description and analysis of group worship in India by Milton B. Singer, "The Radha-Krishna Bhajanas of Madras City," in *Krishna: Myths, Rites, and Attitudes,* ed. Milton Singer (Chicago: University of Chicago Press, 1968), 90-172. The urban situation studied by Singer parallels the urban groups in this book.
3 BC STATS, http://www.bcstats.gov.bc.ca.
4 Sikh traditions are considered in a separate chapter because of their unique history in British Columbia. BC and Ontario are the two provinces with the highest percentages of new South Asian immigrants (http://www.statscan.ca). In BC, Sikhs make up 3.5 percent of the total population and Hindus around 1 percent, whereas in Ontario there are relatively more Hindus than Sikhs. For immigrant Hindu religious groups in Ontario with some very useful Indo-Canadian history, see Milton Israel, *In the Further Soil: A Social History of Indo-Canadians in Ontario* (Richmond Hill, ON: Organization for the Promotion of Indian Culture, 1994).
5 Martin Baumann, "Protective Amulets and Awareness Techniques, or How to Make Sense

of Buddhism in the West," in *Westward Dharma: Buddhism beyond Asia,* ed. Charles S. Prebish and Martin Baumann (Berkeley: University of California Press, 2002), 59.

6 "Sikhing freedom," *Vancouver Courier,* 26 January 2005 (article is now located at http://archive.vancourier.com). Of course, in many cases ethnicity may just as well prevail, as especially noted by Verne A. Dusenbery, "On the Moral Sensitivities of Sikhs," in *Divine Passions: The Social Construction of Emotion in India,* ed. Owen M. Lynch (Berkeley: University of California Press, 1990), 239-61.

7 Paul A. Bramadat and David Seljak, eds., *Religion and Ethnicity in Canada* (Toronto: Pearson Longman, 2005), 230, 225.

8 In *The Graceful Guru: Hindu Female Gurus in India and the United States,* ed. Karen Pechilis (New York: Oxford University Press, 2004), 168.

9 Bruce Matthews, ed., *Buddhism in Canada* (London and New York: Routledge, 2006).

10 Charles Anderson, Tirthankar Bose, and Joseph I. Richardson, eds., *Circle of Voices: A History of the Religious Communities in British Columbia* (Lantzville, BC: Oolichan Books, 1983), 262. This is a basic work on religion in British Columbia.

11 K. Laxmi Narayan, *Indian Diaspora: A Demographic Perspective,* Occasional Paper no. 3 (Hyderabad: Centre for Study of Indian Diaspora, University of Hyderabad, n.d.). See http://www.uohyd.ernet.in/sss/cinddiaspora/occ3.html.

12 In the *Indo-Canadian Oral History Collection,* "made up of two separate projects to interview early Indo-Canadian settlers in Canada, almost all of them British Columbians," by Dr. Hari Sharma, Professor Emeritus of Sociology at Simon Fraser University. See http://content.lib.sfu.ca/icohc/index.php.

13 Field visits of 17 and 20 July 2005 and interviews of 19 July with Swami Lalitananda, and 20 July with Swami Gopalananda. Additional sources are pamphlets and books published by the organization, and the websites http://www.radha.org, http://www.yasodhara.org, and http://www.radhavancouver.org.

14 Arvind Sharma, *The Concept of Universal Religion in Modern Hindu Thought* (Houndmills, Basingstoke, Hampshire, UK, and New York: Macmillan/St. Martin's Press, 1998), 2. The scholar of Bengali mysticism June McDaniel notes its distinct origin in classical Hindu texts and exegesis in "The Hindu Roots of Universalism, and Its Relevance to Modern Religious Studies," *World Association for Vedic Studies Conference,* July 2002; see Infinity Foundation, http://www.infinityfoundation.com.

15 Field visit of 15 January 2006 and a telephone interview with Charles Scott, the current leader of the group. See Polly Trout's 2000 study of Yogananda in the United States. See also http://www.yogananda-srf.org.

16 See http://www.expandinglight.org/who/about/ananda-village.htm.

17 Field visit of 10 February 2006 and conversations with a variety of members. Carl T. Jackson gives a complete account of the society, including history and analysis. Arvind Sharma, *Concept of Universal Religion,* 42-72, discusses the "universalist" views of Ramakrishna and Vivekananda. A fascinating personal account of the order in India is found in *The Ochre Robe* by the singular Austrian Swami Agehananda Bharati (London: George Allen and Unwin, 1961).

18 Steven Vertovec, *The Hindu Diaspora: Comparative Patterns* (London and New York: Routledge, 2000), 162.

19 Field visit of 14 February 2006 and conversations with the temple president, Mr. Indar Narayan Singh; field visit of 4 February 2006 to Then India Sanmarga Ikya Sangam Educational and Cultural Society in Richmond and interview with James G. Reddy, past president; field visits of 25, 26, and 30 July 2006 to Shri Durga Bhameshwari Mandir in Surrey and interview with Yashpal Indarjit Parmar, president of the society, and pandit Rajpal

Sharma; field visit of 27 July 2005 to Arul Migu Thurkadevi Hindu Society (BC) in Burnaby, interview of member, and temple website at http://www.geocities.com/aruldurgavol.

20 Here is an exact parallel to Manmohan Wirk's account of the establishment in 1908 of the first BC gurdwara to house a copy of the Guru Granth Sahib held by a devotee: Manmohan Singh Wirk, *A History of the Sikhs of Victoria, BC* (Victoria: M.S. Wirk, 2005). See also Chapter 2.

21 Such a perception was tentatively noted by Jim Wilson, "Fijian Hinduism," in *Rama's Banishment: A Centenary Tribute to the Fiji Indians, 1879-1979*, ed. Vijay Mishra (London: Heinemann Educational Books, 1979), 86-111. For this reference, I am indebted to Dr. Kam Prasad, most recently of Tokushima Bunri University. Milton Israel, *In the Further Soil*, 10, 38, 43, records similar sentiments.

22 The Bham temple may be seen online at Info Punjab, http://www.infopunjab.com/punjab/travel/bham.htm.

23 A.K. Ramanujan, following Victor Turner, explained the initial breaking of barriers as "*anti-structure*," leading ultimately to "*counter-structure*," in *Speaking of Siva* (Harmondsworth: Penguin, 1973), 34-37.

24 K. Kailasapathy, "The Writings of the Tamil Siddhas," in *The Sants: Studies in a Devotional Tradition of India*, ed. K. Schomer and W.H. McLeod (Delhi: Motilal Banarsidass, 1987), 385.

25 Birth records were confirmed by Verne Deubler of the California Genealogical Society.

26 Field visits to four temples: (1) Hindu Cultural Society and Community Centre of BC in Burnaby on 12 February 2006; (2) Lakshmi Narayan Temple (Vedic Hindu Society) in Surrey on 2 July 2005, and talks with temple president Parshottam (Paul) Goel and secretary Brahma Swarup Varma; (3) Shree Mahalakshmi Temple in Vancouver on 17 July 2005, and interview with Mrs. Chaitanya, wife of temple priest Pandit Prameya Chaitanya; and (4) Victoria Hindu Parishad in Saanichton, Vancouver Island, on 14 August 2005, and interviews with Pandit Parmod Kumar Gaur, temple president Dr. Prasad Chintalapati, and founding member and past president Mr. Gurudutt Jhagra. The Burnaby and Victoria temple websites are at http://www.webpuddy.com/vhp and http://www.victoriahindutemple.com, respectively.

27 Vertovec, *The Hindu Diaspora*, 162-63.

28 A sometimes carping account of this temple and its place in the development of national consciousness is found in Lise McKean, *Divine Enterprise: Gurus and the Hindu Nationalist Movement* (Chicago: University of Chicago Press, 1996).

29 See http://www.webpuddy.com/vhp.

30 See Chapter 3, on Asian Muslims in British Columbia.

31 The temple website is found at http://www.geocities.com/ramkrishnamandir. The temple was visited on 5 August 2006.

32 Milton Israel, *In the Further Soil*, 62, notes that at an Ontario ISKON temple, "the congregation is virtually all Indian."

33 See "New Temple Building Plans under Construction 2007-2009 5420 Marine Drive, Burnaby" at http://www.hindutempleburnaby.com.

34 A rural group of ISKON followers is found in the BC Interior, "Saranagati Village" (or "Saranagati Farm") near Ashcroft. See http://www.saranagati.ca for information on the site as a cooperative (thus joining a long history of rural cooperatives in the province), as well as "Venables Valley School." Since the "Hare Krishnas" are well known, with an extensive Internet presence, and are much-studied, I mention only a study of newer developments in the movement: E. Burke Rochford, *Hare Krishna Transformed* (New York: New York University Press, 2007).

35 Information in this section comes from a temple visit on 8 August 2008.

36 "Kelowna remains one of the least diverse metropolitan areas in the nation, with a visible

minority population of just five per cent": *Vancouver Sun*, 2 April 2008, reporting on census release. See http://www.cbc.ca/canada/british-columbia/story/2008/04/02/bc-most-diverse-province.html. The temple is the only non-Christian religious group in a local listing (http://www.boomtrek.com/canada/summerland/services/churches.html).

37 See http://www.bclocalnews.com/okanagan_similkameen/summerlandreview/lifestyles/22835729.html.
38 See http://www.bkwsu.org/index_html and http://www.nirankari.com/vancouver/index.html.
39 This material is derived from a visit to the Chinmaya Mission in Vancouver on 13 January 2006, and from an unpublished manuscript by Jaya Muzumdar, who now teaches there. I also am indebted to Brahmacarini Robyn Thompson, the main teacher in British Columbia since 1986.
40 Field visit of 23 October 2005 and conversations with members. To illustrate the influence of the Arya Samaj in the Hindu diaspora, according to Hugh Johnston, "The Development of the Punjabi Community in Vancouver since 1961," *Canadian Ethnic Studies* 20, 2 (1988): 11-12, the first priest of British Columbia's largest temple, the Vishva Hindu Parishad, was an Arya-samaji.
41 Kabir's poems were translated into English by Rabindranath Tagore in 1915 and Charlotte Vaudeville in 1957. Much work on the Kabir sect in India has been done by David N. Lorenzen.
42 Information in this section is derived from field visits of 2 and 22 October 2005; interviews with Dr. Das, especially on 8 August 2006; *The Kabir Voice*; and the group website, Kabir Association of Canada, http://www.members.shaw.ca/kabirweb.
43 Field visit of 1 December 2005 and interview with Dr. Avinash Anand.
44 See http://www.themeditationcenter.org and http://www.swamiveda.org.
45 Interviews with Gyan Chand Singhai on 1 September 2006 and Mohan Bangai on 30 July 2006.
46 The bibliography on Ambedkar and the Ambedkar movement is very extensive. For an introduction, see Surendra Jondhale and Johannes Beltz, eds., *Reconstructing the World: B.R. Ambedkar and Buddhism in India* (New Delhi: Oxford University Press, 2004), particularly chapters by Eleanor Zelliot, G. Aloysius, and Maren Bellwinkel-Schempp; see also Sukomal Chaudhuri, *Contemporary Buddhism in Bangladesh* (Calcutta: Atisha Memorial Publishing Society, 1982), and quite a few articles by Heinz Bechert.
47 Vastupal Parikh, *Jainism and the New Spirituality* (Toronto: Peace Publications, 2002).
48 See http://www.gururavidasssabha.org.
49 The Ravidas groups, composed of self-designated Chamars, an "untouchable" (or *dalit*, "oppressed") caste, is included here for its strong reformist strain and also because recent surveys of South Asian religious groups in the United States and Canada have, somewhat ironically, not touched on them, despite many Ravidas associations in these countries. (Mark Juergensmeyer devotes two chapters to the Ravidasis in India and in the United Kingdom in *Religion as Social Vision: The Movement against Untouchability in 20th Century Punjab* (Berkeley: University of California Press, 1982), and the theme is important throughout his book.) A similar lack of notice of *dalit*s in studies of South Asian Christians was cited by Rachel Fell McDermott, "From Hinduism to Christianity, from India to New York: Bondage and Exodus Experiences in the Lives of Indian Dalit Christians in the Diaspora," in *South Asian Christian Diaspora: Invisible Diaspora in Europe and North America*, ed. Knut A. Jacobsen and Selva J. Raj (Aldershot, UK, and Burlington, VT: Ashgate Press, 2008), 223-48.
50 See http://www.gururavidasssabha.org.
51 I owe this and many other points, such as the reference to the British Columbia Human

Rights Tribunal below, to numerous conversations with Jai Birdi, member of the Sabha and president of Chetna Association of Canada.

52 Joseph Schaller, "Sanskritization, Caste Uplift, and Social Dissidence in the Sant Ravidas Panth," in *Bhakti Religion in North India: Community, Identity and Political Action,* ed. David N. Lorenzen (Albany: State University of New York Press, 1995), 113. Schaller also notes variation in self-ascribed religious affiliation, including "Hindu," "non-Hindu," and "Ravidasi."

53 John Stratton Hawley and Mark Juergensmeyer, *Songs of the Saints of India* (New York: Oxford University Press, 1988), 17.

54 *Sahota and Shergill v. Shri Guru Ravidass Sabha Temple,* 2008 BCHRT 269 (http://www.bchrt.bc.ca/decisions/2008/july-aug-sept.htm).

55 Themes for further study are mentioned by Dan Overmyer in the Concluding Comments below. Background can be found in Anderson et al., *Circle of Voices,* and Coward and Banerjee, "Hindus in Canada." Coward's portion of the chapter repeats his earlier work.

56 T.N. Madan, ed., *India's Religions: Perspectives from Sociology and History* (New Delhi and New York: Oxford University Press, 2004), 31-32.

57 Vertovec, *The Hindu Diaspora,* 52.

58 Bramadat and Seljak, *Religion and Ethnicity in Canada,* 232-33, note this for Canada. Diana L. Eck, whose whole *Pluralism Project* was motivated by this in the United States, makes specific note in *A New Religious America* (San Francisco: HarperSanFrancisco, 2001), 18.

59 Charles Taylor, Amy Gutmann, Kwame Anthony Appiah, Jurgen Habermas, Stephen C. Rockefeller, Michael Walzer, and Susan Wolf, *Multiculturalism: Examining the Politics of Recognition* (Princeton, NJ: Princeton University Press, 1994), 63-73. See the final report in 2008 of the Quebec Consultation Commission on Accommodation Practices Related to Cultural Differences (Bouchard-Taylor Commission), available at http://www.accommodements.qc.ca/index-en.html.

60 Robert J. Schreiter, "Summation: Call to Action," in *A Dome of Many Colors: Studies in Religious Pluralism, Identity, and Unity,* ed. Arvind Sharma and Kathleen M. Dugan (Harrisburg, PA: Trinity Press International, 1999), 190.

2   The Making of Sikh Space: The Role of the Gurdwara

KAMALA ELIZABETH NAYAR

From the time Sikhs migrated to Western Canada in the early 1900s up to the present, many issues and events surrounding the community's settlement and development have emerged, most of which centre on the gurdwara (Sikh temple). The gurdwara (literally "door to the Guru") is where a devotee meets with the "Guru" – the revered scripture called the *Guru Granth Sahib*.[1] The scripture not only forms the basis for insight into the true nature of Reality but also plays a central role in Sikh religious worship.[2] Accorded the status of Guru,[3] it is installed on a raised platform covered by a canopied regal throne within the gurdwara. Even today, many Sikhs living in North America "confide" in the scripture for guidance by saying a prayer (*ardas*) in front of the *Guru Granth Sahib* and then randomly opening it to read a sacred passage (*vak*).[4]

Worship of the scripture in the gurdwara is so central to the life of a Sikh that even the British Crown recognized its importance; it allowed Sikh soldiers in the British Indian Army to carry a small version of the *Guru Granth Sahib* during the First World War. Emulating the eighteenth-century innovation of the *safari-bir* (small, travel-sized manuscripts), the British Crown sponsored a limited edition of a remarkably small printed text (2 inches by 2 inches) and distributed it to boost the morale of Sikh soldiers who fought in the war.[5] It also permitted "sacred space" – small gurdwaras – in the Sikh regiments, where the soldiers could recite their daily prayers.

Not only is the gurdwara central to Sikh religious practice, it also has an essential role in community life in village Punjab, just as a Buddhist temple plays a central role in both the religious and cultural life of some of the Buddhist communities discussed elsewhere in this book. Thus, away from their homeland, Sikhs have asserted their religious identity by building gurdwaras wherever they have settled. Despite the many challenges it has faced with migration, the community of 135,310 has successfully created "Sikh space" in British

Columbia,[6] with the gurdwara as the primary medium through which it has established itself in the province.

In light of the gurdwara's centrality in Sikh life, the purpose of this chapter is to examine how the Sikh community has succeeded in establishing sacred, cultural, social, and political space in British Columbia through the gurdwara. In doing so, it delineates the relationship between the conditions surrounding migration and settlement and the pattern of building the BC gurdwaras, and demonstrates how the gurdwara serves as (1) a place for socio-cultural activity, (2) the locus for the Sikh pursuit of social justice, and (3) a base for mobilizing political power. Finally, this chapter also looks at Canadian-born Sikh youth and their perception of the gurdwara as somewhat ineffective in serving their needs.[7]

Establishment of Gurdwaras in Relation to Migration and Settlement Patterns

One of the striking features of the British Columbia cultural landscape is the presence of gurdwaras throughout the province. It is not surprising that Sikhs built gurdwaras according to their settlement patterns. Endowed with the industrious Punjabi character, they were willing to traverse unknown territory under challenging conditions in the hope of finding employment. They also displayed boldness and resiliency in continuing their customs wherever they settled for work, even in the small isolated towns of the North Coast region and on Vancouver Island.

Despite the challenges of living in a new country that did not welcome visible minorities at the beginning of the twentieth century, it was crucial for most newly arrived Sikh migrants to uphold their religious tradition. On many occasions, Sikhs built "home gurdwaras" by transforming a spare room into sacred space. Sabik Singh Dhaliwal, the son of a Sikh pioneer, describes how his father's living accommodation in Vancouver was arranged to create sacred space at a time when no gurdwaras existed:

> My father, Giani Harnam Singh, arrived in Vancouver in 1904. He, and seven or eight gentlemen, rented a house on Gore and East Hastings Street (Vancouver). Some worked at the mill [in the area now called False Creek]; others unloaded the grain at the CPR (Canadian Pacific Railway) at Burrard Inlet. Everything revolved around the train and boats at the Burrard Inlet. They rented the house and all lived downstairs. The *Guru Granth Sahib* was kept upstairs.

Since the scripture is to be revered on a raised platform, the men transformed the top floor into a gurdwara. Certain gurdwaras, such as the Golden Temple in Amritsar, are highly revered because of their connection with important events in Sikh history, but every gurdwara has the same spiritual status because they all enshrine the *Guru Granth Sahib*. The custom of making home gurdwaras is therefore accepted within the Sikh community, as long as the scripture is properly installed and worshipped according to the Sikh Code of Conduct (*Sikh Rehat Maryada*).

Although unique home gurdwaras were established by some devout Sikhs on their initial arrival and settlement, community gurdwaras were also set up beginning in 1906. For the most part, the pattern of building gurdwaras in British Columbia was directly influenced by both the conditions surrounding Sikh migration to Canada and the settlement pattern of the Sikhs as shaped by the Canadian government's practice in managing ethnic diversity. The growth of the Sikh community in British Columbia has also been a factor. On the one hand, such growth has given the community greater resources for building gurdwaras; on the other hand, it has also resulted in factionalism in the community.

Five phases in the development of gurdwaras in British Columbia can be distinguished:

1 the "mill colony" gurdwaras and the Khalsa Diwan Society during the first half of the twentieth century
2 the creation of the Akali Singh Society in Vancouver and Victoria during the 1950s
3 the burgeoning of gurdwaras in small BC towns and the building of actual gurdwara structures in the British Columbia Lower Mainland during the 1970s and 1980s
4 the emergence of the "fundamentalist" and "moderate" gurdwaras beginning from 1998
5 the establishment of "sectarian" orthodox gurdwaras, especially after 1998.

The "Mill Colony" Gurdwaras and the Khalsa Diwan Society

The Sikh pioneers of the first half of the twentieth century migrated to Canada to help fill the dominion's need for manual labour in its natural resource industries, and because Canada had become known in India as an attractive place economically. Although they managed to enter Canada to work, they were not welcomed as citizens and lived for the most part segregated from the general population. Most of the migrants were young men who intended to return to India eventually, and most actually lived at their employment sites in colonies on the mill grounds.[8] Transportation was limited and the mill grounds were often inaccessible, so it was common for mill owners – both Sikh and Euro-Canadian – to build gurdwaras right on site along with bunker-type housing, thus accommodating their Sikh labourers and, in a sense, re-creating Punjabi village life. Joan Mayo, the wife of Mayo Singh's eldest son, observed: "The life of a Sikh revolves around his Temple ... Therefore it was only natural that once the mill and bunkers were erected the next building should be a Temple. Mayo [Singh] built the first official Temple in Paldi in 1919 on the same spot where the present temple is located."[9] The owners made the mill colonies more Sikh-friendly in order to attract Sikh labourers, who were known for their hard work.[10] I refer to these gurdwaras as the "mill colony" gurdwaras.

The mill colony gurdwaras were private organizations since they were built as part of the mill establishments. The labourers constructed these gurdwaras themselves with the wood processed on site. The gurdwaras were simple but were nevertheless places that enshrined the Sikh scripture so that the workers had a place for worship. The first mill colony gurdwara built on BC soil was the one at Fraser Mills in Burquitlam, which no longer exists.[11] Many of the mill colony bunkers and gurdwaras disappeared after the mills closed, but a few such gurdwaras still stand in remote places on Vancouver Island even though the mills are no longer in operation. For example, the Paldi gurdwara near Duncan, constructed in the early 1900s, still stands where the Mayo Company mill operated until 1945.[12]

Besides the mill colony gurdwaras, Sikh migrants in Vancouver formed the Khalsa Diwan Society (KDS) in 1906, as an offshoot of the organization in the Punjab. In 1908, the society bought a lot on West 2nd Avenue and built a gurdwara, referred to as the 2nd Avenue Gurdwara, which was relocated to a new building at Ross Street and Southwest Marine Drive in 1969. The KDS established a second gurdwara in Abbotsford in 1911; in 2004, it was designated as a Canadian historical site by the Department of Canadian Heritage. Although these gurdwaras were not in isolated or segregated mill colonies, they were located close to mills and in areas where Sikhs felt comfortable living.

During the first half of the twentieth century, other KDS gurdwaras – at Abbotsford, Victoria, and New Westminster – functioned under the auspices of the Vancouver KDS. In contrast, the mill colony gurdwaras were privately owned by mill proprietors and some eventually became registered under the *Societies Act* in the 1950s.[13] Although the Sikh community in British Columbia was close-knit and the gurdwaras worked together, over time, the small-town gurdwaras on Vancouver Island actually preferred to be independent from the Vancouver KDS.

The Akali Singh Society
The Akali Singh Society was established in the two major urban centres of Vancouver and Victoria during the 1950s, when the Sikh community grew in size following changes to Canada's immigration law in 1950 in the aftermath of India's independence from the British Crown in 1947. During this period,

Indian immigration into Canada was allowed under the sponsorship system, which worked in favour of Sikhs since most of the earlier immigrants from India had been Sikhs.[14]

Besides the radical change in immigration law, the Canadian government granted Sikhs the right to become Canadian citizens during the 1950s. Now, as members of Canadian society, they experienced pressure to assimilate. During the pioneer days, there had been pressure on Sikhs to remove their turbans, cut their hair, shave their beards, switch to Western clothing, and even assume Anglicized versions of their names in order to find employment. Now many felt that they had to adopt the Western lifestyle in order to be accepted as members of mainstream Canadian society. Consequently, many took on Western appearance, although some were determined to keep the external symbols of their faith.[15]

The increase in numbers of Sikh migrants – predominantly clean-shaven – amplified tensions between the orthodox (those who practise the fundamental principles prescribed in Sikh religious scripture and doctrine) and the non-orthodox Sikhs (those who took on Western appearance). As a result, a small group of orthodox Sikhs broke away from the KDS in 1952 and established the Akali Singh Society in 1953, in order to maintain traditional Sikh practice.[16] (For a discussion of the specific dispute over management of the KDS, see the section "The Gurdwara as a Centre for Mobilizing Political Power" below.)

The Small-Town Gurdwaras and Vancouver Gurdwara Structures

The largest influx of Indian immigrants into Canada occurred during the Trudeau era in the 1970s, following further changes to the country's immigration law (e.g., the expansion of the family reunification program and introduction of the point system). This led, during this decade and the 1980s, to the most extensive development of the Sikh religious landscape in British Columbia.

Many Sikh immigrants found jobs as skilled and unskilled labourers throughout the province. In Canada's thriving resource economy, Sikh communities grew and spread, and gurdwaras were established throughout rural British Columbia. Unlike the earlier small, segregated mill colony gurdwaras, these newer ones were set up in old churches of the mainstream community. The local Sikh communities managed to build gurdwaras even with limited resources in small, remote towns. A handful of families would congregate to pray and would eventually establish a gurdwara, as occurred in Prince Rupert, an isolated town in the North Coast region of British Columbia:

> In the mid-1960s, a few families would get together and listen to the reels [recordings of the recitation of "Japji," the first hymn in the *Guru Granth Sahib*].

We did not have a copy of the *Guru Granth Sahib* in Prince Rupert. We just had the reels to listen to! We eventually ordered the scripture itself in the early 1970s from Singapore. We sent for it by mail. We got it in Prince Rupert by the mail.

By the early 1970s, the Sikh community in Prince Rupert consisted of only four or so extended families that lived in the actual town. There were around thirty to forty Sikh men, who lived in the mill bunkers. The community initially rented a hall belonging to a Catholic church. Once a month, we had the hall from 10:00 a.m. to 12:00 p.m. We would have a local person come and speak about the Sikh religion. We had *langar* [community dining hall] on the floors with some tables and chairs. The food was brought from home. The ladies wore Punjabi suits and the men usually dressed in Western pants and shirts. They all covered their heads. There were about thirty to fifty people who attended this monthly congregation. In 1972, the Indo-Canadian Association was formally established as a registered BC society. One of the chief aims of this society was to establish a Sikh temple. There was some resistance from the inter-religious Indian faction, which preferred a cultural centre instead of a Sikh religious temple.

The Indo-Canadian Association eventually found a suitable property that was previously a church. Four families put up their own properties as collateral to purchase the property. The property cost $38,000, which the community paid off within six months. The society's name was changed to Indo-Canadian Sikh Association on 16 June 1974.[17]

Unlike in the small towns, the Sikh community in the Lower Mainland experienced tremendous growth and could afford to construct gurdwaras according to traditional Sikh architecture – indeed, to build actual traditional gurdwaras. Such construction was tolerated by mainstream Canadian society, which came under pressure to celebrate diversity after the introduction of the Canadian policy of multiculturalism in 1971.

It is important to note that although the gurdwaras today are situated in busy urban centres – for example, the Vancouver KDS Gurdwara on Ross Street and Southwest Marine Drive in South Vancouver, the Akali Singh Gurdwara on Skeena Street in East Vancouver, and the Guru Nanak Sikh Gurdwara on Scott Road in Surrey – at the time the land was acquired and the buildings constructed, they were in fact located in isolated industrial or undeveloped areas. The surrounding areas developed quickly after the gurdwaras were constructed because Punjabis prefered to live close to their places of work (such as lumber mills) and to their gurdwaras.[18] The Guru Nanak Sikh Gurdwara is a good example of how construction of the traditional gurdwara structure was tolerated only in an undeveloped location that was followed by development of the area.

Around 200 Sikh families lived in the Surrey-Delta area during the mid-1970s. The Guru Nanak Sikh Society was registered in 1973 and purchased an old house on 83rd Avenue and 112th Street in North Delta, which it converted into a gurdwara in 1975. Non-Sikh residents complained that the gurdwara ruined the Delta neighbourhood, especially with respect to the congregation taking up all the street parking space.[19] In February 1977, fire damaged the gurdwara beyond repair. Without a temple and without a Delta community centre, the Sikhs – without municipal approval – quickly repaired the gurdwara for worship.[20] The gurdwara was temporarily repaired and re-opened in April 1977.[21] The City of Delta eventually granted the Guru Nanak Sikh Society permission to rebuild it, even as non-Sikh residents near the property lobbied against the project.[22]

Caught between the Guru Nanak Sikh Society and non-Sikh residents,[23] both the City of Delta and the City of Surrey approached the Society to relocate their temple on Scott Road, which forms the border between Surrey and Delta (at that time an unpaved border!). Guru Nanak Sikh Society acquired seven acres of land on the Surrey side of Scott Road in 1973; however, the City of Surrey had previously turned down the Society's proposal to construct a gurdwara at that location. This area was undeveloped and had no sewage system. To defuse non-Sikh hostility toward the construction of a gurdwara in Delta, the City of Delta assured the Society that if it built the new gurdwara on the Surrey side of Scott Road, it would be given access to Delta's sewage system.[24] The Guru Nanak Sikh Gurdwara was built according to traditional temple design and completed in 1981. The location, known as "Scott and 72nd," has since become a major shopping district, with many Sikhs living in the surrounding neighbourhoods.[25]

The "Fundamentalist"/"Moderate" Schism

The split between "fundamentalists" and "moderates" that occurred in the Lower Mainland's Sikh community in 1998 over the use of tables and chairs in the Guru Nanak Sikh Gurdwara's *langar*s echoed the tension between orthodox and non-orthodox Sikhs in the early 1950s. After the 1998 Akal Takht edict prohibiting the use of tables and chairs in *langar*s,[26] gurdwaras that required people to sit on mats in accordance with tradition were branded by the media as "fundamentalist." On the other hand, those that permitted the use of tables and chairs, contrary to the edict, were labelled by the media as "moderate." Thus, the Guru Nanak Sikh Gurdwara is now considered to be moderate, while the newly established temple in Surrey, Dasmesh Darbar Gurdwara, is regarded as fundamentalist. (For a discussion of the specific dispute over management of the Guru Nanak Sikh Gurdwara, see the section "The Gurdwara as a Centre for Mobilizing Political Power" below.)

The schism that resulted in the establishment of traditionalist gurdwaras in the Lower Mainland had repercussions in rural British Columbia. It is now common to find two gurdwaras – one traditionalist, the other moderate – in many smaller centres, such as Terrace, Prince George, and Kamloops. In all cases, orthodox Sikhs, who were outnumbered by non-orthodox Sikhs, felt compelled to create new gurdwaras in their respective towns. Unlike in the 1950s, however, they were able to rely on funds and support from the large base of orthodox Sikhs living in the Lower Mainland.

"Sectarian" Orthodox Gurdwaras

Since the "fundamentalist"/"moderate" schism in 1998, many orthodox but politically moderate Sikhs have distanced themselves from the so-called fundamentalists by establishing "sectarian" gurdwaras. Although Sikhs who are religiously orthodox attend the "fundamentalist" gurdwaras, many of them are politically "moderate." Even more, there are also some orthodox Sikhs, who support the establishment of a separate country of Khalistan but oppose the resort to extreme means to achieve this goal.[27] Sectarian orthodox gurdwaras have, therefore, been established in reaction to the establishment of so-called fundamentalist gurdwaras and their extremist political orientation.

Unlike in the pioneer years, when gurdwaras were non-denominational, the divisions in the 1950s and in 1998 served as a catalyst for the building of gurdwaras according to a specific religio-political orientation. For instance, the Khalsa Darbar Gurdwara in South Vancouver was built according to the rules of the Shiromani Gurdwara Parbandhak Committee, whereas the Gurdwara Amrit Prakash in Surrey was built according to the Damdami Taksal's code of conduct.[28] Meanwhile, the Gurdwara Nanaksar in Cloverdale is connected to a *baba* (a religious preacher-healer). Since these congregations are more specific, consisting of followers of a particular subtradition, they are often smaller in size. Interestingly, these smaller gurdwaras have all been recently established in old churches no longer functioning in areas where there has been a sharp increase in the South Asian population.[29]

Meanwhile, in reaction to the political eruptions within the Sikh community, many baptized and non-baptized Sikhs have simply chosen to distance themselves from the community gurdwaras. They have created their own home gurdwaras, with a room (usually the largest one on the top floor of the house) reserved solely for the scripture, so that they may recite their prayers at home. There is an ironic reversal in the reasons for setting up home gurdwaras. The early Sikh migrants to British Columbia created home gurdwaras because of external factors, such as small community size in an inhospitable society and limited resources. Today, however, home gurdwaras are built because of internal forces, especially divisions related to community members' different religious and political affiliations.

Despite these recent developments, the establishment of gurdwaras has indeed created sacred space for Sikhs, as in village Punjab. As we shall see next, the gurdwaras have also served as the crucial base for cultural, social, and political activities within the Sikh community in British Columbia.

The Role of the Gurdwara in Sikh Community Life

Following the Sikh tradition of *seva* (selfless service), the gurdwara is the centre for community social service, even as it is also a place for religio-cultural functions. Sikhs are obliged to practise *seva* in order to contribute to the community. They have a tradition of providing help to the community at the gurdwara through donations of food, clothing, and money, as well as by assisting in the maintenance of the temple or the functioning of the *langar*. Although the practice of serving others remains a central feature of the gurdwara in British Columbia, its orientation has changed somewhat over the years. Besides helping new Sikh immigrants as in the pioneer days, it now helps also both the culturally alienated seniors and the socially downtrodden.

Home Base for New Immigrants

Like the gurdwaras in the Punjab, which have provided accommodations to itinerant villagers because hotels or motels were not a feature of traditional agricultural society, the gurdwaras in British Columbia have been places not only where people could eat but also where they could stay.[30] In Western Canada, they have played a vital role in assisting new immigrants since the early 1900s, when they were particularly crucial to the newcomers' survival in a foreign land since most Sikh migrants arrived without any connection to a family network. The migrants would often stay initially at a gurdwara, which provided a place to eat and sleep as well as assistance in finding housing and employment.

The gurdwara also served as a home base for new immigrants, especially those who could not speak English or who were illiterate.[31] The latter would go to the gurdwara even for simple matters such as having their mail read to them.[32] The gurdwara also served its members as a conduit to the mainstream society, often in the form of advocacy or as a springboard for building a social network.

The gurdwara's role in providing for immigrants' basic survival needs has declined gradually since 1951, as most immigrants now come to Canada through the sponsorship system and thus already have an established kinship network.

Today, it plays a more important role in providing psychosocial support, as more recent immigrants meet there on a regular basis as a way of creating a home for themselves in their new country.

Gathering Place for Seniors

The gurdwara also serves as a central place for seniors, many of whom were sponsored by their children from the 1970s onward. There they can get together to relive memories of life in the Punjab, be in a familiar environment, and speak with each other in Punjabi.[33] The women often talk about cooking, clothing, their physical ailments, and family life, while the men often play cards and talk about community events or politics in British Columbia and in their homeland. Many gurdwaras operate seniors' groups and some, such as the Guru Nanak Sikh Gurdwara, even have an adjoining seniors' centre.

As in the Punjab, the BC gurdwaras often maintain schools that offer Punjabi and religious or other educational classes. These are mainly for youth, but some gurdwaras offer classes in English as a second language or "survival English" for new immigrants, and these are most often attended by seniors. Volunteers may also assist seniors with such matters as filling out application forms to sponsor family members, paying income taxes, or collecting pensions. Also, it is often through the gurdwaras that new immigrants and seniors become aware of social programs and are able to benefit from them, since they learn about these by word of mouth, even when organizations have Punjabi-language facilities.

Refuge for the Downtrodden

In both the Punjab and British Columbia, the gurdwara serves as a refuge for the marginalized or downtrodden, primarily through its institutions of *seva* and *langar*. Since the gurdwara is open to all, it is not uncommon to find the less fortunate – Punjabi Sikhs, other South Asians, or even Caucasians – availing themselves of both *seva* and, especially, *langar*, chiefly in Lower Mainland gurdwaras. One social service provider comments: "The Sikh temple and its concept of *langar* benefit non-Sikhs as well. Since it is open to all, anyone can go; Sikh or non-Sikh alike. I have come across many youth who reside in BC housing regularly visit gurdwaras for *langar*. I have also talked to several homeless persons who describe the gurdwara *langar* as a good resource for free tasty food."[34] Indeed, the *langar* institution can be viewed as functioning, for some, like the Western soup kitchen.

Religious Ceremonies and Social Functions

Most Sikhs who are economically settled attend the gurdwara mainly for religio-cultural functions associated with either a Sikh rite of passage or religious holidays. The religious ceremonies associated with the four rites of passage are key events in a Sikh's life and are performed at the community gurdwara.[35] There are also many Sikh holy days (such as the birthdays of the ten Sikh gurus and the days when Guru Arjan Dev and Guru Tegh Bahadur became martyrs) or cultural festivals with some religious significance (such as Baisakhi, Divali, and Lohri),[36] during which many Sikhs attend the gurdwara.

Since the gurdwaras were non-denominational during the early 1900s, each gurdwara would host a different Sikh holiday, thereby supporting the operation of every gurdwara for the relatively small Sikh community in British Columbia.[37] Only since the 1950s onward has the community been divided in terms of its religious celebrations and festivities, most notably during the 1999 Baisakhi celebration.

In 1995, the BC government officially recognized the Baisakhi parade for the Lower Mainland, organized by the Vancouver Khalsa Diwan Society Gurdwara, in which many small-town congregations from other parts of the province also participate. Since the 1998 divide between "fundamentalist" and "moderate" groups, however, two separate parades have been held. The "fundamentalist" parade begins and ends at the Dasmesh Darbar Gurdwara in Surrey, while the original, and now, "moderate" parade begins and ends at the KDS Gurdwara on Ross Street in South Vancouver. Ironically, the 1999 Baisakhi celebrations marked the tricentennial of the birth of the Khalsa, which was celebrated by Sikhs the world over as one global community. In British Columbia, however, the Sikh community was divided on this auspicious occasion.

The Role of the Gurdwara in the Fight for Social Justice
In line with the Sikh tradition of fighting against political oppression and social injustices such as the caste system, gurdwaras in British Columbia lobby for the social interests of its members. They have also mobilized the Sikh community against the racist attitude found in past Canadian immigration laws and in restrictions on Sikhs living in Canada.

Lobbying against Immigration Laws
After the anti-Asian riots that occurred in Vancouver in 1907 and the tightening of Canada's immigration policy, two developments brought to the fore the official racial discrimination toward East Indian (predominantly Sikh) migration to Canada: (1) the federal government's proposal to resettle East Indians in British Honduras, and (2) the Canadian immigration requirement of "continuous journey." In 1909, the congregation at the Vancouver KDS Gurdwara, under the guidance of Teja Singh, a Harvard-educated Sikh and Indian-trained lawyer who wrote the society's constitution, rejected the British Honduras resettlement proposal, viewing it as no more than a scheme to expel East Indians from Canada.[38] The KDS likewise protested against the continuous journey

rule, which required passenger ships to come directly from their home ports, thereby making it impossible for an Indian ship to dock in Canada since any ship coming from India had to stop at a foreign port for refuelling. This requirement angered many East Indians, especially because, even though they were from a colony under the British Crown, they were not allowed to migrate to another part of the British Empire, Canada.[39]

This discrimination against East Indians in Canadian immigration law was most evident in the historic *Komagata Maru* incident of 1914, when a Japanese ship was refused permission to dock at Burrard Inlet, Vancouver. The *Komagata Maru* had been chartered by Gurdit Singh to bring 376 prospective Punjabi immigrants to British Columbia. Chartering the ship from Hong Kong was an attempt to work around the Canadian continuous journey restriction. The KDS raised funds to fight the court battle over the docking of the ship but its efforts were unsuccessful and the *Komagata Maru* was prevented from docking by a court order. The ship was subsequently sent back to Hong Kong.[40]

Nevertheless, the KDS continued to function as an advocacy group, lobbying the federal and provincial governments especially on immigration policies.[41] It urged the government to permit the immigration of fiancées, wives, and children, which finally came to pass in 1951 with the institution of the family sponsorship system.

Fighting Racism

Along with the implicit racism in Canadian immigration law during the early 1900s, Sikhs also experienced both legal and informal restrictions, against which the gurdwaras lobbied. The formal legal restrictions included not being allowed to become citizens, to vote, to serve on juries or school boards, to join the military, or to take jobs in public works. Informal restrictions made it difficult for Sikhs living in British Columbia to use public facilities and services, to live outside restricted areas, to acquire an education, to enter professional and other high-status jobs, to get fair wages, and to exercise workplace rights.[42] One example of the gurdwara's lobbying is the official petition by the KDS in 1945, asking that Sikhs be granted the right to vote in municipal, provincial, and federal elections.[43]

During the second half of the twentieth century, the gurdwara continued to work against discrimination and racism. Even in the 1970s, when the policy of multiculturalism enabled many Sikhs to immigrate to Canada, they still encountered a great deal of hostility and racism. Under the multiculturalism policy, however, nongovernmental organizations (NGOs) began receiving funds to serve the distinctive needs of visible ethnic minority groups, through settlement and employment programs, language classes, and advocacy. Initially, the gurdwara functioned as a home base for assisting the early immigrants through such services, but more recently it has become a place for community outreach. Ethno-specific NGOs[44] or personnel from mainstream organizations such as community health centres or hospitals often link themselves to gurdwaras as places where they can connect with immigrants. They go to gurdwaras and the adjoining seniors' centres to establish relations with the community and help bridge the cultural gap between traditional orientation and modern society.[45] In a sense, the gurdwara acts as a liaison between the Sikh community and mainstream institutions.

The Gurdwara as a Centre for Mobilizing Political Power

The gurdwara's history of political involvement is a long one indeed. During early Sikh history, politics revolved around internal disputes regarding succession in the guru lineage and the struggle against Mughal rule and its oppression of Hindus and Sikhs. In line with the Sikh concern over socio-political matters in the secular sphere, the gurdwaras in British Columbia have also been centres for mobilizing political power over issues pertaining to the homeland, to mainstream Canadian society, and to the BC Sikh community itself.

Links with the Homeland

Gurdwaras in British Columbia had especially close links to the Punjab during two periods: the early 1900s, when India was fighting for its independence from British rule, and the late 1970s to early 1990s, when some Sikhs were involved with the quest for "Khalistan" or a separate Sikh state.

In the early 1900s, a gurdwara-based organization known as the Ghadar (mutiny, revolt) party called on Indians, mostly Sikhs, to return to India to fight the British.[46] Although printed in San Francisco, the *Gadr Weekly* was covertly circulated in British Columbia and exhorted Indians to take up the sword:

> Time for prayer is gone,
> take the sword in hand.
> Time is now to plunge in a battle.
> Those, who long for martyrdom,
> will live forever as shining guideposts.[47]

There was tension between Sikhs who aligned themselves with the British Crown and those who opposed it. The politics of the Punjab played out even in Vancouver's Khalsa Diwan Society: Bela Singh and Harnam Singh worked as informants for the British agent W.C. Hopkinson, whose duty it was to spy on Ghadar nationalist party activities in British Columbia. Harnam Singh vanished on 17 August 1914 and was found dead shortly after. After another spy, Arjun Singh, was killed by a Ghadar revolutionary, Bela Singh took revenge by murdering two priests at Arjun Singh's funeral. The Sikh community was enraged by these killings because they took place in the gurdwara. Many believed that the government supported Bela Singh's attack, since he was acquitted on the ground that his actions were taken in self-defence (as argued by Hopkinson). On the day of Bela Singh's trial, Mewa Singh murdered Hopkinson. Mewa Singh was caught, convicted, and sentenced to death. He was hanged on 11 January 1915 and is revered as a martyr in the Sikh tradition; in fact, the *langar* at the Vancouver KDS Gurdwara is named in his honour.

Political linkage between some BC gurdwaras and the Punjab was also related to the Khalistan movement. During the 1980s, Canadian Sikhs felt that the Indian government was marginalizing their compatriots in the Punjab. In response to armed separatist activity inside the Golden Temple at Amritsar, the Sikhs's most significant place of worship, the Indian military launched Operation Bluestar and invaded the temple complex on 3 June 1984. Operation Bluestar spurred many once clean-shaven Sikhs to take the practice of their religion more seriously, and many became orthodox.[48] Some of the Lower Mainland gurdwaras were taken over by pro-Khalistan organizations, which collected funds for the Khalistan movement in the Punjab and lobbied Western governments concerning alleged human rights violations there.[49]

Networking with Mainstream Canadian Society

Indian immigrants were granted the right to become Canadian citizens and the right to vote following India's independence from the British Crown in 1947. This was followed by an expansion of the gurdwara's role as a locus for mobilizing political power in Canadian society. Beginning in the 1950s[50] and steadily growing from the late 1970s onward (after the Canadian government's implementation of official multiculturalism), mainstream politicians' appeal to the ethnic vote through the gurdwara increasingly gained importance. Subsequently, the ethnic vote has also become a valuable political resource for the Sikh community in its efforts to influence mainstream politics at the municipal, provincial, and federal levels. Large Sikh congregations are now viewed by political parties as potential voting blocs, and politicians from the main parties, both Sikh and non-Sikh, commonly give campaign speeches in the prayer halls of gurdwaras.

Just as Sikh leaders use gurdwaras for political purposes in India, Sikhs in Canada participate in gurdwaras as a way to engage the larger polity. There is a major difference, however, between the Punjab and British Columbia in the manner in which gurdwaras are used for politics. In the former, political discussions take place in the *langar*s or in the fields surrounding the temples, whereas in the latter, Sikh and non-Sikh politicians give their speeches in the prayer halls.

In a sense, therefore, mainstream Canadian political involvement in the gurdwara has been disruptive to the concept of Sikh sacred space for worship.[51]

A Political Base within the Punjabi Community
During the pioneer years, the gurdwaras were non-denominational in the sense that they simply functioned according to "what they had remembered back in the homeland," instead of operating from a particular theological or political platform. Indeed, their primary goal was survival in a foreign environment. From 1947 to the present, however, the Vancouver Khalsa Diwan Society has become increasingly concerned with the practice of Sikhism, in the process changing its original orientation. Three major political incidents, which occurred in the early 1950s, during the 1970s, and in 1998, respectively, resulted in divisions along religious and political lines within the BC Sikh community.

In the 1950s, a dispute over the management of the Vancouver KDS Gurdwara, then on West 2nd Avenue, reflected the growing tension between orthodox and non-orthodox Sikhs. From 1906 to 1950, there had been a rule that only orthodox Sikhs could serve on the managing committee. Due to an increase in the number of clean-shaven Sikhs, however, there was much tension from 1948 to 1952 over whether a clean-shaven Sikh could serve. During the management committee elections in 1952, clean-shaven Sikhs were in the majority and thus were able to elect themselves to the committee. In effect, the community suffered a schism when some of the orthodox Sikhs broke away from the KDS and established the Akali Singh Society.[52]

The community became even more divided in the 1970s. Unlike earlier generations of Sikhs, who experienced pressure to assimilate and gave up many of their customs, many of those who arrived during the time of official multiculturalism wanted to maintain the traditional orthodox practices that they had brought with them from the Punjab. Head covering became a contentious issue in the gurdwaras and caused constant tension between earlier and more recent immigrants, between practising and non-practising Sikhs.[53]

Tension between practising and non-practising Sikhs worsened in the wake of Operation Bluestar. Orthodox Sikhs were growing in number, however, and many of them, together with clean-shaven Sikhs who identified with the fight for greater autonomy in the Punjab, became members of pro-Khalistan organizations. Some gurdwaras were taken over by such groups. For instance, the World Sikh Organization (WSO) gained control over the Vancouver KDS Gurdwara, which had previously been run by non-practising "comrade" Sikhs (that is, those with a Marxist orientation). An offshoot of the WSO, the International Sikh Youth Federation (ISYF), gained control over the Guru Nanak Sikh Gurdwara in Surrey. The ISYF was ousted from power in January 1998 through a joint effort of non-baptized communist and pro-Indian Congress Sikhs and baptized Sikhs who opposed the ISYF. In reaction to its loss of control over the temple, the ISYF raised the issue of the use of tables and chairs in the *langar*, even though it had maintained tables and chairs in the *langar* when it had previously been managing the temple.[54]

On 20 April 1998, the Akal Takht issued an edict (*hukam-nama*) against the use of tables and chairs in the *langar*. On 29 May, the newly elected Guru Nanak Sikh Gurdwara management, along with the KDS in South Vancouver and its affiliated gurdwaras, decided not to obey the edict. However, the issue was used successfully by the ISYF to ensure attendance of the followers of the Akal Takht at their newly established Dasmesh Darbar Gurdwara in Surrey. That is, Sikhs began going to this "fundamentalist" gurdwara out of their obligation to follow the Akal Takht. The followers of the Akal Takht in the Lower Mainland, and thus the attendees of the newly established Dasmesh Darbar Gurdwara, which was branded as fundamentalist, in actuality consist of: (1) new Punjabi immigrants; (2) practising but not baptized Sikhs, including those who keep their uncut hair covered (*kesdhari*) or who do not bear any Sikh symbols (*sahajdhari*); and (3) those who are baptized (*amritdhari*), including those who had been originally involved with the joint effort against the ISYF. In fact, opponents of the ISYF manoeuvre saw the raising of the issue on the part of the temple management at the Guru Nanak Sikh Gurdwara in Surrey not only as a way to secure attendance at Dasmesh Darbar Gurdwara but also to channel gurdwara funds for factional interests or for supporting separate statehood in the Punjab.[55]

Although many new immigrants attend the gurdwaras, the real activists in gurdwara politics are the members of the management committees, most of whom have lived in Canada since the 1960s and 1970s and have an established network for political involvement and support.[56] These temple administrators are able to acquire political status and derive economic benefits from their positions, even as they remain in a familiar Punjabi milieu with few language, communication, and cultural barriers. They are considered the community leaders by the media and the political mainstream, even though many Sikhs, especially those who are economically settled in British Columbia, do not regard them as such.

BC Gurdwaras and Canadian-Born Sikh Youth

Although interested in learning about their heritage, many Canadian-born/raised Sikh youth have drifted away from the gurdwaras because of the politics, culture clashes, and lack of proper facilities for learning about the Sikh tradition.[57] Some of these youth consider it futile to build more gurdwaras. A 20-year-old Sikh woman comments:

They are just building gurdwaras but what use is this if the younger generation is not aware of the tradition, religion? If they are not given the intangible aspect of culture and religion these gurdwaras are going to be empty down the road. They do concrete things, such as building new structures, but lack awareness of the need in being involved with the education of religion.[58]

Whether or not this prediction of empty buildings comes to pass, the comment shows how Canadian-born/raised Sikh youth do not find their religious and cultural needs met at the gurdwara. Whether or not they attend a gurdwara, such youth generally experience a malaise with respect to the attendant politics and a culture clash with the management. Consequently, Sikh youth interested in their religion have begun exploring other avenues, including public libraries, postsecondary courses, and Sikh learning centres.

The latter, such as the Guru Nanak Academy in Surrey or the Gurmat Centre in Abbotsford, are modelled on the Western concept of education. Although orthodox Sikhs raised in Canada have established these centres, both orthodox and non-orthodox youth go there to learn Punjabi, Sikh scripture, *kirtan* (devotional singing accompanied by musical instruments), and *gatka* (Sikh martial arts). Interestingly, the learning centres follow the pattern of the sectarian orthodox gurdwaras in that each adheres to a specific sub-tradition in its teaching.

Conclusion

The Sikh community in British Columbia has succeeded in creating sacred, cultural, social, and political space for its members through the gurdwara. Although it has many roles, the driving force of the gurdwara has been and continues to be the practice of *seva* – the principle of selflessly serving others – which has helped to solidify the community in the face of social challenges. During the early 1900s, the Sikh pioneers were quick to establish gurdwaras to aid new immigrants on their arrival in Canada. In a sense, the early gurdwaras were established as non-denominational organizations, bound together by the thread of social activism on behalf of their members.

As the Sikh community grew and developed, and family/clan networks emerged, especially after the sponsorship system was introduced in 1951, there was less need for people to rely on the gurdwara for survival. The gurdwara gradually became a centre for mobilizing the ethnic vote in municipal, provincial, and federal elections, especially after Sikhs gained the right to become Canadian citizens and to vote.

Tension over the religious and political orientations of the gurdwaras' management came to the fore from the 1950s onward. Splinter groups emerged, especially after the 1998 dispute over the use of tables and chairs in *langar*s.

Despite the factionalism, however, the Sikh tradition of service to others continues to characterize all gurdwaras, regardless of their political orientation.

The Canadian policy of multiculturalism has led to a decline in the role of the gurdwara as an agent of advocacy and social assistance, as NGOs began to meet the specific needs of Sikh immigrants in the Lower Mainland. With this, however, came a new role for the gurdwara, that of liaison between NGOs and the Sikh community at large.

Despite the gurdwara's central role in the Sikh community, it has not been very effective in meeting the needs of Canadian-born/raised Sikh youth, causing them to turn to alternative places such as postsecondary educational institutions and Sikh learning centres to learn about their traditions and heritage. As long as Sikhs continue to migrate to British Columbia, however, the gurdwara will continue to be the focus of religious and social activity for many members of the community.

ACKNOWLEDGMENTS

I wish to thank members of the Sikh community who took the time to share their thoughts and experiences. Deserving of special mention are Jagat Singh Uppal (a Sikh pioneer), who kindly read this chapter and offered many useful comments; and Sabik Singh Dhaliwal, the son of Giani Harnam Singh, who also went out of his way to provide materials that would have been difficult to obtain otherwise. Librarians at Kwantlen University and Ryan Gallagher at Surrey Archives were also extremely helpful in finding relevant records.

NOTES

1 The Sikh meaning of *guru* is "Ultimate Reality" or the embodiment of that Reality, such as the Sacred Word. Hence, *guru* as "the embodiment of Ultimate Reality" also refers to the ten personal gurus who uttered the Sacred Word, and the scripture, *Guru Granth Sahib*, which contains the Sacred Word.
2 For an overview of the Sikh tradition, see W.H. McLeod, *Sikhs: History, Religion and Society* (New York: Columbia University Press, 1989), and J.S. Grewal, *Sikhs of the Punjab* (Cambridge: Cambridge University Press, 1991).
3 Some scholars, such as W.H. McLeod, have challenged the belief that Guru Gobind Singh bestowed the status of Guru on the *Guru Granth Sahib*. See McLeod, *The Evolution of the Sikh Community* (New Delhi: Oxford University Press, 1975).
4 Jaswinder Singh Sandhu, "The Sikh Model of the Person, Suffering, and Healing: Implications for Counsellors," *International Journal for the Advancement of Counselling* 26, 1 (2004): 35.
5 Gurinder S. Mann, *The Making of Sikh Scripture* (New York: Oxford University Press, 2001), 125.
6 Statistics Canada, "Population by Religion by Province and Territory (2001 Census)," http://www.statcan.ca. The concept of creating "religious spaces" outside of the homeland is taken from Barbara Metcalf, ed., *Making Muslim Space in North America and Europe* (Berkeley: University of California Press, 1996).
7 The research methodology for this chapter consisted of: (1) an analysis of archival data available from BC Sikh organizations; (2) "participatory observation" by the author at religious

events and programs at various gurdwaras in Greater Vancouver; and (3) semi-structured interviews using open-ended questions with five members of the Sikh community who played a significant role in the establishment of Sikhism in British Columbia. When cited in this study, the interviewees, who requested to remain anonymous, are identified as "Sikh" with a number in order to maintain confidentiality.
8 James Gaylord Chadney, "The Formation of Ethnic Communities, Lessons from Vancouver Sikhs," in *Sikh History and Religion in the Twentieth Century,* ed. Joseph T. O'Connell, Milton Israel, and Willard G. Oxtoby (Toronto: Centre for South Asian Studies, University of Toronto, 1988), 193.
9 Joan Mayo, *Paldi Remembered: 50 Years in the Life of a Vancouver Island Logging Town* (Paldi: Joan Mayo, 1997), 16.
10 Sabik Singh Dhaliwal, personal communication, 27 August 2005.
11 Archival materials concerning the Fraser Mills in Burquitlam are available at Simon Fraser University, Burnaby.
12 For an extensive study of the Paldi community, proposing that family ties have been a source of strength in coping with alienation and the pursuit of upward social mobility, see Archana B. Verma, *The Making of Little Punjab in Canada* (New Delhi: Sage, 2002). The Mayo mill and bunkers were demolished in September 2005 but the gurdwara remains standing: Joan Mayo, personal communication, September 2005.
13 Mayo, *Paldi Remembered,* 17.
14 During the same period, Canadian immigration policy also changed in accordance with the country's need for educated white-collar professionals. While some educated army veterans were permitted to migrate to Canada, most Sikh immigrants came under the family sponsorship program during the 1950s and 1960s; see Hugh Johnston, "Patterns of Sikh Migration to Canada, 1900-1960," in *Sikh History and Religion,* ed. O'Connell et al., 296-313.
15 Tara S. Bains and Hugh Johnston, *Four Quarters of the Night: The Life Journey of an Emigrant Sikh* (Montreal and Kingston: McGill-Queen's University Press, 1995), 58-59.
16 Mahinder Singh Dhillon, *A History Book of the Sikhs in Canada and California* (Vancouver: Shiromani Akali Dal Association of Canada, 1981), 273-74.
17 Sikh 2.
18 James Chadney, *The Sikhs of Vancouver* (New York: AMS Press, 1984), 104-12.
19 "Sikhs in Delta, Group Says Temple Ruins Neighbourhood," *Vancouver Sun,* 16 December 1976, 30.
20 "Surrey Refuses Temple Repair," *Vancouver Sun,* 8 March 1977, 15; "Beach Grove Seawall Seen," *Vancouver Sun,* 15 March 1977, 12; "Sikhs Charge Prejudice: North Delta Temple," *Vancouver Sun,* 22 March 1977, 9.
21 "Sikhs in Delta: Sikhs Break Law with Repair Work," *Vancouver Sun,* 13 April 1977, 20; "Sikhs Rebuild Delta Temple," *Vancouver Sun,* 14 April 1977, 8.
22 The Society did make a request to relocate to 84th Avenue, where they could build a gurdwara on a 1.8 acre site: "Temple Plan 'Most Serious' in History of Council," *Vancouver Sun,* 27 April 1977, 22. Subsequently, the Society was granted permission to repair the fire-damaged gurdwara: "Sikhs Allowed to Repair Temple," *Vancouver Sun,* 3 May 1977, 41; "Sikhs in Delta: Temple Bylaw Gets Nod," *Vancouver Sun,* 14 February 1978, A9.
23 "Sikhs Rebuffed," *Vancouver Sun,* 19 April 1977, 43; "Temple Plan 'Most Serious' in History of Council," *Vancouver Sun,* 27 April 1977, 22.
24 On 17 April 1978, Surrey Council reviewed an application for a land use contract for a proposed Sikh Temple to be built at 7054-120th Street. There was discussion over the use of Delta's sewer service (Surrey Council Minutes, Surrey, BC, 17 April 1978, RES.NO. Q-220, 204). Subsequently, the council on 24 April 1978 reviewed a petition that was concerned about the sewers in the area, objecting to a proposed road from the Sikh Temple to 122 Street

and submitting several questions regarding the building of the Sikh Temple (Surrey Council Minutes, Surrey, BC, 24 April 1978). On 1 October 1978, Surrey Council granted the land use contract 496 to build a Sikh Temple, pending finalization of a sewer agreement with the City of Delta (Surrey Council Minutes, Surrey, BC, 1 October 1979, RES.NO. W-646). On 17 December 1979, Surrey Council adopted the motion for the Land Use contract for the building of the Sikh Temple on Scott Road (Surrey Council Minutes, Surrey, BC, 17 December 1979, RES.NO. X-588).

25 Sikh 5. See also Dhillon, *A History Book of the Sikhs in Canada and California*, 279-81.
26 Akal Takht is the throne of the guru's temporal authority at the Golden Temple of Amritsar. In reaction to Mughal rule and its orientation toward proselytizing (and the martyrdom of the fifth Sikh guru), Guru Hargobind (1595-1644), the sixth guru, developed the concept of *miri-piri* (secular and spiritual), intimating that it is necessary to be concerned with both the religious and the socio-political domains of life. In doing so, he established the *takhts* (thrones), to be built across from the places of prayer; that is, while both domains were to be addressed, they needed to be kept separate.
27 Kamala Elizabeth Nayar, "Misunderstood in the Diaspora: The Experience of Orthodox Sikhs in Vancouver," *Sikh Formations* 4, 1 (2008): 17-32.
28 The Shiromani Gurdwara Parbandhak Committee was set up in 1925 by the Sikh electorate to administer the principal gurdwaras, and issued the *Sikh Rehat Maryada* (Sikh Code of Conduct) in order to distinguish Punjabi Sikhs from other Punjabis. The Damdami Taksal (Damdama School of Sikh Learning) was founded by Baba Deep Singh Shahid (1682-1757), who studied the sacred texts under Bhai Mani Singh (under the supervision of the Guru Gobind Singh) and who also trained in the martial arts. The school specializes in Sikh religious discourse (*katha*) and has its own code of conduct (*rehat maryada*): Harbans Singh, ed., *The Encyclopedia of Sikhism*, vol. 1 (Patiala: Punjabi University, 1995), 587-88.
29 Douglas Todd and Nicholas Read, "Our Religious Beliefs: Less Formal, More Diverse," *Vancouver Sun*, 14 May 2003, A5.
30 Murray J. Leaf, *Information and Behaviour in a Sikh Village: Social Organization Reconsidered* (Berkeley: University of California Press, 1972), 165-67.
31 Mayo, *Paldi Remembered*, 16-17.
32 Sabik Singh Dhaliwal, personal communication, 27 August 2005.
33 Kamala Elizabeth Nayar, *The Sikh Diaspora in Vancouver: Three Generations amid Tradition, Modernity and Multiculturalism* (Toronto: University of Toronto Press, 2004), 194-99.
34 Sikh 4.
35 The four rites of passage are: (1) the naming ceremony performed in the gurdwara, when a person randomly opens the *Guru Granth Sahib* and the first letter of the hymn on the left-hand page becomes the first letter of the child's name; (2) "baptism," the receiving of *amrit* (holy water) as a mark of belonging to the Khalsa (the pure); (3) the marriage ceremony; and (4) the death rite: *Sikh Rehat Maryada*, articles 17-19, 24.
36 Baisakhi (or Vaisakhi) is the Punjabi festival celebrating the harvest at the advent of the month Baisakh (between April and May). The people in the villages participate in Baisakhi by organizing a local fair and participating in the festivities of feasting, singing and dancing. Although Baisakhi is a traditional agricultural festival for Punjabis, it has greater importance for Sikhs. According to tradition, Guru Gobind Singh created the Khalsa Order on the first day of Baisakh in 1699. In the Punjab, many Sikhs go on pilgrimage to Anandpur (the place of the birth of the Khalsa) to celebrate the occasion. In the Lower Mainland, the Sikhs hold a parade that starts and ends at the gurdwara; along the parade route, many Sikhs put up tables and give away food, refreshments, and books. Divali, the festival of lights, is the Hindu celebration of the events of the great epic *Ramayana*. The festival has been given Sikh significance since it was the day Guru Hargobind was released from prison under Mughal rule.

Lohri is the Punjabi festival celebrating the birth of the first male child. While traditionally it has been specifically oriented toward the son, there has recently been a move in the Lower Mainland to include celebration of the birth of daughters.
37 Bains and Johnston, *Four Quarters of the Night*, 70; Mayo, *Paldi Remembered*, 19.
38 Norman Buchignani and Doreen Marie Indra, *Continuous Journey: A Social History of South Asians in Canada* (Toronto: McLelland and Stewart, 1985), 45-60.
39 Ibid., 30-60; Nayar, *The Sikh Diaspora in Vancouver*, 16-17.
40 For a thorough analysis of the *Komagata Maru* incident, see Hugh Johnston, *The Voyage of Komagata Maru: The Sikh Challenge to Canada's Colour Bar* (Delhi: Oxford University Press, 1979).
41 James G. Chadney, "The Formation of Ethnic Communities, Lessons from Vancouver Sikhs," in *The Sikh Diaspora: Migration and the Experience beyond the Punjab*, ed. N. Gerald Barrier and Verne A. Dusenbery (Delhi: Chanakya Publications, 1989), 190.
42 Norman Buchignani and Doreen Marie Indra, "Key Issues in Canadian-Sikh Ethnic and Race Relations, Implications for the Study of the Sikh Diaspora," in *The Sikh Diaspora: Migration and the Experience beyond the Punjab*, ed. N. Gerald Barrier and Verne A. Dusenbery (Delhi: Chanakya Publications, 1989), 142-43.
43 The petition is printed in Dhillon, *A History Book of the Sikhs in Canada and California*, 219-23.
44 Some of the ethno-specific NGOs in the Lower Mainland include Family Services of Greater Vancouver, Multilingual Orientation Service Association for Immigrant Communities, Options, Progressive Intercultural Community Services, and the Surrey-Delta Immigrant Services Society (now called DIVERSEcity).
45 Nayar, *The Sikh Diaspora in Vancouver*, 197-99.
46 Darshan Singh Tatla, *The Sikh Diaspora: The Search for Statehood* (Seattle: University of Washington Press, 1999), 86-90.
47 Ibid., 89. See also Hugh Johnston, "The Surveillance of Indian Revolutionaries," *BC Studies* 78 (1988): 3-27.
48 Nayar, *The Sikh Diaspora in Vancouver*, 139.
49 Tatla, *The Sikh Diaspora*, 151-81.
50 For instance, in 1956 the Akali Singh Society invited MP Harold Winch, who discussed the right of East Indians to vote: Dhillon, *A History Book of the Sikhs in Canada and California*, 274.
51 Nayar, *The Sikh Diaspora in Vancouver*, 172-74.
52 Sabik Singh Dhaliwal, personal communication, 27 August 2005. See also Dhillon, *A History Book of the Sikhs in Canada and California*, 273-74.
53 Joseph T. O'Connell, "Sikh Religio-Ethnic Experience in Canada," in *The South Asian Religious Diasporas in Britain, Canada and USA*, ed. Harold Coward, John R. Hinells, and Raymond Brady Williams (Albany: State University of New York Press, 2000), 191-209. See also Bains and Johnston, *Four Quarters of the Night*, 149-64.
54 Nayar, *The Sikh Diaspora in Vancouver*, 165-66.
55 Ibid., 184-85. Nayar, "Misunderstood in the Diaspora."
56 Nayar, *The Sikh Diaspora in Vancouver*, 173-74.
57 For a discussion of the Canadian-born Sikh youths' malaise with respect to the gurdwaras and their desire for a more Western-style approach to teaching about the religion, see ibid., 179-81.
58 Citation taken from ibid., 181.

3 Religion, Ethnicity, and the Double Diaspora of Asian Muslims
Derryl N. MacLean

> There will emerge from you an *ummah* calling for goodness, enjoining justice, and forbidding the immoral. Such people will be successful.
>
> – Qur'an 3: 104

Over the past thirty years, the Muslim community of British Columbia has expanded rapidly, becoming the third largest non-Christian faith community, following the Sikh and Buddhist communities, with the second fastest growing population among the major religions. Its numbers have risen dramatically from only 1,335 in 1971 to 56,220 in the 2001 Census of Canada, an increase of 125.5 percent since 1991. It is thus a new community in the province, consisting primarily of immigrants and their children. Local Muslims estimate the population to be well over 120,000 now, with more than half being of Asian ethnicity, primarily Indian and Pakistani. Despite the importance and prominence of Asian Muslims in the province's civil society, the community has attracted little attention from academics. To a certain extent, there is a tendency in the study of British Columbia Muslims to assume that they represent a western instance of a much larger Canadian Muslim profile, and then to simply extend to them observations from other Canadian places and persons. This reinforces the impression that there is a seamless Canadian Islam, with little regional variation.[1]

The purpose of this chapter is to recover the configuration of British Columbia Muslims, with a focus on Asian communities and organizations. In particular, I am concerned with possible tensions between ethnic forms of Islam brought to the province by immigrants of Asian ethnicity and the larger overarching assumption of solidarity found in the ideology of the *ummah*, the unified community of Muslims. The term "Asian Muslim" here refers to all Muslims with an ethnicity related directly or indirectly to Asia, encompassing the area from the borders of Afghanistan through South Asia (Pakistan, India, Bangladesh, Sri Lanka), Southeast Asia (Malaysia, Indonesia, the Philippines), and East Asia (China and Korea). The vast majority of Asian Muslims in British Columbia, especially in organizations, is South Asian in ethnicity.

The geographical category "Asian Muslim," however, is descriptive rather than analytical. There is no such self-affirming identity, and a Muslim from North India would probably recognize more cultural continuity with a Muslim from Iran than with one from Indonesia. Indeed, my informants for this study uniformly found the concept of Asian Muslim both unusual and offensive. While the largest Asian Muslim group in the province is South Asian in origin, this geographic term masks significant regional differences in the practice and understanding of Islam. Where relevant, I have specified particular South Asian ethnic or linguistic identities, such as Gujarati or Punjabi.

The focus of my analysis is on formal, spaced religious organizations, since it is here that the representation of the *ummah* is concentrated. As a result, the emphasis is on mosqued Muslims who are committed to membership in an organization, and they are probably a minority of the Muslim population as a whole. I do not include secular Muslims who attend organizations only for high rituals, or not at all, or the smaller groups, especially the Sufi, who meet in homes or rented halls for specific events. Four Muslim religious organizations with significant Asian participation will be discussed in detail: the British Columbia Muslim Association, the Shia Muslim Community of British Columbia, the Ismaili Muslim Community of British Columbia, and the Ahmadiyya Muslim Community of British Columbia.[2]

In what follows, I will draw attention to the presence and activity within these organizations of "double-diaspora" Asian Muslims. I use this term for those Muslims of Asian ethnicity who had relocated initially as communities from some part of Asia to an intermediary location, usually East Africa or Fiji, where the community was reconstituted for a significant length of time before arriving in British Columbia. The definition requires social and not individual movement over a substantial and not ephemeral length of time. Double-diaspora Gujarati Muslims from East Africa often experienced a triple minority: their ancestors were a minority in Gujarat, then in the initial diaspora in East Africa, and finally here in British Columbia. Many of them belong to minority groups within the larger Muslim *ummah* at all locations; thus, they are a minority of a Muslim minority within a non-Muslim context, in origin and in both diasporas. While double-diaspora Muslims are found elsewhere in Canada, they are particularly prominent in the organizations of Asian Muslims in British Columbia. This, I will suggest, has a consequence in the configuration and realization of the *ummah*.

The Question of the Ummah

Throughout their history, Muslims have focused on the importance of the institution of the *ummah*, a word possessing a rich panoply of meaning. Derived from the Qur'anic word for a community, but especially one capable of morality and salvation, the term came to apply more specifically to an ideal global community of Muslims united beyond ethnicity, class, and nationality in the realization of God's plan. It resonates within a pan-Islamic notion that the *ummah* will share certain recognizable beliefs and rituals that will structure and constrain the flux of local cultures, which in turn will nestle in the larger identity as epiphenomena. While there is a difference of opinion on which elements are constitutive of the *ummah*, most Muslims see the lowest common denominator as belief in the Qur'an and the primacy of the prophet Muhammad, as well as certain distinct rituals such as prayer and pilgrimage. In premodern times, the concept was drawn on in specific polities to enable pan-Islamic travel and trade and to constitute institutions, especially on the physical or religious frontiers with non-Muslims.

Modern times have seen the emergence of ethnic nationalisms in the Muslim world, and this has had the consequence of devaluing the pan-Islamic ideal and relegating Islamic solidarity to the level of ideology. At the same time, the concept of a single community of Muslims has been tested by the large-scale diaspora of Muslims to the West. While emigration (*hijrah*) carries with it foundational Islamic elements conducive to the support of an *ummah*, at least in religious terms, it has also led to serious difficulties with conceptualizing the community and realizing it concretely within the new contexts.[3] This is primarily because the Muslim diaspora consisted of numerous ethnic and national groups carrying with them variant cultural expressions of Islam and nationalist or regional notions of solidarity, and doing so in a non-Muslim environment that was at times hostile to Muslims and their institutions.

In Canada, there have been two major challenges to the realization of the *ummah*. The first is the familiar conflict between ethnic versions of Islam, a conflict that persists despite new generations and acculturation. In religious terms, whose Islam will be the cornerstone of the *ummah*? Is it possible to realize a polyvalent *ummah* in practical local institutions? The second challenge is the relationship of the *ummah* to the modernizing, multicultural civil society. In particular, should the *ummah* be understood in isolation from or in partnership with the Canadian environment, and, if so, how?[4]

Origins

Muslims have been in Canada since the nineteenth century, when the 1871 census recorded 13, although their presence in British Columbia is much later. Twenty-four of the South Asians aboard the infamous *Komagata Maru* in 1914 were Muslims, but the community grew only very slowly, recording 136 in 1931 and 1,335 in 1971. The earliest Muslims in the province were South Asians working in the lumber mills or in agriculture, and they shared class location and orientations with the early Sikh community. Following the Second World War, immigration became much more socially diverse, with increasing numbers of professionals arriving from Pakistan and Fiji. The small group of Muslims at this juncture would meet in private homes for religious services and would rely on informal networks to link specific families within the province. As a result, inter-relationships between Muslims were often very personal and the *ummah* had a pronounced ethnic quality.

As the numbers of Muslims in the Lower Mainland increased, so did the need to coordinate their activities. The first formal organization, the Pakistan Welfare Association, was formed in 1963 and then incorporated the following year as the Pakistan-Canada Association (PCA). The original aim of the PCA was to provide a location for religious and cultural gatherings for persons of Pakistani origin. The definition of "Pakistani" had a religious component: the membership was divided into an Islamic Trust restricted to Muslims of Pakistani origin and a Community Trust open to non-Muslim Pakistanis. At some point, a definition of "Muslim" entered into the constitution of the PCA (clause 1.a.iii.3), which had the effect of excluding the Ahmadiyya community as Muslims.[5] The PCA has remained active in the province up to the present, serving as the primary voice for the Urdu-speaking Pakistani community and organizing events such as Republic Day.

At the same time, members of the PCA wished to meet the spiritual requirements of the community of Sunni Muslims beyond those from Pakistan, and in 1964 constituted the Islamic Centre, locating it at the same site as the PCA in Vancouver. The Islamic Centre was dominated by Pakistanis but non-Pakistanis, especially Fijians of South Asian ethnicity, occupied prominent positions.

British Columbia Muslim Association

On 17 November 1966, the Islamic Centre became the British Columbia Muslim Association (BCMA), a large umbrella organization for the benefit of all Sunni Muslims in the province. It maintained a close relationship with the PCA, especially in the 1970s, but shared with the Islamic Centre a founding nucleus of South Asians that included a significant number of double-diaspora Muslims from Fiji. The founding directors of the BCMA, for example, consisted of three Fijian Muslims, one Egyptian, two Pakistanis, and an Indian.[6] The South Asian and Fijian connection of the BCMA remains significant, but the ethnic composition has broadened. Two of the founding directors were mechanics, two accountants, two technicians, and one a civil engineer, which is a fair reflection of the original social composition of the organization.

The objectives of the BCMA, as defined in the original constitution, were similar to those of the Islamic Centre but projected in *ummah* form and extended from Vancouver to all of British Columbia. Among other things, they included the construction and operation of mosques, schools, and senior homes; the production of Islamic literature and libraries to provide information for Muslims and non-Muslims; the service of Islamic life rituals such as marriage and burial; and the encouragement of activities for Muslim youth and women.

The BCMA's initial preoccupation was with the service and preservation of Islamic rituals for the small and isolated Muslim community. There was a particular need to facilitate a properly Islamic funeral and burial in the province, especially in the face of prior opposition by municipalities, and this required special arrangements with funeral homes and cemeteries. In 1976, the BCMA was able to negotiate a block of Muslim burial plots with Ocean View Cemetery in Burnaby, and now there are six such locations in the province. At the same time, it made arrangements with funeral homes for the observance of the requisite Islamic rituals and established a Burial Committee to guide Muslims through the process. Originally, the BCMA provided these services to all Muslims, but as the community expanded and costs mounted, restricted them to Sunni Muslims.

Marriage was another important ritual for the solidarity of Muslims. Initially, Muslim couples would have a civil ceremony and Islamic marriage rituals would subsequently be performed at a home or, after its formation, at the BCMA. Non-Christians had difficulty becoming official Marriage Commissioners, but after much persistence, the first Islamic marriage (*nikah*) took place at the Vancouver Islamic Centre on 5 September 1970. The ritualization of marriage would become a significant function of the BCMA for the larger Muslim community, not only its own members.

The BCMA met initially in a small building in Vancouver, but it intended from the beginning to establish a permanent central mosque in the Lower Mainland. Mosques traditionally have served not only as a location for communal prayer but also as a visible sign of the presence of a vital Muslim *ummah* in a region. They Islamize public space, and this is particularly true of an "assembly mosque" (*jami' masjid*), the primary mosque of a large urban area.[7] A mosque trust fund was established in 1970, but several attempts to purchase or rezone lands in Vancouver and Burnaby fell through due to municipal and public opposition, to the great disappointment of the community. In 1974, a large parcel of land in Richmond was purchased to accommodate a mosque, library, school, and community centre, and the Richmond Mosque opened in 1982. Except for small grants from Saudi Arabia and Kuwait, the building funds were raised entirely by the local Muslim community.

The BCMA aimed to serve the needs of all Sunni Muslims in the province, and thus established mosques and centres in numerous locations. In 1994, these subsidiary sites were decentralized from the Richmond Mosque as Local

Management Committees (LMC) and were given considerable leeway to meet the requirements of local communities, although all BCMA locations share a general orientation and must adhere to the BCMA constitution and operations manual. There are now over ten branches, including prominent mosques in Vancouver (Masjid ul-Haqq), Surrey-Delta (Masjid al-Taqwa), Surrey-East (Masjid ur-Rahmah), and Victoria (Masjid ul-Iman). The oldest and largest of these is the Masjid al-Taqwa in Surrey, which was established in 1979 in an unused Salvation Army church, destroyed by fire in 2000, and subsequently replaced by an imposing and impressive new mosque.

The organization of the mosques of the BCMA is congregational, by which I mean a formal but locally based religious organization with a defined membership electing a governing body and committees of members who hire clergy.[8] This is a departure from mosques in the countries of origin, and it has led to Imams (prayer leaders) increasingly taking on a professional role as clergy. This type of organization also permits the emergence of local qualities in specific communities; Surrey, for example, has always had a significant Pakistani and Urdu-speaking quality to its activities and institutions.

Early members of the BCMA were particularly concerned with providing their children a quality education that would combine Islamic and western principles. Initially, education took place informally on weekends and evenings while funds were being raised for an elementary and secondary school. In 1983, the BCMA founded the Richmond Muslim School, and the following year government-licensed instruction for forty children began in the multipurpose hall. A separate building opened in 1988, with major funding from Saudi Arabia, and provided instruction in the provincial curriculum from kindergarten to grade four. The British Columbia Muslim School (BCMS), as it was now called, expanded rapidly, incorporating Western Canada's first Muslim high school in 1996 and branching into Surrey in 1997. Its purpose is "to provide a superior standard of education, to foster academic achievement and to cultivate an Islamic spirit in each student."[9] It has been signally successful in this combined aim, and in 2005 was a finalist for the Garfield Weston Award for Excellence in Education. It does have a gendered uniform policy, with white hijabs being required for girls in all classes.

Education also included a concern for the proper understanding of Islam by Muslims and non-Muslims, and the BCMA has continued to supply information to the media and the public. It has produced and distributed a popular series of free brochures on Islam with such titles as "Islam and the Environment," "Human Rights in Islam," and "Islam and Homosexuality." Continuing education for Muslims has been provided by a speakers program as well as general courses on Islam offered by the Imams of different mosques and centres.

Women have participated actively in the BCMA from the beginning, although a specific Women's Auxiliary was founded only in 1976. A full-fledged Women's Chapter, similar to other chapters of the BCMA, was formed in 1988 and subsequently expanded to the subsidiary mosques and centres. The Women's Chapter began to publish the *BC Muslim Women's Magazine* in 1998, with articles on such matters as the Internet and alienation in the family, and the effect of war on children. The chapter also provides instruction on women's burial rituals, fundraising, organization of summer camps and educational competitions, dinners for the homeless, and interfaith dialogue.

It should not be thought that the BCMA simply reproduced traditional gender roles brought by Muslim immigrants. Tazul Nisha Ali, current chair of the Women's Chapter, notes of the Richmond mosque, "it was wonderful to be able to come to the Masjid since back home, [sic] women did not worship in Masajid. We frequently went to the Masjid for classes and for just getting together."[10] That is, the mosque (*masjid*, pl. *masajid*) became a spiritual and social centre for women in British Columbia, and this broke with the practice of Muslims in the countries of origin. Women were also able to articulate protest to some effect in the BCMA. When the new Surrey mosque was planned in 1998, little provision was made for the activities of women and children. The women held a large protest meeting and collected a petition of 200 signatures; after some reflection, the design of the mosque was altered.

Since its foundation, the BCMA has been active in both the production and representation of a Sunni *ummah* within the province, and most of the programs discussed above serve the purpose of unity.[11] More than any other group in the province, the BCMA has had particularly close relations with other Sunni webbing and umbrella organizations, including the Muslim Student Association (MSA), the Council of Muslim Communities of Canada (CMCC), and the Islamic Society of North America (ISNA). It participated in a joint board meeting with the CMCC in 1981 and hosted the ISNA Annual Conference in 1994 and the ISNA Canada West Conference in 2000. ISNA, which emerged out of the activism of graduating MSA students, is the most important umbrella organization for Sunni Muslims in North America, and the BCMA's prominent participation in these conferences signifies not only its representation of the Sunni *ummah* in the province but also its stature among Sunni organizations in North America.

The BCMA has sought to represent the provincial *ummah* by hosting international dignitaries from the Muslim world, attending international Muslim conferences, participating locally at interfaith and municipal meetings, organizing guided tours of the mosque for church and school groups, certifying food as *halal* (Islamically permitted), and administering a Muslim Sports Association. The two canonical Eids (festivals) have been convened for all provincial Muslims since 1967, with the Eid al-Fitr, which closes the Ramadan month of fasting, consistently attracting large numbers of Muslims. The Eid al-Adha (festival of sacrifice) has become an ecumenical concern, however, and since 2002 has been co-hosted in public locations with other Muslim organizations, including the Shia.

Certain members of the BCMA, particularly among the Fijian community, wished to be able to represent better the political interests of the *ummah* and, at the same time, encourage Muslims to participate in the political process.[12] After much discussion, an independent Canadian Muslim Federation (CMF) was established in 2000 as the political voice of members of the BCMA. It is now an independent organization concerned with the public and media representation of Islam and the coordination of activities within the *ummah* and with non-Muslim groups.

The representation of the *ummah* has not been without challenges and disputations within the BCMA, which is not surprising given the diversity of groups involved in the organization and the scope of its activities. Some of these arise from the group's congregational organization, which has facilitated the emergence at a local level of particular representations of Islam. There is, for example, a wide range of opinion within the BCMA on the use of its mosques and centres by the Jama'at-i Tabligh, a self-purification movement that originated in India and has spread rapidly throughout the world.[13] The movement has no formal organization but is symbiotic with other Muslim organizations and has used BCMA facilities for a number of its activities.

Perhaps most worrisome for younger Muslims has been a sense that the BCMA works to exclude more progressive elements. While the BCMA has always been a conserving institution, the Itrath Syed incident revealed to some Muslims a worrisome punitive and exclusionary quality. Itrath Syed, a New Democratic Party candidate for the Delta-Richmond East riding in the 2004 federal election and a long-time member of the Richmond Mosque, was publicly rebuked by the Imam of the mosque for her views on gay and lesbian marriage. Ms. Syed's position, explained in a passionate general letter, was that marriage between gay and lesbian couples is a human right guaranteed by the *Canadian Charter of Rights and Freedoms,* which Muslims should necessarily support, while the Imam deemed her position un-Islamic in principle and argued that it would lead to the BCMA's being required to perform gay or lesbian marriage.[14] It remains to be seen whether the BCMA has the will or desire to include progressive or liberal Muslims within the *ummah* represented by their organization.

The BCMA's monopoly on representation of Sunni Muslims has been diminished slightly in recent years by the emergence of new but generally cooperative organizations. The Islamic Heritage Association sponsors the Iqra Islamic

School, founded in 1998 in Surrey and now enrolling around 340 students from kindergarten to grade eight, and the Islamic Information Centre, which opened in 1995 as a multi-ethnic place of worship, instruction, and information. The latter, under Dr. Ali Mihirig, began the popular Canadian Islamic Cultural Expo in Vancouver in August 2005, an outdoor showcase for the *ummah* of British Columbia with booths of nations and cultures, which in its second year moved beyond its Sunni origins and included an Iranian Shia booth. The other major Sunni organization is the Islamic Society of British Columbia, an increasingly active group operating out of the Masjid Al-Hidayah in Port Coquitlam (founded in 2003), with roots in the earlier Tri-City Islamic Centre. It operates the Al-Hidayah Islamic School and organizes study circles, Qur'anic lessons, outreach, and activities for women, children, and youth.

New Organizations

The 1970s and 1980s saw additions to the *ummah* of British Columbia, primarily due to the expulsion of Asians from East Africa. Three new groups arrived: the Ahmadiyya, the Ithna Ashari Shia, and the Ismaili Shia. These groups differ from the BCMA in certain respects. They are sectarian, with two of them being Shia and one being messianic. One of the groups, the Ahmadiyya, consisted mostly of refugees and immigrants from Pakistan's Punjab province, while the other two were primarily double-diaspora Muslims from East Africa with roots in the Kachhi-speaking population of Gujarat and Sindh in western India. By contrast, the double-diaspora Fijian Muslims associated with the BCMA had their origins in the Urdu-speaking population of northern India. All three groups brought to British Columbia, and subsequently maintained relationships with, external bureaucratic organizations. This enabled them to move fairly quickly to set up institutions, and these were not congregational as in the BCMA. The arrival of the new groups both broadened and challenged the provincial *ummah*, making it quite distinctive from other areas of Canada.

The Ahmadiyya Muslim Community of British Columbia

The Ahmadiyya movement was founded in 1889 by Mirza Ghulam Ahmad (1835-1908), a religious scholar, mystic, and reformer from Qadian in the Punjab. He claimed special messianic authority for world religions as the promised Messiah (*masih maw'ud*) and for Islam as the Muslim Mahdi, and began to initiate disciples. After his death, an Ahmadi community came into existence under the leadership of a series of elected successors (*khalifa*), the fifth of which is the current Khalifatul Masih V Hadhrat Mirza Masroor Ahmad, elected in 2003. The community currently numbers around 15 million spread around the world, but is concentrated in Pakistan. It is an organized, bureaucratic, hierarchical, and authoritarian movement, organized at international, national, and regional levels.[15]

While isolated Ahmadis were already in British Columbia in the 1950s, the vast majority of organized members arrived after 1974, when they were declared non-Muslims in Pakistan, primarily for their views on the messianic status of their founder, and restrictions and repression increased. They formed an official organization, the Ahmadiyya Muslim Community of British Columbia (AMCBC), and began meeting in rented halls and homes purchased to serve as mosques in Burnaby and Cloverdale. A disused elementary school on 3.74 acres was purchased in the community of Delta in 1995, and became known as the Vancouver Mission House, the primary location in the province of the movement. The foundation stone for the mosque was laid on 11 June 2005 by the Khalifatul Masih V himself, on his first visit to Western Canada. The mosque was named Baitur Rahman (House of Mercy), and numerous local, provincial, and federal politicians gathered for the occasion.

The community numbers around 1,500 persons in British Columbia, out of a total Canadian membership of 25,000. Most members are from Pakistan, with smaller numbers from India, Fiji, and Africa, although double-diaspora immigration is not characteristic. The Ahmadis have a particular facility for Urdu (their publications and services are usually bilingual) and an ongoing concern for developments in Pakistan. Besides regular and special religious services, the organization provides for its members in such areas as career advice, scholarships, university student associations, and a weekend school for their children.[16]

The representation of the *ummah* is especially important for the Ahmadis, although controversial for other Muslims. Indeed, much of their organization and ideology revolve around the proselytization of Muslims and non-Muslims. This often involves quite modern, evangelical methods. A blitz campaign, "Spreading the Message of Islam," was held in 2006 with seventy different events across Canada, ten in British Columbia. These events consisted of lectures, symposia, and conferences within an interfaith or dialogue context. The British Columbia branch also organizes an annual World Religions Conference at various universities and colleges, inviting speakers from different faiths, usually academics or clergy, to present their views on a specific topic, with Islam being represented by an Ahmadi speaker. The second conference, held at the University of Northern British Columbia on 20 September 2005, concerned "In Search of the Existence of God," while the 2007 series was held at a number of colleges on topics such as "Human Rights and Religion." The Ahmadis place their publications in local libraries and organize Islamic book fairs, presenting Ahmadi views as those of the larger *ummah*.

In short, unlike other Muslim groups discussed in this chapter, the Ahmadis seek to monopolize the representation of the Muslim *ummah* of British Columbia in their own sectarian events, and in the process they look particularly for non-Muslim recognition of the movement as Islamic. This concern with recognition is understandable given the sectarian history and repression. Ahmadis are not permitted to call themselves or their structures Islamic in most parts of the Muslim world, and it is only in the West where this is possible. But the monopolization of Islamic definitions and the active proselytization of other Muslims have meant that they are not inclined to participate, and that they are not welcome, in umbrella organizations and events of the provincial *ummah*. Nevertheless, despite the group's small size, it has succeeded in developing a significant public profile among non-Muslims in British Columbia.

The Shia Muslim Community of British Columbia

The Shia form of Islam, comprising some 15 percent of the world's Muslims, is represented in British Columbia by the Ithna Ashariyah and the Ismailiyah. Both groups depart from the Sunnis with a doctrine of the Imamate, by which spiritual leadership of the Muslim community resides in Imams, genealogical descendants of 'Ali, the cousin and son-in-law of the Prophet. The two Shia groups differ on the precise line of Imams as well as in particular rituals and customs. The Ithna Ashariyah ("Twelver") Shia is so called for its line of twelve Imams, the last of whom disappeared in 878 CE. Until the reappearance of the twelfth Imam at the end of time, the community continues to be led spiritually by legal scholars called *mujtahid*s (popularly, ayatollahs), who reside in Iran and Iraq. Twelvers form the vast majority of worldwide Shia and are located primarily in Iran, Iraq, Lebanon, and the Persian Gulf. They have significant representation in Asia, forming about 20 percent of the Muslim population of India and Pakistan, and important diaspora communities in Africa and the West.

The Ithna Ashari Shia community (hereafter simply Shia) of British Columbia is quite diverse, consisting of Iranians, Iraqis, Lebanese, Afghans, Indo-Pakistanis, and East African Asians. Most participants in provincial Shia organizations and services, however, are of South Asian ethnicity. The numerous Shia groups in the province have been organized since 2005 as the Assembly of Ithna-Ashari Muslim Member Associations (AIMMA), previously known as the Council of Shia Muslim Communities. This group serves as the unified voice of the province's Shia Muslims and works to promote cooperation with other Muslims and the understanding of Islam by non-Muslims. The various Shia organizations, while independent from each other, cooperate in a range of Islamic activities.

The largest Shia organization in the province is the Shia Muslim Community of British Columbia (SMCBC). It is affiliated with and shares the perspective of the World Federation of Khoja Shia Ithna Ashari Muslims, a group formed in 1976 to represent and unite the Khojas after their expulsion from East Africa. The term "Khoja" refers to those Sindhis who were converted to Islam in the fourteenth century by the Persian Ismaili missionary Pir Sadruddin, who gave them the honorific title meaning "lord" or "master." The Khoja Shia Ithna Asharis separated from the Ismailis in the late nineteenth century over the question of religious identity and the role of the Aga Khan as Imam. Both religious communities are primarily Kachhi speakers of Gujarati or Sindhi ethnicity who came to British Columbia from East Africa.[17]

Although the SMCBC is a Khoja organization, it is open to the participation of all Shia. Its chief *mujtahid* for spiritual direction is the Ayatollah Ali Sistani of Iraq, who represents a relatively apolitical position. The Khoja themselves number only about 800 provincially but serve a much larger constituency in their various programs. Initially, the community met in homes for various religious activities and rituals, and audio cassettes of sermons from East Africa featured in this service. In August 2002, the SMCBC opened Az-Zahraa Islamic Centre (ZIC) in a prominent building not far from the BCMA's Richmond Mosque. Highly organized under a constitution, Az-Zahraa operates with an executive and specific committees for youth, seniors, women, burial, and matrimony, among others.

Members of the SMCBC are generally well educated and exhibit a particular interest in wide-ranging discussions within Az-Zahraa and a willingness to adapt and modernize certain traditional institutions. For example, it is the general practice of Ithna Ashari Shia to commemorate during the Muslim month of Muharram the martyrdom at Karbala of the Imam Husayn, the grandson of the Prophet. This is done through lamentations and processions, which traditionally have involved the spilling of one's own blood (*zanjir ka matam*). Az-Zahraa has maintained the spirit of the ritual but has substituted a Muharram Blood Donation Clinic in service of the wider Canadian population. Similarly, the institution of *majalis* (the assemblies held during the month of Muharram) has been expanded to incorporate larger discussions about spiritual and public issues.

The SMCBC operates the Az-Zahraa Islamic Academy, which opened on 2 September 2003 and currently has ten staff and ninety students from Montessori to grade seven in sixteen rooms, a library, a gymnasium, and a computer lab. Instruction is based on the provincial curriculum, which is integrated with Shia Islamic values and beliefs, although the school is open to other Muslims. As elsewhere, there is a concern with developing a larger Canadian context.

This involves participating in the Terry Fox Run, exploring First Nations culture, organizing a food drive for the Richmond Food Bank during the month of fasting (Ramadan), and preparing for a virtual hajj (pilgrimage to Mecca) in the gymnasium.

Outreach, intellectual production, and *ummah* support for the SMCBC is provided by the Academy for Learning Islam (ALI). The outreach program to non-Muslims consists of group tours, presentations at elementary schools, library displays, and book donations. While Shia ritual occasions are reserved for the community, *ummah* formation and outreach focus on important events shared with non-Shia Muslims, such as the two Eids, the Milad un-Nabi, and the fasting month of Ramadan. The Prophet Muhammad Day, for example, held in the gymnasium at Az-Zahraa on 30 April 2006, brought together a panel of three speakers, two of whom were non-Muslim, and attracted an audience of some 500. The ALI also has an active publication program of books and pamphlets that are made available to visitors and on the website.

Although religious tensions between Sunnis and Shias are unfortunately common throughout the Muslim world, especially in South Asia, there are few sectarian problems among British Columbia Muslims. The SMCBC is one of the pillars of *ummah* participation: it invites Muslims to events at Az-Zahraa, participates in the events of non-Shia Muslims, and is one of the primary organizers of the recent custom of a shared Eid al-Adha, the latest of which was held at the Vancouver City Hall. Muslims from other communities have been quick to respond to this willingness to cooperate, and joined with the SMCBC in a common meeting at Az-Zahraa to show the solidarity of the provincial *ummah* to the recent threatened destruction of the Shia shrines of Iraq.

The Ismaili Muslim Community of British Columbia

The most prominent addition to the Asian Muslim presence in British Columbia during the 1970s was that of the Shia Imami Ismaili Muslims, known more simply as the Ismailis. The movement initially diverged from the main branch of the Shia in the eighth century over the choice of Imam, opting in the succession to Jafar as-Sadiq for the elder son Ismail over the younger son Musa.[18] The Ismailis achieved their greatest extent and influence, and a subtle cultural legacy, with the Fatimid Empire, centred on North Africa and Egypt and spreading into Sindh and Gujarat. After the extinction of the Fatimids in the twelfth century, the Nizari form of Ismailism thrived in the western regions of South Asia, where the Imam travelled from Iran in 1848, bringing the Persian title Aga Khan to the institution of the Imamate. The Ismailis prospered after the diaspora of Gujarati commercial classes to East Africa in the late nineteenth century, and it was in East Africa, not India, that the major modern institutions of Nizari Ismailism were enabled.

Alone among the various Shia groups, the Ismailis preserve a living authoritative Imam, currently Prince Karim Aga Khan, forty-ninth in descent from the Prophet Muhammad and the community's guide since 1957. The Imamate is central to Ismailism, and the presence of activist and progressive Imams in Sultan Muhammad Shah Aga Khan III (1885-1957) and Prince Karim Aga Khan IV has legitimized and thus enabled the very rapid modernization of the community. This has been aided by a distinct Ismaili hermeneutic that focuses attention away from the external laws (*zahir*) to their essential spiritual meanings (*batin*).

The Shia Imami Ismaili Muslim community, henceforth known in the province as the Ismaili Muslim Community of British Columbia (IMCBC), began relocating to British Columbia from East Africa in the 1970s, especially after the expulsion of Asians from Uganda in 1972. A later group arrived indirectly via Britain or Europe. Unlike some immigrant groups, the Ismailis arrived with significant communal social capital, English-language skills, an existing hierarchical organization, and a commitment to establishing themselves as Canadian Muslims. As a result, they were able to construct a distinct local presence very quickly. Provincially, they number approximately 15,000, about 80 percent of whom are double-diaspora South Asians of Gujarati or Sindhi ethnicity. There are smaller numbers from Pakistan, India, Afghanistan, Tajikistan, and Syria, and the community is rapidly becoming more multi-ethnic. The Ismailis of British Columbia are prosperous, well educated, and generally endogamous.

The physical centre of the community is found in the Jamatkhana (place of assembly), a location where practices associated with the *tariqah* (the unique Ismaili "way") are practised by members of a *jamat* (assembly). By 1985, the community had dedicated the large Ismaili Jamatkhana and Centre in Burnaby, which has served as the primary location for congregation of British Columbia Ismailis as well as the projection of the *ummah* to the public (Figure 3.1). It was the first such centre worldwide, and to date there are only three (Burnaby, London, and Lisbon), signalling the importance of the province in the larger Ismaili network. The imposing composite architecture of the centre is symbolic of the self-identity of the Ismailis and evokes the legacy of the Fatimids within the larger aesthetic of a global *ummah*. There are currently some seventeen smaller Jamatkhanas throughout the province, including Vancouver, North Vancouver, Surrey, Richmond, Victoria, and Nanaimo.

The Ismailis in Canada have evolved an elaborate administrative system of councils, boards, and committees at the national and provincial levels. The provincial-level administration replicates and is responsible to the national organizations. In British Columbia, there are overseeing Ismaili Council of British Columbia and a number of boards. The Tariqah and Religious Education

FIGURE 3.1   The Ismaili Jamatkhana and Centre in Burnaby. *Photo courtesy of Ismaili Muslim Community of British Columbia.*

Board provides programs for Islamic education and support; the Grants and Review Board is responsible for financial planning and review; and the Conciliation and Arbitration Board assists in reconciling differences among the Ismailis over domestic, commercial, and family matters. All administrative positions are voluntary.

In addition, there are at the international level Apex Institutions pivoting around the Aga Khan Development Network, a collection of agencies and programs working to improve material conditions and opportunities within the developing world. They provide services to people without regard to nationality, ethnicity, or religion. Chief among these are the Aga Khan Foundation (which provides social development for humanity), the Aga Khan University (which provides training and dissemination of knowledge and technology), and the Aga Khan Trust for Culture (which supports the artistic and literary creations of the *ummah*).

Ismailis, both as Muslims and as Canadians, believe strongly in the importance and possibility of realizing a modern and progressive Islam in Canada. As the Aga Khan himself said at the 23 August 1985 opening ceremony at the Burnaby Jamatkhana:

> In the future I hope that the Ismaili Community in Canada, having established the permanency of its home here, will become a part of the reservoir of human talent on which this country can draw, both nationally and internationally. Its members will be men and women who believe in enterprise and freedom, who are inspired by this country's respect for the individual, who will work to build the strength of Canada's economy and democratic institutions. Their spirit will be Canadian.[19]

This orientation toward Islam and Canada has been enshrined as a religious obligation in the Canadian Constitution of the Ismailis, which was published in Burnaby. Indeed, a primary purpose of the Constitution is defined in the preamble as "to enable the Ismaili Muslims to make a valid and meaningful contribution to the improvement of the quality of life of the Ummah and the societies in which they live."[20] That is, the Ismailis are particularly oriented toward an active participation within Canadian institutions as well as cooperation with other Muslims in the realization of the *ummah*.

The Ismailis' concern for philanthropy and social justice has had a major impact in the province. The annual Ismaili Walk for Kids, founded in 1991 by the Ismaili Muslim Council of British Columbia, has consistently raised large sums for local children's programs. The 2006 Walk, in partnership with the United Way, raised over $340,000 for the Success by Six program, which enhances services for young children and families. The World Partnership Walk, founded in British Columbia in 1985 as an initiative of the Aga Khan Foundation Canada, annually raises awareness and financial support for the developing world. Local ambassadors organize walking teams to raise funds and serve as advocates for specific developing countries. In the province last year, the Walk raised over $1.5 million of the total Canadian sum of almost $5 million. The philanthropic ethic accompanies an instinct for volunteerism as a religious and social obligation. It begins at a very young age and continues throughout life as a defining attribute.

Ummah formation is a crucial part of the Ismaili mandate in the province. Religious services are not open to outsiders, either non-Ismaili Muslims or non-Muslims, but rather serve as the reservoir for other *ummah*-recognizing activities. That is, Islamic moral capacities are built by religious service within the various *jamat*s, and are then expended in service to the *ummah* in a large number of areas. All the previously mentioned functions of the Aga Khan Development Network, especially the Trust for Culture, support or recognize the global *ummah*. The Aga Khan Foundation also sponsored a handbook to assist immigrant Muslims in developing an identity as part of the *ummah*.[21] At the provincial level, the Ismaili Council organizes a large annual celebration of Eid-e-Milad-un-Nabi, the birthday of the Prophet Muhammad, which has become a major occasion for all Vancouver Muslims. A popular guest speaker, usually non-Ismaili, is invited to speak on an issue of interest to the larger *ummah*. The 14 April 2007 Eid was held at the Vancouver Law Courts and featured the American calligraphic master Mohammed Zakariya speaking on "The Living Art of Islamic Calligraphy."

The Ismailis also join with other Muslim groups in activities such as the Eid al-Adha, which in 2007 was co-sponsored with the BCMA, the SMCBC, and the Canadian Muslim Federation and hosted by Vancouver mayor Sam Sullivan at the Vancouver City Hall. In other years, the ecumenical celebration of Eid has been held at the British Columbia Parliament Buildings, and the event has become the most prominent ritual in the province for public recognition of the solidarity of the *ummah*. The Ismailis also participated actively with the BCMA and SMCBC in the influential "Spirit of Islam Exhibit," held at the Museum of Anthropology at the University of British Columbia in 2001. This was followed in November 2004 with a manuscript exhibition, "Wellsprings of Wisdom: Persian Contributions to Ismaili Thought," held in conjunction with the Drs. Fereidoun and Katharine Mirhady Lectureship in Iranian Studies at Simon Fraser University, an event that brought together the Iranian and Ismaili communities of the province. Individual Ismailis have also generously supported local programs concerned with pluralism and the broader understanding of the Muslim *ummah*.

Conclusions

The Asian Muslims of British Columbia share certain experiences and responses with other Muslims in the Western diaspora. This is particularly true of the BCMA, with its congregational organization, umbrella affiliations, professionalization of the role of Imam, and occasional disputations of identity among subsidiary centres. It is also true, however, of the other groups discussed in this chapter, especially in the representation of Islam in the public sphere, concern for education and youth services, and choice of a form of architecture that deliberately rejects a regional aesthetic vocabulary. None of this is really surprising or distinctive, although the facility and prominence of the provincial instance of these adaptations is noteworthy.

Nevertheless, the British Columbia Muslim experience clearly has specific local qualities as well, although in flux, and I think it is premature to conceptualize a larger Canadian Islam. This can be seen in the general movement away from ethnic organizations or mosques, the rejection of ethnic or Islamic ghettoization, the muting of diasporic homeland identities, the active participation of Shia Muslims in *ummah* events, the general absence of interest (both Muslim and non-Muslim) in disputations concerning hijab (gendered dress), and the festivals of multicultural inclusion. Indeed, the mechanisms and rituals of *ummah* realization seem particularly close to provincial multiculturalism, with the Muharram blood drives, fundraising walks, interfaith dialogue, and Islamic multicultural expositions.

The particular history, ethnic and religious composition, and timing of immigration surely situate the provincial form of Asian Muslim experience. It is striking that the Muslim community here has no single dominant ethnicity, language group, or religious interpretation. While in much of North America, the percentage of Shia in the overall Muslim population ranges from 15 to 20 percent,[22] in British Columbia, they probably constitute the plurality of Muslims. And these Shia, unlike elsewhere, are themselves represented by various ethnicities, traditions, and orientations. It is thus clearly inappropriate to analyze Islam in this province, as is usually done for Canada, as though Sunnism were normative, or to read the Shia solely in terms of Iranian, Iraqi, or Lebanese orientations. The polyvalence and diversity of the South Asian community is equally striking, with Urdu speakers, who dominate elsewhere, being only part of the mosaic, along with Kachhi, Gujarati, and Sindhi speakers.

It is the prominence of double-diaspora Muslims that has made the provincial Islamic landscape most distinctive, however. While most Muslim populations in Canada include these groups, in this province they dominate the major organizations except for the Ahmadiyya, and thus the overall Muslim configuration. In this respect, they are distinct from other Asian religious groups discussed in this volume. While there is a difference between double-diaspora Muslims from East Africa and Fiji (primarily Gujarati versus North Indian origins), there are still clear similarities – a consequence, I suggest, of the sociology of double-diaspora populations. Having severed ties with the ethnic place of origin, the double-diaspora Muslims have no myth of return (to either India or East Africa or Fiji), no nostalgia of place, and, in consequence, no divided loyalty between the host country and the homeland. This differs significantly from many Sikh, Hindu, and Tibetan groups, where the diaspora appears to have intensified a passion for the politics of the homeland. While larger issues of the Muslim *ummah* abroad certainly concern local organizations, there is little fetishization of homeland, and this facilitates the consolidation of *ummah* identity. Moreover, these groups had previously experienced in the first diaspora a movement away from Indic definitions and practices of Islam, and a movement toward new Muslim identities within the context of a multicultural, multiracial, and multiethnic society. All this had occurred prior to the second diaspora to British Columbia and would be reinforced.

This diasporic configuration has implications, although the evidence is muted rather than definitive. That is, it seems to be conducive to an Islamization process that reverses the usual pattern. While Islamization is normally thought of as a process of constructing Islamists from secularists or pluralists, the process here allows for the realization of the *ummah* by universalizing the consciousness of the double-diaspora experience within the rituals and processes of Canadian multiculturalism as practised in this province. This involves the shunting of ethnic or cultural self-ascriptions from the realm of religious organization to that of cultural association or even the home, and their replacement with those of the *ummah*. This very self-confident movement is significantly different from that noted by other writers in this volume. The Asian Muslim communities appear to be the only faith groups that, for religious and not secular reasons, are moving away from the specifically Asian quality of their religion in the provincial diaspora.

Notes

1 In an example of the neglect of Western Canadian data, the Trudeau Foundation held a conference in Vancouver in 2006 on "Muslims in Western Society." There were no specialists on British Columbia Muslims among the twenty-five featured speakers, chairs, or discussants.
2 I have followed the transliteration customs of particular groups and persons and have not attempted to impose a uniform system. I appreciate the assistance of my graduate student, Marc Corrado, for background research and interviews with the British Columbia Muslim Association.
3 The Prophet Muhammad's emigration from Mecca to Medina, for example, was constitutive of the formation of the original *ummah*. For a discussion of the Islamic implications of emigration, see Muhammad Khalid Masud, "The Obligation to Migrate: The Doctrine of Hijra in Islamic Law," in *Muslim Travellers: Pilgrimage, Migration, and the Religious Imagination,* ed. Dale F. Eickelman and James Piscatori (Berkeley: University of California Press, 1990), 29-49.
4 Shaheen H. Azmi has written of the influence among Toronto Muslims of the Jama'at-i Tabligh, a self-purification movement originating in India and widespread in Canada among South Asians. Many within the Tabligh in Toronto perceived a danger to Islam in a modernizing multicultural Canadian environment and proposed isolation within a "Muslim ghetto" as the solution. See Shaheen H. Azmi, "A Movement or a Jama'at? Tablighi Jama'at in Canada," in *Travellers in Faith: Studies of the Tablighi Jama'at as a Transnational Islamic Movement for Faith Renewal,* ed. Muhammad Khalid Masud (Leiden: E.J. Brill, 2000), 222-39.
5 The original and amended PCA constitution can be found in Salim A. Karim, ed., *A Journey through Pakistan: A Tribute to Its Diversity and Beauty* (Vancouver: Pakistan-Canada Association, 2005), 138-50. A new organization, the Pakistani Canadian Cultural Association, was founded in 2002 to represent all Pakistani Canadians without restrictions of ethnicity or religion.

6 Information on the BCMA is derived from interviews; from Imaad Ali, ed., *Serving the Muslim Community for Forty Years, 1966-2006* (Richmond: British Columbia Muslim Association, 2006); and from Fakrul Alam, "Islam in British Columbia," in *Circle of Voices: A History of the Religious Communities of British Columbia,* ed. Charles Anderson, Tirthankar Bose, and Joseph I. Richardson (Lantzville, BC: Oolichan Books, 1983), 223-31.

7 For an overview, see Gulzar Haider, "Muslim Space and the Practice of Architecture," in *Making Muslim Space in North America and Europe,* ed. Barbara Daly Metcalf (Berkeley: University of California Press, 1996), 31-45.

8 Helen Rose Ebaugh, "Religion and the New Immigrants," in *Handbook of the Sociology of Religion,* ed. Michele Dillon (Cambridge: Cambridge University Press, 2003), 225-39. For a discussion of the problems of congregationalism for American Muslims, see Karen Isaksen Leonard, *Muslims in the United States: The State of the Research* (New York: Russell Sage Foundation, 2003), 106-11.

9 British Columbia Muslim School, *Parents and Students Handbook, 2006-2007* (Richmond: BC Muslim School, 2006), 4.

10 Tazul Nisha Ali, "A Brief History of Women in the BCMA," in *Serving the Muslim Community for Forty Years,* ed. Ali, 52.

11 The term "Sunni" is a residual category for all Muslims not Shia or sectarian in their orientation. They form the majority of Muslims in the contemporary world.

12 See the discussion by Hassan Mallam, "B.C.M.A. Initiates a Political Move," *The Minaret* 2 (2000): 2. This is the official organ of the Canadian Society of Fiji Muslims, centred in Surrey.

13 For an overview of the movement, see the essays in Muhammad Khalid Masud, ed., *Travellers in Faith: Studies of the Tablighi Jama'at as a Transnational Movement for Faith Renewal* (Leiden: E.J. Brill, 2000).

14 See the discussion in the *Vancouver Sun,* 17 June 2004, and the *Arab-American News,* 9 July 2004.

15 Antonio Gualtieri, *The Ahmadis: Community, Gender, and Politics in a Muslim Society* (Montreal and Kingston: McGill-Queen's University Press, 2004). Its American history is discussed in Yvonne Yazbeck Haddad and Jane Idleman Smith, *Mission to America: Five Islamic Sectarian Communities in North America* (Gainesville: University Press of Florida, 1993), 49-78.

16 See, for example, the instruction given to Ahmadi children in Vancouver contained in Waheed Ahmad, *A Book of Religious Knowledge,* 2nd ed. (Athens, OH: Fazl I Omar Press, 1995).

17 For an overview of the Khojas, see Ali Asani, "The Khojahs of South Asia: Defining a Space of Their Own," *Cultural Dynamics* 13 (2001): 155-58. There are other AIMMA organizations that cater to non-Khoja Shia from South Asia. The Aza-e-Hussain Association of British Columbia, for example, coordinates commemorations of the martyrdom of Imam Husayn, following the customary practices of North India.

18 For an overview and bibliography, consult Farhad Daftary, *The Ismailis: Their History and Doctrines* (Cambridge: Cambridge University Press, 1990). For the Canadian data, see Azim Nanji, "The Nizari Ismaili Muslim Community in North America: Background and Development," in *The Muslim Community in North America,* ed. Earle H. Waugh, Baha Abu-Laban, and Regula B. Qureshi (Edmonton: University of Alberta Press, 1983), 149-64.

19 See http://Ismaili.net/speech850823.

20 *Constitution of the Shia Imami Ismaili Muslims: Canada* (Burnaby: Shia Imami Ismaili Community, 1986), preamble. Elsewhere in the same document (5.5c), one of the duties of the Ismaili Councils is to "strive to maintain unity with other tariqahs within the Muslim Ummah, and to seek co-operation and friendly relations with all other peoples."

21 Fariyal Ross-Sheriff, Mali Dhanidina, and Ali S. Asani, *Al-Ummah: Handbook for an Identity Development Program for Immigrant Muslim Youth in North America* (New York: Al-Ummah Corporation, Aga Khan Foundation, 1996).
22 Liyakat Takim, "Multiple Identities in a Pluralistic World: Shi'ism in America," in *Muslims in the West: From Sojourners to Citizens,* ed. Yvonne Yazbeck Haddad (New York: Oxford University Press, 2002), 219.

4 Zoroastrians in British Columbia
RASTIN MEHRI

During a ceremony on the evening of 27 September 1971, the members of a small religious community in British Columbia known as Zoroastrians dedicated a carved sandalwood wall plaque to the people of British Columbia to commemorate the province's centennial (Figure 4.1). At that time the Zoroastrian Society of British Columbia (ZSBC) had a membership of some seventy people – twenty families – and had just registered under the province's Society Act three years earlier. The members had requested the plaque from their mother body, the Trustees of the Parsi Panchayet Society in Mumbai (then Bombay), in their country of origin, India. The ceremony was attended by thirty-one members of the society, along with dignitaries from both the BC Centennial Committee and the High Commission of India in Ottawa. The timing of the ceremony was significant not only for British Columbia's history but also for the Zoroastrians' ancient homeland, Iran.

Jamshed K. Pavri[1] spoke on behalf of the ZSBC:

> For us Zoroastrians, this is a double joyous and important occasion, for coinciding with the centennial celebration of British Columbia, we are also celebrating the 2500th Anniversary of the Founding of the Persian Empire by King Cyrus the Great [in Iran] ... Authentic recorded history begins from the time of King Cyrus the Great who founded the Achaemenid dynasty in 553 BC. When Babylon became part of the vast Persian empire, this noble king terminated the captivity of the Jews.[2]

Pavri then provided an overview of the Achaemenid, Parthian, and Sasanid dynasties – who ruled Iran from 550 BCE until 651 CE – emphasizing that the ancient dynasties in Iran were Zoroastrian. After the fall of the Sasanids to the Arab armies in 651, and due to the ensuing persecution of Zoroastrians, he stated, a group of Persians immigrated to Northern India, where they were

FIGURE 4.1 Plaque donated by ZSBC to the people and province of BC in 1971 with themes from Persepolis flanking dogwood flowers, an emblem of the province. *Photo courtesy of the BC Archives, Victoria*

known as the Parsis, meaning Persians. He also emphasized that despite the passing of centuries, the Parsis were able to preserve their ethnic "identity, religion, history and culture."

In this chapter, I will attempt to explain the factors underlying such a remarkable appreciation of solidarity with a new home country, Canada, in tandem with allegiance to an ancient religion. In doing so, I will introduce some of the complex history and practice of this religion to provide a better understanding of its place in the current multicultural, multi-ethnic, and multi-religious landscape of British Columbia.

The term "Zoroastrianism" is used in the West to refer to the ancient religion founded by the Iranian prophet Zarathushtra (Greek: *Zōroastrēs*). The prophet likely flourished between ca. 1000 and 1200 BCE. His religion spread widely in Iran during antiquity and was made the state religion during the Sasanid dynasty (224-651 CE), remaining thus until the introduction of Islam.[3]

The sacred texts of Zoroastrianism are collected in a book called the Avesta. The *Gāthās*, the most ancient section of the Avesta, consist of seventeen hymns in a part of the Avesta known as *Yasna* (Y) that are held to be compositions by the prophet himself. They portray his thoughts on the dichotomy of good and evil, and his unique vision of cosmic purpose (Y 30). Zarathushtra regarded the *Ahura Mazdā* (Wise Lord) as the one wholly beneficent, omniscient, uncreated, and eternal God, and viewed a demonic being, *Angra Mainiiu* (Evil Spirit) as coexisting with him, wholly evil, similarly uncreated, but doomed at the end to perish (Y 30.5-8). Similar to Judaism, Christianity, and Islam in insisting on the divergence between two opposing principles of good and evil, Zoroastrianism can ultimately be viewed as a dualist religion. It posits one supreme God, whose adversary, like Satan in Judeo-Christianity or *Shaytān* in Islam, is ultimately inferior to him. The struggle between the two irreconcilable principles of light and darkness, truth and deceit, good and evil had begun shortly after creation, a struggle that, according to Zarathushtra's teachings, will end in the elimination of evil at the end of time (Y 30.9-11).[4]

According to Zoroastrian tradition, on the third sunrise after death, a deceased person's good thoughts, good words, and good deeds are weighed in a balance against the bad. If the good outweigh the bad, the soul enters into heaven, referred to in the Avesta as *Vahishtu-anghush,* meaning "the best dwelling" (Persian *Behisht*). Otherwise, the soul descends into hell, seen by Zarathushtra as "the place of worst existence" (Y 30.4). The blessed and the damned will remain in heaven or hell as spirits until the end of time (Avestan *Frashō-kərəti*) and the resurrection, when all souls will be reincarnated and history as we know it will end, since there will be no more striving, suffering, or dying. Zarathushtra called on all people to choose between good and evil, and to emulate *Saoshiiant,* the messianic figure who is due at the end of time to redeem the world (Y 48.10-12).

Zoroastrianism flourished without interruption in Iran under the Achaemenids (550-330 BCE), the Parthians (247 BCE-228 CE), and the Sasanids (228-651 CE), the last Zoroastrian dynasty of Iran. The overthrow of the Sasanid dynasty by the Arabs in the seventh century had a devastating effect on Zoroastrianism. In spite of punitive laws, it maintained a significant presence in Iran until the thirteenth century, but the Safavid dynasty, which ruled Iran from 1502 to 1722, established Twelver Shiism as the state religion and zealously compelled conversions to Shia Islam. Today Zoroastrianism is officially recognized as a minority religion in Iran, and most of the Zoroastrians there – probably around 30,000 individuals – reside in Tehran and in the desert cities of Yazd and Kerman.

Important Rituals and Practices
In contrast to many religions, Zoroastrianism does not regard the material world or the physical body as the imprisonment of the "truer" spiritual self, but rather as a place to oppose and overcome evil. Zoroastrians hold earth,

along with other elements such as water and fire, as sacred and to be protected from pollutants. Disease, suffering, and physical corruption are regarded as attributes of evil, and death as evil's ultimate design. Zoroastrian funeral structures are normally situated on the outskirts of cities and villages, away from the populace. They are open-roofed, cylindrical structures, in the centre of which the bodies are placed, to be disposed of by carrion eaters. They are known as *dūngerwadi*s in India, but in Iran their use was completely abandoned in favour of cemeteries beginning in the 1930s.

In modern metropolitan areas such as Vancouver, it is impossible to maintain a traditional *dūngerwadi*. Alternative funeral methods are used, the most common being cremation by indirect flame. Many modern Zoroastrians believe that since fire obliterates pure and impure alike, it is not prone to pollution; thus, they do not object to cremation by fire. The traditional form of corpse disposal is still preferred by more conservative Parsis in diaspora. Recently, an effort has been made to construct a traditional *dūngerwadi*, known as the "Sky Burial," in a wilderness area in Texas.[5]

All things leaving the body, namely, blood, cut fingernails, and hair, are considered dead and thus tainted by evil. Traditionally, menstruation was viewed as the consequence of the clash between the forces of good and evil, and a menstruating woman as being the victim of evil's assault. As such, she was held to be impure physically – but by no means spiritually – and was excluded from religious functions, specifically those conducted in the sacred space near the consecrated fire.

The breath, similar to blood, is considered impure once it has left the body. Thus, in the presence of the consecrated fire, Zoroastrian priests wear a mouth veil (*padan*) to avoid contaminating the fire. The laity in ceremonies at the temple are expected to be clean before entering the *niyāyish-gāh* (place of worship) – the room where the consecrated fire is kept – and clean, purified water is always made available nearby. Before entering, worshippers are expected to take off their shoes and cover their hair. The exile communities in the West often emphasize the fact that Zoroastrian purity laws are consistent with principles of hygiene.

The Zoroastrian initiation ceremony – known in Iran as *sedre-pūshī* and in India as *naujote* – usually takes place at the age of fourteen but at an earlier age in India. The youth is given the white shirt (*sedre* in Iran, *sudra* in India), together with a sacred cord (*koshti* in Iran, *kusti* in India). They symbolize the armour of the faith that protects the initiated from evil and are a reminder of one's duty to promote spiritual goodness. Having been invested with the sacred cord and shirt, the youth utters the initiation prayer publicly, in the presence of the priest, friends, and family. *Sedre-pūshī* or *naujote* is always a joyful occasion and is often followed by a feast.

Traditionally, the most sacred Zoroastrian festival is *Nōrūz* (new day), which commences at the spring equinox. It is also the most important national holiday in Iran and Tajikistan at present, celebrated by Muslims, Jews, Baha'is, Christians, and Zoroastrians alike. *Nōrūz* is not celebrated by the Parsis, however, since the new year in the Parsi calendar commences in August and is known as *Pateti*.

Diaspora

Zoroastrianism is practised today by some 130,000 people ranging from minorities in Iran (10,000 to 30,000), to scattered diasporic groups throughout Europe, North America, Australia, and the Far East. The largest community of Zoroastrians is found in India (60,000), where they are known as the Parsis, meaning "Persians."[6] The story of the Zoroastrian diaspora in British Columbia is essentially the story of two different communities, the Iranians and the Indians, who make up the present community. The background, history, and reasons for Parsi immigration to North America are documented by J. Hinnells in detail.[7] The following is a brief historical sketch and backdrop necessary for understanding the Zoroastrian immigrant community in British Columbia.

The Parsis

After their migration to India, the Parsis' religious, cultural, and social norms evolved toward Indian cultural requirements, such as Indian dress, festivals, dietary regulations, purity laws, and, most importantly, the caste customs. The adoption of caste played a significant role in preserving and maintaining the Parsis' distinctiveness among Indian communities as it encouraged relative communal isolation. With the advent of British rule in India, the Parsis functioned as middlemen, brokers, and ambassadors, and established bases and settlements in Bombay.

The Parsis' transition from a minor religious community to a wealthy and notable social group in India began in the nineteenth century, when they sought to create for themselves an identity blending an elite Indian Zoroastrian culture with Western notions of secular individualism. As loyal subjects of the British, they prospered as brokers and merchants, gaining fame for their individual wealth and particularly their philanthropy.

The Hindu and Muslim communities' experience of British colonialism in India was similar to that in other regions of the world that had been battered by Western colonialism. By taking advantage of new opportunities through political collaboration, however, the Parsis were able to secure aid and support from the British, who in turn incorporated their authority within colonial rule. Seen as the remnants of a once-great empire, the Parsis aroused both interest and respect in nineteenth-century Europe. This stimulated the Parsi community to advance the study of its own traditions, resulting in the formation of a dynamic scholarly community.[8]

Iranian Zoroastrians

The social situation of the Parsis during the nineteenth and early twentieth centuries bore little resemblance to that of their Persian co-religionists at that time. Until the late nineteenth century, Zoroastrians in Iran (known as Persia at the time) – pejoratively referred to as Fire-worshippers and *Gabr*s or *Gor*s[9] – were subject to abuse, forced conversion, and *jaziya*, a special tax paid by non-Muslims. An unevenly interpreted Islamic structure governed Zoroastrians and other religious minorities as *ahl udh-dhimmī* (Protected People) until the institution of the new civil law codes in Iran in the 1930s. Elders within the minority groups were allowed a measure of control in the internal affairs of their community. This Shia organization legally recognized minorities as inferior – with Zoroastrians being the lowest of all – and regularly subjected them to humiliation and economic disadvantage through enforcement of the *jaziya*.[10] Civic and legal disadvantages were accompanied by fears of violence and conversion of young boys and girls. Conversion amounted to permanent apostasy, but converts to Islam were able to claim inheritance rights to the property of their Zoroastrian kin.[11]

In 1925, the newly formed Pahlavi dynasty under Reza Shah (1878-1944) initiated the modernization of Iran and emphasized Iran's Zoroastrian heritage as the symbol of the Iranian nation. Reza Shah replaced the country's Islamic lunar calendar with the Zoroastrian one, and in 1935 the international community was asked to refer to the country not as Persia but by its pre-Islamic name, Iran (Avestan *airiianəm-vaējah*).[12]

Rapid centralization and modernization in Iran during the 1930s brought about upward social mobility in major urban centres. Many Zoroastrians, who had migrated to Tehran, where the religion expanded from 450 followers in 1925 to 33,000 in 1993, experienced relative prosperity and developed a profound sense of pride in their Zoroastrian culture and heritage. To this day, many Zoroastrians, both in Iran and in the diaspora, consider Reza Shah's reforms very positive for the overall well-being of the community at that time. Secular and middle-class (Muslim) Iranians regarded Zoroastrianism as "uniquely" Iranian and embraced many of its practices, such as the *Sadeh* and *Mehrigān* celebrations in midwinter and autumn.

The advent of the Islamic Republic in 1979 caused much apprehension not only in the Zoroastrian community but also in other minority religious communities in Iran. The Islamic Republic generally slights reminders of Iran's pre-Islamic history and heritage, and its definition of authority (*wilayat ul-faqīh*) intermingles Shia religion and nationalism. Social and economic conditions in

Iran deteriorated after the outbreak of the eight-year war with Iraq in the 1980s, which in part prompted significant migration of Zoroastrians from Iran to Europe, the United States, and Canada.

Zoroastrians in British Columbia
The earliest recorded presence of a Zoroastrian in British Columbia dates back to the 1860s and relates to Maneckji F. Javeri, a Parsi gentleman who stayed briefly in Barkerville, some 450 miles north of Vancouver, prospecting for gold before moving to California. During the 1920s and 1930s, efforts were made by several Parsi notables in Bombay and London to found settlements in Canada, including British Columbia. In 1930, for instance, Sir Homi M. Mehta and his son Jal purchased some 200 acres of land in the province, but later abandoned their plan and returned to Bombay. In 1957, after discriminatory provisions were rescinded in Canadian immigration policy, the first Parsi family, consisting of Hurmusji Engineer, his wife Soonoo, and their son Meherwan, settled in Vancouver. They were followed by Jamshed Pavri, his wife Roda, and their son Yezdi, who arrived in Vancouver in 1958. In 1959, the third Parsi family, Sam and Villie Confectioner, with their children Zarir and Gulshan, immigrated to Vancouver, bringing the total number of Zoroastrians in the province to ten.[13]

The Zoroastrian Society of British Columbia (ZSBC) was registered on 22 February 1968 (the first Zoroastrian association in Canada was the Zoroastrian Society of Ontario, established in 1965). Four months earlier, twenty members of the community in Vancouver had met at the residence of Mr. Pavri to explore the formation of an official registered Zoroastrian body in British Columbia in order that the organization and its generous donors could avail themselves of income tax deductions. Initially, the key members of the small community chose "Zoroastrian Trust Funds of British Columbia" as the society's name, emulating the earliest and best-known Zoroastrian organization in the West, the Zoroastrian Trust Fund of Europe (ZTFE), founded in London in 1861.

A letter to the Registrar in Victoria dated 1 October 1967 introduced the community as the adherents of one of the world's oldest monotheistic religions, and "followers of the Prophet Zarathustra (Zoroaster) in Ancient Persia." The society's rationale emphasized religion:

a) To locate, to watch over and promote the interest and welfare of, and to render necessary service to Zoroastrian residents, primary in British Columbia.

b) To disseminate the knowledge of Zoroastrian religion, especially for the benefit of the younger generation, either by Sunday school(s) or by correspondence courses.

c) To acquire and maintain Burial Ground or grounds in suitable place or places.
d) To defray the expense attendant on or incidental to the performance of burial or funeral rites of Zoroastrians.
e) To provide for or to defray the expenses attendant on or incidental to the performance of rites and ceremonies practiced [sic] or observed by our community at the initiation or introduction [something similar to baptism] of children of Zoroastrians and the marriage ceremonies of Zoroastrians.[14]

The name "Zoroastrian Trust Funds of British Columbia" was rejected by the Deputy Registrar, however, because of a BC law placing certain restrictions on "trusts" and "Zoroastrian Society of British Columbia" was suggested instead. The Deputy Registrar also emphasized that the society's membership must be limited to BC residents.

At their meeting of 8 October, the founding members sought to define not only who a Zoroastrian was but also the society's membership requirements. Debate focused on the permanent but scattered settlement of Parsis throughout the British Commonwealth, and the fact that there had been a significant number of intermarriages with non-Zoroastrians in Canada, despite the objections of many orthodox Zoroastrians. The committee stressed that second-generation Parsis in North America were now exposed to "alien" influences, and that more mixed marriages were likely. In the end, the following definition was agreed on: "A Zoroastrian is a believer or a follower of the religion as propounded by our Prophet Zoroaster and who has signified his willingness to be initiated into the Zoroastrian religion and is also so initiated in accordance with the practice followed by the Zoroastrians, will be considered a Zoroastrian by our Society."[15]

This definition, which was incorporated into the first ZSBC constitution, neither mentions conversion (non-Zoroastrians to Zoroastrianism) nor clarifies what the official "practice followed by Zoroastrians" was to be, other than the view held by orthodox Zoroastrians (discussed below). The meeting concluded with five men being elected to hold office for one year. Rajnikant Pandya (d. 1998), who had become a member of the Canadian Bar Association in 1964, agreed to draft the society's first constitution.

When the ZSBC was incorporated in 1968, its membership consisted of twenty families totalling fifty-one individuals, all of whom were Parsis. ZSBC members made up about 10 percent of the total Zoroastrian population in Canada, which numbered 509 individuals, mostly in Toronto.

Most Parsis came to British Columbia in the wave of South Asian immigrants that arrived in the 1970s (see Chapters 1 and 3). Among them were Parsis from East Africa (two families) and Pakistan (three families), but most came from

India (Gujarat and Mumbai). At the time of the British Columbia centennial celebrations in 1971, the ZSBC had seventy members; by 1978, this number had increased to almost 300. A handful of Parsis from Seattle and Everett in Washington state regularly participated in ceremonies and events in Vancouver, but they were unable to vote in the society's elections.

Up to the 1980s, except for young graduates studying at American and Canadian universities, very few Iranians immigrated to North America. For instance, there was only one Iranian Zoroastrian living in Vancouver in the late 1950s; he married a French Canadian woman and moved permanently to the United States. After the establishment of the Islamic Republic in 1979 and the devastating war with Iraq in the 1980s, many Iranians, including Zoroastrians, immigrated to Canada. Most chose Vancouver or Toronto as their destination, and the former were welcomed into the ZSBC.

Worldwide, Zoroastrians are organized in four formal institutions: the *Parsi Panchayet*, the earliest and main Zoroastrian body in Mumbai; the Zoroastrian Trust Fund of Europe (ZTFE), founded in 1861, and the World Zoroastrian Organization (WZO), formed in 1980, both based in London; and the Federation of Zoroastrian Associations of North America (FEZANA), registered in the State of Illinois in 1987, which is an umbrella organization for Zoroastrians in Canada and the United States. FEZANA's main activities are organizing congresses, youth and humanitarian activities, religious education, scholarships, and various publications. In 2000, there were approximately 4,500 Zoroastrians in Canada, with four local associations, the largest of which was in Toronto. The societies in Vancouver and Toronto are the only formal societies in Canada with Zoroastrian buildings.

Unlike other Zoroastrian associations in North America, which have separated into either Iranian or Parsi associations, the Zoroastrian Society of British Columbia has remained together as one entity.[16] According to its 2008 directory, total membership consists of 1,263 individuals comprising some 450 families. They reside in larger urban centres: North Vancouver (156 families), Vancouver (44 families), Burnaby (33 families), and Richmond (62 families). There are slightly more males than females. The BC community is considerably more youthful than those in the United Kingdom and India, since the newcomers from Iran and India are usually younger, with an average age of 38-45 years. Eighty percent are married and the birth rate is higher than the death rate. As in other Zoroastrian communities around the world, ZSBC members, both Iranian and Parsi, are highly educated professionals with at least one university or college degree.

In contrast to the western United States, where Iranian Zoroastrians are generally more numerous than their Indian counterparts, the population of Parsis and Iranians in British Columbia has been balanced since the late 1990s.

North Vancouver, West Vancouver (the only area in which Iranians are more numerous), Vancouver, Richmond, Burnaby (mostly Parsis), and twenty-two other communities throughout the province had a total of about 450 Zoroastrian families in 2008, with virtually identical numbers of Iranians and Parsis. Most of the Parsis are from communities in India (Mumbai and Gujarat), with smaller numbers from Pakistan and East Africa. Most of the Iranian Zoroastrians are from Tehran.

Among Indian Zoroastrian diasporic communities, the temple continues to occupy a central place in religious activity and for collective solidarity, as it does in India. For members of a relatively small group such as the Parsis, who define their ethnic identity in terms of religion, a physical space for social activities is of immense importance. Meetings and ordinary social functions – such as dinners, games, poetry readings, and trips to parks – reinforce and reaffirm bonds of loyalty and a sense of identity among community members. Such events also provide opportunities for younger members hoping to meet Zoroastrian partners.

In July 1985, an attempt was made to construct a Zoroastrian Centre in West Vancouver. The attempt failed amid controversy, as a newspaper, *The Province*, made clear: "Plans for a Zoroastrian church at Anderson Crescent and Taylor Way in West Vancouver have been withdrawn after a protest by neighborhood residents."[17] Residents opposed the centre and sent a petition to the West Vancouver Municipal Council, citing the issue of traffic congestion. After a short inquiry, the situation was understood to be more complicated. A *Vancouver Sun* article titled "Racism charges levelled as group drops church bid" quoted a resident as stating: "To be really honest with you, they [the neighbours] didn't want an Iranian church in the neighbourhood. It's a high-class neighbourhood. Put yourself in the same position. You've got a $250,000 house and they put an East Indian church in there and the value of your house is going to drop by half."[18]

ZSBC leaders made no statements regarding whether they felt discriminated against, only that due diligence was exercised in designing and creating the plan for the centre and that special consideration was given to preventing any possible hindrance to the neighbourhood, including traffic congestion. In an interview, the president of the Pacific Interfaith Fellowship Association, Aziz Khaki, said: "I have yet to see any non-Christian group to build anywhere in the Lower Mainland without problems with neighbours. They come up with a variety of flimsy excuses, like traffic congestion, as soon as they find out it is a non-Christian, non-white faith. It's the same old story. They always say they don't want to discriminate, but …"

The small Zoroastrian community, then numbering about 140 families, declined to name residents who opposed the building, saying, "It's not our way to do that." Eddie Eduljee, a trustee of the Zoroastrian House, stated: "Our religion is based on peace and harmony, so when we saw it was creating problems we felt it would be best to withdraw and look for a neighbourhood where we would be accepted." In a separate interview, West Vancouver Mayor Derrick Humphreys, who refused to name the complainants, insisted: "There is no bigotry in West Van. We've got a Jewish community centre here, and an Iranian centre. West Vancouver encourages that sort of thing."

In early 1986, with the help of an earlier bequest by Arbāb Rostam Guiv (1888-1980) and his wife, Morvārid Khānum, both prominent Zoroastrian philanthropists originally from Yazd, Iran, the ZSBC purchased a vacant building at 6900 Halifax Street, Burnaby, that had been previously used as an Anglican church, and transformed it into the current Zoroastrian house of worship, the Dar-e Mehr (Court of Mithra).[19]

The Dar-e Mehr is used regularly during ceremonies (seasonal festivals, commemoration ceremonies for the deceased, initiation rites, and New Year celebrations) and for other, less formal social events (poetry readings, games, potluck dinners, lectures, religious classes for young Zoroastrians, and meetings before outdoor excursions). On most Sundays, the Dar-e Mehr is open for a few hours for communal worship. On the first Tuesday of each month, leading members of the community and directors of the Dar-e Mehr – usually seven in number – usually meet to discuss issues pertaining to the community. Every two years, a new president and board members are elected to a maximum term of four consecutive years for any director.[20] A monthly newsletter is distributed to ZSBC members through e-mail, and previous issues are often posted on the society's website.[21]

As J. Hinnells has shown, Parsis are generally very receptive to the opinions and findings of Western authorities and scholarship on Zoroastrianism; in fact, their loyalty to their country of settlement has sometimes taken precedence over communal ties.[22] This remarkable characteristic of the Parsis in diaspora has probably contributed to their successful adaptation to life in North America. In the interviews conducted for this chapter, all Parsis – young or old – expressed much interest in Western opinions and scholarly discoveries on Zoroastrianism.

Nevertheless, many Parsis and Iranians feel discriminated against by British Columbians of European background. ZSBC members who were personally involved in the unsuccessful attempt to establish a Zoroastrian house in West Vancouver feel that the result was due to the xenophobic character of the neighbourhood in the 1980s. The incident is rarely mentioned in any of the ZSBC newsletters, however, and today very few ZSBC members are aware of it or its details. Those who do recall the affair prefer not to discuss it and regard it as unimportant.

The less orthodox or observant Zoroastrians tend to be younger, highly educated, single, and particularly outmarried (married to a non-Zoroastrian) individuals who live in the larger cities in the province, namely, Vancouver, Burnaby, and Richmond. In general, the first generation of immigrants tend to practise their religion more, as doing so preserves a stronger bond with their heritage. Surveys conducted in 2006 and 2007 indicate that more Parsi Zoroastrians pray daily and wear their sacred *sudra* and *kusti* than Iranian Zoroastrians. For the latter, the words of the prayer are more significant than the ritual wearing of the *sedre* and *koshti*, but for most Parsis, the prayer and the wearing of these objects are inseparable.

Marriage and Conversion

Outmarriage and conversion to Zoroastrianism are the two most contentious topics in the Zoroastrian community. In general, most Parsis worldwide have strongly negative attitudes toward outmarriage. A 1988 survey found that 33 percent of Zoroastrian respondents in Britain and 46 percent in California opposed outmarriage. By contrast, only 20 percent of respondents in Chicago and New York, which have the highest proportions of highly educated Zoroastrians, expressed objection.[23] In an online survey conducted in June 2007 and distributed through the e-mail lists of the members of the Zoroastrian News Agency (ZNA) in North America, 80 out of 100 people were positive toward both outmarriages and conversion. Similarly, 77 percent of ZSBC members were positive toward both intermarriages and conversion.

There is in fact no religious or dogmatic instruction in Zoroastrianism that would prohibit conversion, and many reformists argue that Zarathushtra's teachings were universal and that the earliest Zoroastrians were all converts. Compared with Parsis, a greater number of Iranian Zoroastrians in North America and elsewhere accept both converts and outmarriages with non-Zoroastrians, who are then welcomed into the community. Parsis from East Africa, who are relatively few in British Columbia, are said to be more orthodox and more opposed to outmarriage and conversion than are other Parsis.[24] In an interview with me, however, a prominent Parsi *athornan* (priest) who had immigrated to British Columbia from East Africa spoke favourably of intermarriage and conversion to Zoroastrianism.

Since the emergence of Islam as the dominant religion in Iran – and especially since the establishment of the Islamic Republic in 1979 – problems with intermarriages and conversion to Zoroastrianism have become political. According to Islamic tradition, conversion from Islam is apostasy and converting someone from Islam to a different faith is an offence, and both are seriously penalized. The small and ancient Zoroastrian community in Iran is no longer taxed or forcibly converted to Islam, but it is not to allow any Muslim converts into its fold. Marriages between Muslims and Zoroastrians occur regularly in Iran, but they result in the latter's conversion to Islam, otherwise the marriage is not legally recognized by the authorities and government municipalities.

The Parsis in the Indian subcontinent (Gujarat, Bombay, and Karachi) were especially adept in meeting the requirements of their environment. They adapted well to the purity and caste system prevalent in India, and are known for their opposition to any form of conversion to Zoroastrianism. Their main arguments against conversion are that: (1) one is born into a religion according to God's wishes; hence it is incorrect to change; (2) salvation is possible through all religions, so it is not necessary to convert to a different religion; and (3) conversion is linked to missionary acts, and such endeavours have caused a great deal of pain and suffering throughout history.[25]

Since the nineteenth century, the distinction in India between "Parsi" as an ethnic term and "Zoroastrian" as a religious term has been blurred, and in a caste society where social solidarities were, and still are, often defined in terms of religious ties, conversion to a different "ethnicity" is deemed impossible. These facts help explain the dwindling Zoroastrian communities both inside and outside of Iran and India. It is mostly among the new immigrants to BC that the belief in Zoroastrianism as a distinct and exclusive ethnicity is current. Non-Zoroastrians are not allowed to enter *niyāyish-gāh* (the room where the consecrated fire is kept) at the Dar-e Mehr (see Figure 4.2), not because they are not Zoroastrians "ethnically" but because they do not observe Zoroastrian purity laws and hence may jeopardize the purity of the sacred space where important rituals take place.

The earliest documented conversion to Zoroastrianism in India took place in 1906, when Ratanji Dadabhoy Tata (1871-1932), one of the wealthiest and best-known Parsi industrialists, married a French woman, Suzanne (Sooni) Brière, and had her initiation ceremony (*naujote*) performed. Soon after, however, and despite Tata's power and influence, the Parsi Panchayet in Bombay publicly condemned him.[26]

The most recent official initiation of a non-Zoroastrian was that of Joseph Peterson in New York in 1983, which was also controversial. Problems have also arisen regarding children of the outmarriages, particularly in diaspora communities. The Parsi community in India does not accept the children of Zoroastrian and non-Zoroastrian parents into its community, and the same is true

FIGURE 4.2   A worshipper in the presence of the fire during the *Nōrūz* (New Year) ceremony in the Dar-e Mehr (Court of Mithra) in Burnaby. *Photo by Rastin Mehri*

in Britain.[27] Most communities in the United States and Canada admit non-Zoroastrian spouses and their children, but quietly. At a meeting at the Dar-e Mehr in 1997, over 90 percent of the roughly 100 ZSBC members present voted by a show of hands to accept new converts into the society's fold. Today, anyone, regardless of his or her background, is allowed membership in the ZSBC once his or her *naujote* or *sedre-pūshī* is performed by a priest. The society's Constitution and Bylaws, amended and published in 1997, states that non-Zoroastrians are welcomed into the community after their initiation into the religion.[28]

In an interview, a prominent Parsi ZSBC member emphasized that conversion of Muslim Iranians in diaspora who display a unique interest in the ancient Iranian religion should not be permitted, since their apparent interest in the faith is the result of the current inauspicious political atmosphere in Iran as well as the rise in Islamophobia after the terrorist attacks of 11 September 2001. He argued that once the prevailing political situation in Iran changes, loyalty toward and interest in the ancient religion would similarly change. In other interviews, however, two other prominent members of the ZSBC, a Parsi and an Iranian, stated that conversion to Zoroastrianism is justified and must be allowed. One stated that the "good religion" should be thought of in terms of a remedy for many social ills, and that it would be wrong to withhold it from sincere and knowledgeable people. He expressed his pleasure in the rising interest in his ancient faith, which is facing annihilation, and stated that Arbāb Rostam Guiv, the great Zoroastrian philanthropist through whose generous support the Dar-e Mehr was founded, had also emphasized support and welcome of non-Zoroastrians into the community.

Intermarriage and conversion to Zoroastrianism remain controversial in British Columbia and elsewhere. The main roots of this controversy may be traced to the way in which the Parsi and Zoroastrian communities elsewhere define and articulate their ethnic identity. For many Parsis, as well as for many Iranian Zoroastrians, Zoroastrianism does not signify a religious community alone. Many think of it in terms of a cultural designation, and often see conversion as endangering this ethnic identity.

Creating the Zoroastrian Community in British Columbia

The only Zoroastrian periodical in Vancouver is the quarterly *Pake e Mehr* (Messenger of Mithra), founded and edited by West Vancouver resident Dr. Mehrabān Shahrvīnī, an Iranian Zoroastrian who came to Vancouver from Tehran in the early 1980s. *Pake e Mehr* was the first Persian-language periodical in Western Canada. It appears once every two or three months and includes some essays in English. Its aim is to "help expand the Zoroastrian and Persian knowledge and cultures," covering topics as varied as history, politics, language, and upcoming major social events. There are also several websites dedicated to Zoroastrian and ancient Iranian scholarship, cultural issues, and events. One of the most popular of these is the O'Shihan Cultural Organization, maintained by an Iranian Zoroastrian residing in North Vancouver.[29] O'Shihan Cultural Organization belongs to the "reform" groups, which promote conversion and believes that rites and rituals ought to be altered in order to better answer the need of the community at different times. O'Shihan Cultural Organization regularly arranges recreational, scholarly, and cultural events, such as Zoroastrian short-film festivals in different areas in and around Vancouver.

Most Parsis in British Columbia were members of the middle and upper classes in their homelands (India, Pakistan, and East Africa). They are well-educated professionals, often with enough resources to secure residences in middle- and upper-class suburban areas. Members of the ZSBC have been active in many important community service organizations in British Columbia and in Canada at large. In 1992, for instance, the government of Canada honoured Ms. Bella Tata, the ZSBC's first president, with a commemorative medal for community service during its 125th year anniversary.[30]

As with their compatriots in diaspora, Iranian Zoroastrians are proud of their heritage and of their mother tongue, which is linguistically a direct descendant of the "Old Persian" language spoken during the Achaemenid and later Sasanid dynasties (Middle Persian/Pahlavi). They are passionately inspired by their history and the sense of being a unique community that has endured and upheld the ancient Iranian religion despite centuries of hardship and persecution. Most Parsis regard Iran as their true, original, and ancestral homeland, but Iranian Zoroastrians, who believe themselves to have been forced out of Iran following the Islamic Revolution and the eight-year war with Iraq, have stronger ties to that country and grieve at being away from their homeland. Unlike the Parsis, most Iranian Zoroastrians in British Columbia prefer to follow the teachings in the *Gāthā*s rather than later priestly teachings and rituals. They observe ancient festivals, such as *Nōrūz, Mehrigān,* and *Sadeh,* that are not observed by Parsis. Also, most Iranians in British Columbia incline toward the "reform" wing of Zoroastrianism.

Parsis are similarly proud of and inspired by their Zoroastrian heritage. They are an older community in the province, as most Iranians arrived and settled in Vancouver during the late 1980s and early 1990s. Parsis, moreover, are spread throughout the province, whereas most Iranians have settled in North and West Vancouver. Some Parsis define themselves in terms of what they are not: they say that they are not truly Indian, Pakistani, or indeed Iranian, but Parsi Zoroastrian. Most of the ZSBC's members, Parsi and Iranian alike, intend to keep their community together (unlike the community in Toronto, for instance), and are confident of resolving their differences.

Besides religious, cultural, and linguistic differences, a contributing factor in the formation of two separate Parsi and Iranian Zoroastrian associations in North America is the existence of large numbers of non-Zoroastrians (mostly Iranians) who are eager to convert. The Iranian community in British Columbia has risen in numbers since the establishment of the Islamic Republic, but the population is still small compared with that in California or Toronto. Most Iranians in the province are inspired by their pre-Islamic history and show significant interest in the ancient Iranian faith. They are often very quick to stress the uniqueness of their country and culture as a non-Arab civilization, but are generally unaware of the existence of the Zoroastrian centre in Burnaby. Those who know about it usually express disappointment at the reluctance of some ZSBC members to accept converts. Leaders of the ZSBC rarely collaborate with Iranian societies, such as the Iranian Canadian Cultural Association in Vancouver, and neither association takes part in the other's activities.

Many non-Zoroastrian Iranians in diaspora have either sought to join existing Iranian Zoroastrian communities or have formed a society of their own. One example is 'Alī-Akbar Ja'farī (also Jafarey), an Iranian Muslim-born scholar living in California who "returned" to Zoroastrianism long ago (early 1970s). Stressing the forced conversion to Islam experienced in Iran over the last 1,400 years and Islam's intolerance of apostasy, Mr. Ja'farī, now in his eighties, insists that had it been allowed to flourish, Zoroastrianism would never have become a minor religion among Iranians. In order to restore interest in and promote an understanding of the religion, he and his association post information on the Internet and answer phone calls and inquiries. He has studied and translated many Zoroastrian texts and conducted formal conversion and initiation ceremonies for both Iranians and non-Iranians at the Dar-e Mehr in San Jose.[31] His activities have drawn objections from a number of Iranian Zoroastrians, and particularly from orthodox Parsis, who have referred to him as an enemy of the Zoroastrian religion.[32]

The main concern for most Iranians in diaspora – Zoroastrians and non-Zoroastrians alike – is being associated with the Islamic Republic, or of being confused with Arabs. Combating these notions is important to Zoroastrians – as well as to many non-Zoroastrian Iranians – especially with their collective memory of Muslim rule in Iran. Many Zoroastrians view themselves as adherents of an ancient tradition that is similar – or at least linked – to the West and to Western values and traditions. Zoroastrians who are historically informed take great pride in their religion's profound influence on Western religious traditions.

Recently, strong feelings were aroused by the Warner Brothers film *300*, which is loosely based on ancient Greek texts involving the Achaemenid king Xerxes (r. 485-65 BCE) and portrays ancient Iranians as barbarians and demonic figures. The movie generated strong protest not only from the Iranian government and from Iranian communities in North America but also from the Parsi Panchayet Society in Mumbai and Zoroastrian communities worldwide. This incident was an unusual example of solidarity between the Iranian and Parsi communities.

In a recent interview, another prominent Parsi member of the ZSBC stated that she and many other Parsis in the society no longer use the term "Parsi" alone to define their ethnic identity, but rather *Canadian, British Columbian, Irani, Parsi, Zarathushti* (meaning "Zoroastrian" in Persian) – a term also designated by the Federation of Zoroastrian Associations of North America to refer to the members of the community worldwide. She explained that such attempts to redefine ethnic boundaries have helped improve some of the extant (linguistic, cultural, and religious) divide between Iranian Zoroastrians and Parsis in the BC community.

Although the absence of a consecrated pure temple, full-time priest, and permanently burning fire in the Dar-e Mehr means that higher liturgies cannot be performed, the ZSBC community is unique among the communities in North America. Others, including those in Toronto and California, have long been divided into two, each forming new and separate Iranian and Indian associations. In British Columbia, however, both groups have been able to remain together as one community despite their differences, the most significant of which are those of language and those pertaining to ritual observances and the use of separate Parsi and Iranian religious calendars.

NOTES

1 Mr. Pavri (1917-89) was born in Bombay. After living in Hong Kong, he moved with his family to Vancouver in 1958. He was one of the founding members of the BC Interfaith Council, the India Club, the Immigrant Services Society of British Columbia, the Multicultural Society, and the founder of the Gujarati Society of BC, of which he became the first president.
2 "Speech made by J.K. Pavri at the Plaque Presentation Ceremony on September 27, 1971," in *The Proceedings of the B.C. Centennial Celebrations*. The Victoria Archives, Victoria, British Columbia, 1-3.
3 Mary Boyce, *Zoroastrianism: Its Antiquity and Constant Vigour* (Costa Mesa, CA: Mazda Press, 1992), 27-32. For a detailed history of the Zoroastrian religion, belief, and practices, see other works by Mary Boyce in Suggested Readings.
4 The ancient Greek philosopher Plutarch stated in the first century BCE that Persians (Zoroastrians) "have one god and one demon."
5 See http://www.skyburial.org.
6 J. Hinnells, "The Modern Zoroastrian Diaspora," in *Migration: The Asian Experience*, ed. J.M. Brown and R. Foot (Oxford: St. Martin's Press, 1994), 56.
7 See J. Hinnells, *Zoroastrian Diaspora: Religion and Migration* (Oxford: Oxford University Press, 2005).
8 For an interesting exposition of a nineteenth-century Parsi scholar's reflection on his community and British colonial rule, see D.F. Karaka, *History of the Parsis, Including Their Manners, Customs, Religion, and Present Position*, 2 vol. (London: Macmillan, 1884).
9 The term "Fire-worshipper" was first used in the Byzantine Empire to refer to their Zoroastrian counterparts. The term "Gabr," and later "Gor," is an Aramaic ideogram meaning "man" in Pahlavi texts.
10 R. Shahrokh and R. Writer, eds. and trans., *The Memoirs of Keikhosrow Shahrokh* (Lampeter: Edwin Mellen Press, 1994), 33 and 40. See also E. Sanasarian, *Religious Minorities in Iran* (Cambridge: Cambridge University Press, 2000), 19-24 and 43-54.
11 See also Mary Boyce, *A Persian Stronghold of Zoroastrianism* (Oxford: Oxford University Press, 1977), 7-11; and A. Abrahamian, *Iran between Two Revolutions* (Princeton, NJ: Princeton University Press, 1982), 40. Many Zoroastrians lost their lives after converting to new religious movements such as Babism and Baha'ism, which were and are still considered by the Shia ayatollahs as apostates: Boyce, *A Persian Stronghold*, 9.
12 The term 'Iran' (Middle Persian: *ērān-vīj*) is related.
13 J. Pavri, *The Zoroastrian Society of British Columbia 1968-1978* (Vancouver: n.p., 1978), i-ii, and "Contribution of Zoroastrians to the North American Society," *FEZANA Journal* (1997): 30-45. See also B. Tata, "Jamshed K. Pavri (1917-1989): Community Activist Par Excellence," Vohuman.org, http://www.vohuman.org/Article/Pavri,Jamshed%20K.htm; and J. Hinnells "The Zoroastrian Diaspora in Britain, Canada, and the United States," in *The South Asian Religious Diaspora in Britain, Canada, and the United States*, ed. H. Coward, J. Hinnells, and R. Williams (Albany: State University of New York Press, 2000), 35-37.

14 Information in these paragraphs is from Pavri, *The Zoroastrian Society,* 29.
15 Ibid., 25.
16 Primary sources for this study were collected during fieldwork from 2006 to 2008 in Vancouver. In the spring of 2007, Professor J. Hinnells kindly made available to me a modified version of his own survey questionnaire, which had been used by his student Gillian Mehta for a study of Zoroastrians in Europe in 2003.
17 *The Province,* 24 July 1985, A9.
18 All quotations in these paragraphs are from N. Knickerbocker, "Racism Charges Levelled as Group Drops Church Bid," *Vancouver Sun,* 26 July 1985, A14.
19 "Mehr" (Avestan, *Mithra*) is the name of an important *yazata* (angel). In modern Persian, "Mehr" also means "compassion."
20 The ZSBC presidents since the 1997 constitutional amendment are as follows: Bella Tata (1998-2000), Perviz Madon (2000-2), Homi Italia (2002-6), and Sharook Kapadia (2006 to present).
21 See http://www.zsbc.org.
22 Hinnells, *Zoroastrian Diaspora,* 1-31, 134-43, 293.
23 Ibid.
24 Ibid.
25 Ibid., 40-41.
26 Hinnells, *Zoroastrians in Britain,* 19.
27 Ibid.
28 "The Zoroastrian Society of British Columbia Constitution and Bylaws, February 22, 1968 (1997 Amends)," Vancouver, 1997.
29 See http://www.vcn.bc.ca/oshihan/IndexEnglish.htm.
30 Bella Tata was born in Mumbai and grew up in Pune and Bangalore. She immigrated to Canada in 1981 and joined the federal government in 1983, where she is currently Executive Assistant to the Regional Executive Director, Pacific Region, Industry Canada. She was also a recipient of the Queen's Golden Jubilee Commemorative Award in 2002 and the Pacific Federal Council's Community Contribution Award in June 2005. She lives in Vancouver.
31 See Rana Rosen, "Zoroastrians Divided over Conversion, Face a Shrinking Future," Belief.net, http://pluralism.org/news/view/15982.
32 See "The Danger of Ali-Akbar Jafarey," *Ushta Newsletter,* 3 September 2000; and Noshir H. Dadrawala's article "Beware of This False Saviour," http://www.fravahr.org/spip.php?article181.

PART 2

Traditions from Southeast Asia

5 Thai and Lao Buddhism
JAMES PLACZEK AND IAN G. BAIRD

Thailand and Laos are adjacent, independent countries in mainland Southeast Asia. Although there are many similarities between the two nations in language, culture, and religion, their histories and modern-day national structures differ. In Thailand, roughly one-third of the population, over 20 million people, live in the northeast and are ethnic Lao.[1] Their dialects, customs, and festivals are very similar to those of the ethnic Lao in Laos, who make up about two-thirds of that country's six million inhabitants. Thus, there are more ethnic Lao people in Thailand than there are in Laos. The relationship between Laos and Thailand is a complex one. In many ways, it can be compared to the sometimes ambivalent relationship between Canadians and Americans.

Over 90 percent of the population of Thailand is Theravada Buddhist, including virtually all in the northeast. In Laos, the ethnic Lao are also mainly Theravada Buddhists. (See Chapter 6 for a review of Theravada Buddhism.) Over a period of 2,500 years, the different branches of Buddhism have diverged considerably, adding local cultural values and different emphases. In Thailand and Laos, popular practice is dominated by efforts to earn merit toward a better future life. Along with the historical and conceptual differences, there is the powerful drive among all refugees and immigrants to seek comfort by using religion as a basis for building close language-based cultural communities. This tends to divide religious groups along ethnic and national lines. There is some degree of cohesion among the Theravada communities in British Columbia's Lower Mainland, a cohesion that does not extend to their Mahayana fellows unless the event is obviously an interfaith one. In general, Mahayana monks and laity do not attend Theravada events and Theravadins do not attend Mahayana events. As Bandu Madanayake shows in Chapter 6, however, the Sri Lankans do participate more in other Buddhist rituals. Some Theravada events, such as ordinations or demarcations of sacred space, require a minimum number of monks. Other events are enriched and gain prestige according to the number of monks invited. In these cases (see examples below), one finds that monks from Laos, Thailand, Sri Lanka, and Burma (also known as Myanmar) are invited and are considered equivalent.

Thai and Lao Theravada Buddhist practices are largely the same, although there are some differences in the festivals celebrated. For example, the second largest ritual for the Lao each year is *boun that luang*, which is based on an important Lao national symbol, and the festival focused on the story of Prince Vessantara (Lao: *boun phra vet*) is very important in Laos and northeastern Thailand but not emphasized in the rest of Thailand. This chapter reviews Thai and Lao Buddhism in British Columbia, including interactions between the two groups.[2]

Making Merit and Donating

For most Thai and Lao people, the driving force behind Buddhism is making merit (Thai: *tham bun;* Lao: *het boun*). The Thai and Lao urban elites frequently equate merit with the amount of money donated. With the establishment of state Buddhism in Siam (now Thailand) about a hundred years ago, merit making became less a matter of participation than of offering support. Merit making for the modern urban Thai entails limited personal and spiritual effort, and more reliance upon gifts to higher-status monks and monasteries.[3] In Laos and rural areas of Thailand, however, especially the northeast, the older traditions of participation continue.

Contemporary Thais are closely attuned to details of status recognition such as gestures of respect and status symbols. For them, a person's *bun* is "largely knowable through his wealth and especially his merit-making gifts."[4] This is less important for the Lao, but remains a factor nonetheless.

Although Duangsi Tavonesouk, a prominent member of the Lao Buddhist community in British Columbia, often cites the proverb *het dii dai dii* (do good, receive good), she just as often returns to the theme that donating brings one a deep emotional comfort (*khwaam sabaai jai*). She affirms, as do other Lao and Thais interviewed, that most local Buddhists focus on this life; it is mostly the elderly who make merit for the next life. The concept of merit as a kind of travel-mile reward system, so often criticized by Westerners, is not uncommon, according to Duangsi, but it shows a limited understanding of the fundamental Buddhist principle of "non-self." In this view, one should work toward acts of genuinely selfless giving, the ultimate ideal.

Since making merit is a cultural imperative for Thai and Lao Buddhists, they feel a strong need to perform the ritual acts of giving. They do not feel comfortable living in places without monks, as there is literally no "field of merit" for them to fulfill this spiritual need. Thus, they will make great sacrifices of money, labour, and time to support a wat (Buddhist temple-monastery) and its monks.

However, Theravada Buddhists will normally support any legitimate monks available, all the better if they are deemed "good" monks (disciplined, ascetic, knowledgeable, and/or wise). People will travel long distances to offer support to a "good monk," in line with the view that supporting a good monk earns more merit than supporting an ordinary monk. Manote Sappakittipakorn points out that ideally Thais do not give to individual monks; rather, they give to the monkhood in general. There is scriptural support for this. In practice, however, people give donations to the wat in general and also specific envelopes of money to individual monks for their personal use. In interviews with both Thai and Lao Buddhists in British Columbia, the delicate balance between giving more, giving to a better recipient, and hopes for reward is acknowledged, but in the end the emphasis remains on the kind of unattached pure joy of giving that is idealized in the scriptures and accompanying literature.[5]

The Thai Community in British Columbia
No one has exact statistics on the Thai community in the province, but Statistics Canada notes 2,410 British Columbians identified as Thai in the 2006 Census of Canada.[6] The Thai community is much smaller than most of the other communities discussed in this book. People from Thailand tend to arrive as individuals, mostly women who have married Caucasian Canadian men. A few "Thai-Thai" couples have also arrived, with perhaps only 200 to 300 Thai males in the community.

The first Thais arrived in the province in the late 1960s. During this period, public Buddhist activity was limited to trips to the nearest Thai temple, Wat Washington Buddhavanaram in Auburn, Washington, about three hours' drive from Vancouver. A community association was set up around 1986 and lasted several years. The Thai community is strongly divided, however, between factions led by women, and potential community leaders (including some men) who do not want to risk being identified with one faction or another.

Ajahn Chah, one of Thailand's most revered Buddhist teachers, passed through Vancouver in 1978, inspiring a group to promote (unsuccessfully, however) a Thai Forest Tradition monastery in the city. A Thai wat was founded in Vancouver in 1991 and began to function as a community centre. Eventually problems arose (outlined below) and its role as a social centre was greatly curtailed. Partly in response to problems at this wat, a Thai Buddhist Society was registered, but this society was short-lived as well.

In 1995, the first Royal Thai Consulate General was established in Vancouver. It supported the unification of the local community, but it was not until 2005 that the Thai Community Association of British Columbia was established. During its initial phase, some of the original founders resigned or were expelled. The association originally received financial support from the consulate general and had its own office in Burnaby, and membership in mid-2006 was around 370. As of late 2009, two members remain active with one of the wats in Vancouver.

In Thailand, society at the national level functions under the slogan "*chaat saatsanaa, phra mahaakasat*" ("nation, religion, and monarchy"). Among the Thais of British Columbia, these nationalist appeals may appear remote, but when traditional festivals are organized, they attend, often in surprising numbers and sometimes travelling long distances. Clearly, Thais in the province have a need for Thai cultural and religious activities. There is now an official community association (nation), a Buddhist wat (religion), and an active consulate general representing the government, and through it the monarchy. Although the institutions appear to be in place, the community association still struggles to represent the whole community, and up to four Buddhist organizations have been established (see below).

Most Thais live in Vancouver and the surrounding Lower Mainland. There are smaller Thai communities in Victoria, Nanaimo, and Kamloops. Since the phenomenon of Thai women marrying foreigners has become institutionalized in Thailand as a career option, especially in the northeast, Thai women continue to pop up around the province, even in quite remote locations, as they settle in with their Canadian husbands. The only other BC community that has local access to a Thai-related Buddhist wat is Kamloops, which is about a half-hour's drive from Sītavana (Birken Forest Monastery), discussed below.

The Lao Community in British Columbia

The Lao came to British Columbia under very different circumstances from those of the Thais. While the Thais came one by one or in young families with entrepreneurial spirit, almost all the Lao came as refugees, after the communist takeover of their country in 1975. Almost all arrived between 1978 and 1992, and they came as families. The Lao population in British Columbia has a smaller proportion of the old Lao elite than other émigré Lao communities in North America.[7] While the Lao were originally located in various communities in the province, most have gravitated to Surrey and Abbotsford, suburbs of Vancouver. In 1980, the Lao Benevolent Society of British Columbia was registered with a mandate to support the new Lao community, without any political or religious affiliation. Today, the society still organizes some annual social events for the Lao community, but its role has greatly diminished, as there are almost no new arrivals from Laos.

The 2006 Census of Canada recorded a total of 1,590 people in British Columbia who identified themselves as Lao.[8] Champakhome Chanthaphasouk, the head of the Lao Benevolent Society, finds this too low. In the mid-1990s, his group estimated that the Lao population was 2,200, and it has increased since then due to arrivals of Lao families from other Canadian provinces, often attracted by the milder climate. The actual Lao population in British Columbia is probably around 3,000.

While most of the Thais in the province are Buddhist, approximately 15 percent of the Lao population are "Christians" (Protestants, various denominations); most converted from Buddhism when they were in refugee camps in Thailand or out of gratitude to the Protestant families that initially sponsored them to come to Canada. About 25 percent are Catholics whose families converted in Laos during the French colonial era. The remaining 60 percent are Buddhists. While the Buddhists tend to get along fairly well with the Catholics, and frequently interact socially (both groups drink alcohol), the "Christians" interact far less with both groups. Some Lao Buddhists see the "Christians" as religiously intolerant, and they consider their own openness to other faiths to be one of their most important traits. In recent years, some British Columbia Lao have reverted to Buddhism. As one immigrant put it, "I was baptized by my sponsors when I came to Canada, but I was born a Buddhist." Culture and religion are inextricable for Lao Buddhists. This applies to the Thais as well.

In 1984, the Lao Buddhist Cultural Society of British Columbia was established. When it applied for federal charitable status in 1990, the society changed its name to the Lao-Canadian Buddhist Temple Association. The association is a non-profit charitable organization "for religion and heritage," says Bounmy Simmavong, its former president. "We need to show the next generation we are not alone," adds Bounleung Phongmany, another member of the executive committee, who also acknowledges trying to create something for his own generation. During its early years, the association could not organize many religious activities and its financial resources were very limited. Their evening social events (which monks do not attend) usually follow a morning religious event.

Thai Buddhist Centres

Through the 1980s, the only option for Thais who wanted to satisfy their cultural imperative of making merit was to cross the US border to Wat Washington. Although it was at least a three-hour drive, many Thais from British Columbia made the trip. When monks of the Thai Forest Tradition (see below) happened to visit Vancouver, the Friends of Thailand Educational Society would help arrange food offerings and meditation retreats. It was clear, however, that Thais in British Columbia needed a local wat.

Wat Yanviriya
Luang Phor Viriyang Sirintharo (official title, Phra Thep Jetiyajahn) established the first successful Thai wat in British Columbia. ("Luang Phor" is a popular term of respect.) With the help of some BC Thais, he settled on a modest former

Christian chapel in East Vancouver. With Bangkok funding, the property was purchased in the name of Luang Phor Viriyang, and Wat Yanviriya ("Wat Yan" for short) was officially opened in 1992. Perhaps with American models in mind,[9] Luang Phor now has six other Thai wats or Buddhist centres in Canada: three in Ontario and three in Alberta. He personally inspects these wats regularly. Since 2000, he has established Canadian residence in Edmonton, which has become his Canadian headquarters.

In Thailand, wats usually have a management committee, the leader of which is called *makhathayok*, a sort of wat manager. Although a wat committee was set up in Vancouver, Luang Phor's strategy has been to entrust the management of the wat to one person, most likely to avoid dealing with community divisions. This strategy has led to problems in his wats in Ottawa, Edmonton, and Calgary, and especially in Vancouver, where there has been a falling-out with the managers, and Luang Phor has had to find others to manage the wats.

The first managers he selected for Wat Yan were not accepted as community leaders, and conflicts developed within the Thai community. This led to weak support for the wat from the Thai community, and over the years others have stepped in. Early on, the most consistent lay supporter was a Burmese man. A remarkable Vietnamese family currently fills this role. They come daily to offer food, arrange the rituals, and clean up. The head of this family states that it is simply an extraordinary opportunity "to do good." Members of the Thai community come on Sundays. A few also come some weekday mornings, but there is no systematic routine for feeding the monks. Most Thais come to make merit by offering food and cash, and performing the ritualized donation of requisites for the monks. They attend in large numbers on major festival days.

Other Thai leaders invited monks on their own initiative, intending to establish an alternative to Wat Yan. A Thai Buddhist Society was registered in British Columbia around 2001, and invited monks to a residence in Burnaby. Without overall community unity or powerful funding from Bangkok, however, these efforts ended with the monks returning to Thailand. Conflicts also developed at Wat Yan between the managers and the monks, who were at first senior disciples of Luang Phor. Eventually these senior monks were removed. Now only junior monks are assigned to Wat Yan, usually two at a time, and they rotate frequently. Many of the Lao and Cambodian faithful who had attended the wat since the beginning eventually sought a spiritual home elsewhere, as did many long-term members of the Thai community. There were also conflicts over secular use of the wat, such as for Thai-language classes for children or for community meetings. Eventually, all such activities were forbidden, and any such requests had to be forwarded to Luang Phor in Bangkok (now Edmonton), or be dealt with during his regular visits. This pattern is remarkably similar to the management style of Venerable Mongkolthepmolin in the United

States, except that the latter's senior monks have some discretion in dealing with the laity.[10]

Luang Phor may have taken this approach to avoid past problems, such as when one senior disciple, Ajahn Bunthaem, stayed several years at Wat Yan, gained Canadian residency, and on some issues sided with the managers or the congregation against Luang Phor. Although attendance has gone down, Wat Yan has continued to function as a social centre, especially for newly arrived Thais. Also, throughout the entire history of Wat Yan, there has always been a group of dedicated Buddhist faithful who participated and made merit, ignoring the power struggles. In 2004, Wat Yan moved into a new phase. Luang Phor finally released the former managers, and there is now cooperation with leaders of the Thai Community Association. Revenues received are managed by Luang Phor's treasurer in Edmonton.

Luang Phor Viriyang achieved a reputation as a "good monk" decades ago for his exceptionally long career as a meditator and teacher, the standards of his disciples, and the strong support he has been able to inspire for his many projects. He is a classic variety of senior monk who has followed extreme ascetic practices, and has thus attracted religious supporters following a scenario that is virtually standardized in Thailand for famous "good monks."[11] This includes his early asceticism and personal contact with the great Thai Forest Master Ajahn Man (1870-1949).[12] He is now in close contact with the elite and power wielders of the societies he works in. While the classic scenario ends with manipulation of the elderly monks by sometimes unscrupulous managers, Luang Phor Viriyang has avoided this.

At the age of eighty-seven, Luang Phor moves slowly and has difficulty hearing. Overall, however, his vigour is unabated and he has the energy of a youth. He is a walking advertisement for his Willpower Institute philosophy (see below) and approach to life. When asked whether he planned to open any more wats (he has recently looked at sites in Nanaimo and Langley, British Columbia), he replied that if there was a need and conditions were right, he would help. He also said that he was working with scholars in Edmonton to develop a Buddhist university there. He opened a branch of the Willpower Institute in Dallas Texas in 2009. Despite his amazing vitality, Luang Phor's years of personal management cannot continue indefinitely, and it is not clear what his legacy will be when he finally has to relinquish control.

Wat Atammayatarama

Although some BC Thais continued to attend Wat Washington, in 1998 Seattle-area Thais established a new wat in the teaching lineage of the late Buddhadasa Bhikkhu, probably the best-known and most widely respected monk in Thailand. Called Wat Atammayatarama ("Wat Atam" for short), it is located about an hour closer to Vancouver than Wat Washington.[13] Many Lower Mainland Thai Buddhists, including the Thai consul general, go there for special events and festivals. The monks are under the guidance of abbot Ajahn Ritthi Tirajitto. They have already ordained one Caucasian American, and they regularly organize meditation retreats. Ajahn Ritthi is often invited to Vancouver and other places in British Columbia, and the frequency of these invitations has increased noticeably in recent years. Based on his observations during these trips, he notes that the BC Thai groups are unable to get behind any widely accepted community leaders. In 2006, Wat Atam held an event known as *fang luuk nimit* in Thai, the ritual burial of stone boundary markers to demarcate a permanent sacred space that can be used for ordinations and the fortnightly recitations of the rules of conduct for monks. It was an international event, with 80-100 BC Thais, who as a group jointly sponsored one of the boundary stones and participated in the ceremony to drop the stone into its resting place.

Ajahn Ritthi's successes clearly mark him as a monk who is strong in his own practice, capable of maintaining discipline in his wat, and able to inspire Thai groups and individuals. The ritual demarcation of a permanent sacred space and ordination of a successful local-born *farang* (Caucasian) monk are milestones in the rooting of Buddhism in a new culture. Ajahn Ritthi's frequent invitations to British Columbia are for the purpose of conducting rituals on such occasions as an anniversary, a funeral, or the opening of a business. He always turns these events into opportunities for dharma talks, often appointing Phra Santidhammo, his *farang* disciple, to speak simultaneously in English.

His use of such "skillful means" to teach an audience in its own idiom at appropriate moments has inspired a group of BC Thais to work to establish a branch of Wat Atam in Vancouver. In the latter half of 2008, Ajahn Ritthi and his monks came to Vancouver each month to give dharma talks and gauge support for the branch, which was established in November of that year. Under the leadership of abbot Tawatchai Keuket, it is called Buddhapanyanuntarama Buddhist Monastery (BBM) and is located in Burnaby.[14]

Sītavana (Birken Forest Monastery)

Another Thai Buddhist resource in British Columbia is the teaching lineage of Ajahn Chah in the Thai Forest Tradition. This lineage can be characterized as focusing on meditation practice and disciplined application of the *vinaya* rules for monks. In Vancouver, the Friends of Thailand Educational Society has supported occasional visits of Western monks in this tradition for the past twenty years. The international headquarters of the Thai Forest Tradition is in Britain, and there are branches in Europe, Australia, New Zealand, and, most recently, the United States. In Canada, there are affiliate centres in Thunder

Bay and Perth, Ontario, near Ottawa (the newest branch, headed by Ajahn Viradhammo, a senior Canadian monk in this lineage).

The first practitioner of this tradition in British Columbia was Ajahn Sona, a *farang* native of the province who was ordained by a Sri Lankan monk in West Virginia and spent some time with the Ajahn Chah lineage at Wat Paa Nanachaat (International Forest Monastery) in northeastern Thailand. In 1994, he returned to British Columbia and worked with the local Sri Lankan Buddhists for some time (see Chapter 6). By 1998, he had established a site for Birken Forest Monastery (Sītavana) near Princeton. Three years later, the monastery moved to its present location in a forest near Kamloops, roughly a five-hour drive from Vancouver.

Birken has become a Theravada Buddhist anchor point for "serious" Buddhists in the province. "Our ethical rules remain virtually identical from the time of the Buddha," reports Ajahn Sona.[15] Still, Thais are shocked to see such breaches of Thai social tradition as women making offerings directly to monks. Thais have stayed at Birken, including one *anagarika* (Thai: *mae chii;* Lao: *me khao*) "nun" who stayed for several years, but most trainees there are not Thai. In recent years, most of the Thais who go there are from nearby, especially a dozen or so Thai families from Kamloops.

On 29 November 2003, two Caucasian Canadians became the first Canadian-born *bhikkhus* (monks) ordained by Canadians in Canada. Twelve Theravada monks participated in this historic ceremony at Birken.[16] Abhayagiri Forest Monastery in northern California has become the centre of the Thai Forest Tradition in North America and enhances Birken Forest Monastery, an affiliate of the lineage. One of the abbots of Abhayagiri, Ajahn Passano, was the Canadian preceptor for the ordinations at Birken. The Rains Retreat period of late 2009 saw six Caucasian monks in residence at Birken.

Dhammakaya International Meditation Society of British Columbia

Wat Phra Dhammakaya is a very large, very successful, and somewhat controversial Buddhist sect that was established as an independent centre in Thailand in 1970. Dhammakaya is known for modern marketing techniques, for attracting students and leaders of society, business, and government, for focusing on a particular meditation method, and for rituals and ceremonies involving hundreds of thousands of participants, including monks. By 2007, it had over twenty-eight branches in Thailand and over forty internationally.[17] The branch in Seattle has been established for some years and has supported the new branch in Richmond, British Columbia, since 2007. Two monks conduct meditation retreats and the basic rituals that Thais need, and in 2009 they ordained a novice.

The Lao Buddhist Temple

Ajahn Santy Sisombath (Bhikku Kittisaddho) bears the physical scars of war in Laos. He was ordained as a monk in Laos and spent three years in a refugee camp before going to Montreal in 1984. Around 1987, he came to British Columbia, where the Lao community initially housed him in an apartment in Abbotsford. Later, he moved to Vancouver and resided there with support from some Lao and northeastern Thais. At that time, the Lao community was still adapting to the traumatic changes of refugee life. In 1990, Ajahn Santy decided that it was too much of an effort for a few local families to support him, so he disrobed and began adjusting to life as a Canadian layman.

Around 1997, Ajahn Santy decided to re-enter the monkhood. He was on good terms with Ajahn Bunthaem at the Thai Wat Yan, and hoped to be re-ordained by him there. Luang Phor would not allow it, however, as Ajahn Santy's war injuries made him technically unfit to be a monk. He was therefore reordained as a novice at the Burmese temple in Vancouver, and returned to British Columbia after travelling to India. The Lao community eventually arranged for him to travel to Portland, Oregon, to become properly reordained in the Lao tradition. At around the same time, the Lao-Canadian Buddhist Temple Association raised $30,000 and invited a respected Lao monk from Montreal, Ajahn Phouangphanh Mixayphon, to British Columbia. Ajahn Phouangphanh and Ajahn Santy stayed together in a rented house in Surrey for a few months in 1998, but they did not get along, so Ajahn Phouangphanh left and is now at the Lao Buddhist temple in Toronto.

In 2000, the association bought a house in Surrey that became their unofficial temple ("Wat Lao" for short). Even though they had to endure the usual complaints concerning a religious centre in a residentially zoned neighbourhood, they remained there for several years. The Lao community organized a membership and sponsorship system and about 100 families joined, most paying a fixed monthly donation. The building mortgage was paid off in 2004. Members' families are supported in emergencies such as sickness and death, and high school graduates are given small scholarships. Daily meals for Ajahn Santy are supplied by a group of families who rotate on a weekly basis. He eats only one meal per day, in the late morning. Members of the Lao community often compare Wat Lao with Wat Yan, stating that the Lao community offers food to its monk every day, while the Thai Wat Yan relies on non-Thais, as noted above. On occasion the Thai monks have had to prepare their own food. For the Lao, the symbolism of this difference is very significant. The provision of daily food is the most fundamental expression of faith and respect in Theravada Buddhism, generating community solidarity. It is also the most basic method of merit making.

In 2005, the association sold the house in Surrey and bought a piece of rural property in Langley to establish its temple. The new Wat Lao is centrally located between the main concentrations of Lao families in Surrey and Abbotsford. The five-acre property used to be a slaughterhouse, but previous occupants had turned it into a large marijuana cultivation operation. Fire gutted the cinder-block meat-processing building, and the whole property became available at a bargain price. When the association first bought the property, the residence was in serious disrepair and the land was overgrown and full of debris. The house did not even have an occupancy permit, so Ajahn Santy had to be officially designated as the "guard" of the property. Each weekend, however, community members came out and worked at cleaning and repairing. A well and water supply system were installed, and eventually they were able to renovate the burnt-out building into a community hall and religious centre. Lao cooperation in this work was particularly impressive.

The association was unaware, however, of the implications of the fact that the property is included in the provincial Agricultural Land Reserve – it is zoned exclusively for agricultural land use. Despite hiring a consultant to officially rezone the property, it has not been able to officially establish the temple, although Langley officials have advised the association that the municipality is unlikely to object to its operations, provided that it maintains a relatively low profile. Relations with the neighbours, always a potential problem, remain good.

Ajahn Santy is supported by visiting Lao monks, often from the several Lao wats in Quebec, and from Laos, whose travel is sponsored by the Association. In addition, Ajahn Santy is now more confident than before with both Lao and non-Lao visitors. As noted earlier, travelling Theravada monks have stayed overnight at Wat Lao, and this has connected Ajahn Santy with other Lao, Thai, Sri Lankan, and Burmese Theravada monks. He also distributes Buddhist materials from a Taiwanese organization.

Despite these strong links, the relationship between the Lao community and Wat Yan and Luang Phor Viriyang is strained, for several reasons. First, due to historical conflicts and current international relations, Lao people in general tend to be wary of the Thais, who can at times be quite patronizing or insensitive to Lao identity. Then there was Luang Phor's refusal, years earlier, to allow Ajahn Santy to be reordained at Wat Yan. Furthermore, in the late 1990s, when the Lao community began using houses in Surrey as temples, Luang Phor apparently commented that it was unsuitable to have a temple without a *bot*,[18] and that Wat Lao was therefore unsuitable, since it was just a house. Some Lao believe that Luang Phor was concerned that attendance at Wat Yan would go down if Wat Lao were established. When Lao people had earlier frequented Wat Yan, they found it too business-oriented, and they often felt pressured to donate more than they felt comfortable giving. Also, the former manager of Wat Yan would allow monks from there to participate in Lao religious events only if half of the money raised went to Wat Yan. Since the financial resources of Wat Lao are limited, monks from Wat Yan are no longer invited to Wat Lao ceremonies. For example, three Sri Lankan and one Burmese monk attended the Phra That Luang ritual in November 2006, as well as Lao monks from Regina and Calgary, but no Thai monks were invited. According to members of the Wat Lao executive committee, Sri Lankan and Burmese monks accept whatever the Lao community offers them (usually envelopes with $100 each).

The Lao-Canadian Buddhist Temple Association has authorized Ajahn Santy to visit Laos to recruit more monks for Wat Lao. On his trips to Laos, Ajahn Santy found several younger monks with good educational qualifications. They had to apply for visas at the nearest Canadian embassy, in Bangkok, however, or their applications would simply not even be considered. Many of the visa applications were refused. Some Lao suspect that the Thais working for the Canadian embassy view Lao monks as being limited in formal studies, but embassy immigration officials say that the refusals have been largely due to a crackdown on monks by Immigration Canada, for fear that people would use the monkhood to enter Canada and apply for refugee status. In 2007, a younger monk was able to obtain a Canadian visa to come from Laos, probably because he graduated from a Buddhist university in Thailand. One result of this Thai "filter" of new Lao monks over time will be more young Lao monks with training or other experience in Thailand. This in turn may improve the already warm connection between Wat Lao and a local Thai wat, Buddhapanyanuntarama Buddhist Monastery (see above). In 2009 Phra Walaison, a young Lao monk at Wat Lao, had training at the "home wat" of the BBM lineage in Thailand, thus furthering the connection.

The Lao *sangha* (Buddhist community) in Canada has recently established a Canada-wide registered organization to more formally link the thirteen Lao Buddhist temples and twenty-eight Lao monks in Canada. The Lao community in British Columbia is keen to have monks rotated among the different Lao temples in Canada. Ajahn Santy is the secretary of this new organization, but lack of funds has prevented him from achieving much. Some Lao have criticized the Association's executive committee, especially on organizational and communications issues, but it is still generally recognized that the committee has been honest in managing the association's finances and efficient in its work.

The dominant impression one receives in visits to Wat Lao is of the vigorous community spirit, obvious in social relations, in the work they do together, and in the financial risks that they share. This is indicated by the way Wat Lao is managed. Unlike the Thai Wat Yan, Wat Lao is definitely a community effort, with a high level of community participation in management. Wat Lao has a number of subcommittees dealing with various religious and community issues, and Ajahn Santy is not involved in financial management. Wat Lao has paid special attention to maintaining financial transparency. This includes appointing three prominent members of the Lao Benevolent Society of British Columbia to act as auditors for the wat's finances. Without overseas funding, the Lao are building a Buddhist community that will preserve their valued traditions and develop Lao Buddhism as a valid way of life. "We will show we are not primitive," says Bounmy Simmavong, the association's former president.

Bounmy also emphasizes that while the association is officially registered only as a religious organization, the reality is that cultural activities, such as teaching Lao dancing to children, are seen as equally important and are an integral objective of the association. It is also planning to establish a community centre for religious, cultural, and community activities. This is especially important because, as Duangsi Tavonesouk put it, "This generation understands Lao Buddhism and culture well, but we are concerned about what will happen with the next generation."

In most Theravada cultures, youth taking temporary ordination as novices is a standard practice and can function as a rite of passage into adulthood. (See Chapter 6 for examples from the Burmese tradition, where this is most prominent.) In the summer of 2006, British Columbia history was made when a Lao American monk came to Wat Lao and assisted in ordaining three ethnic Lao boys as novices. Unfortunately, Ajahn Santy was committed to attending a national meeting of Lao monks in Toronto and thus the novices would have no trainer at Wat Lao, so two of the novices spent part of their time in the monkhood at Wat Lao Alberta in Edmonton. Despite these problems, it appears likely that other ethnic Lao youth in the province will be able to receive ordination for short periods of time in the future. Ajahn Santy can ordain novices, but a *fang luuk nimit* ritual burial of stone boundary markers remains a goal at Wat Lao before full ordinations can be organized. They have also built a small structure over a pond on the temple's property, which can be used for ordinations.

Ajahn Santy is from a poor family and does not have a high education. Although he speaks Lao perfectly, he is Brou, a Mon-Khmer-speaking minority group in Laos. Many in the Lao community would prefer a better-qualified monk, but most feel that Ajahn Santy's positive characteristics outweigh these social factors. He is a serious monk who is making an effort to constantly improve his practice. As Bounleung Phongmany says, he is "learning from everyone." His frequent contact with other Lao monks, Mahayana monks, and Theravada monks from the various Thai, Sri Lankan, and Burmese traditions has expanded his breadth of understanding of Buddhism. Thongsouk Khantivong, who was a well-educated Lao monk in Montreal before disrobing and starting a family in the 1990s, is helping to guide Ajahn Santy. With this growth,

Wat Lao is becoming a "good temple" in the eyes of many Buddhists in British Columbia.

Thai and Lao Buddhists and Mainstream Society

The very nature of the immigrant experience, especially in the cities, is eventual integration as a natural process. In every society, the education of children is a powerful force for consolidating cultural practices. Thai and Lao children are growing up to be very Canadian. Wat Yan was established as a Thai community wat and continues in that role, with the limitations noted earlier. At major festivals, the *farang* husbands come along with their Thai wives and children. Most enjoy the experience, but those with a personal interest in Thai Buddhism cannot interact further. One suggestion has been to have pamphlets in English to explain the events.

Luang Phor Viriyang has established what he calls the "Willpower Institute" (*sathaaban jittanuphaap*) at his home wat in Bangkok, and is establishing branches of this institute in his Canadian wats. His goal is to promote world peace through meditation. He opens the annual training sessions himself, and graduates take a four-day forest retreat in northern Thailand. By 2007 there were five sets of graduates, and alumni assist in recruiting new trainees. Luang Phor appears to be satisfied that his Thai wats are viable and is concentrating on the Willpower Institute. The Willpower Institute philosophy focuses on rational and practical benefits, such as better concentration at work. Nevertheless, Canadians taking the program appear to be touched in spiritual ways. The volume *haa pii nai khanadaa* consists primarily of written testimonials from graduates of the Willpower Institute, chronicling how the teaching has changed their lives.[19] One Vancouver graduate writes: "Luangphor is my hero – truly. I have never met anyone who lives their life with such absolute authenticity and grace. Most have partitions, or compartmentalize their ways of being, but he is truly a walking work of art."[20]

The situation is more oriented toward mainstream Canadians at Sītavana (Birken Forest Monastery), since the abbot and the other resident monks are English-speaking locals themselves. Since Birken is a genuine forest wat, staying there is automatically a retreat experience. Thai supporters sometimes come on weekends, and a few have stayed for longer periods, but there appears to be less involvement of Lower Mainland Thais in recent years. The movement of Wat Dhammakaya into BC from a Seattle area base parallels the movement of the Wat Atam teaching lineage from the Seattle area to Wat BBM in Burnaby. This fluidity tends to reinforce cross-border Thai social identity, but may limit the outreach of these wats to local Canadians. In late 2009 both wats were still focused on building support within the local Thai community. So far, among

BC Theravada monasteries, only Birken Forest Monastery has also been able to train locals for permanent ordination.

Punnee Intaranuruk has been a Thai regular at Wat Yan. As she sees it, supporting and attending the wat is not an obstacle to acculturation to mainstream Canada, as long as the wat is used in the right way, to "try and make ourselves a better person." Several other Lao and Thai interviewees also voiced this view that being better Buddhists will make them better Canadians.

From time to time, local Canadian or Asian Buddhists have asked to stay at Wat Lao as postulants. So far, the non-Lao residents have not worked out, because they "did not follow the rules," as Duangsi notes. Some of them had personal problems. Ajahn Santy envisions using the spacious property of Wat Lao for retreats and meditation practice, activities popular with mainstream Canadian Buddhists. For example, in 2009 he opened Wat Lao for an intensive week-long meditation retreat led by a Burmese-Canadian layman and a dozen non-Lao participants. As Ajahn Santy improves his English, deepens in his own practice, and strengthens links to other Buddhist centres, the day may come when non-Lao locals might receive good training at Wat Lao, but so far it remains focused on the Lao Buddhist community. Wat Lao is moving into a local Buddhist space in contact with other Theravada monks and with a wide range of other local religious groups, as well as their neighbours. Bounleung emphasizes that the community wants to communicate freely as equals with *all* religious groups in the area, including Sikhs, Muslims, Hindus, and Christians.

Conclusions

The most crucial differences between the Thai and Lao Buddhists in British Columbia relate to community involvement and participation, and the role of culture in Buddhism. At the Thai Wat Yan, a relatively top-down and centralized style of management has been adopted, and cultural activities other than Buddhist rituals have been largely discouraged. As shown above, at least two other Thai lineages have been established to fill this perceived gap. At Wat Lao, the community is devoted to Buddhist practice, and religion is seen as fundamentally linked to culture. These factors indicate a strong future for Wat Lao, especially if it can make a smooth transition to a new generation of Lao monks, which seems possible with Ajahn Santy's cooperation. Building connections with the broader national Lao Buddhist community also adds strength.

Whereas the Lao community continues to bridge its internal differences and build with a single focus, the Thais, despite having a wat with a ritually established ordination space and other formal organizations in place, remain a divided community. This has led some Thais to turn for spiritual recourse to the newer

Thai wats, BBM and Phra Thammakaya, and sometimes to Sītavana (Birken Forest Monastery).

One factor in the future of all these Buddhist centres is their outreach to mainstream Canadians and the education of their children. Wat Yan has cleanly separated Thai community rituals and outreach in the form of the Willpower Institute. It cannot support children's classes. Wat Lao remains focused on the Lao community and has strategies and roles for the next generation. Birken Forest Monastery has successfully ordained several local Canadians and organizes regular retreats for the mainstream society. The newer Thai wats BBM and Phra Dhammakaya were still in consolidating stages in late 2009.

The current virtual explosion of Canadian mainstream interest in Buddhism is developing independently of the Thais and Lao. In the end, getting mainstream Canadians involved may become the link that will attract their own younger generation to their traditions and contribute most to the survival of those traditions. For now, at least, Buddhism remains a central part of the belief systems of most Thai and Lao in the province. With their two very distinct approaches, they will continue working to preserve their cultures and their Buddhist traditions for future generations in British Columbia, as they deal with the pressures of assimilation and internal divisions.

Notes

1 Y. Hayashi, *Practical Buddhism among the Thai-Lao: Religion in the Making of a Region* (Kyoto: Kyoto University Press, 2003), 5. Hayashi (27, 28) records distinctions between Lao and northeastern Thai Buddhist practices in contemporary times. This is most likely due to the ongoing development of nationalist identities in both countries.
2 This chapter builds on work done for J. Placzek and L. DeVries, "Buddhism in British Columbia," in *Buddhism in Canada*, ed. B. Matthews (London: Routledge, 2006), 1-29.
3 Kamala Tiyavanich, *Forest Recollections: Wandering Monks in Twentieth-Century Thailand* (Honolulu: University of Hawai'i Press, 1997), 39-40.
4 R.A. O'Connor, "Siamese Thai in Tai Context: the Impact of a Ruling Center," *Crossroads* 5, 1 (1990): 10.
5 See Russel F. Sizemore and Donald K. Swearer, eds., *Ethics, Wealth, and Salvation* (Columbia: University of South Carolina Press, 1990), especially chapters by Strong and Faulk.
6 Statistics Canada, "Ethnic Origins, 2006 Counts, for Canada, Provinces and Territories (British Columbia)," Ethnocultural Portrait of Canada Highlight Tables, 2006 Census of Canada, http://www12.statcan.ca/english/census06/data/highlights/ethnic.
7 Van Esterik, *Taking Refuge: Lao Buddhists in North America* (Tempe: Arizona State University, Program for Southeast Asian Studies, 1992).
8 Statistics Canada, "Ethnic Origins."
9 See D.M. Padgett, "The Translating Temple," in *Westward Dharma: Buddhism beyond Asia*, ed. C.S. Prebish and M. Baumann (Berkeley: University of California Press, 2002), 205.
10 Ibid., 206-8.
11 J.L. Taylor, *Forest Monks and the Nation-State: An Anthropological and Historical Study in Northeastern Thailand* (Singapore: Institute of Southeast Asian Studies, 1993), 163-64, 202.

12 Tiyavanich, *Forest Recollections*, 155-59, 211, 357.
13 See http://atamma.org.
14 Jim Placzek, one of the authors of this chapter, is the president of the BBM society.
15 See P.D. Numrich, "Theravada Buddhism in America: Prospects for the Sangha," in *The Faces of Buddhism in America*, ed. C.S. Prebish and K.K. Tanaka (Berkeley: University of California Press, 1998), 147-62. See also *Birken Forest Monastery: Our First Ten Years 1994-2004* (Knutsford, BC: Birken Forest Monastery, 2004).
16 See http://www.birken.ca.
17 "Worldwide Centers," Dhammakaya Foundation, http://www.dhammakaya.or.th/centremain.php.
18 Pali *uposatha* (Lao: *sim*), a formal image hall, usually a ritually sacralized space like that described above for Wat Atam. Wat Yan has also performed such a ceremony.
19 *Haa pii nai pratheet khaenaadaa – phra theepiyaajaan* (Five Years in Canada – Luang Phor Viriyang) (Bangkok: Luang Phor Viriyang Sirintharo Foundation, 2005). Other materials on Luang Phor, such as his biography, do not focus so much on practical benefits.
20 Kara Ardan, personal communication, 10 July 2006.

6 Sri Lankan and Myanmar Buddhism
BANDU MADANAYAKE

This chapter discusses Buddhist groups with connections to the lands closest to the origin of the Buddhists – Sri Lanka and Myanmar (formerly known as Burma), as well as a growing connection to India, the original home of Buddhism. These are all Theravada Buddhist groups. I will begin with Sri Lanka and the Buddhist Vihara Society in British Columbia, generally known as the Surrey Buddhist Vihara,[1] which is maintained by Sinhalese immigrants. The objective of the society's founders was to be open to all regardless of ethnicity, but this has eroded over the years. I will explore the place of Sri Lankan Buddhism in the Canadian multicultural mosaic and will touch on the history of immigration of Sri Lankan Buddhists insofar as it affects Canadian multicultural society, since Canada's official policy of multiculturalism addresses some of the well-known issues that historically have faced South Asian religious groups in British Columbia.[2] Following a discussion of Sri Lankan Buddhists in BC, the Myanmar Buddhists are studied in the same way.

Sri Lanka has a population of 20 million, of whom nearly 70 percent are Buddhists, whereas Myanmar has a population of 46 million, of whom over 95 percent are Buddhists. Both Sri Lankan and Myanmar Buddhists follow the Theravada tradition of the teaching of the Buddha.[3] In British Columbia, both Sri Lankan and Myanmar Buddhists live mostly in the Lower Mainland. They are a varied group of people with different occupations, including professionals such as doctors, engineers, and accountants.[4]

History of Buddhism in Sri Lanka
A brief history of Buddhism in Sri Lanka is appropriate at this point. The British called the island nation Ceylon, but the name was changed to Sri Lanka on 22 May 1972. Sri Lanka is situated near the southern tip of the Indian subcontinent and was referred to in history by different names: Tambapanni, Ratnadipa, Serendip, and Sinhale.

Different countries in which Buddhism is practised have adopted different ways of following the Buddha's teaching. The position occupied by Sri Lanka is unique in the history of Buddhism. It has an unbroken recorded history from the time of Emperor Asoka of India in the third century BCE. According to the Sri Lankan chronicles *Mahavamsa* and *Dipavamsa*, Arahant Mahinda, the son of Emperor Asoka, officially introduced Buddhism to Sri Lanka during the reign of the Sri Lankan king Devanampiya Tissa (250-210 BCE). Within a short time, the king and his compatriots embraced Buddhism.[5] They may already have been familiar with the teaching of the Buddha because there are reports that the Buddha visited Sri Lanka in the fifth century BCE.[6]

There are two other important historical events relating to Buddhism in Sri Lanka. First, in the first century BCE, the Mahavihara (Great Monastery) *bhikkhus* (monks) decided to commit to writing the entire Buddhist canon of the Theravada, now known as the Pali Tipitaka – consisting of three categories, *Vinaya, Sutta,* and *Abhidhamma* – and the Sinhalese commentaries. They had the backing of King Vattagamani (89-77 BCE), who ruled Sri Lanka at the time. This historical event took place in Aluvihara in Matale, Sri Lanka.[7] Second, in the fifth century BCE, Bhadantacariya Buddhaghosa came to Sri Lanka from India to translate the Sinhalese commentaries into Pali.[8]

Spread of Buddhism to Europe and North America

From the fifteenth century CE onward, the Portuguese, the Dutch, the French, and the British colonized various Asian countries. Among them were learned persons who were interested in native languages and religions. Some were fascinated by the teachings of the Buddha. They learned Pali, Sanskrit, and Sinhalese, and spread Buddhist teachings in Europe. T.W. Rhys Davids was a key figure; he lived in Sri Lanka from 1866 to 1874, and inaugurated the Pali Text Society in London in 1881. Sir Edwin Arnold published *The Light of Asia*, a poetic translation of the *Buddhacarita* (Life of the Buddha) in 1879.[9]

A glimpse of the Buddha's teachings in Sri Lanka first came to North America in 1893, at the World Parliament of Religions held in Chicago, where the Sri Lankan Anagarika Dhammapala read a paper entitled "The World's Debt to Buddha." He was selected to represent Buddhism at the Parliament by the Theosophical Society in New York formed by Madame Blavatsky, a Russian, and Colonel Olcott, an American, who also gave impetus to a revival of Buddhism in Sri Lanka.[10] According to Venerable Dedunupitiye Upananda ("venerable" is an honorific title given to monks) of the Calgary Buddhist Vihara, Anagarika Dhammapala's diary shows that he visited Canada on this trip to Chicago.[11]

More recent is the remarkable approach by Sri Lanka (then Ceylon) at the San Francisco Peace Conference in 1951, where all the nations affected by the war had gathered to discuss reparations and issues relating to Japan. The Sri Lankan delegation, headed by J.R. Jayawardene (later president of Sri Lanka from 1978 to 1989), told the international community that Sri Lanka renounced any claim for reparations from Japan. His speech, in which he quoted the words of the Buddha from the *Dhammapada* that "hatred does not cease by hatred; it is only appeased by kindness," received wide publicity in the leading newspapers of the United States.[12]

The Surrey Buddhist Vihara

The Buddhist Vihara Society in British Columbia, generally known as the Surrey Buddhist Vihara (SBV), was established on 7 January 1990. By 2001, the Buddhist population in Canada was 300,345, a substantial increase of 83.8 percent from 163,415 in 1991. In British Columbia, the Buddhist population in 2001 was 85,500, an increase of 43 percent from 36,435 in 1991.[13] The increases in British Columbia and other provinces were due to the liberalization of Canadian immigration policy. As these numbers were insufficient to maintain a monk, however, Sri Lankan Buddhists in British Columbia invited monks from Los Angeles and San Francisco for religious rituals. The vihara was established mainly to cater to immigrant Buddhists from Sri Lanka, whose number increased quickly (after the changes to the immigration regulations in 1962) to nearly 500 families today.

Before 1990, there was no place in the province for Buddhist immigrants from Sri Lanka and Myanmar to meet for worship or religious fellowship. According to the SBV's first newsletter, in February 1990, a group of Buddhists met in July 1989 and discussed the possibility of having Buddhist activities in the Lower Mainland (the Greater Vancouver region).[14] Afterwards, they met regularly until a decision was made in November 1989 to draft a constitution. That meeting took place at the residence of Gamini and Sunendra Makawita in Vancouver, and began with an offering (*dana*) being given to Venerable Madawala Seelawimala, a Sri Lankan monk from California.[15] The following January, around twenty-five enthusiastic members of the Lower Mainland's Sri Lankan Buddhist community, spearheaded by Kirthi Senaratne, an engineer, officially inaugurated the Buddhist Vihara Society in British Columbia with a view to establishing a vihara (monastery). Venerable Madawala Seelawimala was elected president and Kirthi Senaratne vice president.

Before the society was established, the late Anagarika Dhammadinna, a Canadian observer of ten precepts (*dasa sil*), had conducted meditation retreats in the province. One participant was the same Kirthi Senaratne mentioned above. When Anagarika Dhammadinna heard about the society's inauguration meeting, she was clearly impressed and wrote from Halfmoon Bay (a tiny community on the BC "Sunshine Coast"): "The unprecedented speed and success with which the society was formed not only shows the need but also that venture was most timely; a long standing hope to be realized."[16]

The aims of the society were to:

- study and practise Buddhism, specifically the Theravada tradition
- promote the study and practice of the teaching of the Buddha through lectures, study groups, publication, retreats, and religious ceremonies
- establish and maintain a Buddhist temple for the furtherance of these aims.

All Sri Lankan viharas in Canada are independent entities. They have no affiliation with Sri Lanka or any international body. Each vihara's administration is vested in an elected body composed of both monks and lay devotees. This body has the authority to invite any monk from Sri Lanka. In almost every case so far, the incumbent monk invites one of his colleagues from his own vihara in Sri Lanka. The president of the Buddhist Vihara Society since its founding, Venerable Madawala Seelawimala, who still resides in San Francisco, continues to be re-elected at the annual general meeting in order to have continuity. He does not have any control over the affairs of the vihara, but he comes each May to help in the *Vesak* celebrations.

The Surrey Buddhist Vihara (mainly Sri Lankan) is located at 13871 64th Avenue in Surrey. It has two buildings. One used to be a house, the other a workshop. The yard has been converted into an asphalt parking lot. The main building is the monks' residence and kitchen. Since the devotees bring *dana* (offerings, such as food) for them every day, the kitchen is used only to make tea. The other building has been renovated to house a large image of the Buddha; it can accommodate sixty to seventy devotees.

The Surrey Buddhist Vihara as a Gathering Place

In Sri Lanka, a vihara is a very important part of the religious and cultural life of any Buddhist. Merely visiting a vihara, set as it usually is amid serene surroundings, provides Buddhists with happiness and fulfillment. It must be said, though, that the vihara in Surrey does not provide the same feeling that one gets from a vihara in Sri Lanka. A ten-year-old boy who recently arrived in British Columbia with his family refused to attend religious services at this vihara because there was no Bo tree (the tree under which the Buddha was enlightened) and it did not have a *dagoba,* a typical Buddhist structure for relics. For the boy, without these familiar things, it was not a vihara. Fortunately, after some explanation, he was persuaded to attend. The older generation, parents who have come to British Columbia after their children had settled here, have had similar feelings toward the SBV. It is difficult for them to rid their memories of the kind of inner tranquillity they were used to in Sri Lanka, for example, on hearing the wind rustling through the leaves of a Bo tree. With a religious culture going back over 2,500 years, it is not surprising that the image of a vihara, associated as it is with a feeling of reverence and peace, is such an important part of people's experience of Buddhism.[17]

Some new immigrants, however, have found the SBV to be an oasis during their adjustment period. For example, Gamunu Ekanayake had a good job in Sri Lanka before immigrating to British Columbia.[18] As he was not sure of the situation in Canada, he secured a two-year leave of absence from his employer and came here with his wife and two sons. During his first six months in Canada, he thought constantly of going back to his job in Sri Lanka. The vihara was very important in helping him resolve this conflict. It has also been helpful to immigrants who come without any relatives or friends, helping them to get through periods of bewilderment and anxiety, and sometimes a sense of hopelessness, particularly if an immigrant is initially unable to find a job.

Monks at the Surrey Buddhist Vihara

Sri Lankans in British Columbia are fortunate to be helped by the monks at the vihara in Surrey. The first resident monk was Venerable Kamalasiri, who served for three months before leaving for Australia. Venerable Somaratana arrived from Sri Lanka in 1993. In 1994, two Western monks, one Canadian and one German, Venerable Sona and Venerable Piyadhammo, were planning to come to Canada from Thailand. Venerable Sona's mother, Irma West, who lived in Coquitlam, asked Kirthi Senaratne whether they could stay at the SBV. Kirthi consulted the board of directors and received its approval. When the two Western monks arrived, they stayed with Venerable Somaratana at the vihara. Both were very experienced meditators and also represented mainstream Canadian society. Many Sri Lankans considered Venerable Sona as a leader in the Theravada Buddhist tradition and had high hopes and dreams. Not only was he knowledgeable in the *dhamma* (teachings; the Sanskrit is *dharma*) and *vinaya* (monastic discipline) but he was also born a Canadian. He could explain Buddhism in a way that ordinary people could understand. Children loved him, as they could easily understand his expressions whether they were born in Canada or elsewhere. He was equally well received by children and adults in the Sri Lankan community.[19]

Venerable Sona's stay at the vihara was marred, however, by various obstacles to his practice of meditation. In addition, it appeared that the two cultures of Sri Lankan and Thai traditions wouldn't go hand in hand, and city life did not suit a monk who was raised in a forest monastery tradition. The Sri Lankan laity were not very much interested in meditation and before long major obstacles erupted, so Venerable Sona and Venerable Piyadhammo left for Pemberton, a small community north of Vancouver, where there was a serene place ideal for meditation in the forest monastery tradition, their first calling. After Venerable Sona left, Venerable Gnanodbhaso stayed at the vihara as a temporary resident (his permanent abode was at the Toronto Mahavihara). Although he was able to give talks on *dhamma* in English, he preferred to do so in Sinhalese. He became a familiar sight to people in the neighbourhood, carrying a fan and, following tradition, looking only immediately ahead of himself when he walked.

It was difficult to find a Buddhist monk with sufficient knowledge of the *dhamma*. In addition, there were structural drawbacks in the vihara society. The president of the society resided in San Francisco and a message circulated saying that the vihara was not controlled by monks (as monks would desire) but by laity, and that it was hard for a monk to work independently. Also, devotees were uneasy about the absence of a permanent monk, and when the directors tried to collect funds, some questioned why they should give money when there were no religious services. The board tried to contact the SBV president in San Francisco, to no avail. Finally, some members used their contacts abroad to invite Venerable Kumbalgoda Sirinivasa and Venerable Mirisse Dhammika to become monks at the vihara. All breathed a deep sigh of relief. The monks now perform many duties for the Sri Lankan community, including conversing with the children in English.

Venerable Kumbalgoda Sirinivasa, who is still in British Columbia, first came to the SBV in 1994. He popularized the sprinkling of *pirit* water (water conveying the efficacy of chanted *pirit* scriptures) on the heads of devotees after Buddha *puja* (service). This was welcomed by some but criticized by others as being a tradition in Singapore and Malaysia but not in Sri Lanka. He also introduced the novel idea of blessings on 1 January. He arranged to bring certain lamps from Singapore that devotees could light on special festivals to beautify the vihara, which brought in a substantial income. Because the vihara was housed in rented premises, Venerable Kumbalgoda Sirinivasa initiated a Buddhist flag drive to raise $200,000 to purchase a new place.

Services Performed by Sri Lankan Monks

Monks at a vihara play a major role in people's lives, in keeping with advice given by the Buddha: *Caratha bhikkhave cārikaṃ bahujana hitāya bahujana sukhāya* "O Bhikkhus, go forth for the benefit and happiness of many."[20] For example, although monks do not participate at wedding ceremonies and do not register marriages, when a woman is pregnant, her relatives invite monks to her residence to bless her.[21] Within a month of being born, a child's first visit outside the home is usually to a vihara for blessings by a monk. This is a long-standing custom among Sri Lankan Buddhists. Some parents bring their young children to the vihara for a first reading of letters. Students go to the vihara before their examinations and monks chant *pirit* (choral chanting of sermons) to give them confidence and clear thinking. The SBV organizes a special *puja* (offering) before the school year starts in September. Some devotees go to the vihara for a special blessing when they purchase a car or plan a holiday. Thus, the vihara is thought of as a place for receiving special blessings and protection against unknown perils or evil.

When a person is hospitalized, monks visit the hospital to chant *pirit* for a speedy recovery. A monk's presence is considered important at the time of death; the monk recites *suttas* (scriptures) and gives a blessing. Following a death, the monk conducts certain rituals at the funeral, gives a sermon on impermanence, and chants:[22]

Aniccā vata saṃkhārā uppādavayadhammino,
Uppajjitvā nirujjhanti tesaṃ vūpasamo sukho

All conditioned things are impermanent. What is born is subject to decay. Having arisen they cease to be. Their subsiding is bliss.[23]

After the monks accept the *mataka vastra* (cloth offering to the monks at the funeral), there is an interesting ritual. In the presence of the monks, relatives pour water from a jug into an empty cup until the water overflows onto a plate. This ritual, referred to as *pan vadima* (pouring water), symbolizes the transfer of merit to the dead. On the seventh day after death, there is almsgiving to the monks. Further almsgiving for the benefit of the dead takes place later.

Festivals and Celebrations at the Vihara

The rich pageantry of Buddhist rituals at viharas in Sri Lanka cannot be matched by the SBV. Due attention is given, however, to the needs of community members in British Columbia who wish to observe various religious festivals with appropriate solemnity. On the day of the full moon every month, many Buddhists observe the *eight precepts* (conventionally understood as to refrain from eight things, namely: killing living beings; taking what is not given; sexual indulgence; false speech; intoxicants; food at inappropriate times; dancing, singing, and playing music; and using high and luxurious seats). Those not observing the eight precepts may participate by performing other religious activities, such as walking or sitting meditation, listening to the *dhamma,* and participating in discussions. On this day, most devotees wear white clothing, although there is no strict dress code inside the vihara.

Venerable Kumbalgoda Sirinivasa, the chief resident monk, says that the most important day of the year is the full-moon day in May. It is called *Vesak,* and is the day, according to tradition, that the Buddha became enlightened, as well as the day he was born and the day of his death. It is hard to tell from the Buddhist literature whether the Buddha was born, enlightened, and passed away on the full-moon day of May, but it is reasonable to assume that these three events took place in May or close to it. Many Buddhists go to the vihara on this day and observe the eight precepts. At the SBV, a colourful *puja* is followed by a special sermon by the head monk.

On full-moon day of July, known to Buddhists as *Esala,* monks are invited to stay at the temple to observe the rain retreat during the time of the monsoon season. There are no monsoon rains in Sri Lanka at this time, but the monks still follow the old Indian tradition of religious service and devotion. They are expected to remain in the same place for three months starting from July, although disciplinary rules allow seven days' absence in the event of an emergency or other important reason. If a monk cannot get back to the temple before the end of the seventh day, he cannot accept the *Kathina* robe, the new robe that devotees offer to the monk at the conclusion of the rain retreat.

Devotees organize a grand festival at the end of the rain retreat. It normally includes an offering to the Buddha and a sermon by a monk who successfully completed the retreat.[24] In Sri Lanka, *Kathina* is a very colourful ceremony that occupies a full night and the following day. Devotees carry the robe in a particular vihara's designated area. The all-night ceremony is not available in British Columbia. On the same day, there is a ceremonial "wishing tree" (*kapruka*) at the vihara. The tree contains all the necessities donated by the laity for the monks – money, medicines, and so on. The full-moon day of July is important for all Buddhists because it was on that day that the Buddha preached his first sermon – *Dhammacakkappavattana-sutta* (Setting in Motion the Wheel of Truth) at Varanasi, present-day Benares in India. As is customary at all viharas, devotees provide the four basic necessities of the monks: robes (*civara*), food (*pindapatha*), shelter (*senasana*), and medicine (*gilana-paccaya-bhesajja-parikkhara*).

Sunday School for Children

Venerable Dhammika revived the defunct Sunday school for children at the SBV in 1995. After he left for Sri Lanka in 2005, the board of directors appointed Venerable Puliyankulame Saranatissa as the principal. Venerable Saranatissa reports that there are seven classes for eighty-seven students in the school. Each class is named after a Buddhist principle of the four "divine virtues" (*brahma-vihara*) and the three sections of the Noble Eightfold Path to enlightenment. These topics, familiar to many Buddhists, are: (1) *metta* (loving kindness); (2) *karuna* (compassion); (3) *mudita* (altruistic joy); (4) *upekkha* (equanimity); (5) *sila* (morality); (6) *samadhi* (concentration); and (7) *panna* (wisdom).

Admission is for children between the ages of three and a half and sixteen years. According to Venerable Saranatissa, a typical day starts with offerings at 12:30 p.m. every Sunday and ends at 2:30 p.m. after paying homage to parents.

There is a half-hour lesson in the Sinhalese language. The school curriculum includes the life of the Buddha, offerings and chanting, the significance of Buddhist events and ceremonies, social and ethical values, practice of non-violence, mutual cooperation, protection, conservation, and gratitude toward the environment, respect for parents and elders, attending to the sick, and anger and stress management through meditation. In order for the students to practise public speaking, singing, and recitation of poetry, there is a student society meeting every month. Past students often participate in this event and speak of their experiences and of the benefits of attending the school. A newsletter is published every three months to provide students with an opportunity to develop writing skills.[25]

Changes to the Pioneers' Original Vision

At the inception of the Buddhist Vihara Society, founder Kirthi Senaratne's vision was to open the vihara to all Buddhists regardless of ethnicity and nationality, and not to cater only to the Sri Lankan community. He wanted to provide services to mainstream Canadians who embraced this faith or to those interested in learning the teachings. His vision gradually faded because, as he put it: "What seems to be lacking in the group is the enthusiasm to overcome suffering as the Buddha had recommended. An essential component of his recommendation is tranquillity and insight *bhavana* (meditation). This aspect is almost non-existent in the group."[26]

Due to his continuous efforts, however, meditation sessions have been started with the help of the resident monks. In 1992, the Thai Buddhists found a place and established a vihara based on Thai tradition. On 28 February 1993, the Myanmar and Sri Lankan Buddhists jointly established a vihara in rented premises at 15681 82nd Avenue in Surrey.[27]

Changes in Practice

In many ways, Buddhist practices in British Columbia are similar to those in other viharas in Canada and Sri Lanka. The offerings to the Buddha at the Surrey Buddhist Vihara are conducted in Pali, which is the universal language of the Theravada Buddhist tradition. Not many understand Pali, but a number of the words are familiar to devotees who are familiar with the Sinhalese language, as many words are similar. This way of chanting *gathas* (verses) is not so welcome for non-Sri Lankans, however. Venerable Puliyankulame Saranatissa's translation of the Pali texts into Sinhalese is helpful to most who attend the vihara, but no serious attempt has been made to encourage non-Sri Lankans to attend the vihara regularly. Since Venerable Saranatissa's arrival in 2005, relations with at least the Hindi-speaking devotees have improved, and the chanting of the *Bojjhanga Sutta* of the *Anguttara Nikaya* (one of the Tipitaka texts) every day from 10 July to 12 August 2006 encouraged more people to participate in the vihara's activities.

It is not certain whether providing religious services in Pali and Sinhalese alone will do, as second- and third-generation Sri Lankans may not be able to understand a sermon delivered in these languages. Some argue that most Sri Lankans speak Sinhalese at home, but will this level of proficiency be sufficient for understanding Buddhism's doctrinal concepts? If the monks were to give sermons in English, such comprehension would not be an issue, so ultimately, if the vihara is to be of continued benefit, Canadian monks will need to be ordained, just as Sinhalese monks were ordained long ago on the advice of Arahant Mahinda of India to King Devanampiya Tissa of Sri Lanka in the third century BCE.

The Indian Buddhist Society of Canada

Another Buddhist group expanding in British Columbia is the Indian Buddhist Society of Canada (IBSC). Its approximately fifty members attend the Surrey Buddhist Vihara for their services and spiritual guidance. The society was registered on 18 August 2006, with signatories Yaspal Mehay, Khushi Ram, Kamlesh Ahir, Kulwant Sandhi, Mohan Bangai, Sutey Prakash Ahir, and Satish Aujila. Like the SBV, it has no affiliation with any other group in Canada or overseas. The society is planning to establish a vihara on its own when it has enough funds, and to invite a monk from India. It recently celebrated Buddha Jayanti, the 2,550th anniversary of the passing away of the Buddha, at the Raja Bear Creek Hall in Surrey.

This community is inspired by the example of the renowned Dr. B.R. Ambedkar, the first Minister of Law of independent India. He was the chairman of the drafting committee of the Indian Constitution and is considered responsible for the Fundamental Rights and Directive Principles of State Policy enshrined in this constitution. After many years of study and research, and following visits to Sri Lanka, Myanmar, and Thailand, Dr. Ambedkar is quoted as saying: "My religious conversion was not inspired by any material motive. There is hardly anything I cannot achieve even while remaining an Untouchable. There is no other feeling than that of a spiritual feeling underlying my religious conversion." To celebrate the anniversary of Buddha Jayanti, many other people also became Buddhists in Nagpur, India. Dr. Ambedkar had earlier received help from the Buddhist Society of India. One of the significant aspects of Buddhism is that it is not based on caste. The Buddha said: "By birth is not one an outcaste; by birth is not one a Brahmin; by deeds is one an outcaste; by deeds is one a Brahmin."[28]

The IBSC is providing financial support to the Punjab Buddhist Vihara Society, which held opening celebrations for the Takshila Maha Buddhist Vihara on 6-8 October 2006 in Ludhiana, Punjab, 400 kilometres from the ancient Taxila University, which is now located in Pakistan. Donations from Australia, Canada, Korea, Thailand, Taiwan, the United States, Vietnam, and some countries of the Middle East were coordinated by Venerable Chander Bodhi of the Punjab Buddhist Society in the United Kingdom.[29] A related outreach by Venerable Bodhi, who is able to deliver *dhamma* talks in Punjabi, led to the founding of the Indian Buddhist Society Toronto, which celebrated its first Buddha Jayanti in 2007. The close relationship, noted in Chapter 1, between the Ambedkar Buddhists in British Columbia and the Shri Guru Ravidass Sabha in Burnaby is demonstrated by the enthusiastic reception of recent dharma talks by Venerable Bodhi at Guru Ravidas gurdwaras in Toronto and Burlington, Ontario.[30] The aim of the various societies in India is to promote the vision of Dr. Ambedkar and its connection to all *dalit* ("oppressed," indicating "untouchable" status).[31]

Myanmar Buddhism

Myanmar is surrounded by five countries – Bangladesh, China, Laos, India, and Thailand. Many writers have called it the Land of the Pagodas (monasteries). Most of the population is Buddhist (89.5 percent), but there is religious tolerance of other groups. After the Third Buddhist Council in India, Emperor Asoka sent a mission to Suvarnabhumi – specifically, Lower Burma, or Mon Country – in the third century BCE.[32] The first known kingdoms of Myanmar were founded in the fifth century CE. These non-Burmese kingdoms were influenced by Hindu and Buddhist ideals,[33] but King Anawrahta, who founded the first major kingdom on the banks of the Irrawaddy River at Pagan, north of Yangon (formerly Rangoon), embraced the Theravada tradition of Buddhism with the help of a Mon monk, Shin Araham. He overthrew the Mon capital of Thaton in 1057 in order to obtain Theravada scriptures.[34] This king had a cordial relationship with Sri Lanka, another Theravada country, and there were exchanges of pilgrims and knowledge of the *dhamma*. Given that the Buddhist images found in Sumatra, Java, and Celebes belong to the Andhra (South Indian) style of the second and third centuries CE, it would appear that Theravada Buddhism had spread in Southeast Asia by that time.

Immigration and the Manawmaya Theravada Buddhist Society

Since the changes to the immigration regulations in 1962, many professionals from Myanmar have settled in Canada.[35] There are about 1,500 people from that country in British Columbia, and 80 percent of these are Buddhists.[36]

The Crystal Mountain Tibetan Buddhist group invited U Thilawunta, a monk from Myanmar, to Canada in 1989. The group held meditation sessions on Galiano Island and has built a pagoda there. The meditation sessions continued in Abbotsford.[37] In 1991, the Myanmar Buddhists incorporated as the Manawmaya Theravada Buddhist Society. The society's purposes are very similar to those of the Surrey Buddhist Vihara, namely, to study and practise Theravada Buddhism and "to establish a place of gathering and worship for Theravada Buddhists," including accommodations for monks. The constitution specifically sets forth the society's goals: "To promote fellowship, cooperation and understanding amongst Theravada Buddhists and their families and affiliates regardless of ethnic backgrounds" and to "refrain from any political affiliation or organization." The first directors were Myat Htoon, Reggie Tun Maung, Tin Maung Kyi, Phyu Win Noronha, and Becky Lynn Marie Brechin.

After informal conversations, the boards of directors of the Buddhist Vihara Society in British Columbia and the Manawmaya Theravada Buddhist Society decided on 6 December 1992 to establish the Buddhist vihara mentioned above for both Sri Lankan and Myanmar Buddhists. Venerable Kamalasiri, representing Sri Lankan Buddhists, and U Pannabhaso, representing Myanmar Buddhists, were involved. This arrangement lasted until 1 August 1994. The Manawmaya Theravada Buddhist Society then established its own monastery in April 1994 at 252 East 65th Avenue, Vancouver, and purchased the property in 1996. Inadequate space combined with zoning issues led the society to purchase the former Baptist church at 13260 108th Avenue in Surrey in 2002.[38] Myanmar Buddhists do not call their Buddhist centre a temple or vihara; instead, they prefer to call it *phonegyikyaung* – a school for *bhikkhus* or simply a monastery.[39] It has been difficult to engage monks for the monastery. After the first monk left, another monk came from Chicago. The chief abbot is U Pannao Ba Tha, and the assistant abbot is U Sandha.

Services Performed by Myanmar Monks and Lay Practices

The *sangha* (monks) play a very important part in Myanmar Buddhism. Throughout the centuries, they have earned the respect of the laity as they follow strictly the *vinaya* (code of monastic discipline) and provide advice and guidance to laypeople. Myanmar Buddhist rituals are similar to those found in any other Theravada Buddhist vihara, but emphasis is placed on meditation. Monks at the monastery limit themselves to spiritual activities and are not involved in the business of the society. They may influence the society through board members, however.

At its monastery, the Manawmaya Theravada Buddhist Society celebrates events such as the Myanmar New Year, *Vesak, Kathina,* and the festival of lights.

Most celebrations are called *Pwe*. The *Kason* festival is the most important; it is the first full-moon day in May, commemorating the birth, enlightenment, and death of the Buddha, just like the Sinhalese *Vesak* festival. On the full-moon day of *Waso* in July, devotees commemorate the first sermon of the Buddha. On that day, monks in Myanmar begin the three-month rain retreat, meditating, reading, and carrying out other religious activities. The end of the rain retreat is marked by the festival of lights, when devotees donate new robes to the monks and decorate their houses with lanterns, candles, and electric lights. Some of these religious activities are not carried out in British Columbia. In Myanmar, they also decorate public buildings at this time. Young people play an active role; in fact, young couples avoid getting married during this season in order to participate in spiritual observance. In Myanmar, parents send children who have not yet reached their twenty-first birthday to become *samanera* (novices) at monasteries for seven days, although some stay for only two days.[40]

For the Myanmar New Year in April each year, devotees come to the monastery to offer *dana* (alms) and to spend time in meditation. At midday, they share their meals with friends and others. A striking feature of this celebration is paying respect to elders. A young devotee will wash the head of an older person, usually one who is over seventy-five years. The elder is presented with new clothes, medicines, and other necessities.[41] Monks who visit hospitals or private residences provide spiritual comfort to patients by reflecting on the teaching of the Buddha and chanting *pirit* (blessing).

Most Myanmar families pay homage and recite the five precepts before they retire for the night. Buddhism is thus a vital part of their daily living. Mrs. Mitzi Tun observed, however, that after she immigrated to Canada, she became more aware of the true nature of Buddhism and now follows the teaching of the Buddha.[42]

A noticeable difference between the Myanmar monastery in Surrey and the Sri Lankan Surrey Buddhist Vihara is the lack of Sunday school facilities at the former. According to Ken Sai, however, there is a special program for children on *Vesak* (full-moon day in May) and at the *Kathina* ceremony after the rain retreat. In summer, children may be ordained as novice monks in the monastery for a few days or more and observe the eight precepts. Ken himself was temporarily ordained for two weeks at Mahasi Temple in Mandalay City, Myanmar, at the age of ten. At the time, he was happy for the opportunity to understand why one follows the teaching of the Buddha. First, he was taught the *Kalama Sutta*, which contains the counsel given by the Buddha to the people of Kesaputta in India, who came to him confused about the various doctrines being preached. Explaining their right to doubt, the Buddha stated: "When you know yourselves – these things are moral, these things are blameless, these things are praised by the wise, these things when performed and undertaken, conduce to well-being and happiness – then do you live and act accordingly." Ken says that "this experience really stuck in my head."[43]

The Myanmar monastery in Surrey ordains five to ten novices each year. This reflects the practice in Myanmar and shows the importance placed on young people. Children are also taught the value of meditation at an early age. The general thinking throughout Myanmar is that Buddhism is meditation. As far as rituals are concerned, the practices at the Surrey monastery and those in Myanmar differ in some respects because of inadequate numbers in British Columbia and also certain city bylaws. According to Ken Sai, there are two types of Buddhists: those who practise Buddhism without rituals and those who practise Buddhism as an integrated part of Myanmar culture, including rituals.

Sri Lankan and Myanmar Buddhists and Canadian Multicultural Society
Assimilation into mainstream Canadian society is not a difficult problem for Sri Lankan Buddhists because English is a familiar language. Some of them, born before Sri Lanka's independence from the British, were educated entirely in English. The selection criteria for immigration as applied by the Canadian High Commission in Colombo consider how well an immigrant might integrate into Canadian society. Immigrants who are qualified professionals usually obtain jobs immediately on arrival.

The situation is different for refugees who arrived in Canada after 1983. Many were not professionally qualified, and their lack of English-language skills hampered them in dealing with mainstream Canadian society. Since both Canada and Sri Lanka are Commonwealth countries, Tamils and Sinhalese from Sri Lanka used to be able to enter as visitors and claim refugee status in Canada. The process has been changed, however, and citizens of Sri Lanka now have to obtain visitor's visas to enter Canada.

On the whole, Sri Lankan Buddhists are full participants in mainstream Canadian culture and society, having a separate identity only with regard to their participation in activities relevant to Buddhism. The principles of Buddhism – kindness, love, compassion, tolerance, and respect for equality and human rights – are not inconsistent with basic Canadian values.[44] Also, Buddhism encourages friendship and goodwill toward all, so Sri Lankan Buddhists have no difficulty adjusting to Canadian values and multiculturalism. They consider Canada as their country and home, and see in its multiculturalism the same views that they hold: tolerance, social and ethnic harmony, and the eschewing of discrimination and violence.[45]

Naturally, Buddhists would like to see the universality of the Buddha's message become better known in Canada, but this will have to wait until there is greater awareness of Buddhist values. This is not a problem because Canadians have a long tradition of democracy and an innate, deep-seated sense of tolerance. These positive aspects of multiculturalism have helped small groups such as the Sri Lankan Buddhists pursue their aspirations within the broader Canadian society.

In general, the foregoing observations also apply to immigrants from Myanmar. Both countries gained independence from Britain in 1948. Since Myanmar (at that time Burma) was also under British rule, English was prevalent, and those who immigrated to Canada did not have any difficulty assimilating into Canadian society. Some Myanmar immigrants have married Canadians, and English is the mother tongue of the younger members of the community in British Columbia. Myanmar Buddhists have joined Canadian clubs, socialize with other Canadians, and entertain as other Canadians do. They still adhere to Buddhist teaching, but being a small community, they have little influence on political life.

Conclusion

Sri Lankan and Myanmar Buddhists in British Columbia have established monasteries that, although not identical to those in their home countries, engage in a wide range of religious activities. Unlike the simple desire to "make merit" described in Chapter 5, these activities are more like those described by Wendy Cadge in her study of a Thai wat in Philadelphia, involving listening to teachings, refuge and precepts, prayer and *puja,* chanting, merit transfer, protection, purification and blessing, enjoying friends, and celebrating major Buddhist holidays, in addition to donations.[46] Although it appears from this survey that Sri Lankan and Myanmar Buddhists are well adjusted in their new home in British Columbia, this should not give us the false impression that the adjustment is without difficulty. For many, immigration is a traumatic experience at first. Some immigrants from Sri Lanka may come from extended families that provide considerable support and empathy in all of life's many challenges, and find it very daunting to be alone in a new country. An organization such as the Surrey Buddhist Vihara is therefore very important to them.

After an immigrant has become established, however, the need for this type of support diminishes, unless he or she desires a continuing connection with a religious and ethnic group like the Buddhist vihara. The nucleus of the Surrey Buddhist Vihara consists of people who wish to actively participate in Buddhist religious activities as practised in Sri Lanka. Many other Sri Lankan Buddhists do not necessarily wish to be associated with formal religious worship. The hope of the pioneers of making the vihara society a microcosm of Canadian society by being open to all regardless of ethnicity or nationality has not succeeded because there are insufficient Canadians (apart from immigrant Buddhists from other countries) who were already Buddhists in British Columbia. In addition, almost all such Canadians were already established in one meditation group or other.

The Sri Lankan and Myanmar viharas may function as a bridge between the familiar country of origin and the new country, or even as a means of maintaining cultural identity (see also Chapters 2 and 8). The extension of this function to future generations appears likely, as young people are receptive to Buddhist practices and values, unlike the Sikh youth mentioned toward the end of Chapter 2, who may be wary of the motives of the older generation.

To a Sri Lankan Buddhist, the vihara is always a familiar, and welcoming place. It is a place where there is no feeling of being discriminated against or of being an outsider. Such organization of religious communities along ethnic lines does not pose a threat to Canadian values; in fact, that they can exist without tearing the nation's cultural fabric shows the strength of Canadian values and democracy. As A.K. Warder observes in the acclaimed book *Indian Buddhism*: "There is a general underlying assumption that beyond the immediate aim of individual peace of mind or more probably in essential connection with it, lies the objective of the happiness of the whole of human society and the still higher objective of the happiness of all living beings."[47]

NOTES

1 *Vihara* means a dwelling where the Buddhist monks live, and also the place where an image of the Buddha is installed.
2 For a succinct overview, see Paul Bramadat, "Foreword," in *Buddhism in Canada*, ed. Bruce Mathews (New York: Routledge, 2006), xii.
3 The term "Theravada" means "school of elders;" it is followed in Sri Lanka, Myanmar, Thailand, Cambodia, and Chittagong in Bangladesh.
4 My thanks are due to all participants. In particular, I wish to thank Ken Sai for introducing me to the Myanmar community.
5 K.M.D. De Silva, *A History of Sri Lanka* (Colombo: Vijitha Yapa Publications, 2003), 9.
6 Mahanama, *Mahavamsa*, ed. W. Geiger (Colombo: Government Publication Bureau, reprinted 1960), 3-9.
7 De Silva, *History of Sri Lanka*, 57.
8 Nanamoli, *Path of Purification* (translation of *Visuddhimagga* by Buddhaghosa) (Colombo: Semage, 1956), xvi-xvii.
9 John William Cousin, *A Short Biographical Dictionary of English Literature* (London: J.M. Dent and Sons, 1933), 13.
10 Rick Fields, *How the Swans Came to the Lake: A Narrative History of Buddhism in America* (Boston: Shambala, 1992), 132-33.
11 Interview with Upananda Dedunupitiye, 6 August 2006.
12 J.R. Jayawardene Centre, http://www.jic.net/jrj/biography.html.
13 Statistics Canada, 2001 Census of Canada.
14 Palitha Palliyeguru, "Editor's Corner," *Buddhist Vihara Society Newsletter*, February 1990.
15 Interview with Gamini Makawita, 28 January 2006.

16 Note from Anagarika Dhammadinna, *Buddhist Vihara Society Newsletter,* February 1990.
17 Interview with Sudu Vatagodakumbura, 10 February 2006.
18 Interview with Gamunu Ekanayake, 28 January 2006.
19 Interview with Kirthi Senaratne, 6 February 2006.
20 "Mahāparinibbānasutta," in *The Dīghanikāya,* ed. T.W. Rhys Davids and J. Estlin Carpenter. Pali Text Society Publications; v. 22, 52, 67 (London and Oxford: Pali Text Society, 1890-1911), 2.157.
21 Interview with Venerable Kumbalgoda Sirinivasa, 10 February 2006.
22 Interview with Venerable Mirisse Dhammika, 20 June 2005.
23 Leon Feer and Caroline A.F. Rhys Davids, eds., *The Saṃyutta-nikāya of the Sutta-piṭaka,* vol. 1 (London: H. Frowde, for the Pali Text Society, 1884-1904), 105.
24 Interview with Venerable M. Dhammika, 20 June 2005.
25 Interview with Venerable Puliyankulame Saranatissa, 19 June 2006.
26 Interview with Kirthi Senaratne, 10 February 2006.
27 Interview with Kirthi Senaratne, 10 January 2006.
28 Godwin Wijesinghe, *A View of the World* (Battaramulla, Sri Lanka: Banu Graphics, 2004), 65.
29 See http://punjabbuddhistsociety.com/index.htm.
30 See http://www.ambedkartimes.com/buddha.htm.
31 Interview with Yaspal Mehay, 10 July 2006. See also the discussion of Ambedkar Buddhists in Chapter 1.
32 A.K. Warder, *Indian Buddhism* (Delhi: Motilal Banarsidass, 1970), 265.
33 P.A. Church, *A Short History of South East Asia* (Singapore: Asian Focus Group, 2006), 109.
34 R.R. Noble, *Buddhism: A History* (Fremont, CA: Jain Publishing Group, 1951), 114.
35 R. Arthur and S. Baya, *Canada's Immigration Heroes and Countrymen* (Toronto: Touche Base, 2000), 28.
36 Interview with Ken Sai, 15 December 2005.
37 Interview with Win Aung, 4 February 2006.
38 See the Manawmaya Theravada Buddhist Society website at http://www.mtbscanada.org.
39 Interview with Myat Htoon, 6 February 2006.
40 Interview with Reggie Tun Maung, 8 February 2006.
41 Interview with Myat Htoon, 4 February 2006.
42 Interview with Mitzi Tun Maung, 4 February 2006.
43 Interview with Ken Sai, 8 January 2006.
44 Interview with Tissa Kannangara, 28 January 2006.
45 Interview with Godwin Wijesinghe, 12 February 2006.
46 Wendy Cadge, *Heartwood: The First Generation of Theravada Buddhism in America* (Chicago: University of Chicago Press, 2005), 74-84.
47 Warder, *Indian Buddhism,* 157.

7 Vietnamese Buddhist Organizations
Cam Van Thi Phan (Thích Nữ Trí Khả)

Mái chùa che chở hồn dân tộc,
nếp sống muôn đời của tổ tông.

These two lines are from "Nhớ Chùa" (Remembering the Pagoda), a famous poem written in 1949 by Venerable Master Thích Mãn Giác, styled Huyền Không, to express the importance and influence of Buddhist teachings and practice in the Vietnamese tradition and people. Translated loosely as "the [Buddhist] pagoda's roof shields the people's spirit, an everlasting custom [that has been passed down] from our forefathers," they poetically affirm the intricate and dynamic role Buddhism has played in shaping the spiritual foundation and philosophical vision that extends and influences Vietnamese popular customs, educational system, and political life and assists in creating a "Vietnamese identity" that stands strong against external domination and cultural assimilation. Consciously or unconsciously, many Vietnamese have been influenced in their daily lives by Buddhist concepts and customs that seem to have become assimilated naturally into the Vietnamese lifestyle. It is therefore not surprising that shortly after the first group of immigrants settled in British Columbia, a couple of dozen lay Buddhist followers gathered at a small house to chant and hold dharma talks. According to Ms. Nga Bích Nguyễn, one of my interviewees, who has been living in Vancouver for over twenty-four years, the Vietnamese people during the early 1980s were quite at a loss as to how to adapt to and handle their loneliness and homesickness in a new, foreign environment.[1] She recalls that during those early years, the Vietnamese community was not as connected and active as it is today; the temple, however, was one thing that connected them and brought about a sense of common origin, shared culture, and group solidarity through participation in religious activities. The Vietnamese "Buddhist Temple" established in Vancouver by the Vietnamese people became a centre for all social activities, for Buddhists and non-Buddhists alike. The word "temple" is an overstatement for the facility where the group assembled weekly. Rather, Phước Long was an ordinary house-turned-temple religious centre that held the soul of the young overseas Vietnamese community and blazed a trail for other Buddhist organizations that followed.

Before reviewing the formation of the Vietnamese Buddhist community here, however, it is essential to have a general outline of the history of Buddhism in Vietnam and the development of the Vietnamese migrant community in British Columbia.[2]

History

Although there is a lack of authentic historical data on the precise date that Buddhism entered Vietnam, the historian and Buddhist monk Lê Mạnh Thát, in his *Lịch Sử Phật Giáo Việt Nam* (History of Vietnamese Buddhism), tells us that it could have taken place as early as the second or third century BCE.[3] It is believed that the first group of Buddhist monks to enter Vietnam were part of the missionary fleet that Indian emperor Ashoka (270-232 BCE) sent to disseminate the Buddha's dharma to places beyond the Indian borders, such as Africa, Central and West Asia, Southeast Asia, and Giao Châu, which is modern-day Bắc Ninh Province in the north of Vietnam. To trace these 2,000 years of Vietnamese Buddhist history and condense them into a couple of paragraphs is a virtually impossible task for any Vietnamese scholar who wants to relate the unique role of Buddhism in shaping Vietnamese tradition and history.

Suffice it to say that Buddhism in Vietnam has been influenced by both India, particularly in its early history, and China, but has nonetheless developed its own distinctive characteristics, thanks to the contributions of a number of outstanding monks over the centuries. Vietnamese Buddhism today is predominantly Mahayana Buddhism, the same type of Buddhism examined in the discussions of Japanese Buddhism in Chapter 10 and Chinese Buddhism in Chapter 12. Vietnamese traditionally attribute the formation of their own *Thiền* sect to a king, Trần Nhân Tôn, who, after his abdication in 1293, became a great Buddhist scholar and founder of the first indigenous Vietnamese *Thiền* sect, called Trúc Lâm, which unified the various pre-existing Chinese *chan/thiền* traditions into one cohesive "Vietnamized" system that has become the main practice in Vietnamese Buddhism to the present day.[4]

Although *thiền* is dominant, it is not the only form of Buddhism practised by Vietnamese. Pure Land Buddhism (Tịnh Độ Tông) and Tantra (Mật Tông) are also part of the Vietnamese Buddhist tradition. These alternatives to *thiền* attracted followers by granting magical powers to heal or call down rain and by promising absolute salvation in the next life, all of which seem to the general population to be more practical and beneficial than the complicated *thiền*, paradoxical *công án*,[5] and obscure metaphorical language. Together, all these forms of Buddhism claim the allegiance of 70-80 percent of the Vietnamese population, according to a 1960 census. However, in a more recent 1999 census done by the United States, the CIA claims that now only 9.3 percent of the population are Buddhist,[6] while according to another American statistic, half of the Vietnamese population are "nominally Buddhist."[7]

Over the centuries, Buddhism has penetrated Vietnam's popular culture to the extent that Buddhist themes appear in traditional Vietnamese opera, music, and folktales, and Buddhism is now seen as a Vietnamese religion more than one with Indian or Chinese origins. In the response to the challenge of French colonial rule, in the twentieth century many Vietnamese turned to Buddhism to assert their pride in their indigenous culture. This cultural nationalism inspired the formation of many Buddhist associations throughout the nation. In 1948, these associations were brought together under an umbrella organization called the United Buddhist Vietnamese Association (UBVNA). In 1951, the UBVNA joined the World Fellowship of Buddhists (WFB), which was founded in Colombo in 1950 and currently includes representatives from thirty-five nations.

Despite its growing unity, Vietnamese Buddhism encountered hard times in the twentieth century, even after the end of French colonial rule, since neither the Diệm regime in what was until 1975 a separate country in the south nor the communist regime, which now controls the entire country, was particularly friendly toward Buddhism. After the communist unification of Vietnam, many Buddhists joined the exodus that resulted in the creation of Vietnamese exile communities around the globe, including British Columbia.

Immigration to Canada

According to a former Vietnamese exchange student, now in her fifties, the first wave of Vietnamese settlers in Canada came between 1950 and the 1960s and '70s, when several students received scholarships to study at universities in Quebec. The second wave occurred after 1975, when the communists gained control of South Vietnam and a large number of southerners fled the country by boat, hoping to make a new life in foreign non-communist nations. This phenomenon shocked the world at the time, not because it was unprecedented in history but because of the large number of people who risked their lives travelling in tiny underequipped boats with barely sufficient supplies of food and water on the wide-open seas, suffering great losses. Among the humanitarian countries that received these boat people was Canada, one of the migrants' most favoured destinations.

The Vietnamese population in Canada grew dramatically between 1978 and 1982, after the federal government passed a law in 1976 that allowed any non-profit organization or group of at least five adult citizens to sponsor an individual or family of refugees.[8] In 1979, Canada alone took in 19,859 Vietnamese, and in 1980 accepted another 25,541; another 60,247 arrived between 1988 and 1990.

Most of these immigrants took up residence in the four largest provinces, with British Columbia becoming home to 13 percent of the overall Vietnamese refugee population, according to 1991 Canadian statistics. The third major wave, which started after 1982 and continues today, was stimulated by a family reunification program through which those who already have Canadian citizenship are able to sponsor relatives who are either in Vietnam or still living in transit camps. The Canadian government accepted more than 34,400 new immigrants between 1983 and 1986. Since 1995, however, the immigration rate has decreased greatly, with only about 4,000 new immigrants arriving per year. In 1996, there were about 22,000 people with Vietnamese ethnic identity in British Columbia, and a plurality (about 43 percent) claimed to be affiliated with a Buddhist organization.[9] In the most recent Census of Canada (2006), the Vietnamese population was recorded to have grown by 3 percent annually, reaching approximately 27,200 in British Columbia alone, with 48 percent of the 151,000 Vietnamese spread across Canada recorded as being Buddhist.[10]

The Religious Landscape

Even for a religion that advocates the cultivation of the mind and heart and devalues superficial rites and possession of material objects, constructing and maintaining a pagoda or monastery is considered essential for cultivating good karma and, from a cultural standpoint, helps in preserving a long tradition. Like many other Asian communities, the Vietnamese, on arriving in Vancouver, immediately established a Buddhist centre by temporarily transforming a residential house into a "sacred chanting hall" where Vietnamese of the Buddhist faith as well as those of other faiths would gather to celebrate religious and national holidays. As Ms. Nguyen states, this "small and humble semi-pagoda" was a product of the migrants' effort to rebuild their lives and strengthen Vietnamese pride and sense of community by establishing a bond with one another through shared beliefs and values. Upholding Vietnamese customs and values was possible through the existence of this public facility, which provided space and opportunity for the older generations to interact with the younger generation through weekly events and annual grand festivals. The Vietnamese Buddhist population grew as monks, nuns, and lay followers came to British Columbia and other provinces, and more temples were needed to fill the spiritual demand.

As a child entering the monastery, I often heard from senior masters the phrase *Chỗ nào chúng sinh cần con sẽ đến* (wherever there are [suffering] people [in need of the dharma], I will gladly go to that destination [to expound the teaching and help them]). This quotation best describes the distribution of Vietnamese pagodas and associations throughout British Columbia. Most of these institutions are located on the east side of the Greater Vancouver region, with one pagoda in each of Surrey, Richmond, Burnaby, Langley, and Mission, plus two pagodas in Victoria and one in Nanaimo. None are found in West or North Vancouver or in communities in northern British Columbia, where there are few Vietnamese.

Temples
According to Ms. Nguyen, the Phước Long temple, the predecessor of the current Chân Quang Temple, was established in 1982 under the guidance of Venerable Thích Nguyên Trí (who has now moved to the United States). In 1989, the temple, after many changes of address, settled permanently at its current location at the corner of East 1st Avenue and Commercial Drive, on the east side of Vancouver. Under the guidance of the Most Venerable Thích Tâm Châu, the acting president, and Master Thích Chân Hoà, the current abbot, the Chân Quang Temple is the largest and one of only two officially recognized Vietnamese Buddhist institutions in British Columbia.[11] With its convenient location five minutes away from a bus stop, this rectangular red-brick building with yellow tile roofing and two majestic stone lions at its front steps is a testament to the integration of Western and Eastern cultures – signifying the Vietnamese people's vigorous efforts to adapt to the Canadian lifestyle while trying to preserve their forefathers' tradition.

A successful transformation from dancehall to religious institution created this weekend gathering place for more than 100 Vietnamese Buddhists. Testifying to its role as the heart of the Vietnamese community, during special religious events such as *Vesak* (Buddha's birthday) and *Ullambana* (Ancestor Day), as well as secular holidays such as the Lunar New Year, the temple attracts over a thousand pious devotees as well as spectators. On weekdays, the temple is open from the first gong of the early morning chant at 5:30 a.m. and closes after the evening chant at 5:00 p.m. On weekends, especially Sunday, when a public ceremony is held, the temple is extremely busy, with a tight schedule that starts with a short ceremony of praying for ancestors at 10:00 a.m., continues with a forty-five-minute public ceremony and a half-hour sermon, and ends with a complimentary vegetarian meal at noon.

Besides the Chân Quang Temple, there are three other active Buddhist organizations in the Greater Vancouver area. The Thiền Tôn Buddhist Association is headed by Venerable Master Thích Nguyên Tịnh, who is the most senior of the Vietnamese Buddhist monks living in British Columbia. He resides with his only disciple at the association's main facility, a small house on Renfrew Street. The association has been active since the early 1980s. Its circle of followers is smaller and more intimate than that of the Chân Quang Temple, and it is especially popular among the older group of lay devotees. Although I was not granted an interview, I learned from speaking with relatives of mine who are ardent members of the Thiền Tôn association that it conducts short, fifteen-minute chants for the public every Sunday afternoon, followed by a short sermon and vegetarian lunch. Due to the small capacity of the house, the religious activities here are relatively low-key and attendance at each gathering has stabilized at around twenty people. Because of his advanced years, the master has become less active and now concentrates more on his own spiritual cultivation. Nevertheless, he is one of the most respected masters and the person from whom the monastic community occasionally seeks advice.

The Bảo Lâm Buddhist Association is the only religious society in the Greater Vancouver area headed by an ordained Buddhist nun. Recently moved from busy Knight Street to a more residential neighbourhood on St. George Street, this association has been active since 1998. At first, its gatherings were held on the main level of a lay devotee's house on Victoria Drive. Within a year, it was able to purchase a house at its current location, and it has attracted a small group of about twenty people weekly. Because it does not want to be in conflict with other temples, which hold public ceremonies on Sundays, the Bảo Lâm association's gatherings are held every Saturday afternoon and include sutra recitation, a dharma talk by the abbess, and a light vegetarian meal. The association is quite popular among Buddhist laywomen, who often seek guidance and counselling from the abbess about sensitive feminine issues and family problems.[12] The main ceremonial hall is quite small, but the solemn Buddhist images and vibrant decorations create an aura of joyfulness and vivacity. Entering the Garden of Peace and Happiness (in the backyard), one is led into a state of tranquility by the artistic design of the handmade lotus pond and the dozens of aromatic flowers and trees. (I happen to be associated with this organization and am also a disciple of the president and head nun, Reverend Thích Nữ Tịnh Pháp.)

The Hoa Nghiêm Temple is the only Vietnamese Buddhist association located in Burnaby. Headed by Venerable Thích Nguyên Thảo, the temple was established in 1996.[13] After many moves, it finally purchased a strip of farmland in 2002 and has been renovating the area, with plans to rebuild the current structure to give it the typical Asian curved-roof style of architecture. Passing down a long and bumpy road, visitors are led into the spacious temple grounds and welcomed by the five-coloured Buddhist flag at the entrance gate. Converted from a farmhouse, the main hall is quite spacious and is able to hold about a hundred people in both the upper ceremonial hall and the lower dining hall. The abbot and two young ordained monks and several nuns reside there and hold services for the public on Sunday mornings. The service includes public chanting, a dharma talk given by the abbot, and a free lunch. On weekends, there are also Vietnamese-language classes for the children and a beginner's

FIGURE 7.1 Gleaming floors at Chân Nguyên Temple are a testament to the effort of its community. *Photo by Cam Van Thi Phan*

Mandarin class for all ages. Behind the main hall are rows of blueberry bushes, preserved to bring in revenue for the temple. The Hoa Nghiêm Temple can be said to be the most active Buddhist association as far as participation in Vietnamese community events is concerned. Especially during the Lunar New Year, the temple's volunteers sell sticky rice and participate in the *Chợ Tết* (New Year Market), an exhibition of Vietnamese music, food, and entertainment at a cultural centre (chosen each year), reconstructing the lively and joyful atmosphere of markets during the Lunar New Year festivals in Vietnam.

Venerable Thích Viên Giác, a prominent Buddhist monk and leading poet in the local Vietnamese community, established Chân Nguyên, the first Vietnamese temple in Surrey, some seven years ago in 2003.[14] Situated in a quiet neighbourhood, the temple is unrecognizable as such from afar. A first-time visitor would be amazed, however, at the majestic decoration in the main ceremony hall and meditation room, creating a solemn and sacred atmosphere. The Chan Nguyen Temple, as the abbot describes it, is both a dharma centre and a training institution, with the hope of educating and producing knowledgeable and virtuous future religious leaders. There are currently three monks, three nuns,[15] and seven novices, ranging from elementary school age to college students, living and training at the institution. Although it is a training centre for ordained disciples, the abbot also holds a public ceremony for laypeople every Sunday morning, starting at 7:00 a.m. or 8:00 a.m., depending on the season. The service includes a walking meditation routine followed by sitting meditation exercise, then chanting of sutras (in Vietnamese and English) and a dharma discussion. It concludes with lunch at 1:00 p.m. The sermons are given in Vietnamese and English, as the members attending consist mostly of Canadian-raised Vietnamese youth and Caucasian practitioners. The abbot, with a goal of harmonizing both Eastern and Western cultures, has also designed many new and interesting atypical activities that integrate Buddhist philosophy with Western festivities, such as performing compassionate acts of serving free food to the homeless on Thanksgiving, and educating the younger lay followers and the Canadian-born Vietnamese youth about the spirit of sharing on Halloween.

The Lâm Tỳ Ni (Lumbini) Temple, also in Surrey, was originally a Korean cultural centre that was turned into a Vietnamese Buddhist centre in 2004 by Venerable Thích Tịnh Trí and his disciple, Thích Nữ Trí Nghiêm.[16] Venerable Thích Tịnh Trí immigrated to Canada in 1990. In 1996, he moved to Victoria and established the Pháp Hoa Temple (now known as Hải Triều Âm Temple and managed by his disciple, nun Trí Nghiêm), where he lived and provided religious services to the community until he moved to the Lower Mainland in 2002. He established the Lâm Tỳ Ni Temple on 57th Avenue in Surrey. Two years later, he moved the temple to 16837 94A Avenue, where he continues to provide weekend public services for the Vietnamese laity in Surrey. The main building is quite spacious and, after being renovated by skilful volunteer laymen, bears the appearance of a Vietnamese temple, with the lotus-designed iron gates, colourful Buddhist flags, and a solemn Avalokitesvara Bodhisattva image standing in a lotus pond surrounded by a garden of flowers and mini stupas. On entering the main chanting hall, one is amazed by its cleanliness and artistic decorations, from the black bronze Buddhist statues in the centre to the Buddhist scriptures, skilfully etched on precious sandalwood, that line the side walls. Although located in the rural northeastern section of Surrey, the temple's participants and membership are comparable with those in more urbanized areas, with about fifty lay devotees participating at gatherings every weekend and a few hundred at grand festivals. Notably, two-thirds of the participants are middle-aged people and teenagers who have the means to commute to the rural areas. The abbot is trying to find a way to help those elders who do not drive to attend these events. The weekend sessions (on Saturday and Sunday) begin at 11:30 a.m. with recitation of a sutra, followed by a dharma talk given by the abbot, and ending with a vegetarian meal provided by the nun Trí Nghiêm. Other services include chants on the fifteenth and first of every lunar month, during which the number of participants is double that for ordinary weekend services. Besides the traditional services that are provided by all Buddhist temples, the Lâm Tỳ Ni Temple is well known for the traditional exquisite Vietnamese cuisine (hard to find elsewhere) and handmade Vietnamese traditional dresses, which Trí Nghiêm makes to keep Vietnamese tradition alive and earn income to support the temple's activities. In the future, with the help of visiting monks from Vietnam, the abbot intends to provide additional services, such as language or home economics classes for Vietnamese youth and more dharma talks and recitation sessions for the middle-aged and older members.

Located on Vancouver Island are two temples headed by Venerable Thích Pháp Ấn, Vạn Hạnh Temple and Hải Ấn Temple.[17] The first is a small house in a suburb of Victoria, while the latter is nestled in downtown Nanaimo. Both are in quiet neighbourhoods and were founded by the Most Venerable Thích Thiện Nghị, the Vạn Hạnh Temple in 1990 at its current location and the Hải Ấn Temple a few years later. The temples were managed by pious laity until 1993, when Venerable Thích Pháp Ấn was assigned by the Most Venerable Thích Thiện Nghị, his teacher, to become abbot for both temples. Humbly standing among rows of residential houses, the Vạn Hạnh Temple is immediately recognizable, with flowing Buddhist flags at the wooden entrance gate. At the end of a row of pink roses stands an Avalokitesvara Bodhisattva statue over one and a half metres in height, gazing calmly at visitors. A miniature bronze Maitreya statue in the back garden watches over the practitioners, who sit quietly in meditation beside the small fishpond. The main ceremonial hall was formed by breaking down the walls between the many small rooms of the former residence, so that it can accommodate around thirty to forty people.

The design of the Hải Ấn Temple is a little different, with the Avalokitesvara Bodhisattva statue placed in the back garden, overlooking a spacious green lawn, while visitors are welcomed by the dangling bunches of grapes at the entrance gate. Public ceremonies on Sunday morning commence at 10:30 a.m. at the Hải Ấn Temple and finish before noon so that the abbot can return to Victoria in time to begin the session at the Vạn Hạnh Temple at 2:00 p.m. The schedule is similar for both temples: recitation of a sutra, meditation exercise, and a dharma talk, ending with a light meal provided by the laity. By request, there is also a Pure Land recitation session from 8:00 p.m. to 9:30 p.m. on Wednesdays at the Vạn Hạnh Temple. Although attendance at both temples fluctuates between ten and fifteen people at each gathering (due to the recent increased migration to the Lower Mainland of British Columbia and other provinces), the abbot's peaceful composure and affable smile provides assurance that he is unaffected by this change and does not wish to relocate to an area with a larger Vietnamese population. On the contrary, with the support of the

FIGURE 7.2   Vạn Hạnh Temple in Victoria is located in a residential neighbourhood, which is typical of many temples mentioned in this book. *Photo by Cam Van Thi Phan*

current members, he is preparing to construct a new and larger building at the Victoria location, one that will have an Asian architectural appearance.

Lay Associations
The Huyền Quang Vietnamese Buddhist Youth Association in British Columbia is a well-known lay Buddhist organization. It is headed by Mr. Đời Chí Lê and Ms. Tâm Hạnh, who graciously permitted me to interview them in the midst of teaching their classes at the Collingwood Neighbourhood House.[18] This lay association, which aims to educate youth in both religious teachings and virtuous conduct, represents a unique characteristic of Vietnamese Buddhism. It was originally established in Vietnam in 1945 by the United Vietnamese Buddhist Association in order to create a proper, fun, and constructive environment in which to educate Vietnamese youth. The program's structure is modelled after the secular academic school system. A child is taught basic Buddhist principles as well as proper conduct, and advances through three levels and nine ranks. These youth organizations were traditionally affiliated with Buddhist temples, with the head abbot or abbess acting as chief adviser.

The situation is quite different in Canada, however. The Vietnamese Buddhist Youth Association in British Columbia was established in 1995 and is located on the second floor of the Collingwood Neighbourhood House on Joyce Street in Vancouver. It holds its services every Sunday from noon to 4:00 p.m. The numbers of children attending (ages six to twenty) fluctuates between fifteen and twenty. The main instructors, Mr. Lê, Ms. Tâm Hạnh, and three instructors in training conduct a chanting ceremony, teach Vietnamese language and Buddhist philosophy, and serve a light lunch at each gathering. As this is a nonprofit organization, the young people are asked to pay only a $10 lunch fee each month; activities such as the annual camping trip, attendance at the World Annual Buddhist Youth meetings, and training programs for leaders are financed by fundraising activities.

Since we are discussing lay associations, we should also mention a lay group that is not technically "Vietnamese" because its members are not ethnic Vietnamese but that bases its practice on the Vietnamese *Thiền* (meditation) tradition as developed by the Vietnamese monk Thích Nhất Hạnh. The Mindfulness Practice Centre of Vancouver was founded in 1998 by Jeannie Seward Magee and John Magee, who were inspired by the teachings of Master Nhất Hạnh (referred to by the members as "Thầy," meaning "master") during a retreat at Plum Village, the place in France where he teaches. They felt that his methods would be beneficial and suitable to a Western audience and wanted to share their experience with their fellow British Columbians. They currently meet at 382 Main Street in Vancouver, in a space offered by the Bentall family rent-free. Facilitated by Harreson Sito, the group meets for a couple of hours every Monday to participate in a variety of exercises, including stretching yoga, sitting and walking meditation, tea meditation ritual, and listening to or reading from the Thầy's books. The weekly sessions end with "community sharing," a unique exercise that allows participants to freely share their problems and thoughts concerning their daily life or religious practice with other participants, and to ask or give advice in a safe and constructive atmosphere. The session ends with participants going to Chinatown for dinner (Harreson revealed that a vegetarian diet was not a requirement for joining the group). The number of participants varies from three to ten people, ranging in age from students in their late twenties to office workers in their early forties.

Cao Đài Association
Besides Buddhist and Catholic Vietnamese (discussed in Chapter 8 in this book), British Columbia also has a few followers of a new Vietnamese religion. Cao Daiism (Đại Đạo Tam Kỳ Phổ Độ, "Third Revelation of the Great Way") claims that it is a syncretic belief system that encompasses the quintessence of all religions.[19] Centred in the southern province of Tây Ninh, Cao Daiism is

an amalgam of ideas and philosophy from Christianity, Buddhism, Daoism, Confucianism, and Western nineteenth-century romanticism. It was first propagated by Chiêu Văn Ngô (1878-1926), who claimed to have received a revelation directly from "God," the creator of the universe and mankind, about the unification of all beliefs and spiritual teachings. According to his revelation, the formation of other religions and the birth of religious leaders were all of God's handiwork. The world is divided into three periods of revelation, in which different messiahs were sent by God to serve humanity and to found the many branches of the Great Way. Each messiah preaches according to the needs and customs of each period and nation they encounter; however, the teachings are of the same truth and from only one source, which is "God." Humanity's inherent weakness has brought about division and conflict through misinterpretation of God's intention; the revelations to Chiêu Văn Ngô and the introduction of Cao Daiism represent the last period in which God has given his final injunction to unite all religions, end worthless conflict, and treat all one's fellow human beings as one's sisters and brothers. While advocating the renunciation of wealth and the control of greed and desire, this religion emphasizes that people have great responsibility toward themselves, their families, and society. Followers believe in reincarnation and practise meditation, yet they also perform divinations and worship Daoist deities, Confucius, Jesus Christ, and famous secular figures such as Victor Hugo and Julius Caesar.[20]

The Cao Đài organization in British Columbia, although formed fairly early in 1980, was not well known within the Vietnamese community at first. It was not until 1991 that it was able to purchase a house in the quiet Vancouver neighbourhood of Kensington as its main office. The organization's membership is relatively small, approximately fifty followers, but one of the leaders says that it is increasing slowly but steadily as new Vietnamese migrants come from other parts of Canada. The association holds public services every Sunday (attendance reaches over a dozen people on normal days and over fifty on special holidays). These services consist of public chanting, dharma discussion, and a vegetarian lunch, much like the services in Buddhist temples. The society is headed by Mr. Thu Văn Đặng, a lay leader who is seen as the highest authoritative figure for Cao Daiists in British Columbia.[21]

Tradition and Adaptation

Vietnamese Buddhism is both a manifestation of the distinctive Vietnamese culture and a part of the global Buddhist community. As such, it both reaches out to the broader community and invites non-Vietnamese into its own. Thiền Master Nhất Hạnh's Plum Village in France is a prime example of such inclusiveness, as is a recent trend of inviting dharma masters from other ethnic groups to hold talks and conduct special rituals at local temples or in private homes. These gatherings are quite popular and participants sometimes number in the hundreds. Communication and language problems are overcome by local translators. Some sessions may last for several hours due to a three-stage (e.g., Tibetan-English-Vietnamese) translation process.[22] Because of language barriers and limited resources, however, the Vancouver Vietnamese Buddhist community is still finding it difficult to reach out to local non-Vietnamese communities and to interact in a significant manner with other religious denominations or even with the other local Buddhist associations discussed elsewhere in this book.

The local Vietnamese Buddhist community has also had to adapt to the Canadianization of its members without losing touch with its Vietnamese foundation. Although they are in British Columbia and not Vietnam, the temples all celebrate important Vietnamese religious holidays, such as *Phật Đản* (*Vesak*) and *Vu Lan* (*Ullambana*), as well as national holidays such as the Vietnamese *Tết* (Lunar New Year). It should be noted that although the Vietnamese *Vu Lan* festival has many similarities to the *Ullambana* of other Buddhist denominations (especially the Chinese and Japanese), in which the monks and laypeople chant, offer food, and make prayers (every day for one to two weeks) for the deliverance and salvation of suffering ancestors and relatives in hell, it has also become the unofficial Vietnamese "Mother's Day." This association goes back to *Thiền* Master Thích Nhất Hạnh's famous piece "Bông Hồng Cài Áo" (A Rose in Your Pocket), which he wrote after a trip to Japan in 1962. It highlighted the *Ullambana* festival's concept of "filial piety" and praised the Japanese tradition of wearing a red flower to indicate that one's mother was still alive or a white flower to indicate that she had already passed away. When attending a *Vu Lan* festival, therefore, do not be surprised if someone comes up to give you a white or red rose.

As a way of maintaining a connection with the younger generation, the Chân Nguyên Temple even celebrates Western holidays such as Halloween and Thanksgiving. When a celebratory date falls on a weekday, when most of the Buddhist laity are busy, most local temples hold the celebration on a weekend or a weekday evening instead of sticking to the traditional date. Through such adaptations, the Vietnamese Buddhist community in British Columbia has, on the whole, maintained a distinct religious identity that still embodies the values and customs that originated in Vietnam, but has also made some adjustments to better fit into its Canadian setting.

Vietnamese Buddhists in a Multicultural Society
Within the Vietnamese Buddhist community, there are clear differences in attitudes toward Buddhism in general and Vietnamese temples in particular.

Among the middle-aged and older generations, attending religious rituals is a habitual necessity that enables them to connect with their tradition and community. Temples also act as educational and cultural centres for the Canadian-born Vietnamese youth, whose knowledge of Vietnam and her culture comes from history textbooks and documentary films that present only a small and dark portion of Vietnam's 4,000-year history. Among the younger generation, it seems that attending temple services is more of a cultural obligation than a matter of religious sincerity, although there are a few young people who fervently help out at the temples, and in recent years some Vietnamese youths born and raised in British Columbia have decided to leave the household life to enter the monastic order. Other young people accompany their parents to Buddhist rituals but also, either out of curiosity or influenced by friends, attend rituals and worship services of other religious denominations. As one laywoman commented, her twenty-six-year-old son, while still identifying himself as a Buddhist, also attends social functions and volunteers for activities organized by the local Christian churches or other religious dominations, actions that she fully encourages.

The Vietnamese lay community has recently become active in providing social services, sometimes on an individual basis, at other times working with local Buddhist associations to perform humanitarian deeds for their fellow Vietnamese. Besides supporting these local associations, they provide financial help to renovate and repair damaged religious sites, famous pagodas, relic stupas, and large monasteries in Vietnam and neighbouring Asian regions, and to help sponsor the livelihood and study fees of monks and nuns in Tibet and Thailand. Many volunteers willingly sacrifice time and money to set up compassionate relief programs for the poor and sick in Vietnam.

An important clue to the health of the Vietnamese Buddhist community is the monastic order, consisting of monks, nuns, and a growing novice population. The monastic order in British Columbia is relatively small, consisting of no more than twenty monks and nuns, all of whom follow the Mahayana tradition and are easily identified by their brown or gray/brown robes. Similar to the *sangha* in Vietnam, the *sangha* in British Columbia consists mostly of middle-aged monks and nuns. The expression *nhất tăng nhất tự* (one monk, one temple) to some extent accurately describes the situation in the past, when there was a shortage of monks and nuns in the province, but the situation has improved. More Vietnamese youth (those under twenty-five years of age), mostly males, are entering the *sangha,* now more than a dozen youths. Moreover, talented monks and nuns from Vietnam are sometimes invited to take up residence for a couple of years as assistants to the abbot/abbess in two of the Buddhist associations in British Columbia, although this phenomenon is more common in other provinces.

Supplementing the traditional monastic community are a few elderly women who go through ordination rituals, usually performed in Vietnam, that certify them as ready to enter the monastic community. They then return to Canada and, instead of living in a temple, live with their families in their own homes or in a personal residence called an *am* or *thất* (loosely translated as "cultivation hut") and perform their own individual religious practices. They do not engage in any outreach activities. These nuns are difficult to contact (especially for the laity) because of their preference for leading quiet lives and their reluctance to make public appearances. The Vietnamese Buddhist community is very supportive and treats them with great respect, as shown by the invitations to religious festivities and functions that they receive from local temples.

Another healthy feature of the Vietnamese community is the cooperative relationship between the different temples and associations. In accordance with the concept of *lục hoà* (the six ways to live in harmony) expounded by the Buddha to teach monastics how to function in large groups, the competition that naturally exists among different religious denomination, sects, and schools becomes secondary to the greater aim of solidarity and unity. Especially in times of natural calamities in Vietnam or other parts of the world, all Vietnamese Buddhist temples simultaneously hold relief drives to collect donations, which they entrust to the Canadian Red Cross. On special Buddhist ceremonial days, many of the head monks and nuns from different temples come together to hold grand public rituals at a local temple or a rented auditorium. At other times, monks and nuns may gather to offer prayers and recitation at the funeral of a deceased layperson whose last wish was to invite the entire monastic community to his or her burial service in order to offer the *trai tăng* ritual. (This is the offering of the four essentials – food, clothing, medicine, and money – to a group of four or more monks or nuns in order to gain merit for the living family and/or its deceased members.)

Economic Factors

The sustenance of a temple or monastery in Vietnam was never a major issue for its monastic residents because they did not need to worry about paying property taxes or the monthly water and electricity bills, which amount to no less than a thousand dollars even for the smallest association in British Columbia. This issue initially proved to be a challenge for the Vietnamese temples in the province, because tradition dissuades monks and nuns from working in non-religious occupations to earn income, and financial support from the laity was relatively weak due to the economic problems common among new immigrant groups. Facing this harsh reality, most temples that do not receive sufficient donations have learned to be more self-reliant and have found ways to generate revenue to cover temple maintenance and the monks' daily expenses. Besides conventional religious services such as chanting at funerals or performing esoteric rituals for the sick, which usually bring a small gratuity, monks and nuns have recycled pop cans, grown commercial crops on temple property, and sold vegetarian food, religious items such as necklaces with Buddha images or recitation beads, and books to cover their expenses. Some have been fortunate enough to hold charity concerts or vegetarian dinners, generating funds for larger projects such as renovation of existing temples or construction of new pagodas.

In some extreme cases, especially among a few monks and nuns who have recently settled in the community and are not very well known among the laity, and those who choose to live secluded lives in individual huts, monastics have no financial assistance at all and must take up different minimum-wage jobs to support themselves, such as picking floral leaves, working in recycling depots, or doing take-home sewing jobs. Is this an indication of how the monastic community is gradually adapting to the independent Western lifestyle, or is it a sign of the religion's decline, as believed by some lay Buddhists who oppose monastics' becoming involved with secular work and neglecting their spiritual cultivation? The answer to this question will become clear only with time.

Contemporary Issues

Given the rapid changes of the new millennium and the number of youth growing up and being educated and immersed in Western culture, Vietnamese religious leaders in British Columbia have three major challenges: (1) how to preserve Vietnamese culture through the establishment of permanent facilities and, if money permits, the construction of a traditional Vietnamese-style temple with a traditional appearance; (2) how to transmit the dharma to the younger generation and encourage them to participate in religious activities; and (3) how to provide intermediate and higher education in Buddhist studies and philosophy for novice monks and nuns and others who are interested in Buddhism.

The establishment of a stable and traditional-style temple would not only promote the stability of the religious community but also be a visible sign of the importance of Vietnamese culture in British Columbia. The short-term goal for most temples is to relocate to a building where a large number of people can gather for religious ceremonies and dharma talks without provoking complaints by neighbours. Because most temples are located in residential neighbourhoods rather than in areas specifically set aside for religious activities, they have difficulty opening language classes for young children, holding large meditation classes or classes on Buddhist studies in English or Vietnamese, or freely celebrating Buddhist holidays according to Vietnamese tradition. In addition, these Vietnamese temples have had to endure unfriendly gestures, verbal attacks, and property damage caused by anti-Buddhists who live within their neighbourhoods. Because of the pacifist nature of most Buddhists, they have chosen to bear such discrimination in silence, in the hope that time will win them acceptance or that they will soon have an opportunity to relocate to a friendlier and more tolerant area.

The second concern within the Buddhist community is the unenthusiastic response on the part of most Vietnamese youth (ages fifteen to thirty) toward attending temple services or participating in religious festivals. They lack the motivation to learn and understand the importance of a religion that helped shape Vietnamese culture, values, and history. After speaking to many religious leaders, immigrant parents, and Vietnamese youth, I have concluded that there are three main reasons that youths born and raised in Canada rarely attend Buddhist temples and lose interest in Vietnamese religions in general.

First, finances are a very important issue for the individual families, who generally came to Canada as "boat people," without money or resources. To help their families financially and pay for their own daily expenses, many youths work long hours seven days a week and attend temple services only in times of family crisis or personal difficulty. Second, there are youths who associate Buddhism with backwardness, and who believe that this "old-fashioned tradition" belongs to their parents' and grandparents' generations and is not suited to the modern lifestyle.

The last reason that large numbers of young Vietnamese are not interested in the temple or in Buddhist rituals is the simple fact that the religious activities and the paraphernalia involved are uninteresting and excessively complex, making them difficult to comprehend. The youth feel uncomfortable attending these rituals mainly because of the language barrier and complicated taboos. The rituals and dharma talks at the temples are usually conducted in Vietnamese, but most youths growing up in British Columbia have insufficient knowledge of the language and are unable to comprehend what is being said and done at the ceremonies. This problem arises from a lack of centres that can provide Vietnamese-language classes for the younger generation, who are taught to communicate in English at school and who rarely interact with their overly busy parents at home. It is but natural that they lose interest in attending rituals and ceremonies that they do not understand and therefore do not see as important. Moreover, misinterpretations of certain Buddhist concepts have dissuaded many youths from entering religious premises. For example, the term *tội,* loosely translated as "sin," is often applied liberally by adults to all actions that appear to go against social protocols, such as wearing skirts or short-sleeved shirts or speaking and laughing loudly on temple grounds. Although the Buddhist conception of *tội* is quite different from the Christian's "sin," most people do not understand the difference and subconsciously attach the image of falling into hell to the term *tội*. Thus, fearful of committing a "sin" and reaping an unpleasant afterlife, some naïve youth refrain from entering the Buddhist temple altogether.

Another concern, especially in the monastic community, is the lack of a proper religious training institution in Canada. It is generally recognized that novice monks and nuns in Canada do not have as much religious training and education as those of former generations, or even as much as their counterparts in Vietnam. Most novices are trained at their respective monasteries in a one-master, one-student format; some are sent to study and train temporarily at a credible religious institution in Vietnam or in other countries, such as Taiwan, India, or Japan, where the Buddhist educational systems are well-developed. Another option for novices is to seek advancement at academic institutions in Canada while simultaneously educating themselves about Buddhist doctrines. In Vietnam, there are nationally acclaimed universities where monks and nuns can earn master's degrees and doctorates in Buddhist studies. Such programs (taught completely in Vietnamese) cannot be found anywhere in Canada – or even in the United States, where the *sangha* community is many times larger, socially active, and politically influential.

On a positive note, it must be said that technology has aided the development of a flourishing *sangha* community by enabling most temples to upload their information to websites and conveniently interact and exchange information rapidly with people around the world. More popular in the United States and gaining increasing acceptance by monks and nuns in Canada is an MSN-like program called Paltalk, which senior nuns introduced to the author after a 2002 An Cu retreat held at the Bat Nha Temple in Calgary. The nuns reported that, since long distance phone calls were costly and sending letters was time-consuming, interacting through this program was much more convenient and enjoyable. Buddhist lectures are also conducted live every day by masters from around the world (some of these lectures require preregistration and have a format similar to online university seminars). Paltalk also makes it possible for a layperson to attend a live Buddhist chanting ceremony or participate in discussion groups on a variety of topics related to Buddhism. Of course, such programs and lessons cannot compare with actual person-to-person lectures, but for monks and nuns who live in regions that do not have a proper facility or educational institution, especially where Buddhism is still new, Paltalk provides a way for people from different countries and nations, whether lay or monastic, to come together and learn from competent masters. It is not inconceivable that the Internet may one day replace temples and religious institutions and become a place for Buddhists and non-Buddhists alike to exchange information and accumulate knowledge.

If we want to be optimistic, we may say that the younger generation of monks and nuns, who lack a traditional education and have limited literacy in their mother tongue (although most can speak fluent Vietnamese), may nevertheless be an asset to the Buddhist community in the new environment, in which more than just religious knowledge is required to successfully propagate the religion. Such monastics may be able to communicate more easily with younger audiences and attract a wider range of individuals interested in exploring and learning about the uniqueness of Vietnamese Buddhism.

Conclusion

Although Vietnamese Buddhists are a fairly new community in British Columbia and have encountered minor setbacks, they have established a fair number of religious institutions and developed a noticeable presence in the province. From small houses turned into temples to the increasing number of lay and monastic practitioners, Vietnamese Buddhism is certainly finding a way to adjust to the new environment while safeguarding its long tradition. Certain customs and rituals have been somewhat modified to suit the Western lifestyle. Nevertheless, the temple remains firmly at the centre of the community, and leads in upholding Vietnamese values and beliefs. While providing a place for religious cultivation, the temples are also the main public space for large gatherings on national holidays and grand festivities. The laity, largely consisting of middle-aged and older women (very few men), habitually attend weekend religious services at the local Buddhist temples and perform various meritorious deeds. Even the younger generation, although intimidated by or uninterested in becoming involved in religious activities, still drop by the temple on special festivals or family occasions. It is fortunate that almost all the temples and Buddhist associations in British Columbia are headed by ordained monks or nuns, compared with other provinces, where there are more temples than monastic individuals to head them, and an increase in the number of young novices and acolytes has brought hope for the preservation and transmission of the tradition. Finally, no one can deny that Vietnamese Buddhism in British Columbia is unique and is still gracefully evolving into a distinctive tradition no less worthy of respect and study than its parent in Vietnam.

Notes

1 Interview with Ms. Nga Bích Nguyễn, 16 February 2006.
2 I have been a part of the Vietnamese Buddhist community for eight years and have interacted with most of these groups in both private and public. The study of the monastic order presented special challenges. In a gradually modernizing but still conventional Buddhist *sangha* (this has been variously translated as community, monk, or order) that still abides by the long tradition of a patriarchal monastic hierarchy, a relationship based on absolute

reverence from novice to senior and nun to monk is required and expected. I sincerely welcome all constructive comments that can enhance the quality and reliability of this study.
3 Lê Mạnh Thát, *Lịch Sử Phật Giáo Việt Nam: Tập 1* [History of Vietnamese Buddhism] (Hue, Vietnam: Nhà Xuất Bản Thuận Hoá, 1999).
4 *Thiền* is the Vietnamese word for what is called *dhyana* in Sanskrit, *chan* in Chinese, and *zen* in Japan. It refers to meditative Buddhism.
5 *Công án* are words, phrases, or questions given by a *Thiền* master to his student, usually holding no empirical logic and withstanding all common reasoning, to "shock" the student and force him or her out of habitual ways of thinking.
6 CIA website, https://www.cia.gov/library/publications/the-world-factbook/geos/vm.html. The statistics given on this website are suspicious and should be read with caution.
7 See website, http://www.state.gov/g/drl/rls/irf/2007/90159.htm.
8 Louis-Jacques Dorais, *The Cambodians, Laotians and Vietnamese in Canada,* Canada's Ethnic Group Series No. 28 (Ottawa: Canadian Historical Association, 2000), 8.
9 Statistics Canada, http://www.statcan.gc.ca.
10 Colin Lindsay, *The Vietnamese Community in Canada* (Ottawa: Statistics Canada, 2001).
11 Interview with Venerable Thích Chân Hoà, 11 January 2006.
12 Interview with Venerable Thích Nữ Tịnh Pháp, 7 February 2006.
13 Interview with Venerable Thích Nguyên Thảo, 10 January 2006.
14 Interview with Venerable Thích Viên Giác, by Dr. Don Baker and me, 2 October 2005.
15 These elderly nuns reside in Thôn Đoài (a small cottage) in Mission, where it is possible for monastics to pursue self-cultivation without being disturbed by outsiders.
16 Interview with Venerable Thích Tịnh Trí and Venerable Thích Nữ Trí Nghiêm, 9 August 2006.
17 Telephone interview with Venerable Thích Pháp Ấn, 7 February 2006.
18 Interview with Đời Chí Lê and Ms. Tâm Hạnh, 19 February 2006.
19 Surprisingly, they do not include Hinduism, Shinto, or the Islamic tradition.
20 Merdeka Thien-Ly Huong Do, *Cao Daiism: An Introduction* (Perris, CA: Cao Dai Temple Overseas, Center for Dai Dao Studies, 1994).
21 Interview with Thu Văn Đặng, 8 February 2006.
22 The dharma master speaks in Tibetan. His words are translated into English by another master, and translated into Vietnamese by a lay follower.

PART 3
Traditions from East and Central Asia

8 Korean Religiosity in Comparative Perspective
Don Baker

Although Korea is overshadowed on maps by its much larger neighbours China and Japan, and shares many cultural elements with them, it has managed over the last couple of millennia to nurture a distinctive culture of its own. This culture is reflected in the Korean language, in Korean food, in Korean music, and in Korean religiosity. This chapter focuses on the distinctive religiosity of Korean Canadians in British Columbia, especially on the role that Korean religious organizations play in helping Koreans who live in the province to maintain ties to Korea. It will show how different the Korean Canadian religious experience is from the Chinese Canadian experience described in Chapters 11 and 12 or the Japanese Canadian experience described in Chapter 10.

Koreans comprise one of the largest Asian communities in British Columbia. In 2006, Statistics Canada estimated that the over 50,000 Koreans living in the province were the fourth largest community in British Columbia with roots in Asia, behind only the Chinese, East Indians, and Filipinos. Over one-third of all Koreans in Canada live in the province, mostly in the Vancouver area, and only Ontario has more residents of Korean ethnicity. No one who has driven down North Road, which serves as the border between the Vancouver suburbs of Burnaby and Coquitlam, and noticed the Korean supermarkets, restaurants, and shops on both sides of the road would doubt that there is a substantial Korean presence in our province.

Similar to what we have seen in most of the other Asian Canadian communities, one religion tends to be pre-eminent in the BC Korean community. As is clear from the many signs on streets and buildings around the Lower Mainland advertising Korean churches, that religion is Protestant Christianity. There are also many Koreans living in British Columbia who are Catholic or Buddhist. A goal of this study was to discover what role Protestant Christianity plays in the Korean community, and to find out whether Catholicism and Buddhism play the same role. I wanted to see whether Korean Canadians use religious organizations more to adapt to Canadian society or to provide an enclave to which they can retreat from Canadian society when they feel the need to speak Korean, eat Korean food, and be with fellow Koreans. I also take brief looks at some other Asian Canadian communities to see whether their religious organizations, particularly Christian ones, play the same role in their communities that such organizations play in the Korean Canadian community.

Such an investigation has relevance beyond the relatively small Korean community in British Columbia. The role that religious organizations play in this community can shed light on the relationship between ethnicity and religious orientation in general. In particular, this chapter and the others in this book can help determine whether a close connection between ethnic identity and religious affiliation will help or hinder social cohesion in Canada. Will a society divided along ethno-religious lines have a heightened risk of erupting into conflicts over fundamental beliefs and values? Or will such a diverse society flourish because of the wide range of options it provides for dealing with the various social problems that Canada will undoubtedly encounter in the years ahead?

Before we can answer such broad questions, however, we need to gain more information about the various religious organizations in Canada and the communities that support them. This chapter focuses on one such community. Although, as noted above, the 2006 Census of Canada found only a little over 50,000 Koreans living in British Columbia, Koreans themselves insist that their community is at least 70,000 strong. (This larger figure may include the estimated 15,000 or so Korean ESL students who spend some time in Vancouver every year.) They also say that as many as 35,000 of those Koreans are Protestant Christians. This would mean that half of the Koreans living in the province are Protestant Christians, which is more than twice the rate in South Korea itself. (The 2005 South Korean census found that 18.3 percent of South Koreans were Protestant Christians, with another 10.9 percent Catholic and 22.8 percent Buddhist.) Catholics may make up another 15 to 20 percent of the local Korean population, according to estimates given me by local Korean Catholic leaders. This, too, would surpass the percentage of Koreans in Korea who are Catholic. There appear, however, to be only 2,000 or so Korean Buddhists in British Columbia, less than 5 percent of the Korean Canadian community here and far below the percentage of Koreans in Korea who are Buddhists. Such discrepancy between religious affiliations in Korea itself and the religious affiliations of Koreans in British Columbia suggests at first glance that the latter may have gravitated toward Christianity in order to help them assimilate to Canadian culture, which has more Christian than Buddhist elements. A close examination of Korean religious organizations in the province shows, however, that such is not the case. Instead, Korean houses of worship, whether Protestant, Catholic, or Buddhist, have provided places for Koreans to be Korean more than to help them become Canadian.

Protestant Christianity in the Korean Canadian Community

My research assistant, Daniel Unsok Pek, identified over 170 Korean churches in British Columbia in 2006, most of them in the Lower Mainland. Both he and I heard that there were several small churches not on our list. Most of our informants told us that, in 2006, there were at least 200 churches in British Columbia. It would be safe to assume that the number has grown since then.

Almost all of these churches are Protestant churches. (There is one Korean Catholic Church, with three affiliated chapels, and there are also four Korean Buddhist temples.) Korean churches are found all over the Lower Mainland. My small community of New Westminster, for example, had at least sixteen Korean churches the last time we counted, while Surrey, across the Fraser River, had at least thirty-three. There were thirty Korean churches within the city limits of Vancouver, another twenty-seven in Burnaby, and sixteen in Coquitlam. Even outside the Lower Mainland, Koreans have their own congregations. We found three Korean churches in Victoria and another four in Nanaimo. Even Kamloops and Kelowna have a couple of Korean congregations each. Most of these churches are relatively new. The history of Korean Christianity in British Columbia is less than half a century old.

The oldest Korean congregation in the province celebrated its fortieth anniversary in 2006 and now occupies its own impressive church building in Burnaby. Its beginnings were much more humble, however. In 1966, six recent Korean immigrants began meeting once a month for worship and fellowship in a borrowed room in the Vancouver School of Theology. Their young pastor, the Reverend Sang-Chul Lee, had graduated from the school in 1963 and then returned to Korea. In 1965, he was invited back to Canada by a United Church pastor in Richmond who needed someone who could speak both English and Japanese to minister to a Steveston congregation. Korean friends he had met as a student asked whether he could lead them in Korean-language worship services when he wasn't busy with his church in Richmond. At first they met just once a month, but soon they were meeting every Sunday afternoon in borrowed facilities at the Canadian Memorial Church. That same congregation also formed the nucleus of the original Vancouver Korean Association, and the Reverend Lee served as its first president.

Sang-Chul Lee stayed in Vancouver for only a few years. He moved to Toronto in 1969 to serve as pastor of a church there, and eventually rose to the post of moderator of the United Church of Canada from 1988 to 1990.[1] The congregation he helped found in British Columbia survived and grew, however, and at one point had as many as 300 adults on its membership rolls. Today it is one of thirteen Korean United Church congregations in Canada, although still the only one in British Columbia. The congregation is also aging. When I interviewed him on 16 February 2006, the pastor, Jong Chul Woo, told me that when he came to that church three and a half years earlier, after eleven years as pastor at a Korean church in Montreal, 80 percent of the people in his pews were retired. He has begun to revitalize the church, and attendance has grown from around 60 people who attended Sunday services regularly when he first came to 130 or more adults by early 2006. He has also hired a youth minister to help him serve the 20 young people who attend English-language services in the church as well as to teach the 20 children who attend Sunday school.

In many ways, the Vancouver Korean United Church is a Canadian church for Koreans rather than a Korean church that happens to be in Canada. Unlike many other Korean churches, both in Korea and in Canada, this church does not have any formally designated elders helping the pastor (there was an elder system when he arrived, but Pastor Woo abolished it). Moreover, unlike most Korean churches, the Vancouver Korean United Church does not hold worship services at dawn on weekdays. In one more break with Korean Christian tradition, it is not evangelical (although Pastor Woo says that it is still more evangelical than most Canadian United Churches). It does not have its own mission program but instead contributes to the mission fund of the United Church of Canada.

On the other hand, this church is well aware of its Korean identity. Its congregation celebrates such traditional Korean holidays as the autumn harvest festival and the day of the first full moon of the new year by engaging in traditional Korean games. Moreover, the congregation remains overwhelming Korean. There is no program for reaching out to non-Koreans. The only non-Koreans who attend services are the spouses of Korean members of the congregation.

There were not many Koreans living in British Columbia in the 1960s and into the 1970s, so it wasn't until 1974, eight years after the founding of the Vancouver Korean United Church, that another Korean congregation appeared. This one was more Korean in its identity. There is no United Church in Korea. There, unlike in Canada, where the Presbyterians and the Methodists merged to form the United Church in 1925, Presbyterians and Methodists maintain strong, separate denominational identities. Of the two, the Presbyterians are by far the stronger. Far more Korean Protestants identify themselves as Presbyterians (there are at least eighty-five Korean Presbyterian subdenominations in Korea) than as Methodists or as members of any of the many other denominations into which Korean Protestantism is divided. It is therefore not surprising that the second Korean church to appear in British Columbia was the Vancouver Korean Presbyterian Church (Figure 8.1), established in 1974. Under its fourth

FIGURE 8.1 The Vancouver Presbyterian Korean Church on Vancouver's West Side.
Photo by Don Baker

pastor, in 2006 it had 900 registered members and 500 adults regularly attended Sunday worship services. A hundred adults usually attended Wednesday evening services (another feature of Korean Christianity), and around 20 to 70 came to weekday dawn prayer services, which are held a couple of times a week.

Like the Vancouver Korean United Church, the Vancouver Korean Presbyterian Church has its own buildings, which it purchased from the Mount Pleasant Presbyterian Church. Unlike many of the newer Korean Presbyterian churches in British Columbia, it is a member of the Presbyterian Church in Canada, which is a legacy of the Canadian Presbyterian congregations that did not join the United Church in 1925. Korean churches now comprise five of the nine largest congregations in the Presbyterian Church in Canada. In order to make the large number of Korean Presbyterians in Canada feel at home, two separate presbyteries for Korean Canadians have been established, one in Eastern Canada and the other in Western Canada. In 2008, the head of the western Korean Canadian Presbytery, which embraced eleven churches in British Columbia, was Kim Kyŏngjin, the pastor of the Vancouver Korean Presbyterian Church.[2]

This pastor is what Koreans call a member of the "1.5 generation," that is, Koreans who may have been born in Korea but who immigrated to Canada at a young enough age to attain native-speaker fluency in English. His fluency in

English has enabled Pastor Kim to reach out to other English-speaking Koreans, giving him a more youthful congregation than at many other Korean churches. Around half of those who attend worship services at the Vancouver Korean Presbyterian Church are under twenty-five years of age. This church maintains its Korean identity not only through the Korean Canadian identity of its congregation but also through its Korean-language school for Koreans born in Canada and through its interest in North Korea. It has begun providing assistance to an Institute of Technology in an area in China, just north of the North Korean border, that is heavily populated by ethnic Koreans, and is also considering providing assistance for North Korean technical education.

The next Protestant churches to be established by and for Koreans in British Columbia were less mainstream Canadian in their orientation. The year 1976 saw two new Korean churches established in the province, the Korean Baptist Church and the Vancouver Full Gospel Church. The Korean Baptist Church is a member of a distinctively non-mainstream Canadian denomination, the Southern Baptist Convention. (There are now at least thirteen Southern Baptist Korean churches in British Columbia.) The Vancouver Full Gospel Church has its own church building between Deer Lake and Highway 1 in Burnaby. At least seven more Korean Full Gospel churches have opened in British Columbia since 1976. The pioneer church alone had a membership of around 200 in 2006. Full Gospel churches, which are both evangelical and Pentecostal, make up one of the major denominations in Korea. Some of the Korean Full Gospel churches in Canada are members of the Pentecostal Assemblies of Canada. Others are members of the American Full Gospel Church, and still others see their connection with the Yoido Full Gospel Church Mission in Korea (the world's largest congregation) as their primary affiliation. No matter what their formal affiliation is, they have many things in common, including an experiential and exuberant approach to spirituality.

Presbyterian churches, Baptist churches, and Pentecostal churches are not the only Korean churches found in British Columbia. There are also at least twenty-two Korean Methodist churches, a few Holiness churches, one Seventh-day Adventist church, some Korean Christian and Missionary Alliance churches, a Salvation Army congregation, and even a Korean Lutheran church and a Korean Mennonite church, plus some Korean churches with no denominational affiliation (see Figure 8.2).

The first Korean Methodist church in British Columbia was formed in 1983, whereas the largest and most influential one was founded six years later. The latter is the Kwanglim Methodist Church in Canada, which is visible beside Highway 1 in Surrey. It attracts around 750 people to its Sunday services, which are held in both Korean and English. In fact, it attracts so many that it planted

FIGURE 8.2   A Lutheran church in New Westminster, which, in addition to holding its own worship services, also provides space for two Korean congregations: the Korean Youngnak Presbyterian Church as well as the Vancouver Seventh-day Adventist Church (the Korean language sign on the right identifies this church as the home of those two Korean congregations). *Photo by Don Baker*

another church in Coquitlam, the Disciple Methodist Church, which itself had a membership of around 500 in 2006.

The very name of the Kwanglim Methodist Church signals its Korean identity to Koreans, since it is also the name of one of the more famous Methodist churches in Korea itself, which also happens to house the largest Methodist congregation in the world. Kwanglim Methodist tries in many ways to maintain and promote its Korean identity. Since its congregation consists mostly of relatively recent immigrants (those who have arrived in Canada within the last five to ten years), it works hard to help them and their families adjust to life in Canada. It offers both Korean-language classes for the children born here to whom Korean is a second language, as well as "silver school" English classes for older Koreans who may have joined their adult children in Canada and are having trouble with English as well as how daily life in Canada differs from daily life in Korea. The church also sponsors a number of Korean cultural events. The head pastor, Reverend Kim Taewon, explained that it was an important mission of his church to help the children maintain both a Korean and a Canadian identity.

Like other Korean church groups, Kwanglim Methodist also reaches out to the mothers and children of "lonely goose families." "Lonely goose" is a name Koreans apply to families in which the father stays in Korea while his wife lives in Canada with their children so that the latter can obtain a Canadian education. These mothers are often lonely and also worried that their children will become too Canadianized. Attending a Korean church with their children gives them a chance to meet with other Koreans and feel almost like being back in Korea, and it gives their children a chance to be socialized in Korean manners and customs. Kwanglim Methodist is basically a Korean church in Canada rather than a Canadian church for Koreans. It does not try to attract non-Koreans to its services, even though it is situated in a residential neighbourhood in which many Canadian Christians probably live. It is also determined to maintain its Korean cultural identity.

According to its pastor, Kwanglim Methodist is affiliated with the Korean Methodist Church instead of a Canadian denomination only because the formation of the United Church of Canada left it no Canadian Methodist churches it could associate with. Given its focus on Korean Christian culture and its lack of interest in attracting non-Koreans to the congregation, however, Kwanglim Methodist appears to be a good example of what is seen so often in Korean churches in British Columbia: the creation of a religious refuge, of a sanctuary where Koreans can flee to escape the pressures of living in what is for them an alien culture.

Another example of a church established as an oasis of Korean culture for Koreans in British Columbia is the non-denominational Grace Community Church, established in 2003 by Park Sin-il, who had served as pastor of Kwanglim Methodist from 1997 to 2003. His young church has quickly become the largest Korean church in the province. There were only 100 families in the beginning, but by 2006, 1,100 adults were attending services on an average Sunday, along with 250 young men and women at youth services, and 280 children. In 2007, needing a larger worship hall for his still-expanding congregation, he purchased a building that had been an automobile dealership and transformed it into his new church hall. By 2008, Grace Community Church had grown so large that Pastor Park needed the help of four assistant pastors and had to hold four different services on Sundays in order to accommodate the entire congregation. The church also holds weekday 6:00 a.m. prayer services (popular with Korean Christians) in four different locations around the Vancouver area, ranging as far north as West Vancouver and as far east as Port Moody.

Park Sin-il represents the dynamic evangelism that is so characteristic of Korean churches. His church dispatches members of the congregation to the Vancouver International Airport, to the Koreatown shopping malls, and to public libraries to approach people who appear Korean to invite them to Sunday services. Their proselytizing is not confined to the Lower Mainland. In 2006, donations from the congregation also supported four missionary couples in Muslim countries. He told me that in 2006 one sixty-nine-year-old elder from the church moved to Afghanistan to proselytize.

Not all Korean Christians in British Columbia attend Korean churches. Some find the churches' demands on their time (weekday dawn prayer meetings, Wednesday evening services, Friday 10:00 p.m. mini-revival services, cell group meetings on weekday evenings to study the Bible together, and so on) rather daunting. Instead, some attend a church like Willingdon Church in Burnaby. Although it is not a Korean church, Koreans make up a sizable proportion of the congregation. Since 1985, there have been Korean-language assistant pastors either translating English-language services or leading services in Korean. (Other language ministries at Willingdon Church are Mandarin, Cantonese, Russian, Japanese, French, Arabic, and Romanian!)

With the conspicuous exception of Willingdon Church, most churches with services in Korean are ethnic enclaves to which Koreans retreat to escape the pressure of living in Canadian society. It is not the only exception, however. One Korean pastor, Don Tong-eun Kim, moved from being pastor of a Korean Seventh-day Adventist church in New Westminster for seven years to serving as the pastor of the multicultural Oakridge Seventh-day Adventist Church in Vancouver. The forty Korean families in the latter congregation in 2006 did not constitute the majority. There are a few other Korean pastors ministering to non-Koreans in British Columbia. A few Korean pastors are active in missions to First Nations peoples. Faith Evangelical Lutheran Church in Surrey is led by a Korean pastor who, with the help of a non-Korean associate pastor, offers services in Chinese and Spanish as well. Another Korean church in Surrey, Revival Church, has a Sunday afternoon service in Japanese. There is also a Korean mission to Japanese ESL students along Robson Street in downtown Vancouver. These are exceptions, however. The vast majority of Korean pastors in British Columbia live in a Korean world, preaching and praying in Korean to Koreans in Korean churches.

Most Korean Christians and the churches they attend are in the Lower Mainland. Fewer than 20 of the 170 churches that my research assistant and I have identified are on Vancouver Island or in the Interior. There are three Korean churches in Victoria and four in Nanaimo. Both Kamloops and Kelowna have two Korean churches each. Most of these congregations are young and relatively small, however, and only the oldest of the eleven churches outside the Lower Mainland – twenty-year-old Victoria Korean Church – has more than 200 members in its congregation.

Besides churches, Koreans in the Lower Mainland have developed a number of other institutions that together create a Korean Christian culture. There are Korean Christian bookstores, a Christian school for Saturday morning language and culture classes, a weekly Korean-language Christian newspaper as well as columns by pastors in some of the secular Korean-language daily newspapers, Korean-language sermons broadcast by local Korean-language radio stations, and seminaries (some accredited, some not) to train additional Korean pastors. There is also a special program for Korean lay Christians at the theological schools based at Trinity Western University in Langley. The director of the Korean Worldviews Study Program, Paul Yang, is a former physics professor from a major university in South Korea.

The Lower Mainland also has four *kidowon*, retreat centres that are very popular with Christians in Korea. In that country, prayer centres tend to be found in the mountains and provide two or three days of intensive prayer and Bible study away from the distractions of city life. In the Lower Mainland, the prayer centres are found in Surrey, Langley, and Burnaby. I was able to visit the Burnaby Kidowon, Holy Spirit Prayer Centre. It functions more as a place for intensive praying than for actual retreats. The pastor is a woman (unusual in Korean churches, although women comprise about 60 percent of Korean congregations) who worked for twenty years at the famous Yoido Full Gospel Church in Seoul. In 2006, she told us that her ministry was a healing ministry. She said that people come to her centre for the miracles that occur there. Unlike *kidowon* in Korea, there are no facilities for people to stay overnight. She holds 5:00 a.m. worship services every weekday, however, which attract an average of twenty or so worshippers. She also holds daily 9:00 a.m. and 10:30 a.m. services.

In visiting various Korean churches around the province and finding out when they were established and how many people attend their services, we began to notice a pattern. The earliest Korean churches tended to affiliate with Canadian denominations, either the United Church of Canada, the Presbyterian Church in Canada, or the Pentecostal Assemblies of Canada. As the number of Korean churches exploded (there were only seventy Korean churches in British Columbia twelve years ago), the newer churches tended to affiliate with Korean denominations, such as the Korean American Presbyterian Church, or with denominations, such as the Southern Baptists, that are stronger in Korea than in Canada. The vast majority now act as Korean churches that happen to be in Canada rather than as Canadian churches that happen to minister primarily to Koreans.

As their community in British Columbia has grown and the number of churches has multiplied, Korean Protestants have withdrawn more deeply into their own ethnic community, preferring to worship in the Korean language and in the Korean style rather than mix with Christians from non-Korean denominations. Most Korean churches in British Columbia are places of cultural refuge, places that provide a Korean cultural religious experience for those who miss their native land and culture or, in the case of the second generation, want to affirm their connection to the culture of their parents and ancestors.

Korean Catholics in British Columbia
Catholics, on the other hand, do not appear to want to withdraw into a Korean sanctuary on Sundays. At the main Korean Catholic church in British Columbia, I was told that there were 8,000 to 9,000 Korean Catholics in the province in 2006. (This was the size of the mailing list of St. Andrew Kim Catholic Church in Surrey.) Only about 2,500 to 2,700 attended Sunday Mass either at St. Andrew Kim, at one of the mission stations that the parish has established (one in North Vancouver and the other on Cambie Street in central Vancouver), or at the International Catholic Student Centre on Robson Street in downtown Vancouver. There is no Korean Catholic church on Vancouver Island, so St. Andrew Kim dispatches a priest once a month to offer Mass in Korean in a church in Victoria for the small (about 100 strong) Korean Catholic community there.

If these numbers are correct – if at most only 2,700 out of 9,000 Korean Catholics in the province attend the Korean Catholic church – then the rest attend Sunday Mass in English, at non-Korean churches. Why would Catholics be so different from other Korean Christians, more willing to break out of the "religious sanctuary" that churches provide? There are probably a couple of reasons. First, Catholics are less likely to find a Korean-language church near their homes. There are not as many Korean priests as there are Korean Protestant ministers. The celibacy requirement and the long period of required training keeps the number of Korean priests down. Fewer priests mean fewer churches.

Second, there is less variation in Catholic worship across cultures than there is in Protestant services. A Korean Catholic who knows enough English to understand what is going on at an English-language Mass will feel almost as at home as he or she would during a Korean-language Mass. The fact that Roman Catholic churches around the world all belong to the same religious organization, under the overall authority of the Pope in Rome, means that services follow the same basic format worldwide, and that the manner in which the congregation participates does not vary that much from one cultural or linguistic community to another. The relative uniformity of Catholic services throughout the world means that a Korean Catholic attending Mass at any Catholic church in the Lower Mainland would experience the comfort of a familiar ritual and would therefore have less incentive to drive all the way out to St. Andrew Kim in Surrey or to drop by one of its two mission stations.

There may be a third reason that Korean Catholics are likely to attend their local church rather than go out of their way to attend Korean-language services at one of the three locations available in the Lower Mainland. The official policy of the Archdiocese of Vancouver is that there are no real "ethnic parishes." Instead, there are parish churches, some of which serve a congregation that is dominated by members of a specific Asian Canadian community. Catholics are encouraged to go to their local church, which most, though not all, of British Columbia's Korean Catholics do.

St. Andrew Kim differs from the typical Canadian parish in many ways. The church building was not particularly Korean-looking, but a sign in Korean and English at the entrance announced that it was St. Andrew Kim Parish Church. The church bulletin is printed in Korean, and the three priests and two nuns who serve in the parish are all Korean. Most of the Masses, including the sermons, are in Korean. It is no surprise that most of the non-Korean Catholics in the neighbourhood attend another Catholic church, rather than the one that is officially their parish church.

Although St. Andrew Kim is under the authority of the Archdiocese of Vancouver, it acts like a Korean church in Canada rather than a Canadian church for Koreans. The priests and nuns are borrowed from the Catholic Church in Korea, and it promotes Korean culture along with the Catholic faith. Like many Korean Protestant churches, St. Andrew Kim has Korean-language classes for the second generation and hosts classes in traditional Korean music. It also celebrates Korean as well as Canadian holidays.

Other Asian Catholics in British Columbia

The ambiguous status of St. Andrew Kim Catholic Church, which is institutionally a Canadian church but culturally a Korean church, is shared with other Catholic churches in British Columbia that serve Asian Canadian congregations. In 2008, ten Catholic churches in the Vancouver archdiocese offered Masses in at least one Asian language, ranging from Vietnamese and Filipino to Cantonese, Mandarin, and Korean.[3] A couple of churches in Victoria also offered a Sunday Mass in an Asian language. Some of these Vancouver churches are clearly ethnic churches. One mentioned in Chapter 11, Richmond's Canadian Martyrs Catholic Church, is obviously a Chinese church despite its name, since most of the weekend Masses there are in Mandarin and Cantonese, Chinese New Year is celebrated there, and its website is in both English and Chinese.[4] It would be safe to assume that most of the 1,200 families it serves are Chinese Canadians. St. Francis Xavier Church in Vancouver is another predominantly

Chinese parish. It identifies itself on its website as a "Chinese Catholic Centre."[5] St. Joseph's Parish in Vancouver is now predominantly a Vietnamese parish, although it used to serve the Filipino community.[6] Filipino Catholics now comprise the bulk of the congregation of what must have once been an Irish church, St. Patrick's, near the corner of East 12th Avenue and Main Street in Vancouver, although they can also attend a Mass in Tagalog once a month at Holy Trinity in North Vancouver.[7]

More typically, in accordance with the official preference for geographically rather than ethnically based parishes, Asian-language Masses are offered once or twice a month at churches that otherwise serve an English-speaking congregation. Laotian Catholics can find a Mass in their native language in Surrey once a month, and Indonesians can gather at Guardian Angels Parish in Vancouver a couple of Saturday evenings a month for Mass in their language.

The Catholic Church, as befits its claim to be a universal church, has worked hard to rein in the tendency of immigrant communities to retreat into their own ethnic and linguistic enclaves come worship time. It does not appear to have been totally successful, however. Some of the Catholic churches serving Asian immigrants, including St. Andrew Kim, are more like outposts of the church back in the home country than Canadian churches that happen to have Asian immigrants in their congregations. Nevertheless, even Catholic parishes with predominantly Asian congregations are, at least institutionally and often also culturally, more integrated into Canadian society than most Korean Protestant churches.

Korean Buddhism in British Columbia

The same cannot be said about the three Korean Buddhist temples in British Columbia, all of which are affiliated with specific head temples in Korea. Their monks and nuns all come from Korea, and they ensure that their rituals are identical to the rituals at Buddhist temples in Korea. They see their role as providing a Buddhism that Koreans can feel comfortable with. Little effort is made to coordinate their activities with the non-Korean temples in the province, such as the Vietnamese, Japanese, or Chinese temples described in Chapters 7, 10, and 12, respectively. They realize that Korean Buddhists would not experience the comfort of home if they tried to promote a pan-Asian Buddhism in British Columbia, since various Asian countries have developed their own separate and distinct Buddhist traditions over the centuries. Nor do they try to attract any non-Koreans to their services, even non-Korean Buddhists, although a few non-Korean spouses of Koreans do attend occasionally.

The largest Korean Buddhist temple in British Columbia, Seogwangsa in Langley, looks like a temple would in Korea (Figure 8.3). Although it has been open for only a little over a decade and did not open its Korean-style worship

FIGURE 8.3   Seogwangsa, a Korean Buddhist temple in Langley. *Photo by Don Baker*

hall until 2002, it attracts up to a thousand worshippers on Sundays. It also advertises in the local Korean-language press whenever it celebrates a traditional Korean holiday (in a traditional Korean way). For example, every December, a large advertisement invites Koreans to visit the temple to eat red bean porridge on the winter solstice (actually, on the Sunday closest to it), just as they would in Korea. The temple also provides Korean-language classes for second-generation Korean Canadians, and teaches traditional Korean folk music.

The other two Korean Buddhist temples in British Columbia, one in Burnaby and one in Coquitlam, cannot compete with Seogwangsa's Korean architecture and five clerics. They are housed in standard Canadian houses and attract much smaller crowds, although their services represent mainstream Korean Buddhism just as much as the services at Seogwangsa do.

New Korean Religious Movements

There is a fourth group in the Lower Mainland, one not affiliated with mainstream Korean Buddhism. Between thirty and a hundred Won Buddhists meet on Sundays for worship services in a house in Surrey. Won Buddhism is a new religion with Buddhist roots. It was founded in the first half of the twentieth century and has no institutional ties with mainstream Korean Buddhism. In

Korea, it is considered an urban Buddhism for the middle class. Unlike traditional Korean Buddhism, it allows its priests to marry and it gives women a major role in rituals and temple leadership. (The only clerics for the BC group are two nuns.)

Although Won Buddhism is a missionary form of Buddhism, with English-language publications presenting its message to non-Koreans, it does not appear to be attracting non-Koreans to its services here. Each time I have attended a service in Surrey, I have been the only non-Korean present. Similar to most Korean Christian churches, the community remains a Korean religious institution in Canada rather than a Canadian institution serving Koreans. The entire service is in Korean, and the meals served afterwards feature traditional Korean foods. Clearly, Won Buddhism provides for its adherents in British Columbia the same refuge from the alien character of Canadian life that Korean Christianity provides.

There are two conspicuous exceptions to the tendency for Korean religious organizations in British Columbia to focus on the local Korean community. One is a group that claims not to be a religion but instead teaches techniques for enlightenment and provides spiritual guidance. Dahn World originated in Korea in the early 1980s but moved its headquarters to Sedona, Arizona, in 1997. It operates a centre in North Vancouver.[8] Despite its roots in Korean martial arts (the founder used to be a martial arts teacher) and in a Korean new religion that worships the legendary first Korean (named Dan'gun), and despite the fact that many of its practices are similar to those of the internal alchemy school of pre-modern Korea, Dahn World attracts many more non-Koreans than Koreans in British Columbia. When the founder gave a public address in Vancouver in September 2006, there were few Koreans among the 500 or so in the audience.

The Unification Church, now also known as the Family Federation for World Peace and Unification, is another religious organization that has Korean roots but attracts mostly non-Koreans in British Columbia.[9] Only four families out of the hundred people that make up the Lower Mainland congregation are Korean. For many years, the Unification Church has considered itself a global religion, not a Korean religion. The founder and leader, the Reverend Sun Myung Moon, is from Korea but he has lived in North America since 1971. Moreover, the Unification Church has attracted followers in Japan, North America, and Europe and is no longer a Korean religious organization, despite its Korean origins.

The same cannot be said of another group with global ambitions, Maum (Mind) Meditation Centres. Maum Meditation Centres have been established across Canada and the United States as well as in Japan, Australia, Italy, Germany, France, and Chile. Altogether, there are 124 Maum Meditation Centres around the world, with possibly as many as 200,000 people attending them.[10] The centre I visited in 2006, however, located in a house in Burnaby not far from the Metrotown area, attracts mostly Koreans, although I was told that there were three non-Koreans among the thirty or so who practised meditation there.

The Maum Meditation organization says that it is spiritual, not religious, and says that it is not a lay Buddhist organization, although much of the language it uses to describe the goal of its meditation techniques sounds similar to what Buddhists say. Maum meditation teaches an eight-stage approach to meditation, based on the assumption that our memories form our individual minds and that to rise above our individual existence and become one with the infinite universe, we therefore need to clear our minds of those memories that keep us tied down to the finite realm. Although the teachers usually use Korean as their medium of instruction, the practices in themselves require little use of language and so, theoretically, are open as much to non-Koreans as to Koreans. Maum Meditation may soon join Dahn World and the Family Federation for World Peace and Unification as Canadian spiritual organizations that happen to have originated in Korea, rather than Korean religious organizations that happen to serve Koreans outside of Korea.

Korean Canadians themselves will increasingly gravitate toward religious and spiritual institutions that function as outposts of Korean culture on the Canadian landscape. During the many interviews we conducted for this chapter, we were told by several pastors that in the last ten years the nature of the Korean community in British Columbia has changed. Those who moved to Canada twenty or thirty years ago recognized that they had left their old country and their old culture behind. They were therefore more willing to assimilate into the Canadian mainstream even on Sundays, and to form or join churches that had close ties to Canadian churches, such as the United Church or the Presbyterian Church in Canada. More recent immigrants, however, often see themselves as temporary residents of Canada, staying only as long as necessary to obtain a Canadian education for their children. In some cases, the father of the immigrant family continues to work in Korea, dropping in on his family in Canada only occasionally and reminding them that their real home is across the Pacific. Moreover, the Internet and the availability of Korean radio and TV broadcasts and Korean films on DVD enable the newer generation to maintain cultural contact with their homeland in ways unavailable to their predecessors. As a result, newer immigrants often feel more like Koreans in Canada than like Canadians who happen to be Korean. Many of them maintain ties with their churches in Korea, in many cases even continuing to make regular financial contributions to what they consider their home church. It is not surprising that such sojourners seek out Korean churches in British Columbia, since in their minds they have not really left Korea.

Non-Buddhist Japanese in British Columbia

As we have seen, the Korean community in British Columbia is overwhelmingly Christian. The Japanese community, on the hand, is predominantly of Buddhist background (see Chapter 10). As a result, little attention has been paid to Japanese Christianity. For example, a recent study of Christianity and ethnicity in Canada took note of Chinese, Korean, and Filipino evangelicals but said almost nothing about Japanese Christian communities in this country.[11]

Although the Japanese Christian community in British Columbia is small, it merits our attention, if only to shed comparative light on the role that Christianity plays in the somewhat larger Korean community.[12] Japanese have been in British Columbia a lot longer than Koreans have (the first Koreans did not settle here until the early 1960s, whereas Japanese have been here for well over a century). Because of the predominance of Buddhism, however, there are not very many Japanese churches in the province. I have been able to identity only eleven Christian churches that specifically serve Japanese congregations. I was able to interview only four pastors. To my surprise, I found the same tendency among Japanese Christians as that found among Korean Christians: the earliest immigrants, if they were Christian, tended to gravitate toward mainstream Canadian churches, whereas later immigrants are drawn to denominations that lie at the margins of Canadian Christian culture.

The oldest Japanese congregations in the province are the Japanese United Church (founded in 1897) and Holy Cross Japanese Anglican Church (founded in 1903). According to the interim pastor I interviewed in 2006, Holy Cross has been through some rough times. The church it used before the Second World War was confiscated and given to an Anglo-Anglican congregation. (There were actually two Japanese Anglican churches in Vancouver back then.) The congregation did not get its own church again until 1955, and has never recovered the vitality it had before the war. The Japanese United Church also had its church taken away when Japanese were expelled from the West Coast in 1941. In fact, there were seven Japanese United Church congregations in the province back then; all lost their churches and it was not until the 1960s that they again had a church of their own. The current pastor, Reverend Maki Fushii, arrived from Japan in 2004, after serving as a chaplain at the International Christian University in Tokyo. She told me that in 2006 there were around sixty people in her congregation, thirty to forty of whom attended Sunday services regularly. She said that most were elderly Japanese who immigrated to Canada after they retired. They came to the United Church because it reminded them of the United Church of Christ in Japan, although there is no formal affiliation between the two denominations (the United Church of Christ in Japan is the result of a forced merger of Japan's Protestant Christian denominations in 1940).

A third church I visited is also relatively old. The Vancouver Japanese Gospel Church, which, despite its name, is in New Westminster, is slightly over fifty years old. It was founded by Canadians who ministered to interned Japanese in the 1940s. Although it is a Japanese church, it has two pastors: a Canadian who doesn't speak any Japanese and another who is a Japanese immigrant. It is the largest of the Japanese churches I visited, with close to a hundred people attending Sunday services (including four or five non-Asians who live nearby). Services are held in both Japanese and English (for those Japanese born in Canada), at the same time but on separate floors of the church building.[13]

The other Japanese church I visited in 2006, the New Westminster Free Evangelical Church, also had a Canadian pastor. Jacob Friesone had been a missionary in Japan for thirty-five years and was very comfortable leading services in Japanese. He held English-language services on Sunday morning (which several English-speaking Japanese Canadians attend), and Japanese-language services afterwards. About twenty-five people attended the latter regularly, including a few Koreans and Chinese.

Who goes to the Japanese churches in British Columbia? I was told by several pastors that recent immigrants who were not Christian before they moved to Canada made up the majority of the congregations (except in the case of Holy Cross Japanese Anglican Church, which attracts an older crowd). Becoming Christian and joining a Japanese church do not appear to be ways for them to assimilate into Canadian society, however. If that were the reason they became Christian, we would expect them to go to a Canadian church, or at least to a Japanese church in a major Canadian denomination, such as the United Church. Instead, most Japanese churches are non-mainstream. In the Lower Mainland, besides those that I visited plus one more Japanese United Church in Surrey, there are a couple of Japanese Mennonite congregations and a Japanese Baptist Church.

The Japanese tendency to use religion as a cultural sanctuary indicates that Koreans are not unusual in this respect. Nor is this tendency confined to Christians and Buddhists. One of the new Japanese religions discussed in Chapter 10, the Konkōkyō, serves a similar function. (The Institute for Research in Human Happiness, on the other hand, has begun to attract many non-Japanese to what was mostly a Japanese congregation, and the same is true of Sōka Gakkai.)

Another new Japanese religion, one that shares the desire of Won Buddhism to grow beyond its national roots into a world religion, has, like Won Buddhism, found itself occupying a niche in an ethnic enclave in British Columbia. Founded in the middle of the nineteenth century, Tenrikyō is one of Japan's oldest new religions. With roots in the distinctively Japanese indigenous religion of Shinto, it has had difficulty attracting non-Japanese. Like Won Buddhism, Tenrikyō is a missionary faith and publishes materials (including newsletters and its scriptures) in English, but such materials appear to be read mainly by overseas Japanese who don't read Japanese. Tenrikyō has an outreach program in Vancouver, in the form of a Japanese Education Centre that offers Japanese-language classes. It attracts over 530 students a year, but the nearby Tenrikyō worship centre usually has no more than thirty-five to fifty people at its monthly worship services. They tend to be either Japanese Canadians or the spouses of Japanese Canadians. Tenrikyō provides a place for Japanese to be Japanese rather than helping them assimilate into Canadian society. In this respect, it appears to be no different from the other Japanese new religions discussed in Chapter 10.

Conclusion

This survey of Korean religiosity in British Columbia, supplemented by a look at other Asian Catholics, Japanese Christians, and followers of Tenrikyō, suggests that some worship halls for Asian-Canadian congregations may be promoting religious separation along ethnic lines in British Columbia, despite our boast that we have an unusually multicultural society in the Lower Mainland. If this hypothesis is correct, we need to temper our boasting a little. After all, when religious communities are organized along ethnic lines, they can hinder broad social cohesion at the same time that they cushion the individuals and families who join them from the trials and tribulations of a culturally pluralistic society.

Although it may hinder social cohesion, providing a cultural oasis is not necessarily bad for Canadian society overall. Separate and distinct religious ethnic communities are more than just visible institutional reminders of ethnic diversity. They also create space for those who enjoy spending time with others in Canada who share a similar culture and similar beliefs and values. In doing so, they also reinforce those beliefs and values.[14] This can be good for Canada, by providing it with a healthy range of alternatives for dealing with whatever problems society as a whole may encounter. In other words, religious ethnic enclaves make Canadian society more flexible.

We need to be aware, however, that a society divided along cultural lines runs the risk of conflicts resulting from those very differences in beliefs and values. This risk is particularly great when ethnic and cultural differences are reinforced by religious institutions. Religious beliefs are among those least amenable to compromise, yet compromise is essential for democracy to function. Compromise is difficult to achieve in such fundamental value-based conflicts as those concerned with the moral acceptability or unacceptability of abortion or same-sex marriage, or over women's rights and the roles of husbands and wives within a family. Individuals with a strongly held minority religious opinion that, say, same-sex marriage is immoral, or that women do not have the right to choose their own husbands but should marry whomever their parents select for them, may feel that they have to go along with whatever the majority decides, but if such like-minded individuals come together in a group bound by both ethnic and religious ties, they may become emboldened to speak out and resist the majority view. The majority might fight back, leading to social conflict rather than the social cohesion that helps members in a society work together for the benefit of all.

This potential for conflict can be increased by the often conservative nature of overseas communities compared even with their compatriots back home. Whereas they might have been more open to change if they had stayed in their home country, when they settle overseas they often join a religious organization composed of people like themselves as a way to relax in the familiar comfort of the culture they left behind. The problem is that they define that culture as it was when they left it, not as it has become since then. They therefore become resistant to change and can become a drag on the society of their adopted country, making it more difficult for that society to change and adapt to new situations.

As a democratic society, we obviously do not want to suppress minority religious organizations or force minority ethnic groups to assimilate to such an extent that they lose the sense of their own ethnic identity. Not only would that be undemocratic but it would also undermine the roots of Canada's greatness, the diversity of its people that gives it such a wide range of talents, expertise, and ideas to draw on. We cannot pretend, however, that Canada is a homogeneous society. Studies such as this are necessary to remind us of just how diverse we are. We – Canadians in general, but particularly Canadians in policy-making positions or in a position to influence those who make policy – need to be aware of the ethno-religious diversity of Canadian society. We need to keep in mind the advantages and disadvantages of such diversity in order to keep Canada on the right side of the fine line between healthy diversity and unhealthy incompatibility.

ACKNOWLEDGMENTS

This chapter is based on interviews with the leaders of the various religious organizations discussed. I was assisted in this research by Daniel Unsok Pek, a doctoral student in Korean philosophy at the University of British Columbia.

Notes

1. For more on the remarkable story of Sang-Chul Lee, see Sang-Chul Lee, with Eric Weingartner, *The Wanderer: The Autobiography of a United Church Moderator* (Winfield, BC: Wood Lake Books, 1989).
2. For a list of these churches, see http://www.presbyterian.ca/about/contact/churches/486.
3. See http://www.rcav.org/parishes/languages.html for the Lower Mainland and http://www.rcdvictoria.org/parishes for Victoria.
4. See http://cmartyrs.rcav.org.
5. See http://www.sfxchurch.ca.
6. See http://www.stjosephvancouver.ca/eng.
7. Mark G. McGowan, "Roman Catholics (Anglophone and Allophone)," in *Christianity and Ethnicity in Canada*, ed. Paul Bramadat and David Seljak (Toronto: University of Toronto Press, 2008), 62. McGowan writes that there are seven parishes in the Vancouver area besides St. Patrick's that have a substantial Filipino presence.
8. See http://www.dahnyoga.ca/html/kitsilano.html.
9. See http://www.vancouverfamilychurch.org.
10. See http://eng.maum.org.
11. Bruce L. Guenther, "Ethnicity and Evangelical Protestants in Canada," in *Christianity and Ethnicity in Canada*, ed. Bramadat and Seljak, 378-83. There is also a brief mention in that book of Japanese United Church congregations by Greer Anne Wenh-In Ng, "The United Church of Canada: A Church Fittingly National," 208.
12. The 2006 Census of Canada found 41,585 people in British Columbia who identified themselves as Japanese and 51,860 who identified themselves as Korean.
13. See http://www.japanesegospelchurch.com.
14. Helen Rose Ebaugh and Janet Saltzman Chafetz, *Religion and the New Immigrants* (Walnut Creek, CA: Altamira Press, 2000), use the phrase "reproducing ethnicity" to describe a similar process by which Asian immigrants in the United States create islands of their native culture through their religious institutions.

9 Tibetan Religions
MARC DES JARDINS

In 1971 and 1972, 228 Tibetans were brought to Canada as part of a special program arranged by the Indian and Canadian governments and the Tibetan government in exile to help resettle the population of refugees from the Land of Snows. These expatriates made their homes in different communities across the country. Among them was Geshe Khenrab Gajam (*dge bshes mkhan rab dga' byams*)[1] (1928-93), a scholar-monk of the Gelug (*dge lugs*) School of Tibetan Buddhism. He accompanied the Montreal group and became the spiritual director of the Ontario and Quebec Tibetan communities. It was not until much later, in the 1980s and late 1990s, that Tibetans settled in British Columbia, where they comprise at most a hundred families at present.

Among the refugees sent to Alberta were another religious hierarch, Jetsunma Chimey Luding (*rje btsun ma jigs med lus lding*) (b. 1938), with her husband and three of their children. Jetsunma is the sister of the current head of the Sakya School of Tibetan Buddhism. Despite being part of the Tibetan nobility and a member of the prestigious Khön clan, she was a nun before leaving her homeland. The invasion of Tibet by the People's Liberation Army in 1959 forced her to resettle in India, where she abandoned monastic life and married Mr. Rinchen Luding, a member of another branch of the Khön clan and brother of the holder of the Ngor lineage of the Sakya. Despite her elevated social position in Tibet and her rigorous schooling and training in the most arcane lore of the Sakya religious tradition, Jetsunma did not become the spiritual guide of the local Tibetan community. In fact, it was only in the early 1980s that she began to teach Buddhism, and only after repeated requests from her brother, the forty-first Patriarch of the Sakya, Ngawang Kunga (*Nga dbang kun dga' theg chen dpal bar phrin las sems dpal dbang*) (b. 1945). Most of her students are not Tibetan but Westerners interested in studying the teachings of her school and venturing into its religious and meditative practices. For decades, Jetsunma

Luding has worked as a seamstress by day while continuing the spiritual practices she had cultivated earlier. She still gets up every day at 4:30 in the morning and teaches on evenings and weekends.

As we shall see, Tibetan religions[2] in British Columbia were "imported" by families to Canada as a cultural product of a specific ethnic community. The ritual practices and beliefs associated with their land of origin continue to be important in the daily lives of members of the Tibetan community, but the community was not purposefully or even wholly instrumental in the spread and adoption of their religions by Canadians. Other factors contributed more significantly to this.

The spread and establishment of the Land of Snows's religions, chiefly Buddhism, was a gradual process that has evolved over the last thirty years. Two factors may have contributed to the initial progress in North America. The first was the romantic image that people in the West had of Tibet as a forgotten Shangri-La, an image that was sustained and popularized by the accounts of adventurers and travellers, such as Alexandra David-Neel, and former British officers who visited Tibet, such as Augustin Waddell. Later writers in other genres, including mystics (Theosophical Society, Lobsang Rampa, etc.) and travel writers, further contributed to the spread of these very Western cultural ideas in the public's imagination. Issues and implications of these phenomena are discussed by Donald Lopez in his *Prisoners of Shangri-La*.[3]

The second factor was the diffusion of Buddhism to North America, where it became a countercultural icon in the late 1960s and early 1970s. This phenomenon was not restricted to Buddhism but touched other Indian religious traditions as well, as discussed in Chapter 1. Popular heroes, writers, and poets of the counterculture began to study Buddhism with the misconceptions, shared by many, that viewed it as a philosophy rather than a religion. It was with this misunderstanding, which some attribute to Protestantism and its disregard for ritual,[4] that a young Tibetan Tulku,[5] Chogyam Trungpa (1940-87), began to spread Buddhism in North America, the Tibetan Way. Trungpa associated with popular persons of the time, such as the poet and activist Allen Ginsberg (1926-97), and other influential intellectuals, such as Anne Waldman (b. 1945) and William S. Burroughs (1914-97). As noted in Chapter 1, the interest in intellectual countercultural movements in North America in the 1970s coincided with an increase in immigration from Southeast Asia, which also brought Tibetan refugees to Canada. Trungpa's understanding of the psychology and culture of young North American intellectuals helped him present Tibetan Buddhist ideas and institutions in a format inspiring enough to cause a vast number of students to flock to him and adhere to his organization. The Shambhala Organization, formerly known as the Vajradhatu (its centres being named Dharmadhatu) is one of the oldest and most influential Tibetan Buddhist societies in the West, with branches, centres, and offices in most major North American cities. Its headquarters in Nova Scotia oversees 150 centres worldwide, 30 of them in Canada. Its Vancouver branch opened in the early 1970s and contributed significantly to the spread and continued presence of Tibetan Buddhism in British Columbia. Tibetan religions are important within the Buddhist world of the province. A little over one-third of all its Buddhist centres are of Tibetan persuasion, and several Western Buddhist and non-Buddhist organizations (i.e., non-Tibetan or without an Asian lineage) have adopted Tibetan techniques of meditation within the curriculum of their regular practices.[6]

The initial spread of Buddhism in the West was linked to the sustained visits of Tibetan religious figures from the community in exile, but since the liberalization of religious practice in China, beginning in the late 1980s, and the revival of Tibetan culture, a wave of new lamas has begun to change significantly the dynamics of Tibetan religions in British Columbia. Until very recently, Tibetan masters from territories within the borders of present-day China were not able to travel overseas. Today, however, Han Chinese patrons, both in China and abroad, provide financial support to monasteries and institutions in Tibetan areas and invite their masters to come to Canada, to stay permanently or to establish a dharma centre. This has revitalized monastic life in Tibetan territories. For Tibet-born lamas, it also brings new possibilities for true improvement of their current conditions and social standing. Vancouver is now visited regularly by Tibetan masters from Golok (*mgo log*; Ch. *guoluo*) and other Tibetan territories. Many of these lamas have either an excellent command of Chinese or attendants who are fully conversant in that language; in some cases, their teachings are translated into English.

Given the complexity of the phenomena and the changes still taking place today, I will introduce the British Columbia scene using categories unique to Tibetan religions, focusing on the implantation of Tibetan Buddhist lineages and schools in the Greater Vancouver area as well as the province at large. It is not exhaustive because these communities and their centres continue to move, some are dissolved, new ones are created, and others branch out. The popularity of Tibetan religions in Canada and the rest of the world is such that many of these organizations will continue to exist and thrive. I will also attempt to interpret the social and religious significance of these phenomena, and will discuss the broader implications of this research for future studies. I will first introduce the topic of lineage demarcations and types, and then proceed to the complex syncretism of these organizations, which use teachings, tenets, and practices from other lineages or sublineages of Tibetan Buddhism.

The general sectarian divisions in which Tibetan religions are typically placed are:[7]

- those of the Bön (*bon*) traditions (of which there are at least two main movements in contemporary Tibet – see below) associated with the kings of pre-Buddhist Tibet[8]
- the Nyingmapa (*rnying ma pa*), the "[Followers of the] Old [tradition of Buddhism]," established during the first spread of the dharma in Tibet (sixth to eighth centuries CE)[9]
- the Sakya (*sa skya*) School, which has recorded transmissions of teachings from the first spread of the dharma and continued to incorporate later transmissions from India until the late thirteenth century[10]
- those under the generic term "Kagyü School," which is one of the most popular outside Tibet and is represented by several important lineages and subsects[11]
- the Gelug School, founded at the beginning of the fifteenth century by Tsong Khapa (*tshong kha pa blo bzang grags pa*) (1357-1419) and to which the present fourteenth Dalai Lama (b. 1935) belongs; the most influential school inside as well as outside Tibet.

The foregoing list of schools attempts to follow a historical sequence in Tibet. It does not reflect their chronological presence in British Columbia.

The Sakya School

The first important Tibetan Buddhist teacher to appear in British Columbia was Jetsunma[12] Chimey Luding (*'chi med 'od gsal rig 'dzin bhu-khri 'phrin las dbang mo*) (b. 1938). She is the sister of the present head of the Sakya lineage, holder of the throne (*sa skya khri 'dzin*) Ngawang Kunga Thegchen Palbar Trinley Samphel Wanggi Gyalpo[13] (*Nga dbang Kun dga' theg chen dpal bar phrin las sems dpal dbang gi rgyal po*) (b. 1945).

Jetsunma came to Canada in 1971 and settled in Vancouver in 1973. She was accompanied by her husband, Luding Sey Kusho,[14] member of a branch of the Khön clan heading the Ngor tradition, together with three of their children. Thus, both husband and wife are members of the Tibetan nobility, tracing their ancestry to one of the first Tibetan families to have embraced Buddhism in the eighth century. Jetsunma is the mother of an important reincarnated master of the lineage, Luding Shabdrung Rinpoche (b. 1967), who is not only continuing the family tradition of perpetuating the Sakya lineage within the clan, but also upholding the scholarly tradition of this sect in acting as a lineage holder (Sanskrit *ācarya;* Tib. *slob dpon*), transmitter, and instructor. As mentioned earlier, it was not until the early 1980s that Jetsunma began teaching and conferring empowerments. Her centre on Beckwith Street in Richmond is the site of regular practice sessions and empowerments. Her husband, Mr. Luding, assists while Jetsunma conducts the ritual.

This centre has seen its fair share of monks and eminent Tibetan lamas of the Sakya tradition. In all cases, however, the teachers are Tibetan, despite Jetsunma's having several advanced Western students who have followed her for well over a decade. The members of the Sakya Tsechen Thubten Ling Centre are currently working on several projects, including one to build a Sakya monastery to replace the centre. Another important goal is to have regular Tibetan lamas come to Vancouver to teach and train students. The centre also supports the construction of a nunnery in India and has a retreat centre on San Juan Island in Washington State. Regular activities include the practice of the Green Tara ritual every Sunday morning, which is open to everyone, and of the Feast Offering ritual (*tshogs*) of Vajrayogini for those who received the empowerment to the practice. Green Tara, a feminine manifestation of Avalokitesvara, the Bodhisattva of Compassion, is the protectress of Tibet. She is a peaceful deity and is propitiated daily by many Tibetans of all denominations. In Tibet, her cults are widespread and are as common as those of Guanyin (see Chapter 12). In China, Jetsunma is commonly believed to be an emanation (*sprul sku*) of this Buddhist deity, although she has never discussed or confirmed this belief.

One of the most important activities organized by the centre was the visit of Jetsunma's brother, the present head of the Sakya School, to Vancouver to confer the Uncommon Lamdre teachings. The empowerment and teachings on this seminal system of the Sakya took about a month and was conducted at the Asian Centre of the University of British Columbia. Over a hundred students attended the long ceremony, which is essential to enable one to practise the Tantric system for which the Sakya school is famous. Receiving this empowerment from the head of the tradition is considered as most auspicious. Students from all over North America came to this ceremony.

The Sakya Tsechen Thubten Ling is regularly attended by a small group of students. This organization is a branch of the larger Sakya School, and the teachings and empowerments are given by the foremost representatives of the tradition in Tibet. Those wanting to become masters in the tradition will seek to receive Buddhist teachings and empowerments from Jetsunma and the visiting lamas at her centre in Richmond. Although the general atmosphere of the settings is fairly convivial, the religious authority and pedigree of the centre's teachers makes this a place of religious learning sought not only by Western students of the tradition but also by Tibetans. The importance of the master's personal teaching and that of the spiritual energy transmitted through his master-disciple lineage in the Tibetan tradition parallels that found in the Hindu and Jain traditions examined in Chapter 1. For serious students of this form of Buddhism, fostering a close personal connection between disciple and master is considered a requirement for spiritual realization.

With the building of the monastery on the same location, the centre in Richmond will become an international landmark for the Sakya School.

The Kagyü Tradition

The Oral Lineage (*bka' brgyud*) of Tibetan Buddhism is a traditional lineage of teachings and practices that have come down from India to Tibet through unbroken successions of masters.[15] The two main streams of this tradition find their sources in Tibet in the saintly characters of Khyungpo Nanjor, "the yogi from Khyung po" (*khyung po nal 'byor*) (b. 984), and Marpa Chökyi Lodro (*mar pa chos kyi blo gros*) (1012-97), the Translator[16] (*lo tswa ba*). The first was a Tibetan yogi who wandered to India seven times in the pursuit of Buddhist teachings. The accounts of his tradition, known as the Shangpa Valley branch of the Kagyü, or Shangpa Kagyü, relate that he had four root-masters, two of whom were women who imparted to him the secret yogic teachings and practices that are characteristics of this particular sect.[17] This lineage has existed among the Kagyü at times as a distinct sect as well as an "insider" tradition, a set of instructions kept separate within another existing branch of the Kagyü. Thus, the Karma Kagyü branch, besides possessing its own sets of teachings and practices, also carries the Shangpa tradition in its midst. This lineage is among the most popular in the West because of the charisma of one of its lineage holders, the late Kalu Rinpoche.[18]

The second stream of the Kagyü is the most widespread, and became divided into many branches and subsects. Marpa Chökyi Lodro was a layman who travelled to India four times.[19] He associated with two main masters, Maitripa (fl. tenth century) and Nāropa (1012-1100), who conferred on him Buddhist Tantric teachings. Marpa spent about sixteen years with Nāropa, learning a host of yogic practices, of which the Kagyü have developed a specialty. In Tibet, members of this school will customarily spend three years and three months in retreat, learning the meditative practices of the order. Although rituals are important to the school for various reasons, the most devoted of its monks and nuns will favour eremitic life, and some will spend all their lives in caves, in hermitages, or in the solitude of the mountains. Foremost among their saints is Milarepa (*mi la ras pa*) (1052-1135), the cotton-clad Mila, whose biography has been translated several times into Western languages.[20] Despite major difficulties and obstacles, most of which were imposed on him by his tyrannical master, Marpa, Milarepa remained steadfast in his pursuits and focused on the practice of meditation to gain enlightenment. His story, popular in the West, has influenced and inspired a number of converts to Tibetan Buddhism. It is not uncommon to hear among them the name of Milarepa as a source of inspiration for their spiritual pursuits and practices. Many of these have embarked on the traditional Kagyü road to self-perfection and have become monks and nuns and have completed the traditional long retreat. Some are currently following this process in the various hermitages in North America, Europe, and Asia. Others have become full-time teachers and translators.[21] One of these Kagyü retreat centers was created on the summit of Mount Tuam on Saltspring Island in 1975 for such a purpose. This hermitage, Kunzang Dechen Osel Ling (*kun bzang bde chen 'od sal gling*), hosted the first three-year retreat ever held in Canada in the early 1980s.

Kagyü Kunkhyab Chuling

The first Tibetan Buddhist centre in Vancouver, Kagyü Kunkhyab Chuling (KKC) (*bka' brgyud kun khyab chos rling*), was founded in 1972 as the North American headquarters for the Kagyü School in general and the Shangpa lineage in particular. The late Khyabje[22] Kalu Rinpoche (1905-89), who is recognized within this tradition as an emanation of Jamgon Lodru Thaye,[23] was holder of the Shangpa Kagyü lineage as well as of many other teachings from the Kagyü and Nyingma schools. In his formative years, he spent twenty-two years in retreat. He followed part of the Tibetan community into exile and founded a new monastery in Sonada, West Bengal. Kalu Rinpoche attracted many Western students and was subsequently invited around the world to teach Buddhism, confer empowerments, and educate new lamas in his tradition. He established important retreat centres in France, and dharma centres throughout the world. The centre in Burnaby was founded with the help of Western disciples of this master, and has been operating under the direction of various Tibetan teachers, all of the same lineage. The contribution of this centre to the spread of Tibetan Buddhism in the Lower Mainland as well as to the rest of North America has been very substantial. Shortly after the creation of the centre, the master Tsenjur Rinpoche (b. 1939) became its first permanent resident-lama. Under his leadership, important hierarchs of the Kagyü School besides Kalu Rinpoche visited the site, such as the late sixteenth Gyalwa Karmapa Rangjung Rigpei Dorje (*rang byung rig pa'i rdo rje*) (1924-81) and other key figures in Tibetan Buddhism. The centre organized empowerment ceremonies, which are important in initiating practitioners into the lore and system of the Tibetan Tantras of this school. It also provided Buddhist practitioners and students with sustained schooling in Buddhist teachings, ritual practices, and communal festivities. The latter consist mostly of regular ritual feast offerings (tsok: *tshogs*) to the dharma protectors and to important tutelary deities (*yidam*), training in the practice of Shinay (*zhi gnas*), Calm Abiding Meditation, ritual meditation on Chenrezig (*spyan ras gzigs; Avalokitesvara*), and the Green Tara (*sgrol ma*). The resident-lama also provides tutoring and counselling for those engaged in the Preliminary Practices (*sngon 'gro*) and more advanced practices such as the Rite of Severance (*gchod*), the practice of Tantric cycles such as Cakrasamvara, Yangdak Heruka, and others. The importance of this centre is reflected not only by these various teaching and training activities but, most importantly, by the formative influence it has had on contemporary key figures among Westerners in their roles as translators, scholars, activists, and other professionals who have continued to sustain Tibetan Buddhism in North America by creating new organizations or supporting traditional ones. Most Kagyü centres in the area of Vancouver and British Columbia in general had initial relationships with the KKC, which housed Tibetan lamas for a time before they established their own centres, or served as a training school for new members before they branched off to found another Kagyü centre in the province.

Although the main ethnic background of the regular members of the centre has been North American Caucasians, members of other ethnic groups, particularly Han Chinese, have increased in number. This is in keeping with changes in Vancouver's multicultural and multi-ethnic population. More research needs to be conducted in this regard.[24]

One of the most important branches of the KKC is the retreat centre on Mount Tuam on Saltspring Island named Kunzang Dechen Osel Ling (KDOL) (*kun bzang bde chen 'od sal gling*). It was established in 1975 to serve as a training centre for those who wish to complete the traditional three-year retreat. It also supports individuals engaged in shorter or longer retreats. Regular activities, including children's camp, are organized during the summer. They provide a unique environment that fosters long-term meditative endeavour under the guidance of experienced teachers. While Tsenjur Rinpoche has been on a six-year retreat that will culminate in 2008, the resident-lama has been a Westerner by the name of Lama Tara. She was part of the first group of practitioners who undertook the three-year retreat in the early 1980s. On completion, she remained on Mount Tuam to help support and train two other three-year retreatants. She has now completed a total of three traditional retreats and is still residing at KDOL. This makes her one of the most experienced Westerners in the meditative practices of the Shangpa and Karma Kagyü (two important branches of the Kagyü School) in North America.

The three-year, three-month, three-week retreat is a traditional form of training in yoga and asceticism common to several schools of Tibetan Buddhism.[25] In the Kagyü tradition, it follows a strict regimen of gradual practices, during which students learn the liturgies and the ritual practices of the sect.[26] It culminates in the advanced yogic practices of the Six Yogas of Naropa (the Six Yogas of Nigumas, for the Shangpa Kagyü), for which the Kagyüpa (i.e. the followers of the Kagyü) are most renowned in Tibet. These are strenuous yogic practices that train the adept to bear the rigours of winter cold (Heat Yoga [*gtum mo;* Sanskrit *candali*]), to remain awake while dreaming (Sleep Yoga [*rmi lam*]), and other important and difficult exercises.[27] Although, in theory, one can attain enlightenment while performing these retreats, the first round of three years is, in practice, an apprenticeship period. For the serious adept, it is generally considered that longer periods of practice, such as six years or, better, twelve years, are more conducive to attaining realization.[28] The core of Kagyü teachings is learned through the three-year retreat. To become a lama (i.e., a teacher) in the tradition, it is mandatory to have completed at least one three-year retreat. To become a lineage holder, other requirements are necessary. These comprise the territory of reincarnated lamas (*sprul sku*), of doctors of divinity (*dge shes*), and other charismatic figures of Tibetan Buddhism. Although some Westerners have become recognized teachers within the Kagyü schools, none within this lineage has yet been recognized as a lineage holder.[29]

At this point, it is difficult to identify how other Kagyü centres of British Columbia besides the KDOL are indebted to the KKC for helping them along the way. Over many years, the KKC has invited several Kagyü and Nyingma/Kagyü masters to visit and dispense teachings and empowerments. Most have come and gone, but some who have come have revisited the KKC and eventually established new centres and organizations that are independent of the KKC.

The Shambhala Organization

The second oldest Tibetan Buddhist organization in British Columbia is the Shambhala organization, previously known as the Dharmadhatu (then also called Vajradhatu, founded officially in 1973).[30] It was created by Chogyam Trungpa (*chos kyi rgya' mtsho*) (1940-87), the eleventh Trungpa reincarnation heading the Surmang Monastery in Kham (Eastern Tibet-Western Sichuan). The Vancouver centre was founded at the end of the summer of 1974. Chogyam Trungpa visited Vancouver in 1975 and generated enough interest to attract members and new students. Later in the same year, the organization rented a fourteen-bedroom house at 3183 West 5th Avenue (and Trutch Street). Subsequently, the centre was moved to a private house on West 22nd Avenue, which received the visit of the sixteenth Karmapa. Following a brief move, the centre was transferred to the present location at 3285 Heather Street in the late 1970s.

The evolution of the Vancouver and Victoria centres (the latter was also founded in the late 1970s) is tied to the growth of the organization. As new programs were implemented by Trungpa Rinpoche in North America, they were gradually incorporated in the local centres. The dynamism of the organization relied on Trungpa's vision of how to import Tibetan Buddhism to the West. His familiarity with Western ideas and attempts to incorporate them in his methods of teaching and training made him a very successful teacher.[31] He did not hesitate to indulge in other Buddhist arts, such as ikebana (Japanese flower arranging), which were foreign to Tibetans but popular in the West. I believe that his most successful strategy was to include Westerners in his organization and place them in key positions. Also key are the ties that are still maintained with the traditional Tibetan institutions in exile as well as in China. From the inception of the organization, key figures such as the late sixteenth Karmapa, his present incarnation (the seventeenth), the masters of the Surmang Monastery in Kham, and other members of the Kagyü and Nyingma lineages have been regularly invited to visit and give teaching and empowerments.

The Shambhala organization is the largest group of Western Buddhists in the world. It includes many different smaller organizations, such as the Naropa University, the Dorje Kasung Organization, the many Shambhala centres and retreat centres (five in North America and one in France), the Nalanda Translation committee, and various art schools; and it also cooperates with several monasteries outside and inside traditional Tibet. The Shambhala centres in Vancouver and Victoria, following other centres, organize activities for children, the practice of arts, the study of the Tibetan language, meditation training, festivals and celebrations, ritual chanting, conferences, study groups, and a host of other Buddhist activities. The Shambhala organization is now headed by the eldest son of Chogyam Trungpa Rinpoche, a recognized reincarnate, the Sakyong Jamgön Mipham Rinpoche (b. 1962),[32] who is the holder of the Kagyü Shambhala lineage.[33]

Other Kagyü Organizations

Nalandabodhi

Nalandabodhi was founded in 1997 by the seventh Dzogchen Ponlop Rinpoche (b. 1965), who is heir to both the Nyingma and Karma Kagyü traditions. He is a graduate of the Karma Shri Nalanda Institute at Rumtek (Sikkim) (now the headquarters of the Karma Kagyü in exile) and has completed courses of study in English and comparative religions at Columbia University.

The Karma Shri Nalanda Institute currently coordinates related activities that include a translation committee (Nitartha Translation Project), a monastic university (i.e., a Shedra, *bshes grwa*), Tibetan calendar, Tibetan art (Thangka project), computer software (dictionaries, word processor, digital data bank and programs), and Nalandabodhi International, which is to be found in at least seven countries, with centres in four Canadian metropolises (Montreal, Toronto, Vancouver, and Halifax). The Vancouver centre has regular events consisting of the study of the Buddhist Path according to vehicles (Mahayana and Theravada), Calm Abiding Meditation (*zhi gnas*), Tibetan-language instruction, Vajrayana practice with the corresponding Feast Offerings and the Protector Propitiation ceremonies, and community events. Besides training in the

Karma Kagyü School, advanced disciples are also trained in the Great Perfection (*rdzogs chen*) system of the Nyingma.[34] The resident-lama of the Vancouver centre is Lama Rabten (*rab brtan*), who arrived in 2002.

One of the most important masters who comes to Vancouver regularly and is sponsored by Nalandabodhi is Khenpo Tsultrim Gyamtso Rinpoche (*mkhan po tshul khrims rgya' mtsho*), born as Sherab Lodro (*shes rab blo gros*) in 1934. He is a Kagyü abbot (*mkhan po*) and a fully trained master in the Great Perfection. He has given Pith instructions on Togal (*thod rgal*) and Trekchö (*khregs gchod*), advanced visionary practices of this tradition, to North American students, teachings that are rather difficult to acquire even in Tibet. Western students therefore have an advantage over many Tibetan monks in that, besides benefiting from higher education, they also have access to teachings that are generally restricted in normal monastic settings to advanced practitioners. These opportunities are often lost, however, to many of them who do not have the commitment and time or who have not developed the ability to benefit from the teachings and put them into practice.

From the very beginning, this has been a recurring problem for both Tibetan lamas and Westerners. The former, hoping to establish a support base of committed students and recreate monastic communities in foreign lands, were at first pleased with the level of instruction of their new disciples. This enthusiasm subsided when many students showed little intention of completing the Preliminary Practices (*sngon 'gro*), which are required for more advanced training in Buddhist Tantric meditation. The same students would request initiation into Tantric cycles without the proper traditional prerequisites, and would continue to discard actual regular practice. Despite this sobering resistance, some Westerners have learned Tibetan and have spent extensive periods in intense practice, thus fulfilling the traditional requirements that made them masters within the confines of their lineages. After leaving India, Nepal, or the isolation of their monastery and retreat centres and going back to a Western environment, many have had to abandon their monastic commitments for lack of a supportive community as well as general cultural settings that were not conducive to keeping vows of celibacy or wearing Tibetan Buddhist garb in public.

Some universities have benefited from these specialists, for many have since completed advanced degrees and secured teaching positions in such institutions. The general trend among Western Buddhists, however, has continued to be that a small core of students supports a centre with a visiting or resident-lama, attending regular sessions of practice and teachings; at the same time, there is a floating population of seekers who visit one or more dharma centres or monasteries in search of a spiritual master or a path, or just to learn more about Buddhism.

Among the problems faced by Westerners is difficulty in communication. Tibetan lamas operate within a system of cultural references that is mostly alien to their students. This has made it difficult for teachers to effectively convey their expectations to students as well as to fulfill the latter's hopes. Masters have also been unable to understand the religious needs of many of their students in a Western context, and consequently have failed to appropriately address some important issues regarding ethics, sexual identity and behaviour, and social problems within families, such as divorce, family dynamics, and others. Despite these incongruities, however, the most successful Tibetan lamas have been either (1) those who were able to adapt to Western culture and worldview, or (2) high hierarchs who came into limited direct personal contact with Westerners, maintained the distance of their rank, and used the same didactic methods used in their own monasteries. The latter are charismatic leaders who have been essential in attracting the world to their religion.

The Thrangu Vajra Vidhya Buddhist Association
The Thrangu Vajra Vidhya Buddhist Association is on Wallace Crescent in Vancouver but is currently building a Tibetan-style monastery in Richmond. For a number of years, the spiritual head of the association was the abbot of the Shambhala organization's principal monastery, Gampo Abbey in Nova Scotia.[35] The ninth Khenchen Thrangu Tulku[36] is an important Karma Kagyü master who founded monasteries and retreat centres in India, Sikkim, and North America. Although linked to the Shambhala organization, he has developed his own network of supporters and students and slowly built his association. He currently has forty-three centres, some of which are monasteries and nunneries, in fourteen countries. His influence is greatest with the Chinese communities in Taiwan, Hong Kong, Malaysia, Thailand, and Vancouver. His seat monastery in Tibet is the Thrangu Gompa in Kham, but he has been visiting the West since 1976. He has an important place within the Karma Kagyü lineage since he, together with the late Karmapa, was instrumental in setting up the curriculum of studies of the order. He has authored twenty-two books published by Namo Buddha Publications based in Boulder, Colorado and created in 1989, and his organization has published study material in the form of audio CDs and tapes, video tapes, DVDs, and print materials. The groundbreaking ceremony of his new monastery in Richmond was held on 9 October 2004, a few months after the Dalai Lama's visit to Vancouver in May. The association's hope is to make this monastery the official seat of Khenchen Thrangu Rinpoche in North America.

As mentioned earlier, the involvement of members of the Vancouver Chinese community has created a new dimension in the transplantation of Tibetan Buddhism to British Columbia. Relations between Western non-Chinese

Buddhists and Chinese Buddhists have not been entirely smooth, particularly when some empowerment ceremonies and teaching ended up being translated only into Chinese. The Vancouver Chinese community is a multinational one, with members coming from Taiwan, mainland China, and all over Southeast Asia. The language of preference has changed over the years from various Cantonese dialects to the now mainstream Mandarin. The latter is used by many members of the Vancouver and Richmond communities who are active in the association but speak English only minimally. It will be interesting to see how the association evolves, and how relations develop between the native English speakers and the Mandarin speakers.

Rimay Tsar Tsar Chokor Namgyal Ling Centre

Gyalten Rinpoche (*rGyal brtan sog 'dzin*) (b. 1969) is a newcomer to Vancouver. He is an official reincarnation from the Tsar Tsar (Ch. *chacha*) Monastery in Kham, in contemporary West Sichuan Derge Prefecture (Ch. *dege xian*), in the A phyug (Ch. *axu*) pasture land. He was identified at his birth as the new head of the Tsar Tsar lineage and was schooled and trained in Kham, at his monastery. This makes him a different type of Tibetan lama from those to whom the disciples in the West have been accustomed. He was born in China, trained there, and maintains his loyalty to his monastery. Although he has travelled on foot to Lhasa and Nepal, an epic journey retold in the movie *Is It Karma?* by Geoff Browne (2004), a local Vancouver film producer, he is not a member of the hierarchy of the Tibetan masters in exile. His relationships with them are yet to be determined.

Tsar Tsar Gyalten Rinpoche has been written about in the local Lower Mainland press.[37] He was the disciple of the abbot of the Tsar Tsar Monastery, the eighth Drubgen Tulku, Yizhin Norbu (*grub chen sprul sku yig bzhin nor bu*). He spent five years studying the monastic codes (*'dul ba;* Sanskrit *vinaya*), and he completed the traditional three-year retreat twice, which entitled him to become a retreat master (*bsgrub dpon*). It is not certain whether or not he acted in this capacity before he left on his pilgrimage and subsequent visits to Nepal, India, and Vancouver. With the help of Taiwanese patrons, Gyalten Rinpoche established the Rimay Tsar Tsar Chokor Namgyal Ling Centre on Millstream Road, in the British Properties area of West Vancouver. The centre regularly performs the ritual of Dharmapala Mahakala[38] in order to make the centre successful and to get rid of potential obstacles to its establishment. Regular teachings are organized, and include the practices of Tara and Chenrezig (*spyan ras gzigs*), both Bodhisattvas of Compassion, Manjusri (Wisdom), and Vajrasattva. Gyalten Rinpoche has recently published a book, an introduction to his tradition of Buddhism.[39]

The Nyingma Tradition

The Nyingma tradition has a strong presence in British Columbia, with over six centres and several Rimé masters incorporating practices and teachings from this lineage, as in the case of the Kagyü School. This school is said to be the oldest Buddhist sect in Tibet, and it traces its founding to the thaumaturge Padmasambhava (late eight century) and to King Trisong Debtsen (756-97). This division of Tibetan Buddhism was best described by Tucci,[40] and its traditional history by Dudjom Rinpoche (1991). In Tibet, this sect has specialized in the performance of rituals of exorcism, curing, and others with a "worldly" orientation.

The main teachings of the Nyingma lamas in the West and in the Vancouver area consist of training in the Great Perfection (*rdzogs chen*) as well as the practice of short Tantric propitiation rituals (Sanskrit *sādhana*) from the Terma (hidden treasure text) literature. To my knowledge, thorough training in the ritual lore of Mahayoga is not provided. This system of meditation emphasizes practices that eschew the performance of ritual and are grounded in the theory of "primal purity" or "primeval spontaneous realization" (*ye nas lhun gyis grub pa*).[41]

The Nyingma tradition most represented in Vancouver is that of the Palyul Monastery (*dpal yul dgon*), located in Kham (Western Sichuan) in the Palyul dzong (Ch. *Baiyu xian*). This tradition has re-established itself in exile at the monastery of Mindroling in South India, but contemporary masters are currently raising funds for and visiting the original monastery in Sichuan. Heads of different lineages have congregated at the Indian monastery and have visited the West, establishing centres of their respective branches of the Nyingma tradition as well as representing the Mindroling tradition of Central Tibet.

Many of these, particularly Penor Rinpoche (*Pad ma nor bu*) (b. 1932), current head of the Palyul lineage, visit British Columbia regularly. This master has helped set up several centres now headed by younger lamas. One of the latter, Ogyen Tulku (*U rgyan 'gyur med dbang rgyal*) (b. 1956), is a master of the Palyul lineage who also visits Vancouver regularly. He has established a centre at Oak Street and West 49th Avenue in Vancouver, and has consecrated the site several times while conferring empowerments and delivering a commentary on the Heart Sutra, among other teachings. The other master, Latro Lama (*bla khro bla ma*), is the resident teacher at the Nyingma centre on Blundell Street in Richmond. Both centres receive strong support from members of the local Chinese community and teachings are often presented in Mandarin.

Siddhartha's Intent and the Sea to Sky Retreat Centre

The last of the Five Great (Buddhist) Treasure discoverers of Kham and the founder of the Rimé movement was the master Jamyang Khyentse Wangpo

(*'Jam dbyangs mkhyen brtse'i dbang po*) (1820-92). He was influential in initiating a religious trend that successfully competed with the hegemony (religious and political) of the Gelugpa sect in Eastern Tibet. One of his present reincarnations, Dzongsar Khyentse Rinpoche (*rdzong gsar mkhyen brtse*) (b. 1961) is the founder of Siddhartha's Intent, based in Vancouver. Although Dzongsar Rinpoche does not live in Vancouver, he did settle in the Squamish area for a while, where he opened the Sea to Sky Retreat Centre in 1995 (construction began in 1993). This centre is still in operation and offers regular retreat sessions. The umbrella organization of Siddhartha's Intent has centres throughout the world. It produces tapes and teaching materials, and publishes texts (Yashodhara Publications in New Delhi), maintains a website (http://www.siddharthasintent.org) and a membership roster, and has diversified in producing and supplying dharma items and organizing dharma tours, fundraising, outreach programs, education, and others. It offers intensive retreats, study of the seminal texts of Madhyamika, empowerments, and the practice of Tantric *sādhana* such as Avalokitesvara. It is a far-reaching, influential, and well-structured organization that, despite having grown deep roots in British Columbia, has managed to remain inconspicuous to the local population. The present Dzongsar Rinpoche (recognized reincarnation of the late Dzongsar Khyentse Rinpoche mentioned above) was a student of the late Dilgo Khyentse Rinpoche (*lDil mgo mkhyen brtse*) (1910-91), a Nyingma hierarch and head of the Shechen (*Zhe chen dgon* in Derge Prefecture, Sichuan province, founded in 1735) lineage, which is one of the six main Nyingma head institutions in Kham. The latter was instrumental in first introducing his school to the West, and opened monasteries in France and other Western countries. Dzongsar Rinpoche (also known as Khyentse Norbu) is best known for his movie *The Cup* (2000), which won critical acclaim worldwide.

Lotus Speech Canada
Another disciple of the late Dilgo Khyentse Rinpoche who was a student at Shechen Monastery and is now heir of the Northern Treasure lineage (*byang gter*) is Changling Tulku Rinpoche (*gTsang gling sprul sku*). Although he does not reside in Vancouver, his organization, Lotus Speech Canada,[42] is based in the city. In 2005, Changling Tulku Rinpoche gave teachings and empowerment of the Vajrakila practices according to the Northern Treasure tradition. His organization planned a series of guest lecturers from six Tibetan institutions who visited Vancouver to confer further empowerments and give Buddhist teachings. Besides those from his own lineage, Changling Tulku Rinpoche imparts to his students the teachings and practices from the two main Nyingma masters, Longchen Rabjam (*klong chen rab 'byams*) (1308-64) and Mipham Jamyang Gyatso (*mi pham 'jam dbyangs rgya mtsho*) (1846-1912). Teaching

sessions are hosted by the Heather Street Shambhala Centre and other Buddhist communities throughout British Columbia.

Tibetan Buddhist Clear Light Retreat Centre

Besides Palyul and Shechen in the Kham area, the important Kathok Monastery (*ka' thog rdo rje'i gdan*) (founded in 1159) from the same region has also established a branch in British Columbia. This institution, like others that head religious lineages, specializes in the transmission of a corpus central to the Great Perfection system, the Longchen Nyingthig (*klong chen nying thig*). This system of meditation is recognized as the quintessential system of attainment by the Nyingma tradition, and is therefore extremely authoritative. As part of establishing its presence in Canada, two reincarnated lamas have regularly visited a retreat centre in Qualicum Beach on Vancouver Island. A third reincarnate, Tulku Karzang (*sprul sku skal bzang*) (date of birth unknown), a lay master, is the resident-lama. The Tibetan Buddhist Clear Light Retreat Centre (ca. 2001) regularly hosts the acknowledged leader of this centre, Lingtrul Rinpoche (*gling sprul ka dag chos dbyings rdo rje*) (b. 1955), who heads the Traling Monastery (*khra gling dgon*), a branch of Kathok, in the Golok areas of Northern Sichuan/Southwestern Qinghai. The second regular visitor is Loga Rinpoche (*bLo gros bstan pa'i rgyal mtshan*) (b. 1952), present head of Kathok. The centre has so far concentrated on the transmission and teaching of the Preliminary Practices (*sngon 'gro*), transference of consciousness, and other basic teachings of this tradition. It hosts regular activities for its members and newcomers.

Nyingma Buddhist Meditation Centre of Victoria

The Yeshe Khorlo Centre was founded in 1995 by Gangteng Tulku Rinpoche (*sGang steng sprul sku*)[43] (b. 1955), the present head of the Gangteng Monastery (*sgang steng dgon*) (founded in the fifteenth century) in Bhutan. Like other Nyingma establishments and lineage-holding institutions, this monastery specializes in the transmission of the rituals and teachings associated with the Treasure Discoverer Pema Lingpa (*Pad ma gling pa*) (1450-1521). As such, it has focused its schooling on prayers, meditation systems, rituals, and its unique practice of the Great Perfection. The centre has had several resident-lamas, including Lama Chhimi Kinley (*'Chi med sprin las*) (b. 1965) and Lopon Sang-ngag Yeshe (*bLo dpon gsang sngags ye shes*) (b. 1957). The former arrived in 2000 and returned to Bhutan in 2006 to complete a three-year retreat. Teacher (*blo dpon*) Sang-ngag Yeshe was schooled in Bhutan at a Drigung Kagyü Monastery and completed his studies at Namdroling in Bylakuppe, India, where other contemporary Nyingma masters have spent time. The centre organizes regular activities in both Victoria and Vancouver, and hosts the Gangteng Tulku Rinpoche during his visits.

The Gelug Tradition

This reformist tradition was founded in the fifteenth century by the Tibetan scholar-monk Tsong-kha-pa (*bLo bzang drags pa*) (1357-1419). From the sixteenth century onward, it became the dominant sect and held temporal power over the country until its ouster by Chinese forces in 1959. The present head of the Tibet government in exile is the fourteenth Dalai Lama, who has been living in Dharamsala in North India for over forty years. He visited Vancouver in 2004 and inaugurated the Contemporary Tibet Research Program of the Institute of Asian Research at the University of British Columbia. The head of the Gelug sect, a position that is held for seven years and is also living in exile, is the holder of the throne of Gaden (*dGa' lden khri pa*), the head monastery of the order founded by Tsong-kha-pa in 1409. The 101st head of the order is Venerable Lungrig Namgyal (*lung rigs rnam rgyal*) (b. 1927), who was enthroned in 2003.

With the establishment of small Tibetan refugee communities throughout the world, which were for the most part accompanied by a spiritual representative of the Gelug School, Venerable Lungrig Namgyal quickly established an international network of contacts. In the late 1970s, important Tibetan lamas began travelling the globe, imparting teachings and enthusiastically conferring empowerments. Consequently, the Gelug centres need not be numerous in one location such as Vancouver but can accommodate many students. These large centres provide entry for many Westerners, male and female, to the world of Buddhist monasticism.

Teaching activities are fairly standard in Gelug centres and consist of exposition of the Graded Path to Enlightenment as detailed in Tsong-kha-pa's *Treatise* as well as the shorter versions composed by contemporary masters. Although the tradition is fairly homogeneous and the explanations are virtually identical, diversity within the tradition can be found in its numerous Tantric lineages. The Nyingma sect emphasizes the study of the Great Perfection, the Kagyü, that of Mahamudra; and both require their students to spend a fair amount of time completing the Preliminary Practices (*sngon 'gro*). The Gelug, however, have different requirements, including understanding of the Graded Path, the practice of ethical conduct and morality, the taking of the Bodhisattva vows, and the practice of the Path of Tantra in a gradual manner. Masters will come to present teachings on Tsong-kha-pa's *Treatise*, then confer Tantric empowerments of the main Tantric deities of this sect. Some will spend a greater amount of time explaining the Tantric practices, with regular practice sessions held in the centres. These consist of basic meditation, such as *śamatha* (*zhi gnas* in Tibetan: Calm Abiding Meditation), the monthly offering ritual (*tshog*) to the masters and the Tantric deities of the sect, and practice sessions of characteristic Tantric rituals of the sect, such as Vajrayogini, Cakrasamvara, or Yamantaka.

The latter are elaborate ritual cycles that are believed to help practitioners attain enlightenment in this very body. They are complex systems of meditation that involve lengthy rituals of various sorts, the recitation of mantras, visualizations, and yogic practices in the more advanced stages of practice. Most of the rituals associated with these particular Tantric cycles performed in Canada are simplified. The same texts are also used in Tibet for those already familiar with their complete cycles or for those who just want to keep the commitment to the meditational deities.

Although the situation is now changing with the coming of younger Gelug masters, the original lineage of dissemination in the West seemed to have been associated with the reformist and polemical lama Pha-bong-kha-pa (*Byams pa bstan 'dzin 'phrins las rgya mtsho*) (1878-1941). His intransigence toward other Buddhist sects and his outright condemnation of the practices of the old Bön religion were reflected in his disciples' controversial practices and outspoken sectarian attitudes. Although his disciples' students have not, in general, continued this trend, some have carried on some controversial practices, which has brought open condemnation from eminent Gelug masters such as the Dalai Lama himself (see below).

Among the earliest centres established in British Columbia were those of Zazep Tulku (ordained name: *Byams yangs thub bstan blo gros*) (b. 1948) in Vancouver (Zuru Ling Tibetan Buddhist Society, registered in 1986) and Nelson (date not available). Both were established after the creation of the Gaden Choling Mahayana Buddhist Meditation Centre in Toronto. Zazep Tulku is the thirteenth reincarnation of Lama Chubdak,[44] a fourteenth-century Kagyü master and founder of the Zuru monastery in the Zadoh region of Kham. Although the monastery was originally a Kagyü institution (it has apparently been rebuilt as such), the eleventh Chubdak reincarnation (*Kun chog bstan 'dzin*) (1871-1934) incorporated Gelug practices and studies at the institution. Zazep Tulku has lectured and taught those for a long time. He has also taught extensively throughout Canada, and is probably one of the most well known lamas in this country, particularly in British Columbia. Although most of his students are Westerners, there are now an increasing number of overseas Chinese disciples from the Vancouver region who provide substantial financial aid to various projects in Tibet.

Thubten Choling Dharma Centre

A second important Gelug teacher who has been working for a long time in British Columbia, particularly on Vancouver Island, is Jhampa Shaneman (b. 1950), a British Columbian who became a monk in the early 1970s and spent a good deal of time in India. He was the disciple of the senior tutor of the Dalai Lama, the celebrated Ling Rinpoche (alias Thupten Lungtok Namgyal

Thinley 1903-83). He spent over three years in retreat on a mountain in the vicinity of his teacher's residence in Dharamsala. His spoken Tibetan is very good, and in his capacity as a translator and a facilitator, he has helped many Tibetan lamas, regardless of sect, to settle in British Columbia. Although Lama Jhampa has not completed a Tibetan monastic degree (*dge shes*), he has been authorized by the Dalai Lama to teach the various levels of Tibetan Gelug practices. His knowledge and understanding of commentarial literature as well as the oral lore of many practices central to the Gelug lineage of his root-master have made him a strong teacher in this tradition. Besides focusing his Tantric practices on the cycles of Yamantaka (Thirteen-Deity Circle, *dkyil 'khor*) as well as Pha-bong-kha-pa's Solitary Hero (*Ekavira*) form and Vajrayogini (*Na ro mkha' spyod*), he studied and wrote a book on Tibetan astrology that was published in 2003.[45] Lama Jhampa travels extensively between Mexico and British Columbia. He has founded three Buddhist centres on Vancouver Island, one of them, the Thubten Choling Dharma Centre, in his native Duncan. A Buddhist stupa dedicated to people suffering from sickness was built on the property in 1995. Besides teaching and supervising short retreats for students of the Gelug lineage, Lama Jhampa operates four different websites dedicated to various aspects of Tibetan Buddhism.[46] His contributions to the establishment and development of Tibetan Buddhism in British Columbia are significant. The fact that a Westerner trained in the meditative practices of the Gelug lineage has been allowed by an important personality of the Buddhist clergy to transmit the teachings is a landmark. Very few Westerners have established themselves as serious teachers and practitioners recognized by Tibetan lamas.

Foundation for the Preservation of the Mahayana Tradition
One of the early masters of Lama Jhampa was Lama Thubten Yeshe (*bla ma thub bstan ye shes*) (1935-84), a meditation master of the Gelug School who was a charismatic teacher to many Westerners. Lama Yeshe created the Foundation for the Preservation of the Mahayana Tradition in 1975.[47] This organization, headed by a student of his, Thubten Zopa Rinpoche (b. 1946),[48] has over sixty centres worldwide, six monasteries (Italy, France, Australia, India, and Nepal), and four nunneries (Taiwan, India, Nepal, and Italy). After the passing of Lama Yeshe, a young Spanish boy was recognized as his reincarnation. Lama Tenzin Osel Rinpoche was born in Bubion, Spain, in 1985. Although the Foundation has only one official centre in British Columbia that is located at 150 Mile House, its incorporation of Westerners as part of the greater Gelug tradition makes it an important and rapidly growing organization in Western countries.

Several smaller satellite Gelug centres have been established in British Columbia, but are not be dealt with here for lack of space.

The New Kadampa Tradition (NKT)

The New Kadampa Tradition, based at the Manjushri Kadampa Meditation Centre in Ulveston, England, is an important movement in the West. It was initiated by a disciple scholar-monk of Trijang Rinpoche, Geshe Kalzang Gyatso (*bsKal-bzang rgya-mtshob*) (b. 1931). He is the author of over fifteen books on Buddhist philosophy and advanced Tantric and yogic practices. The quality of his translations and writings on the Gelug tradition is such that they are among the finest expositions of this school's ritual texts in translation and path. He has created an organization that is essentially composed of Westerners, which trains students in the traditional Gelug curriculum of study and practices and also offers support for monastics and regular Buddhist activities for the laity. The organization has a publishing house (Tharpa Publications) and an extensive network of temples, dharma centres, and affiliated local groups. Most of the dharma centres have resident teachers (mostly Western monks or nuns) who conduct rituals on a monthly basis and provide teaching and basic training in meditation. The Greater Vancouver centre, the Tilopa Buddhist Centre, extends its activities to twelve locations, including Prince George. Victoria has its Bodhichitta Centre and Abbotsford its Dorje Chang Centre. The latter hosts the former's website.[49]

This important organization represents a landmark in the transmission of Tibetan Buddhism to the Western world in that it possesses a genuine lineage as well as a complete curriculum of study and practices of a branch of the Gelug School. Its students are mostly Westerners who take vows and contribute to the organization through volunteer work; they also make up the bulk of the support staff. The only other organization that parallels it is the Shambhala organization (see above).

Like the Shambhala organization, it is not free of controversy. The head of the NKT, Geshe Gyatso, ran into trouble with his own institution, the Sera Monastery, in 1996. In Tibetan religion, protective deities are regularly propitiated to help with the mundane aspects of religion. These entities are either local deities converted to Buddhism or subjugated spirits that are bound by vows (*dam can*) to protect the followers of the master's sect.[50] The cults associated with these involve daily propitiatory rites in order to "put in action" the activities of the protectors. One such deity, Dorje Shugden, had been handed down to Geshe Gyatso through spiritual transmission from his master. Heads of other sects of Tibetan Buddhism have loudly denounced it as a protector that targets non-Gelug sects and their adherents. This forced the Dalai Lama to intervene and forbid the practice of propitiating Dorje Shugden. The order was not followed by Geshe Gyatso, who to this day has not only refused to stop the practice but has also transmitted it to his Western students. This created a schism with other sects as well as within the Gelug community, since many of the latter's monks propitiated Shugden.[51] This is Tibetan politics, where religious discourse and practices are political statements. As we have seen, however, this has not prevented the NKT from becoming one of the largest and most successful Tibetan Buddhist organizations in the West.

Bön Religion

Tibet is not only Buddhist but also the land of the Bön religion. This religion is associated with the kings of ancient Tibet and has been practised continually, even after Buddhism became the state's official religion.

Today, the Bönpo are found in the border regions, where, before 1959, neither the Chinese nor the Tibetan government in Lhasa had much power. Bönpo lamas are considered ritual specialists par excellence in Tibet. They conduct rituals to expel bad luck, exorcise, cure sickness, and deal with other negative events affecting families. Despite this specialty, the Bönpo have monasteries where monks and non-celibate lamas study philosophy, practise asceticism, learn the various ritual traditions, and carry out the same activities that one can find in the competing Buddhist monasteries. The Bönpo also have scholar-monks who graduate with the degree of Doctor in Divinity (*dge bshe*), like their Buddhist counterparts. There are several important Bönpo monasteries in Kham and Amdo. The largest Bönpo monastery in the world, and now the most important of its main institutions, is the Nangzhig Monastery (*sNang zhig dgon*) in the Northern Prefecture of rNga ba (Ch. *Aba xian*) in Sichuan province. This institution of learning, which possesses a college for Bön studies (*grwa sa*) and a training institute for meditative and ritual practices (*sgrub grwa*), has the authority and the tradition of conferring the high degree of *geshe*. Its population of monks is over 900, and Bönpos come from the entire Tibetan world, including Central Tibet, to study and obtain this degree. From this institution, a young Bönpo scholar-monk, Geshe YongDong (*g.Yung drung*) (b. 1969), came to settle in the Comox Valley of Vancouver Island, where he established the Sherab Chamma Ling Tibetan Bön Buddhist Centre.[52] Geshe YongDong has written eight books plus essays and poetry (in Tibetan), and has established a curriculum of study and practice for his students on Vancouver Island. He has also taught at Vancouver Island university (then called Malaspina College) in Nanaimo and at different locations on the Island and in Vancouver, the United States, and France. He has well over 200 students, all of them Westerners, and with their help he has established a retreat centre on Gabriola Island. Over the last few years, Geshe YongDong has trained his students in the Preliminary Practices of Bön (*sngon 'gro*) in nine parts. He has also given a course on "Death and the Intermediate State," on the Great Perfection systems of Bön, and on the practices of the deities Chamma, Sipa Gyalmo, Sherab Marwa, and others.

He intends to invite other accomplished Bönpo lamas to the centre to help teach the growing number of students.

Sponsored by Thomas Kefferputz, a disciple of the Menri abbot, eminent Bönpo masters have visited the Vancouver region, including the thirty-third abbot of the Menri Monastery (*bkra shis sman ri dgon*), now located in India, Lungtok Tenpai Nyima (*Lung togs bstan pa'i nyi ma*) (b. 1927); Chongtul Rinpoche (b. 1967), a senior master at Menri; and Geshe Tsugphud, who graduated from Menri in the early 2000s. The latter has lived on the North Shore of Burrard Inlet for several years, and has been working in concert with the Squamish Nation on religious and spiritual exchanges. In 1994, Thomas Kefferputz also invited three members of the Squamish Nation to visit Tibet and several Bönpo monasteries.

Bönpo masters are relatively rare in Tibet, let alone in the West. Regular visits to Vancouver by the abovementioned masters and others will help make British Columbia fertile ground for the growth of this rare Tibetan religion in the West.

Conclusion

Unlike the religious groups to which members of the Sikh, Sri Lankan, and Korean communities belong, which are characterized to a great extent by the ethnic cultures of their adherents, Tibetan Buddhism has not flourished in British Columbia based on the recreation of a foreign culture and community in local soil but has depended on non-Tibetan adherents. Religion in this community is central to its rise and establishment in the region. Tibetan lamas belonging to the community in exile from their homeland were instrumental in starting groups and centres where Tibetan Buddhism was taught and practised. In the beginning, the vast majority of members and students in these centres were Canadian- or American-born and newly converted to Buddhism. Their enthusiasm fuelled the development of retreat centres, study groups, and organizations.

Since 2000, Buddhists from the large Chinese community in Vancouver have also supported the development of new leaders from the two Tibetan communities: the diaspora and the younger generation of Tibetan masters coming from mainland China to spread the dharma and Bön to the West. This has created a division along language lines – English and Mandarin Chinese. As is the case with other Chinese religious community centres (see Chapter 12), where an organization's sponsors are predominantly Chinese (either residing permanently here or travelling between Vancouver and China) and where the participants are also of the same language background, little effort is made to involve non-Chinese members. The same is true of Chinese Christian churches that are self-sufficient (Chapter 11). These findings may help demonstrate how segments of the Chinese community are still largely dependent on overseas support, and may also point to the social functions of such religious organizations that provide networks for Chinese speakers who speak no English. The Tibetan Buddhist community is also relatively fragmented. Groups operate independently for the most part, although a number of students attend empowerments and teaching sessions at other centres when an eminent master visits the region. There is also a population of eclectics who, in the spirit of Buddhist ecumenism, associate with different groups. In the long run, however, serious students will usually focus their practice by choosing one root-guru with whom they will establish a lifelong relationship.

This fragmentation of the Tibetan Buddhist community nurtures sectarianism, which is quite apparent with some students. This may or may not reflect the student's perception of his or her master's attitude toward other groups, but it reflects a tendency in Tibet for sectarian boundaries to be important, despite the Buddhist faith's general claim to impartiality with regard to sects, creed, family clans, and communities. Tolerance is definitely a common characteristic of most members of a Buddhist group with regard to others of the same faith. Although violence has not yet manifested itself, public protests over the New Kadampa Tradition's propitiation of the deity Dorje Shugden have made news around the world.

Fragmentation within the same sect is also common. Tibetan religions emphasize the primacy of the guru, and this has led to the creation of groups within groups and factions. In Tibet, where the Non-Sectarian School (*rigs med*), an ecumenical movement that practises and accepts teachings from all lineages of Tibetan Buddhism, is prominent, this has been demonstrated by the multiplicity of sects, monastery traditions, and lineages. In regions where the Gelug sect is dominant, such as Central Tibet, this fragmentation was created when people followed one master at the expense of another. Hence, even within a single monastery such as Drepung or Sera, disciples will study almost exclusively with one master and his major students.[53] The resulting factions within monasteries have sometime erupted in riots and violence.

The single most important problem involving those Westerners who have taken monastic vows is how they are to be supported. Many former monks and nuns have had to "give back" their vows because there was no support, monastic precinct, and monetary help in Canada to enable them to continue. The projected creation of two monasteries in British Columbia (one Sakya and the other Kagyü) will certainly help. It is not certain, however, that this help will benefit Western monks and nuns and that the monasteries will not become havens for Tibetan monastics in exile. The two organizations that have been most successful and reliable in regard to helping Western monks and nuns are those that have empowered Westerners to become representatives of their tradition – the Shambhala organization and the New Kadampa Tradition. Both

have had their share of controversies, and one wonders whether
in Tibetan society is often found in the ambit of religion, is not
issues. This will need to be investigated further.

The dominant organizations in Vancouver are Shambhala, t
Kagyü groups, the NKT, and Zuru Ling. The new organizations that have sprung up from the Chinese community, although popular and influential in their own milieu, have yet to prove themselves. Restriction of the language of instruction to Mandarin will contribute to their isolation from Western Buddhists who do not know the language, and may lead to the marginalization of these organizations. Only time will tell how the local scene will evolve in British Columbia.

Notes

1 The Tibetan transliteration scheme used in this chapter will follow the Standard Extended Wylie system and will not be preceded by any other indications. Chinese transliteration will follow standard Pinyin with "Ch." preceding the entry.
2 There are a number of different religions and popular cults in Tibet. The latter are only beginning to be studied. After the five main schools of Buddhism and their numerous subsects, the most important denomination is Bön, a religion associated with the early kings of Tibet. There are also a number of Tibetan Muslims. Although there has been and still is intense proselytizing by different Christian groups, the number of Tibetan converts to Christianity is unknown. See Abdul Wahid Radhu, *Islam in Tibet: Tibetan Caravans* (Louisville, Kentucky: Fons Vitae, 1997), and Marku Tsering, *Sharing Christ in the Tibetan Buddhist World*, 2nd ed. (Upper Darby, PA: Interserve USA for Tibet Press, 1997). Two Tibetan religions have been imported into British Columbia, Buddhism and Bön.
3 Donald S. Lopez Jr., *Prisoners of Shangri-La: Tibetan Buddhism and the West* (Chicago: University of Chicago Press, 1998).
4 Gregory Schopen, *Bones, Stones, and Buddhist Monks: Collected Papers on the Archaeology, Epigraphy, and Texts of Monastic Buddhism in India* (Honolulu: University of Hawai'i Press, 1997).
5 Tulku (*sprul sku*), literally "magical body," is a recognized status in Tibetan traditional society. It denotes a person to whom is attributed a past life in the person of a former saint who has deliberately reincarnated into the body of the present holder of the title. This title involves important social benefits, from ownership of vast monastic estates, records, and treasures, to facilitated access to elite education and political position. See Melvyn C. Goldstein, "The Circulation of Estates in Tibet: Reincarnation, Land and Politics," *Journal of Asian Studies* 32, 3 (1973): 445-55. For a Tibetan guide to recognizing reincarnation, see Jamgon Kongtrul Lodrö Tayé (Ngawang Zangpo), *Enthronement: The Recognition of the Reincarnate Masters of Tibet and the Himalayas,* trans. Hugh Leslie Thompson (Ithaca, NY: Snow Lion Publications, 1997).
6 Friends of the Buddhist Order, founded by a Western Buddhist, Sangharakshita (Dennis Lingwood, b. 1925), uses practices from the Gelug and Nyingma schools such as Refuge Tree visualizations, ritual to Tara, and other characteristically Tibetan Buddhist techniques. Among his Tibetan masters, Sangharakshita counts the late Dhardo Rinpoche (*thub bstan lhun grubs legs sangs*) (1917-90), Chatral Sangye Dorje (*bya bral sangs rgyas rdo rje*) (b. 1913), Dilgo Khyentse Rinpoche (*dil mgo mkhyen brtse*) (1910-91), and Dudjom Rinpoche (*bdud 'joms 'jigs 'bral ye shes rdo rje*) (1904-85).

in this chapter, the terms "sect," "sectarian," and "cult" are used without their pejorative connotations. "Sect" and "sectarian" refer to a particular school or branch of a traditional Tibetan religious organization that conceives of itself as different and separate from other religions (such as Bön, Daoism, local cults) or co-religionists. These sects may or may not have a unique corpus of writing of its main scholars or founders. The word "cult" refers to a set of distinctive ritual practices organized within the broader corpus of religious teachings. The Tantric cycles of Vajrakila or Hevajra, for instance, are good examples of this use of the word.

8 See Karmay's 1972 translation of Shardza Trashi Gyaltsen for a good introduction to the history of Bön: Samten Gyeltsen Karmay, *A Treasury of Good Sayings: A Tibetan History of Bon* (reprint) (Delhi: Motilal Barnasidass, 2001).
9 See Dudjom Rinpoche's history of early Buddhism in Tibet: Dudjom Rinpoche Jikdrel Yeshe Dorje, *The Nyingma School of Tibetan Buddhism: Its Fundamentals and History* (Boston: Wisdom Publications, 1991).
10 For an introduction to the history of the Sakya lineage, see Chogay Trichen, *The History of the Sakya Tradition* (Bristol, UK: Ganesha Press, 1983).
11 For a very general history of the Kagyü, see Victoria Huckenpahler, ed., and Khenpo Könchog Gyaltsen, trans., *The Great Kagyü Masters: The Golden Lineage Treasury* (Ithaca, NY: Snow Lion Publications, 1990). To my knowledge, most of the above schools still lack critical appraisals of their social and political history.
12 "Jetsunma" (*rje btsun ma*) is an honorific title commonly used among Tibetans and now increasingly by Westerners, such as Rinpoche (Precious). In ancient Tibet, it was used for addressing superiors, whether they were religious or political figures. Today, it is used almost exclusively to denote reincarnated masters or lineage holders.
13 A brief bibliography is available through the official website of Jetsunma's centre, at http://sakya.thinkbig.ca/lama-trizin.html.
14 His personal name is Rinchen Luding. "Kusho" (*sku gzhogs*) is another honorific title, mundane in orientation but also used for monks or religious figures of a lesser degree than a *rinpoche*. His brother was the head of the Ngor Monastery's Sakya lineage, the Luding Khen (*mkhan*) Rinpoche. The son of Luding and Jetsuma is the successor and present holder of the throne of the Ngor Monastery. He occupies one of the most senior posts in the Sakya order. His monastery has well over a hundred branch temples and monasteries.
15 For a brief introduction to the various sects of this school, consult Tulku Thondup Rinpoche, *Buddhist Civilization in Tibet* (London: Routledge and Kegan Paul, 1987), 48-56.
16 This branch is also commonly known as the Dagpo (*dvags po*) Kagyü, from the main disciple of Marpa, who was a scholar and physician from the Dagpo Valley (*dvags po lha rje*). He was also known as Gampopa (1079-1153): Jampa MacKenzie Stewart, *The Life of Gampopa: The Incomparable Dharma Lord of Tibet* (Ithaca, NY: Snow Lion Publications, 1995).
17 For biographical details of the Shangpa lineage, see Nicole Riggs, trans., *Like an Illusion: Lives of the Shangpa Kagyü Masters* (Newport, UK: Dharma Cloud Press, 2002).
18 Kalu Rinpoche (*Kar ma rang byung kun khyab phrin las*) (1905-89). See a brief biography: François Jacquemart, *Paroles et visages de Kalou Rimpotche, Lama du Tibet* (Saint-Cannat, France: Claire lumière, 2003).
19 See his biography in Nalanda Translation Committee: Chogyam Trungpa, *The Life of Marpa the Translator* (Boston: Shambhala Publications, 1986).
20 For example, see Lobsang Lhalungpa, trans., *The Life of Milarepa* (Boston: Shambhala Publications, 1984); W.Y. Evans-Wentz, *Tibet's Great Yogi Milarepa* (Oxford: Oxford University Press, 1928); and Jacques Bacot, trans., *Milarepa, ses méfaits, ses épreuves, son illumination, traduction*, vol. 2 (Paris: Ed. Bossard, Les Classiques de l'orient, 1925).

21 Some of the most accomplished translators are from Vancouver or have spent three years at the Mount Tuam retreat centre. See, for instance, the translations of Richard Baron (Chokyi Nyima), as well as the new website for translators of Tibetan at http://www.lotsawahouse.org/school/index.html.
22 The title *skyabs rje* (refuge lord) is traditionally conferred on heads of spiritual lineages and sects.
23 'jam mgon kong sphrul blo gros mtha' yas (1813-99). See Richard Barron (Chökyi Nyima), trans. and ed., *The Autobiography of Jamgon Kongtrul: A Gem of Many Colors*, a Tsadra Foundation Series book (Ithaca, NY: Snow Lion Publications, 2003).
24 This chapter does not include any research on the ethno-cultural backgrounds of the participants at the various centres dealing with Tibetan Buddhism in British Columbia. It will, however, include general remarks on the nature of the population of regular participants. It is my hope that these remarks will be challenged in future studies of the implantation of Tibetan religious movements in British Columbia.
25 The followers of Bön also have several three-year retreat programs. Nothing has been published on this yet: Marc des Jardins, "A Preliminary Field-report on the Bonpos of Songpan," Master's thesis, McGill University, 1994. I hope to provide in the near future a descriptive analysis of contemporary three-year retreats in Bönpo hermitages in Tibetan territories in Sichuan and Qinghai provinces.
26 For a manual of guidelines and practices to be followed during the Kagyü three-year retreat, see Ngawang Zangpo, *Jamgon Kongtrul's Retreat Manual*, trans. Hugh Leslie Thompson (Ithaca, NY: Snow Lion Publications, 1994).
27 *The Six Yogas of Naropa and Niguma* has been the subject of several translations and studies. See Glenn H. Mullin, *The Six Yogas of Naropa: Tsongkhapa's Commentary* (Ithaca, NY: Snow Lion Publications, 2005); Tson-Kha-Pa Blo-Bzan-Grags-Pa, *Tsongkhapa's Six Yogas of Naropa*, trans. Glenn H. Mullin (Ithaca, NY: Snow Lion Publications, 1997); Dalai Lama Dge-Dun-Rgya-Mtsho, *Selected Works of the Dalai Lama II: The Tantric Yogas of Sister Niguma*, Glenn Mullin, and Zasep Rinpoche, eds. (Ithaca, NY: Snow Lion Publications, 1985).
28 Twelve years is a recurrent number in Indo-Tibetan Buddhist hagiographies. Many Buddhist saints of ancient India were known to have attained Buddhahood after the systematic practice of certain Tantric cycles, chief among them Cakrasamvara, Hevajra, Vajrayogini, and Guhyasamaja. See Keith Dowman, *Masters of Mahamudra: Songs and Histories of the Eighty-Four Buddhist Siddhas* (SUNY Series in Buddhist Studies) (Albany, NY: State University of New York Press, 1986).
29 Some schools, such as the Drigung Kagyü ('dri gung bka' brgyud), do not recognize even very experienced practitioners as potential masters. The organization is based on such a hierarchy to prevent any offshoots. The recognized reincarnated lamas within the lineage are the sole dispensers of empowerments and legitimate teachings. See John H. Crook and James Low, *The Yogins of Ladakh* (Delhi: Motilal Banarsidass, 1997).
30 The information came partly from current members of the Shambhala organization who have been members since the organization's establishment in Vancouver. I would like to thank Geof Bannof, Dale Timble, and Martin and Virginia Evans for their kind help.
31 He attended Oxford University from 1963 to 1967 on a Spaulding scholarship, where he studied comparative religion, philosophy, and fine arts. This no doubt contributed significantly to his understanding of Western culture.
32 Born Ösel Rangdröl Mukpo ('Od sal rang grol mug [?] po), also formal head of the aristocratic Mukpo clan. He was born in India and later joined his father in the West, where he was educated. He was recognized as the reincarnation of Mipham Jamyang Gyatso (*mi phams byams yang rgya' mtsho*) (1846-1912), an influential master, whose thirty-two volumes of

writings are studied by both Nyingma and Kagyü lamas. Right now, it is difficult to tell whether the Sakyong lama will develop his influence strictly in the West. It will be important to follow his career and the relations that he will develop with the new reincarnation of his father which has already been found in Tibet and the other Tibetan hierarchs of the different schools of Tibetan Buddhism.

33 This is a new lineage added to the traditional Trungpa tradition. Its source lies in the revealed "mental treasures" (*dgongs gter*) that Chogyam Trungpa began to receive during his retreat in 1968 in the Taktsang (*stag tshang*) cave (Tiger's Den), a famous hermitage of the Kagyü in Bhutan. The Shambhala tradition consists of various ritual and meditative practices along the traditional way of Tibetan Buddhism. The success of this lineage will depend on its continued use and recognition by other members of the Kagyü lineage such as the Karmapa and his senior tutors.

34 For some references on the Great Perfection tradition, see Samten Gyaltsen Karmay, *The Great Perfection Rdzogs Chen: A Philosophical and Meditative Teaching in Tibetan Buddhism* (Hanover, Germany: Brill Academic Publishers, 1989); Klon chen pa Dri med 'od zer, Tulku Thondup Rinpoche, and Harold Talbott, *Buddha Mind: An Anthology of Longchen Rabjam's Writings on Dzogpa Chenpo* (Buddhayana Series) (Ithaca, NY: Snow Lion Publications, 1989). See also Dudjom Rinpoche Jikdrel Yeshe Dorje, *The Nyingma School of Tibetan Buddhism: Its Fundamentals and History* (Boston: Wisdom Publications, 1991).

35 The present abbot is Pema Chödron (born Deirdre Blomfield-Brown in 1936), an American Buddhist nun, author of seven books, and a disciple of the late Chogyam Trungpa from 1972 until his death.

36 Karma Lodrö Lungrik Maway Senge (*kar ma blo gros lung rig rma ba'i seng ge*) (b. 1933).

37 Katharine Hamer, "Buddha of Suburbia: Tibetan Pilgrim in West Van," *North Shore News*, 17 March 2002.

38 Wang Yao, "The Cult of Mahakala and a Temple in Beijing," *Journal of Chinese Religions* 22 (1994): 117-26.

39 Kyabje Gyalten Sogdzin Rinpoche, *Hearing Happy News from the Dharmadhâtu: Teaching to Bring Understanding in Spirituality, Humanity, and Tibetan Buddhism* (Vancouver: Rimay Tsar Tsar Chokor Namgyal Ling Centre, n.d.).

40 Guiseppe Tucci, *Religions of Tibet*, reprint ed. (Berkeley: University of California Press, 1988).

41 Samten Gyaltsen Karmay, *The Great Perfection Rdzogs Chen: A Philosophical and Meditative Teaching in Tibetan Buddhism* (Hanover, Germany: Brill Academic Publishers, 1989).

42 Founded and registered with the government of British Columbia in 2005 as a charitable organization: See http://Lotusspeech.ca.

43 I have not been able to ascertain his personal or religious name besides this title.

44 His biography can be found on the official website of his organization at http://www.zuruling.org.

45 Jhampa Shaneman and Jan Angel, *Buddhist Astrology: Chart Interpretation from a Buddhist Perspective* (Ithaca, NY: Snow Lion Publications, 2003).

46 These websites bear the names of the topics to which they are devoted. They are: http://www.buddhistconsulting.com; http://www.yamantaka.org; http://www.vajra-yogini.org; http://www.buddhist-astrology.com.

47 See http://www.fpmt.org.

48 His biography can be found at http://www.fpmt.org/.

49 See http://www.meditateinvictoria.org/index.html and http://www.dorjechang.ca/index.html for the websites of the Victoria and the Abbotsford centres.

50 See the study by René de Nebesky-Wojkowitz, *Oracles and Demons of Tibet: The Cult and Iconography of the Tibetan Protective Deities* (London: Oxford University Press/Mouton, 1956).

51 On the history of this cult, see Georges Dreyfus, "The Shuk-den Affair: History and Nature of a Quarrel." *Journal of the International Association of Buddhist Studies* 21, 2 (1998): 227-70.
52 The official website is found at http://www.sherabchammaling.com.
53 Georges B.J. Dreyfus, *The Sound of Two Hands Clapping: The Education of a Tibetan Buddhist Monk* (Berkeley: The University of California Press 2003), 321-24.

10 Traditional and Changing Japanese Religions
Michael Newton

This chapter focuses on the Japanese religious organizations in British Columbia and the varied ways through which they entered and adapted to Canadian society. Among the first Asian immigrants to British Columbia, the Japanese have brought, directly and indirectly, a variety of religious traditions, practices, values, and beliefs that continue to influence Canadian society today. A number of these Japanese religious traditions have taken root in British Columbia, but through different routes. Some, such as the Pure Land Buddhist groups, have come directly from Japan, whereas others, such as the Zen Buddhist groups, have come indirectly, through the United States.

At first glance, the two streams appear to be quite different. The religious organizations that trace their origins directly from Japan have a membership that is largely Japanese Canadian. The older organizations played an important role in maintaining a connection to Japan and Japanese culture for their members. Groups that originated in or have a strong connection with a religious organization in the United States consist largely of non-Asian converts, and the connection to Japan and Japanese culture is much weaker. The Japanese Canadian religious organizations recognize that the traditional supportive role that they played is no longer as important as before, and are beginning to reach out to the Canadian community at large.

During the interviews for this chapter, it became clear that all the religious organizations face similar challenges, such as how to deal with zoning regulations, involve laypeople in roles that normally would be filled by a priest or minister, capitalize on the Internet as a way to become known to the public, generate funding, and train new leaders. Here, I will look first at the Buddhist organizations: Japanese Pure Land, Zen, and Nichiren. At the end, I will discuss some of the non-Buddhist religious organizations.

Jōdo Shinshū and the Buddhist Churches of Canada

Two denominations of the Japanese form of Pure Land Buddhism can be found in British Columbia: Jōdo Shinshū and Jōdoshū. Pure Land Buddhism is based on Mahayana scriptures and writings that describe *sukhāvati,* the Pure Land, as an ideal environment, created by Amitabha Buddha, for attaining enlightenment. The first Japanese religious tradition established in British Columbia was the Jōdo Shinshū (Pure Teaching of the Pure Land) form of Buddhism, also known as Shin Buddhism. In keeping with its focus on laypeople, Shin Buddhism's teachings offer an approach based on faith and a relatively uncomplicated practice. A Shin Buddhist should have *shinjin* (an entrusting heart) and recite the name of Amida Buddha (Amitabha in Sanskrit), the Buddha of the Pure Land, with deep gratitude. Once a sense of *shinjin* has arisen, all religious actions, including recitation of the *nembutsu* (mindful of Buddha) *Namu Amida Butsu* (Homage to Amida Buddha), are seen as expressions of gratitude.[1] In Japan, the Pure Land denominations remain distinct and separate from other Buddhist denominations such as Zen and Shingon, but in the Buddhist traditions from Vietnam and China, a range of religious practices are often found in one organization. (See Chapters 7 and 12 for examples of Buddhist organizations that embrace a variety of religious practices.)

The first known Japanese immigrant arrived in British Columbia in 1877. Immigration from Japan remained steady until the early 1900s, when the Canadian government requested that the government of Japan voluntarily restrict emigration. Immigration picked up again toward the end of the 1920s, then stopped during the Second World War. In 1904, a group of Japanese Buddhists living in Vancouver made a formal request for a priest from Nishi Hongwanji, head temple of Jōdo Shinshū in Japan, and in 1905 Reverend Senju Sasaki became the first resident Shin Buddhist minister in British Columbia.[2] In 1909, this group of Japanese Buddhists incorporated as the Nihon Bukkyō-kai, with a membership of around 650.[3]

Over the years, until the Second World War, a number of buildings were either constructed or renovated for religious purposes in Vancouver and the surrounding area, but with the invocation of the War Measures Act in 1942, first- and second-generation Japanese Canadians were removed to internment camps and the British Columbia Security Commission disposed of their buildings and properties, including religious buildings. During this time of extreme hardship, Buddhist faith and practice were kept alive in the internment camps by the dedication of Shin ministers and believers. Several years after the war, Canadians of Japanese descent were allowed to return to the West Coast, and in time, religious centres were re-established in Vancouver, Richmond, Abbotsford, and elsewhere in the province.[4]

There are seven main temples in British Columbia. Three are in the Lower Mainland: the Vancouver Buddhist Church, the Steveston Buddhist Temple, and the Fraser Valley Buddhist Temple. There are also three temples in the Interior: the Vernon Buddhist Temple, the Kamloops Buddhist Temple, and the Kelowna Buddhist Temple. In addition, there are several fellowships, smaller Shin Buddhist groups, scattered throughout the province. The temples are part of a cohesive and strong provincial organization, which meets twice a year and deals with common issues such as fundraising. Each temple is fairly autonomous in its programming and other major decisions, although the recruiting of new ministers is the responsibility of the bishop, who oversees all the Shin Buddhist temples in Canada. The British Columbia temples are also part of a national organization, the Buddhist Churches of Canada, and there is a strong connection with the Jōdo Shinshū organization in the United States, the Buddhist Churches of America, and, of course, to the head temple in Japan, Nishi Hongwanji.

It is not possible to describe all the Shin Buddhist temples of British Columbia in detail here, but a look at the two larger temples in the Vancouver area will provide some insight into how Shin Buddhism has adapted to Canadian society and how it is practised today. The present location of the Vancouver Buddhist Church is on Jackson Avenue. The Methodist church building on the Jackson Avenue site was purchased and renovated in 1954, and the present building was constructed in 1979. In addition to the *hondo* (main worship hall), the building also has underground parking, a gym, and classrooms on the second floor. There is no minister's residence, but there is a large commercial kitchen off the gym. The *naijin* (altar area) is quite traditional, with most of the decorations and religious objects imported from Japan. The *geijin* (seating area) is reminiscent, however, of a typical Christian church, with pews and windows. In Japan, the seating area of a Shin temple usually has either tatami or, in some cases, chairs, but never windows. Windows would be considered a distraction, drawing the believers' attention away from the *naijin*. Another structural difference from a typical Japanese temple is that the *naijin* is raised much higher than the *geijin*, reflecting the raised altar area found in a Christian church. The present minister of the Vancouver Buddhist Church, Reverend Tatsuya Aoki, commented that a highly raised *naijin* is not in accord with Shin Buddhism's strong sense of equality between the minister and the congregation.

The Steveston Buddhist Temple is located on Garry Street in Richmond, and there are some striking differences between it and the Vancouver Buddhist Church. Completed in 1963, it is a handsome and relatively new building on an open acreage. Like the Vancouver Buddhist Church, it has a worship hall, large commercial kitchen, gym, classrooms, offices, and parking. The *geijin* has pews and windows that overlook a large lawn. The *naijin* is quite different, however. The raised altar has a large statue of Amida Buddha and the altar area itself is spare, without as much of the traditional furniture and religious decorative objects found in a typical Japanese Jōdo Shinshū temple.

Historically, Jōdo Shinshū temples played a vital role in the Japanese community, both spiritually and socially. As visible immigrants or sons and daughters of immigrants, Japanese Canadians needed an organization and facilities that would provide safe and welcoming places where they could meet and socialize. Besides sporting events and dances, plays and concerts were held in the gyms, various hobbies and language classes were taught in the classrooms, and meals for large groups were served at various functions. The Japanese Canadian community has changed greatly in the past twenty years and temples no longer play a social role to the same degree as before. The gym at the Vancouver Buddhist Church is rented to outside groups, and the gym at the Steveston Buddhist Temple is used on some weeknights for community bingo. The temples all have active *fujinkai* (women's auxiliaries), which support the temples, organize events, and often provide food for special occasions. There are still social events, both events for the members of the particular temple and special gatherings open to all Shin Buddhists in the province.

The typical worship service performed at the temples reflects the influence of, and adaptation to, Christian society in British Columbia. It has many of the elements of a congregational Christian service. A temple member welcomes people from a podium at the front of the seating area and generally chairs the service. *Gāthas* (Buddhist hymns) are sung, incense is offered by representatives from the congregation rather than just the minister, a collection is taken, and closing remarks and announcements are made.[5] These practices are in addition to the *nembutsu,* traditional chanting of various Buddhist scriptures and a dharma talk by the minister. Although most temple members have Japanese ancestry, most are not fluent in Japanese and services are largely carried out in English. Parts of the Buddhist sutras are chanted in Sino-Japanese. Services are also conducted periodically at the Nikkei Home, an assisted-living residence for Japanese speakers in Burnaby.

In keeping with the tradition of Buddhism in Japan, an important function of Shin Buddhist temples in British Columbia is conducting funerals and memorial services. A memorial service is offered every month and is usually the best-attended service of the month. The service is dedicated to individual family members who died during that particular month in the past. The names of individuals who will be remembered are published in advance in the temple newsletter, and relatives and surviving friends are encouraged to attend the memorial service. In a recent Vancouver Buddhist Church newsletter, for example, around a hundred names were listed for January and around eighty-five for February. Besides regular services and memorial services, there are also special events such as New Year's Day, Shinran Shōnin Memorial Service, Buddha's Birthday, and Buddha's Enlightenment. The main temples offer Sunday school or dharma school for children and periodic classes and discussion groups for adults. There are also cultural and artistic activities that vary from temple to temple.

Jōdo Shinshū shares some of the problems affecting other religious groups in British Columbia. One that surfaced in all the interviews was a concern about the decline in membership. Among other factors, high rates of intermarriage for Japanese Canadians, lack of interest on the part of youth, busy lifestyles, and almost no proselytizing outside the Japanese Canadian community have resulted in a marked drop in both attendance at weekly services and membership. This issue is widely recognized and various approaches for dealing with it were mentioned in the interviews. One informant suggested that, although the temples have dharma schools for children, more educational programs should be offered for adults. Another proposed offering meditation classes and general courses on Buddhism for members, and also advertising these and making them available outside the community. Another suggestion was to change the general approach from one of passive participation, where members just listen to the dharma talk, to one of active participation by encouraging members to talk about their faith and be more involved.

Another issue is difficulty in recruiting and retaining ministers. Most of the Jōdo Shinshū overseas ministers, or *kaikyōshi,* in Canada come from Japan. The training of ministers involves *tokudo* (formal priest ordination), which must take place in Kyoto, usually after completing an undergraduate or graduate degree and at least one year of additional study at a recognized seminary in Japan or at the Institute of Buddhist Studies in Berkeley, California. Those training to be ministers must have knowledge of the Japanese language and competency in the various Jōdo Shinshū services and rituals. This is in addition to the academic study of Buddhism. Most ministers now also have a master's degree from a certified university. To train someone from Canada is an expensive proposition and few Canadians apply, so the bishop relies on recruiting from Japan after first trying to get ministers from the Buddhist Churches of America. Ministers from Japan have to deal with cultural and language difficulties, and sometimes must be willing to accept a lower income than in Japan. In addition, because of the shortage of ministers and declining membership, ministers often serve at more than one temple. Today, Jōdo Shinshū is starting to consider how it can reach out beyond the ethnic community. In August 2005, the head of Nishi Hongwanji, Reverend Ohtani Koshin, and his wife came to Canada to celebrate the centennial of the Buddhist Churches of Canada. Part of his message was a plea to continue to propagate the dharma in this country.

Jōdoshū and the Tozenji Buddhist Temple
Relatively new in Greater Vancouver is Jōdoshū, another branch of the Japanese Pure Land tradition, represented by the Tozenji Buddhist Temple in Coquitlam, a striking building influenced by traditional Japanese temple architecture and landscaping. It was built through the dedication and enthusiasm of Reverend Hashimoto Zuicho, a Jōdoshū priest of the Seisan branch of this sect. Reverend Hashimoto was invited in the early 1980s to give a lecture at a Jōdo Shinshū temple in Kamloops, and was inspired to create a temple in British Columbia by his interactions with a Japanese Canadian who had grown up in a Seisan Jōdoshū temple in Wakayama, Japan. Through his efforts and donations from his supporters in Japan, the main building of the Tozenji Buddhist Temple was completed in 1991.[6] Tozenji is the only Seisan Jōdo temple outside Japan, although at present it is not formally recognized by Zenrinji, the head temple of the Seisan Jōdo branch.[7]

Additions to the temple continue. A large Japanese bell and bell tower were installed in 1993, and recently a *Kannon do* (chapel dedicated to the Bodhisattva of Compassion) was constructed and a beautiful statue of Kannon installed. The grounds are spacious, with a large parking lot, ornamental cherry trees, and gardens. The main building contains a worship hall, reception area, offices, activities room, gym, traditional Japanese tearoom, and priest's residence. What makes this temple different from the Jōdo Shinshū temples in Vancouver is partly its Japanese aesthetics. The hall is spacious, and with its high wood ceiling and paper shoji doors covering the windows, it has the feel of a small Japanese neighbourhood temple. The main altar is traditional in style, as are the services. The outside of the buildings as well as the landscaping and gardens are also Japanese in style. Unlike the Jōdo Shinshū temples, which reflect congregational church architecture, Tozenji has the ambiance of a newly built temple in Japan.

There is only one part-time priest, Reverend Keith Snyder, and he does not reside at the temple. As a result, there is not the full program of services and activities that would be found in a Japanese temple. From the beginning, the temple has celebrated four yearly religious events: the Enlightenment Day of Shakyamuni Buddha, New Year's Eve, *hanamatsuri* (Buddha's birthday), and Tozenji Day, when *segaki* (the hungry ghost festival) is held. There is also a monthly ceremony in honour of the Bodhisattva Kannon on the eighteenth of each month, and a Buddhist study group meets once a month. Memorial services, baby blessings, and other ceremonies are performed by request. Like the Jōdo Shinshū temples, Tozenji offers the community a variety of cultural activities, such as Shorinji Kempo karate classes and the tea ceremony.

The temple is an incorporated society with a board of directors composed of both Japanese and non-Japanese members. Membership in the temple is formally around forty people, although many people, particularly Japanese from Japan, come when they need a service, even though they are not members. These services are offered on a donation basis. Membership is not solicited, in the spirit of letting people decide if and when they would like to join. Most of those who use the temple for religious ceremonies and services are *issei,* first-generation Japanese, who either have an ongoing relationship with the temple through its cultural activities or visit for a specific ceremony. Second- and third-generation Japanese Canadians seldom make use of the temple. Tozenji's sources of income include fees for cultural activities, offerings for ceremonies, membership donations, and donations from group excursions of Seisan Jōdoshū believers from Japan. This income is not enough to sustain the temple, however. Reverend Hashimoto has collected some funds to support its operations, but there is concern about how Tozenji can sustain itself in the future.

Tozenji is a new temple that offers a great deal to Japanese living in Vancouver and to the local community. In the future, Reverend Snyder would like to see daily services, more classes, and other events offered, and to have the temple open for longer hours. For this to happen, membership will need to grow to provide enough volunteer help, and another priest would be needed to share the workload. Tozenji is certainly a facility that has great potential.

Japanese Zen Tradition

The Zen school of Buddhism began in China and spread in different forms to Korea, Vietnam, and Japan. The focus of traditional Zen Buddhism is meditation rather than the study of Buddhist scriptures or devotional practices. In Japan, two denominations are particularly strong, the Rinzaishū, which emphasizes *kōan* study and the Sōtōshū, which stresses *shikantaza,* "just sitting."[8] Students meditate by repeating these *kōan* over and over, deepening concentration. The student presents answers to the *kōan* and the teacher judges whether the student has had true insight. In *shikantaza,* students meditate by constantly refining their awareness of the present moment.

Both traditions are found in British Columbia. In modern Japan, however, most Zen priests, after a period of training in a monastery, marry and provide pastoral care to the laity by performing funeral and memorial services for parish members. Zen Buddhism in the West has largely returned to a focus on meditation, not only for the priests but also for lay members.[9] Even though the two traditions maintain distinct institutions in North America, many Zen students practice both *kōan* and *shikantaza.* The Rinzai groups will be discussed first, then those belonging to the Sōtō lineage.

Zen Centre of Vancouver

The oldest Zen group in British Columbia, now known as the Zen Centre of Vancouver (ZVC), was formed in the 1960s by students of Denkyo Kyosan

Joshu Sasaki-roshi, the present abbot of Rinzaiji Zen Center in Los Angeles and the longest-lived Zen teacher in North America.[10] Joshu Sasaki-roshi trained in the Rinzai Zen tradition at Myōshinji, Kyoto, and he is still teaching at the age of ninety-eight.[11] Students of his have established a number of centres throughout the United States and Canada. In the 1970s, the Zen Centre of Vancouver was registered as a nonprofit charity and rented a house. Joshu Sasaki-roshi continued to visit Vancouver to lead *sesshin* (intensive meditation retreats) until the early 1980s. Around this time, the group was able to purchase a house to use as a Zen centre. Reverend Eshin John Godfrey Osho, the current resident priest, trained under Joshu Sasaki-roshi and took up residence in 1985.[12] In the late 1990s, the centre moved to its current location in Vancouver's East Side, near the Nanaimo SkyTrain station.

The centre occupies a medium-sized home on an average Vancouver lot. The main floor has been renovated into an open and spacious meditation room, meeting area, kitchen, and bathroom. Reverend Eshin and his partner, who is also ordained, live upstairs, and a basement suite is rented out for added income. The altar, at one end of the meditation room, is quite simple, in keeping with the rest of the room, which has the black cushions typical of Zen meditation around the walls and very little else to distract the meditator.

Since he arrived in 1985, Reverend Eshin has been leading all ZCV religious activities, but recently two other people were ordained by him and are training under his guidance. Over the years, the number of meditation sittings at the ZCV has increased. Today, there are four early-morning weekday sittings, two evening weekday sittings, and mid-morning sittings on Saturdays and Sundays. There is also a work-practice period on Sundays, when members help clean the centre or work on special projects. There is a full day of sitting meditation one Sunday a month. The ZCV also holds four seven-day *sesshin* a year. The house is too small for residential retreats, so the *sesshin* are held at a facility on Galiano Island. In addition to regular religious services, Reverend Eshin also conducts weddings, memorials, funerals, and ceremonies for particular reasons, such as adoptions or abortions. There are no special activities for children, who are welcome, however, on workdays and at ceremonies.

The ZCV is a registered nonprofit society with three directors. The centre's operations are divided into administration and practice. Administration is carried out by the three directors and others who have special knowledge or skills to help direct the society and make the necessary business decisions. Board meetings are open to all members. The practice area is Reverend Eshin's responsibility, although Rinzaiji, the home temple, sets the standard and ways of conducting practice and ceremonies. There are around thirty members who have a commitment to the centre. There is no active recruitment of members, so new people learn of the centre mainly through the Internet and the ZCV website.

The ZCV's main concern at present is finding an adequate facility for practice, a place that is large enough to hold local residential retreats and where residential students can live and train. The group had considered buying a property in the countryside to have in addition to the city centre, but decided that financial resources would be better spent on one larger facility in the city. Another issue is the amount of time that Reverend Eshin devotes to the centre. He works part-time, but as the centre grows and his responsibilities increase, the members may have to consider how to support him as a full-time priest.

Shinzanji of Victoria

In a large private home in a quiet area of Victoria is the Rinzai temple, Shinzanji. Founded in 1999 under the auspices of Shinzan Miyamae-roshi, the temple is run by Reverend Eishin Melody Cornell, an ordained priest and wife of Miyamae-roshi. When not in Canada, Miyamae-roshi teaches at Gyokuryuji, a Rinzai temple located in Gifu Prefecture, Japan. The *zendo* (meditation room) in Victoria is a spacious room in the lower floor of the house, with large windows that overlook part of a garden in a green residential area of Victoria. Shinzanji is a registered nonprofit organization of about thirty members, with a large mailing list of former members who have moved away but stay in contact.

The practice at Shinzanji is not typical of a Japanese training temple or of a parish temple, yet has elements of both. In order for the practice to be accessible to everyone, the temple has regular weekly sittings of two twenty-minute periods, with walking meditation between periods. Members can work on *kōan* and have *sanzen* (private interviews) with Reverend Eishin and with Miyamae-roshi when he is in town, but there are no long meditation retreats. Regular services are held, in which members chant in Sino-Japanese, and special ceremonies such as *jukai* (receiving the precepts) and *tokudo* (priestly ordination) are held periodically. Shinzanji has a strong social and cultural aspect as well. There are community hikes, picnics, garden parties, and a monthly gathering at a local coffee shop. Once a month, a movie with a Buddhist theme is shown and members discuss the movie afterwards. The temple also has ikebana classes, Japanese tea ceremonies, and pottery shows. Shinzanji also has a close relationship with the Victoria Nikkei Cultural Society, performing ceremonies for the society and sharing the temple space and activities such as tea ceremonies and ikebana classes.[13]

Membership fees at Shinzanji are nominal, and the group holds concerts and other fundraising events to help pay for Miyamae-roshi's travel expenses. Reverend Eishin describes the members of Shinzanji as quite close, like a family, which may make it difficult for new people to join. The group is exploring ways to be more open to newcomers, such as creating a buddy system or setting up a website. Its future direction will depend largely on whether Miyamae-roshi decides to reside in Victoria full-time or continue dividing his time between Japan and Canada.

Victoria Zen Centre
The oldest Zen organization in Victoria, the Victoria Zen Centre, is connected with the Joshu Sasaki-roshi lineage. It was established in 1980 when a group of people were inspired by a talk given by Sasaki-roshi at the University of Victoria. Today, the centre rents a large home on three and a half acres in East Sooke, about forty-five minutes from Victoria. Various programs and classes are offered both at the centre and at other locations in the city; the long-term goal is to make the centre available for residential practice. The resident monk, Reverend Eshu Karl Martin, lives at the centre with his family; since November 2005, he has been supported financially by the members. The membership made it a priority to employ a priest full-time to enable him to commit fully to the centre's needs, teaching and supporting the greater Buddhist community on Vancouver Island.

The Victoria Zen Centre has an innovative approach to teaching Zen Buddhism. People who are curious can attend a beginners' group at the University of Victoria or an eight-week introduction to Zen meditation, during which students are introduced to longer periods of meditation, posture awareness, chanting, bowing, formal eating practice, retreats, and what it means to join the *sangha,* or community of practitioners. Those who have completed this course can attend the Sunday sittings at the centre as well as all intensive retreats. Individuals with a background in another meditative tradition can have a two-hour orientation with Reverend Eshu instead. Private instruction is also available. The centre also offers a four-week course called the Fundamentals of Zen Practice, which introduces the basic teachings of Zen Buddhism, focusing on repentance, the three-fold refuge, the five precepts, and the Bodhisattva vows. Like many other Zen organizations, the Victoria Zen Centre offers monthly one-day intensive sittings, five-day residential retreats, private meetings with the resident priest, and various ceremonies, including weddings and funerals. It is unusual, however, in following a detailed fee schedule for most activities other than the beginners' group.[14] Membership is also organized into categories, each of which has clearly specified fees and entitlements.

Besides his duties as resident priest and Buddhist chaplain at the University of Victoria, Reverend Eshu is involved in inter-*sangha* work. He helps other Buddhist groups arrange venues for talks and assists them when he can through his position as chaplain. He sees his current challenge as developing two streams of practice, one for people with careers and family and one for those who wish to engage in residential training.

Lions Gate Buddhist Priory

The Lions Gate Buddhist Priory in Burnaby is part of the Order of Buddhist Contemplatives, an international organization focused on the practice of Sōtō Zen meditation, with monasteries, priories (local temples), and meditation groups in Great Britain, Canada, Germany, the Netherlands, and the United States. This international order was incorporated in 1983 by Reverend Master Jiyu-Kennett, an ordained British woman who had practised Buddhism in Malaysia and Japan. In 1970, she established a training monastery in northern California, called Shasta Abbey. Two years later, she founded what would become Throssel Hole Buddhist Abbey in the north of England. She taught and trained monastics and laypeople until her death in 1996.[15]

In the late 1970s, a group of laypeople from the Vancouver area who had been visiting Shasta Abbey regularly decided to form a local chapter. Priests from Shasta Abbey visited periodically to support the group. In 1984, the priory was officially established in Vancouver. The name "Lions Gate" was chosen to reflect the region without being connected to a particular city. Reverend Kōten Benson, the head of the priory, came from Shasta Abbey in 1986 and resides full-time at the priory. Today, the Lions Gate Buddhist Priory occupies a mid-sized house in a quiet residential area of Burnaby. The living room and dining room of the house have been converted into the meditation hall and altar area. The kitchen serves as a kitchen for the two resident priests and also as a communal kitchen for temple activities. The meditation hall is empty except for cushions and several small altars, and connects to the old dining room, where the larger main altar is set up.

In 2003, the priory purchased 160 acres of land near Lytton, and named the property Dragon Flower Mountain. Several residential retreats in this rural setting are held each year, and there are discussions about how to increase the use of the facility. The mortgage is paid off and improvements are gradually being made. This pattern of first establishing an urban centre and then creating a rural retreat facility is one that has also been followed by some of the larger Zen centres in the United States.[16]

The priory has a full schedule of services and meditation. Meditation and a short morning service are held most weekday mornings. On Saturdays and Sundays, meditation is followed by either a full morning service or temple cleaning and morning service. On weekday evenings, there is meditation and evening service or meditation and classes. The last Saturday of the month features a day retreat. Dharma talks and classes are given by Reverend Kōten at certain times, and he is available for private interviews. Besides weddings, funerals, naming of children, house blessings, and memorials, there are special celebrations for various Buddhist events, such as *segaki* (the hungry ghost festival). For *sesshin* (intensive meditation retreats), members usually visit Shasta

Abbey, although with the Dragon Flower Mountain property this may change. A wide range of formal and monastic Sōtō Zen ceremonies are conducted at the priory.

The priory has no formal connection with any other Buddhist group in British Columbia, but Reverend Kōten is involved in interfaith activities and occasionally gives talks on Buddhism and meditation to outside groups. Although the priory is incorporated under British Columbia's Society Act and has ten to fifteen people listed officially as members, there is no requirement to officially join the priory and very little encouragement to do so. Everyone is welcome to participate in the activities. Members are those who consider themselves to be members, financial or legal connections aside. Decisions regarding practice and services are made by the priests; other decisions about the organization are made in consultation with the members. The financial situation of the priory is precarious, but the members manage to support both the temple and the two priests.

Several other active Zen organizations, such as the Mountain Rain Zen Community in Vancouver and the Vancouver Zen Sangha on Vancouver Island, are similar in size to the Zen groups already discussed.

Zen Groups outside Major Urban Centres

There are over half a dozen small, unaffiliated Zen groups scattered throughout British Columbia, including groups in Terrace, Bowen Island, Prince Rupert, and Prince George. Generally, they are run by lay leaders with years of experience at a Zen centre in the United States or Japan. One such group is in Kelowna, where the Zen tradition is represented by Reverend Unzan William Bates. Another group, on Saltspring Island, was started by Peter Levitt, a lay practitioner. In 1986, the University of British Columbia received a donation of meditation equipment from the Sōtōshū-affiliated Komazawa University in Tokyo. Leonard Angel, then at UBC's Philosophy Department, now at Douglas College, and Shotaro Iida of UBC's Department of Religious Studies established the UBC Zen Society with the aim of introducing meditation to students, faculty, and staff and providing a place for experienced meditators to practise on campus.[17]

Nichiren Tradition

In addition to Pure Land and Zen Buddhism, which Japan shares with other East Asian countries, Japan developed its own distinctive approach to Buddhist practice, known as Nichiren Buddhism. The founder of this branch of Japanese Buddhism, Nichiren Daishonin (1222-82), was one of the most colourful and dynamic personalities in Japanese history. According to Nichiren, the Lotus Sutra teaches the only true way to salvation, and chanting the formal title of the Lotus Sutra is the sole means of attaining enlightenment. In Japan today, the Nichiren School is divided into several branches, of which Nichiren-shū and Nichiren-shōshū are the largest.

Nichiren practice and belief are summed up in the "three great secret laws." The *daimoku* (sacred title) is the practice of chanting *namu myōhō renge kyō* (salutation to the Lotus Sutra). This is chanted quickly and repeatedly, sometimes for hours at a time. The *gohonzon* (object of devotion) is a mandala that was created by Nichiren and has been blessed by a Nichiren priest. It represents the Buddha-nature possessed by everyone, and the three bodies or forms of Buddha. Practitioners usually chant facing the *gohonzon*. The third element is the *kaidan* (sacred platform or sanctuary), where the *gohonzon* is installed. Although the Nichiren School is not the largest Buddhist group in Japan, it has been very active. Shortly before the Second World War and afterwards, new lay groups based on Nichiren's teachings resulted in several large religious movements. One of these movements is Sōka Gakkai.

Sōka Gakkai
Sōka Gakkai (Value Creation Society) was founded in Japan in 1930 by Tsunesaburo Makiguchi and his colleague Josei Toda. After the Second World War, Sōka Gakkai experienced a period of very rapid growth in Japan, and today is the largest lay organization among the Nichiren-derived groups. SGI, Sōka Gakkai International, was started in 1975 to help organize and assist the society's international membership. In 1992, however, an ongoing and complex conflict led to Sōka Gakkai's and SGI's leaving the Nichiren-shōshū to become completely independent groups. The SGI charter states that it has a mission "of contributing to peace, culture and education based on the philosophy and ideals of the Buddhism of Nichiren Daishonin."[18] SGI is a nongovernmental organization recognized by the United Nations, and is involved in humanitarian relief, peace awareness, environmental protection, education, and literacy work.[19]

There was already a small group of Sōka Gakkai followers in Vancouver by the late 1960s, but in 1975 the group was large enough to rent office space at Arbutus Street and West 12th Avenue. In 1988, it bought land at Marine Drive and Cambie Street, where the present building was completed in 1990. The SGI Canada Vancouver Culture Centre is spacious, welcoming, and quite modern in design instead of reflecting traditional Japanese architecture. Although there are some hints of Japanese aesthetics, the design and layout of the building are more like a modern Vancouver community centre. This is in keeping with SGI's intention not to emphasize its Japanese heritage in order to make itself more accessible to people of all cultures and backgrounds.[20]

One point that makes SGI unique among the Japanese Buddhist groups in British Columbia is that the main place of group practice is in individual members' homes. Individual members belong to a district, which is made up of ten to fifteen members. District meetings occur in private homes and usually begin with fifteen to thirty minutes of group chanting of the *daimoku* and chapters of the Lotus Sutra before the altar and *gohonzon*. This is followed by another hour of activities, usually a discussion of a selected topic related to practice and life, with the goal of bringing the principles of Nichiren's teaching to bear on life in a practical way. A district meeting is also where non-members are introduced to the organization and its teachings. Its purpose is largely to help members support each other and promote deeper understanding of the teachings. From the beginning, small meetings in individuals' homes have been SGI's foundation; the rest of the organization is built to support the activities of these small meetings.

There are fifty-six districts in British Columbia, each with its unique characteristics. Some may consist mostly of immigrants or non-English speakers, others mostly of English speakers born in Canada. This helps to facilitate study and reflects immigration patterns in British Columbia over the last ten years. The ideal district, however, has a balance of men and women of all ages, and people from a wide variety of backgrounds. SGI emphasizes being together with different ethnic groups, although some gatherings of non-English speakers cut across districts.

SGI is also unique in that there are no priests; it is entirely a lay organization. Everyone participates as a volunteer, including those in leadership positions. Leadership at various levels is taken on by members who show enthusiasm and the necessary skills and knowledge. Usually, members are nominated by their peers for leadership positions and then interviewed by members of long standing to ensure that they understand the level of commitment and responsibility that the position entails. People usually come to SGI after first encountering it on the Internet or hearing about it from friends or family. They are encouraged to attend district gatherings or visit the main centre for at least three months before being considered for membership. Once a person is committed to chanting the *daimoku* on a daily basis, he or she is asked to fill out an application form and demonstrate some understanding of the practice.

In addition to the district gatherings, there are a number of other religious, administrative, and social meetings. There are groups for children and youth; a chorus; a band; a hip-hop dance group; a gay, bisexual, and transgender group; and groups that help support the functioning of the centre by taking care of cleaning and correspondence. SGI also works with other organizations to increase awareness of social issues.

One big challenge for SGI in British Columbia is the shift to a community-based district organization, rather than having members attend meetings in the district where they were first introduced, regardless of how far it is from their homes. The organization is asking members to join the district closest to where they live. This contributes to the growth of roots in the local community and encourages less driving. Asking members to change districts is a sensitive issue, and the leadership expects it to take six months to a year before members feel comfortable with this change.

There are also plans to eventually build centres in Surrey and other areas so that members do not have to come into Vancouver to attend larger events. Even more than the Buddhist Church of Canada, SGI has dropped Japanese cultural traditions to meet the challenge of practising in a Canadian environment. It provides a supportive and intimate environment, a wide variety of cultural and social activities, and venues where members can engage in activities such as environmental and human rights advocacy.

Nichiren Shōshū and the Nichiren Buddha Hokkekyō Dharma Centre

A Nichren-shōshū group is based at the Nichiren Buddha Hokkekyō Dharma Centre in Duncan, on Vancouver Island. Its leader, Mr. Henry Landry, is a recognized lay guiding teacher. He has been given the title *Ajari* (Communicator) by the High Priest of Nichiren Shōshū. The centre is located in Mr. Landry's home, and although the membership is small, there are various events throughout the week: chanting on Wednesday, meditation on Friday evenings, and a course called Discovering Your Buddha Nature on Sundays. A priest from Nichiren Shōshū visits about four times a year, and members may choose to receive Nichiren Buddhist precepts and take vows.

Non-Buddhist Organizations

Besides the Japanese Buddhist organizations, there are at least six Japanese religious organizations with a presence in British Columbia: Konkōkyō, Seichō No Ie, Mahakarikyō, Reiyūkai, Tenrikyō, and the Institute for Research in Human Happiness. Tenrikyō is discussed in Chapter 8. In general, all these organizations have small memberships of mostly Japanese and Japanese Canadians, but are looking for ways to attract members who do not have Japanese background. It is not possible to examine all the groups in this chapter, so I will focus on the oldest and one of the newest to provide an idea of the structures and challenges facing these groups.

Konkōkyō

Konkōkyō derives from the Shinto tradition and was founded by Konkō Daijin (1814-83), a farmer in a small farming village in Okayama Prefecture, Japan.[21] Thinking that he may have offended the deity Konjin, Konkō Daijin sought Konjin's forgiveness and, while in prayer, discovered that Konjin was a benevolent deity who desired to bring peace and happiness to the world. This deity was renamed Tenchi Kane No Kami (Golden God of Heaven and Earth, also referred to as God the Parent) and came to speak through Konkō Daijin.[22] Over time, Konkō Daijin became a conduit between villagers and Tenchi Kane No Kami, relaying their requests for advice on daily problems and activities and, in turn, the deity's advice and blessings. This was the start of *toritsugi* mediation, the act of mediating between believers and Tenchi Kane No Kami. This mediation became one of the main religious activities of Konkōkyō.

Konkōkyō believers first arrived in Canada in 1926. By 1929, there were two groups of believers, one in Vancouver and one in Ucluelet on Vancouver Island. Both groups were without ministers and remained independent of each other until 1939, when the Ucluelet group came by boat to Vancouver for the first joint service. It was at this time that an official minister of Konkōkyō from Seattle began to visit and hold services.

Members of Konkōkyō were sent to internment camps in British Columbia and Alberta during the Second World War. After the war, most of the members migrated to Calgary and Ontario. Only about 40 percent of the original members from Vancouver returned, which severely limited the growth and prosperity of the Vancouver Konkōkyō organization. In 1958, the Vancouver members formally regrouped under the direction of Reverend Fumio Matsui from Seattle; in 1966, they obtained official recognition from the provincial government. At the same time, they also obtained recognition as a formal church from Konkōkyō headquarters in Japan, and the Vancouver group became known as the Konkōkyō Church of America, Vancouver Branch.[23] The church did not have a permanent home but met for services at the Vancouver Japanese Language School. After a series of visiting ministers from Seattle, the Vancouver church welcomed its first resident minister in 1989 – Reverend Roderick Hashimoto, who continues in that position today. In 1991, the church purchased its first home with financial help from Konkōkyō members in Japan; in 2000, it moved to its present location in Vancouver, a medium-sized house whose downstairs has been renovated into a meeting area with an altar, while upstairs is home for the minister and his family.

The main hall seats around thirty people. There are two altars, one for Tenchi Kane No Kami and one for the ancestors of the members. A prayer service is held daily at the church, the doors of which are kept open for members as much as possible. In the spring and fall, large memorial services are conducted, but there are also smaller monthly memorial services, during which the names of people who died that month are recited before the ancestral altar. Reverend Hashimoto also performs funerals, weddings, groundbreaking ceremonies, home blessings, and car blessings. The main practices, however, are individual prayer and *toritsugi* mediation, when the minister relays the believer's words to Tenchi Kane No Kami, who then replies through the minister. Reverend

Hashimoto describes these mediation experiences as being very humbling, where he, as the minister, has to open his heart and trust.

There are around thirty families or a hundred church members throughout British Columbia. Most are in their late sixties. Around twelve people regularly attend the memorial services and ten of the other services. When Reverend Hashimoto first arrived, the numbers were double these, but as old members pass away and few new members join, the membership is in decline. This is partly because the church had no resident priest until 1989, so the children of the early members had no one to teach them and support them in the Konkōkyō faith. Reverend Hashimoto is trying to introduce the faith into the lives of the children and grandchildren of the original members in a way that is relevant. The church members form a close-knit group that survived as a largely lay organization until relatively recently, and there is reluctance to accept people who are not of Japanese background. Also, Konkōkyō is passive about seeking converts, although Reverend Hashimoto does offer *toritsugi* mediation to all who ask for it.

Institute for Research in Human Happiness

The Institute for Research in Human Happiness (IRH) is a relatively new religious movement in Japan. It was founded in 1986 by businessman Ryūhō Ōkawa, a graduate of the University of Tokyo. In March 1981, Ōkawa had a profound religious experience that led him to renounce his business career. Five years later, he founded an organization known as Kōfuku no Kagaku to promote his teachings and support followers. In Japan, Kōfuku no Kagaku has around twenty training centres and many branches. There are also branches in the United States and Europe, where the English name Institute for Research in Human Happiness is used.

IRH teachings include basic ideas from Buddhism but also the many writings of Ryūhō Ōkawa, who has published 400 books.[24] Some of the distinctive teachings include faith in the Eternal Buddha, Lord El Cantare, who is a guide of humanity, and a teaching called the Fourfold Path: Love, Wisdom, Self-Reflection, and Development or Progress. IRH teaches that through spiritual development, we experience happiness. The main religious activities include prayer, study, and meditation.

There is no permanent IRH temple or centre in British Columbia, so meetings are held in private homes. The husband-and-wife team of Tsuneo and Toyomi Yamazaki facilitate meetings in the Greater Vancouver area. The IRH group in Vancouver is small and most of the members speak Japanese. Mr. Yamazaki is very interested in having meetings conducted in English as soon as there are enough English-speaking members. As he points out, he and all the local members are lay members with jobs and families, and so are unable to commit to IRH work full-time. Most people come to IRH through word of mouth, although it does host occasional public events such as workshops and showings of IRH teaching videos. Occasionally, it sets up an information booth at large public gatherings. The Greater Vancouver members meet three or four times a month in private homes to study, discuss, and practise the teachings of Ryūhō Ōkawa.[25] Readings from the magazine *IRH Monthly* are used to generate discussion, and sometimes an IRH video is shown. Members are encouraged to study the teachings of other religious traditions and focus on how those teachings are interrelated. At home, members may pray using the IRH prayer book, study, and meditate to music.

IRH is relatively new to British Columbia and faces several challenges. There is no full-time leader who can ensure that IRH teachings and activities are publicized. There is no permanent place to hold and promote IRH activities. Finally, there is the challenge of language. Most members are Japanese speakers, although the Yamazakis are working hard to make IRH known to English speakers. If IRH is to become well established in British Columbia, it will be by increasing the number of English speakers and integrating them fully into the organization.

Conclusion

Given the extraordinary diversity of Japanese religious organizations in British Columbia, it is difficult to come to many conclusions that apply to all of them. Nevertheless, some issues and characteristics are shared by most groups. For example, all face many long-term challenges in building viable organizations. While the larger and older organizations have designated buildings for meetings and religious activities, and the smaller groups meet in private homes and apartments, all groups have to deal with the mundane issues of zoning and building codes. The smaller and newer groups struggle to find appropriate places to rent, since buying in hot real estate markets of Vancouver and Victoria is not financially feasible. Finding an economical space near public transit where public gatherings can be held is an ongoing issue for organizations that do not own a building.

All groups consist mainly or entirely of lay members, who are very much involved in the decisions and operations of the organizations. Organizational structures are egalitarian, with elected boards and various committees. Groups that have priests or ministers frequently divide responsibilities, with the priests largely in charge of the practice forms and teaching but sharing administrative and other responsibilities with lay members. Some groups, like Sōka Gakkai International, have a set of criteria for membership, whereas membership in other groups is very loosely defined. In many of the Zen groups, an individual who calls herself a member is considered a member, whether or not she signs a form or makes donations. For some groups, membership is a legal formality that is required in order to obtain nonprofit status but has little relevance in terms of participation in religious practice. Given that the lay membership, and sometimes the priests and ministers as well, have families and jobs, the ritual calendars and events are often adjusted to enable as many as possible to attend. For example, *rōhatsu,* the day commemorating the enlightenment of the Buddha by Zen Buddhists and traditionally celebrated on 8 December, might be celebrated on a regular meeting night.

With one exception, all groups surveyed are completely open to all members of Canadian society. In general, liturgy and the language spoken is largely English, religious texts have been translated into English, and religious forms and settings are simplified compared with those of similar groups in Japan. The organizations that traditionally catered to Japanese Canadians are exploring ways to make themselves more accessible to the Canadian public. No group engages in active proselytization, but almost all are welcoming of anyone, regardless of ethnicity, who is interested in joining. The organizations make themselves known through low-key advertising of special events, a listing in the Japanese-language newspapers and phone book, word of mouth, and a website.

Most of those interviewed stated that new members largely find out about the group through the Internet, where practically every group has a presence. Some, like Shinzanji in Victoria or Tozenji in Coquitlam, have a minimal presence through the website of the mother organization in Japan; others, like the Buddhist Church of Canada and the Victoria Zen Centre, maintain large and comprehensive websites with schedules, teachings, and links to related organizations. E-mail is used not only for practical communication among members but sometimes also for religious purposes.

The leaders and teachers of most groups come from outside Canada, usually from Japan or the United States. Even the Buddhist Church of Canada, the oldest and largest of all the groups studied, does not provide a complete training program for those who wish to become teachers or priests. With the exception of SGI, all the larger groups require that upcoming teachers and priests do some training and study outside Canada. Very few of the leaders of any group are originally from Canada, most coming from either Japan or the United States.

In contrast to the dynamic growth due to immigration seen in the Chinese and Korean religious organizations in Greater Vancouver, most Japanese religious organizations that rely on Japanese nationals and the Japanese Canadian community suffer from shrinking membership. Few people immigrate from Japan these days, and the descendants of Japanese immigrants tend to marry outside the Japanese Canadian community, which makes it difficult for them to continue in the Japanese religious organization that they grew up in. Those religious organizations that have fully integrated into Canadian society and do not rely on immigration to bolster membership, such as SGI and the various Zen organizations, are prospering. All the groups studied have, to a greater or lesser degree, successfully overcome the problems of becoming established in Canadian society. As acknowledged by their leaders, however, there are new challenges to overcome, such as attracting new members, developing and maintaining financial security, and training or finding teachers and leaders. Japanese religious traditions have been in British Columbia for over a hundred years; how they continue to change and adapt will determine whether they survive for the next hundred.

Notes

1 There are many websites and much literature in English published by Hongwanji International Center, Kyoto. For an academic view, try Esben Andreasen, *Popular Buddhism in Japan: Shin Buddhist Religion and Culture* (Honolulu: University of Hawai'i Press, 1998).
2 Largely as a result of adapting to North American culture, a Jōdo Shinshū priest is usually referred as a minister and the temples are called Buddhist churches, although this terminology is changing. Today the word "temple" seems to be preferred.
3 For a detailed history of Jōdo Shinshū in Canada, see Terry Watada, *Bukkyo Tozen: A History of Jodo Shinshu Buddhism in Canada 1895-1995* (Toronto: HPF Press and Toronto Buddhist Church, 1996).
4 For more information about this period, see Akira Ichikawa, "A Test of Religious Tolerance: Canadian Government and Jodo Shinshu Buddhism during the Pacific War," *Canadian Ethnic Studies* 26, 2 (1994): 46-69.
5 From Vancouver Buddhist Church – Family Dharma Service 2002/03 September 4 sheet.
6 See http://tozenji.at.infoseek.co.jp/zuicho.htm.
7 For information in English on the Zenrinji, see http://www.eikando.or.jp/English/eikando_e.htm.
8 For a popular introduction to both schools and Zen meditation practice in general, see Robert Aitken, *Taking the Path of Zen* (New York: North Point Press, 1982). For *kōan*, see Chapter 7.
9 For an introduction, see Richard Hughes Seager, *Buddhism in America* (New York: Columbia University Press, 1999).
10 Rinzaiji Zen Centre's website gives a description of the centre and an essay on Joshu Sasaki-roshi's fascinating life. See http://www.rinzaiji.org/about/index.html.
11 "Roshi" is an honorific Japanese term for a teacher of Zen Buddhism.
12 "Osho" is a term that denotes permission to teach in this tradition.
13 The purpose of the Victoria Nikkei Cultural Society is to participate in the promotion of the Japanese Canadian heritage though cultural, educational, artistic, and other activities. The society sponsors community activities that are for the benefit of the Nikkei community in the Greater Victoria area and offers outreach activities that involve and benefit the community at large.
14 See the Victoria Zen Centre's website for details, at http://www.zenwest.ca.
15 For more information about her interesting and unusual life, see her autobiography, Jiyu Kennett, *The Wild White Goose, The Diary of a Female Zen Priest* (Shasta Abbey, CA: Shasta Abbey Press, 2002).
16 See "Zen and Its Flagship Institutions" in Seager, *Buddhism in America*.
17 I would like to thank Dr. Leonard Angel and Dr. Graham Good for this information.

18 See http://www.sgi.org/english/SGI/charter.htm.
19 For a recent introduction to Sōka Gakkai and SGI, see Richard Hughes Seager, *Encountering the Dharma: Daisaku Ikeda, Soka Gakkai, and the Globalization of Buddhist Humanism* (Berkeley: University of California Press, 2006).
20 For an overview of Sōka Gakkai in Canada, see Daniel A. Metraux, *The Lotus and the Maple Leaf: The Soka Gakkai Buddhist Movement in Canada* (New York: University Press of America, 1996).
21 See the excellent Konkōkyō website at http://www.konkokyo.or.jp/eng/index.html.
22 In English, the expression "Principle Parent of the Universe" or "Principle Parent" is used.
23 The name Konkōkyō Church of America was officially changed to Konko Churches of North America in 1987.
24 Ryūhō Ōkawa's best-known book is *The Laws of the Sun* (New York: Lantern Press, 2001).
25 Official website: http://www.kofuku-no-kagaku.or.jp/en.q.

11 Christianity as a Chinese Belief
Li Yu

The Chinese community's existence in British Columbia has spanned over a century and a half, beginning with the arrival of the first Chinese on Vancouver Island in 1858. From only a few hundred people in the early days, the community has grown into the second largest ethnic group in the province. According to the 2006 Census of Canada, its population of 377,500 accounted for 9.2 percent of the total population of British Columbia.[1] This growth has been due more to the continuous arrival of new immigrants than to the natural growth of the local Chinese community.

As will be discussed in Chapter 12, the Chinese in British Columbia today come from a variety of geographic and social backgrounds. Unlike the early immigrants, who were mainly from rural Guangdong, Chinese immigrants after the Second World War came from all over the world. In the last decades of the twentieth century, most were from Taiwan, Hong Kong, and other parts of Southeast Asia, and in recent years, the People's Republic of China has become the largest source of Chinese immigrants to British Columbia.[2] Also unlike early immigrants, most of whom were single males and physical labourers, today's Chinese immigrants often come with their families and had been engaged in a variety of professions and occupations in their countries of origin.

The Chinese in British Columbia no longer aggregate in Chinatowns but are dispersed throughout the province. Most still prefer to live in urban areas, however. According to the 2006 census, over 94 percent live in the Greater Vancouver area and nearly 3 percent in Victoria, while only about 3 percent live in all inland areas of British Columbia, the highest urban-living ratio of all ethnic groups in the province.[3]

As the Chinese community has expanded, a fairly complete and independent service system serving mainly Chinese has grown in recent decades. This system includes numerous Chinese groceries, shops, bookstores, restaurants, educational institutions, entertainment amenities, and religious facilities. The major service language is not English but Mandarin or Cantonese. The Chinese community also has its own mass media, consisting of two Chinese radio channels (FM 96.1 in Mandarin and AM 1470 in Cantonese), two Chinese TV channels (Channel 229 Talent Vision in Mandarin and Channel 230 Fairchild TV in Cantonese), three large Chinese newspapers (*World Journal*, with Taiwan background; *Ming Pao Daily News* and *Sing Tao Daily*, with Hong Kong background), and numerous small newspapers, most of them with China background.

Closely related to social change within the community is the rapid growth of Christianity among the Chinese of British Columbia. The 2001 Census of Canada found that Chinese Christians in the province, including both Protestants and Catholics, totalled 86,575, or 24 percent of the total Chinese population, making Christianity the largest religion in the community. In comparison, Chinese Buddhists in British Columbia totalled only 53,185 in the same year (roughly 14 percent), while another important Chinese religion, Daoism, had 660 believers (less than 0.02 percent).[4]

Christianity among the Korean and Japanese Canadian populations in British Columbia is discussed in Chapter 8. In this chapter, I investigate the major factors that have contributed to the growth of Christianity among the Chinese in recent decades. I will show that the continuous growth and dispersal of the Chinese population, and social and psychological problems among the new immigrants, such as culture shock, identity crises, and job and family pressures, have all led to Christianity's greater role in Chinese social life. Responding to the changes, Christian churches have adjusted their mission strategies to meet the needs of Chinese immigrants. The most important driving force, however, is the fact that after the Second World War, more Chinese churches became self-supporting, independent churches, and Chinese missionaries replaced Caucasian missionaries, gradually transforming Christianity in the community from a Western religion into a Chinese belief. But before starting our investigation, let us survey the general situation of the Chinese Protestant and Roman Catholic churches in British Columbia.[5]

Chinese Protestants in British Columbia

Like the Chinese population in general, the Chinese Protestant churches in British Columbia are concentrated in the Greater Vancouver area. According to *Truth Monthly*, a major local Chinese Christian newspaper, by March 2006 there were 110 Chinese Protestant churches in the province – 45 in Vancouver, 12 in Burnaby, 22 in Richmond, 11 in Coquitlam, and 20 in Surrey, Victoria, and the BC Interior. There are also twenty-six Chinese Christian newspapers, magazines, radio stations, and theological education and research organizations in the Greater Vancouver area.[6] It should be noted that these numbers refer only to mainline Protestant churches and institutions and do not include other denominations, such as Jehovah's Witnesses or Seventh-day Adventists. In 2001, there were 54,880 Chinese belonging to all Protestant denominations, accounting for 15 percent of the 365,485 Chinese in British Columbia that year.[7]

Before the Second World War, Protestant missions in the BC Chinese community were predominantly Methodist,[8] Presbyterian, and Anglican. Today, almost all denominations in the province at large can also be found in the Chinese community: Baptist, Alliance Church, Lutheran, United Church, Anglican, Methodist, Presbyterian, Evangelical Association, Mennonite Brethren, Seventh-day Adventist, Amazing Grace, and so on. Some of the denominational churches, such as the Presbyterian Church and the United Church, were established by Caucasian missionaries in the late nineteenth century or early twentieth century; others, such as the Mennonite Brethren, were daughter churches that separated from corresponding Caucasian denominational churches and became independent in the 1960s or 1970s. Still others, such as some Baptist and Alliance churches, were formed in recent decades by Chinese immigrants from Hong Kong, Taiwan, or the United States.

Occasionally, Chinese Protestant churches will join a mission association of their denomination, ceding part of their administrative independence to the association. Many others choose not to join any association, remaining independent in finance and administration but still keeping their denominational identity. It is estimated, however, that over half of the Chinese Protestant churches in British Columbia have no denominational identity and are completely independent, both financially and administratively.[9]

Some denominations, such as the Anglicans and Seventh-day Adventists, are highly organized in national or international networks, and their churches are usually affiliated with the larger national or even global body. For example, the Vancouver Chinese Seventh-day Adventist Church, located on Oak Street in Vancouver, is affiliated with the British Columbia Conference, the Union of Canada, North American Division, and the Seventh-day Adventist General Conference, with headquarters in Washington, DC. The church is tightly woven into the global network and has little financial and administrative independence.[10] The denominational complexity of Chinese Christianity in British Columbia reflects, to a certain extent, the increasing diversification of the Chinese community in the province at large.

Many Chinese Protestant churches grow rapidly and are capable of producing several generations of descendant churches in a short period. The Pacific Grace Chinese Church at 1587 Frances Street in Vancouver is a good example. This church began as a Chinese fellowship in the British Columbia Conference of

Mennonite Brethren Churches' largely English-speaking Pacific Grace Mission Chapel. The fellowship grew rapidly in the 1960s with increased Chinese immigration, and started a separate Chinese service in 1973. In 1977, the Caucasian Pacific Grace Mission Chapel disbanded, and the Chinese took over the church building and changed its name to Pacific Grace Chinese Church. It produced a daughter church, the Burnaby Pacific Grace Chinese Church, in 1990. One year later, the daughter church became economically independent and began to form its own congregation. In 1995, it produced its own daughter church, the Port Moody Pacific Grace Chinese Church, which attained financial independence in 1998.[11] The growth of Protestant Christianity in the Chinese community of British Columbia continues, especially among new immigrants, and the proportion of Protestants in the total Chinese population of the province is expected to increase.

Chinese Roman Catholics in British Columbia
The Roman Catholic Church began its mission among the Chinese in British Columbia early in the twentieth century, but its growth was very slow. In 1931, there were just 93 Chinese Catholics in the whole province.[12] By 1941, there were 274, just 1.5 percent of the 18,619 Chinese at the time.[13] The 1970s saw more rapid growth,[14] and the 2001 census counted 31,693 Chinese Catholics, nearly 9 percent of the 365,485 Chinese in the province and equal to nearly 58 percent of the total number of Chinese Protestants.

It is interesting that although the Chinese Catholic population is fairly large, there is only one ethnic Chinese parish, St. Francis Xavier Church in Vancouver, plus three multi-ethnic parishes with high ratios of Chinese worshippers: St. Theresa's Parish in Burnaby, Corpus Christi Parish in Vancouver, and Canadian Martyrs Catholic Church in Richmond.[15] Considering that there are only 1.7 times more Chinese Protestants than Catholics but over a hundred Protestant churches, it is natural to wonder where large numbers of Chinese Catholics worship. One explanation is that, unlike their Protestant brethren, many Chinese Catholics usually attend their local Catholic churches, whether or not these have services in Chinese. In addition, Catholic parents normally have their children baptized shortly after they are born. The children are counted as part of the Catholic population, whether or not they continue going to church after they are grown.

There are many Chinese Catholic organizations and clubs in British Columbia. For example, the Chinese Catholic Society of UBC, also known as CATSO or *Tinching*, was founded in 1997 by a group of young Catholics from the Lower Mainland. It is one of the largest Chinese Catholic student organizations in the province and is also an active member of St. Mark's College at the University of British Columbia.[16] Chinese Catholics also have an important annual event, the Western Canada Chinese Catholic Living Camp (WCCCLC), which is jointly organized by lay Catholics from many parishes in the province. This camp is held every year during the Labour Day weekend. Its purpose is to help young Chinese Catholics strengthen their faith.[17]

From a Western to a Chinese Belief

The history of both the Chinese community and Chinese Christians in British Columbia spans a period of around a century and a half. Soon after the first group of Chinese immigrants arrived in 1858, missionaries from local churches undertook mission work among them. Methodist missionaries were the first. For example, Edward White reached the Chinese in New Westminster, on the banks of the Fraser River, as early as 1859. Reverend A.E. Russ held services for Chinese Christians in an unused barroom at the corner of Government and Harold Streets in Victoria in 1866, while his wife opened a night school for the Chinese.[18] Mrs. Monk, a local pastor's daughter, began teaching the Chinese about Christianity on Vancouver's Hastings Street in the early 1860s.[19]

Anglican missionaries also began working among the Chinese very early on. George Hills, the Bishop of British Columbia, "made an important beginning amongst the Chinese" in Victoria in 1860, while John Sheepshanks had regular contact with some Chinese in New Westminster and instructed them in Christianity. Another Anglican missionary opened a school for Chinese immigrants at Williams Creek in the Central Interior in 1869, and about ten of them came to the school to learn English and Christianity.[20]

Thus, an important feature of Chinese Christianity in British Columbia, unlike the other Asian religions discussed in this book, is that it originated in the local Chinese community instead of being brought over by immigrants from their places of origin.[21] Local Caucasian missionaries brought Christianity to the province's Chinese community, and the history of Christianity in this community before the Second World War is largely a history of mission work by Caucasian churches and missionaries.[22] The Christianity seen in the Chinese community today, however, is quite different from that of those early years.

Before the Second World War, the missionaries who worked in the Chinese community were mainly from the three major Protestant denominations in Canada: the Methodist (United Church after 1925), Presbyterian, and Anglican churches. In the 1920s, Catholics and a number of other Protestant denominations, such as the Baptist and Mennonite Brethren churches, joined in the mission to the Chinese community, but they could not shake the dominant position of the three major denominations. In 1941, there were 1,591 Chinese in the United Church, 735 in the Presbyterian Church, and 440 in the Anglican Church, whereas there were only 371 in all the other denominations, including Catholics and Baptists.[23]

It is worth mentioning that the three major denominations as well as the Roman Catholic Church in Canada also sent missions to China in the late nineteenth and early twentieth centuries. The Presbyterian Church of Canada had three missions in China: the Formosa mission (established in 1870), the North Henan mission (1888), and the South China mission (1902). The Methodists concentrated mainly on Sichuan, where they started their West China mission in 1892. At first, the Anglican Church of Canada sent missionaries to join the British Anglican mission to China, but it established its own independent diocese in Henan in 1909.[24]

The Canadian Catholic Church, most of whose missionaries to China were French Canadians from Quebec, began its organized mission to China in the 1920s. It took over the work of French missions in Shandong, Suzhou, and Manchuria under a Vatican-sponsored arrangement. English Canadian Catholics also set up a small mission station in Ningbo in 1925.[25] From the 1870s to the 1950s, the three main Canadian Protestant churches and the Canadian Catholic Church sent over a thousand missionaries to China.[26]

The Canadian churches were actually more concerned with mission work in China than in the Chinese community in Canada, especially in British Columbia, drawing criticism from those who did practical mission work in the province's Chinese community. One reason that the missionary J.E. Gardener, who started the organized mission of the Methodist Church in the BC Chinese community in 1885, gave up this work and left the province was the lack of moral support from the church and Canadian society.[27]

Most of the province's Chinese before the Second World War were poor and uneducated lower-class people who were discriminated against by mainstream Canadian society. Public opinion of Chinatown was that it was a place full of sin and backward customs such as gambling, opium smoking, polygamy, and human trafficking, and that the Chinese living in Canada had a negative influence on society's morals. This view was shared by the churches, which argued that their mission was important because it would bring salvation to the sinful Chinese and enhance their moral standards, benefiting Canadian society in general.[28]

Mission work in the Chinese community thus reflected the needs of mainstream society rather than those of the Chinese. Since they viewed Christian missions as an external assimilating power, most Chinese had no interest in Christianity, and although the missionaries made great efforts to evangelize the Chinese, the results were not very impressive. By 1921, the total number of Chinese in British Columbia was around 23,600, but in all of Canada no more than 700 were baptized Christians.[29] In 1931, around half of the Chinese in Canada – a total of 27,139 – lived in British Columbia, but only 1,969 (7.2 percent) were Christians.[30]

Ten years later, in 1941, Chinese Christians numbered 3,135, or 17 percent of the total Chinese population. This sharp increase, however, was not due to greater interest in Christianity on the part of the Chinese but, rather, to the effects of the Chinese Exclusion Act passed by the House of Commons in 1923.[31] This act caused the total number of Chinese in the province to decline to 18,619 in 1941 (only around 68 percent of the Chinese population of 1931), a steeper decline than in any other province.[32] When many Chinese left British Columbia, the percentage of Christians among those who remained rose, since they were more likely to remain in Canada during this period of exclusion.

The postwar repeal of the Chinese Exclusion Act, the revision of immigration laws, and the adoption of a multiculturalism policy by the federal government led to a dramatic change in the Chinese political and social position in Canada. Christianity in that community also began to change. The old Caucasian denominational missions withdrew one by one, and turned over their work to their Chinese congregations. As early as the mid-1950s, the United Church discontinued organized missions to the Chinese community. It was followed by the Presbyterians in 1962 and the Anglicans in 1967.[33]

During this period, many self-managed Chinese churches also came into being. Many new ones were established by Christians among the immigrants coming from Asia, or by local Chinese Christians who separated from Caucasian denominational churches. For example, the Vancouver Chinese Alliance Church (VCAC) began as a Chinese Bible study fellowship in the Tenth Avenue Alliance Church in the 1960s. In 1966, when the group had grown to around seventy and a Chinese pastor, Zhao Shichang, came to Vancouver, the Chinese members decided to form an independent Chinese Alliance church. They bought land on Knight Street and constructed a church building. The VCAC is now the largest Chinese Alliance church in the province.[34]

Another example is the Vancouver Chinese Baptist Church. In 1968, a group of fifteen people from Hong Kong formed a Chinese Baptist fellowship in Vancouver. They invited Reverend Jonathan Cheung to be their pastor and David See-Chai Lam to be one of their advisers.[35] Regular Sunday worship service began a month later under the current name, Vancouver Chinese Baptist Church. In July 1969, the church was constituted as the first Chinese Baptist church in Vancouver. As the number of members increased, a bigger church building was needed. In January 1979, the church purchased and moved into its present building at 7474 Culloden Street in Vancouver.[36]

The Evangelical Chinese Bible Church has a similar story. On 5 March 1972, 30 to 40 worshippers came together for the first Evangelical Chinese Bible Church Worship Service on the premises of the Evangelical Free Church. With Reverend John Sun from Taiwan at the helm, the church grew to around 350 worshippers within ten years. By 1992, it had become one of the largest

Chinese churches in British Columbia, with twelve fellowships and over 700 members.[37]

Beginning in the late 1980s, even as Hong Kong, Taiwan, and other parts of Southeast Asia have continued to be major sources of Chinese immigrants, more and more people have come from China as it has reopened itself to the outside world. A major impetus during this period was a series of political incidents in Greater China. The 1989 Tiananmen Square incident, the 1996 Taiwan Strait missile crisis, and the 1997 handover of Hong Kong to China caused large-scale Chinese migration to Canada. Many of the immigrants from China in the 1980s and early 1990s were students, with some refugees. After the federal government revised the immigration laws in 1994, independent and business immigration became the major form of immigration from China, Hong Kong, and Taiwan, and Chinese Christian churches became even more prosperous. They tried not only to meet the religious needs of the new immigrants but also to be the first public organization through which they could establish social connections in Canada. In 1997, a group of Mainland Chinese, most of whom had been baptized in British Columbia, established the Chinese Christian Gospel Church in Burnaby, the first Mainland Chinese immigrants' church.[38]

The rise of Chinese self-managed churches in the postwar period indicates that Christianity had changed from an external assimilating force into a project of the Chinese themselves. The churches became Chinese ethnic churches, and Christianity became a Chinese belief system. This historical transformation is one of the major factors behind the growth of Christianity in the Chinese community of British Columbia in recent decades.

Reaching the Chinese

At first, the most important way for churches in British Columbia to attract the Chinese was to open schools to teach English. Chinese went to the evening schools, day schools, and Sunday schools run by churches because English-language skills could greatly increase their opportunities in Canada. For the churches, these English classes partially solved the problem of a shortage of missionaries who could speak Chinese. After the Second World War, however, language education for new immigrants was taken over by secular educational institutions. Also, since almost all the churches serving the Chinese are now ethnic churches, few still use English classes to attract the Chinese.

Chinese immigrants during the postwar period were no longer mainly lower-class people from rural Guangdong; they came from all over the world and from different social backgrounds. They initially went to churches with various motives. Some new immigrants without jobs and friends wanted to establish social connections. Wives of *taikong* (space) families from Taiwan, Hong Kong, and China felt lonely in their incomplete families and looked for spiritual support in their churches.[39] Some educated people from China who were disillusioned with the atheist and communist teachings they had been taught from childhood went to church out of religious curiosity.

Today, the churches' major challenge is no longer how to attract people but how to deal with their different needs, how to keep them in the church, and how to transform their social or psychological concerns into religious belief. After 1995, when independent and business immigrants comprised the majority of new immigrants to British Columbia, many churches began changing their mission strategy with the Chinese from China. They helped them adjust to the new environment, resolving problems and overcoming difficulties in their everyday lives. For example, the Amazing Grace Christian Fellowship in New Westminster teaches new immigrants to drive, helps them move house, and provides them with housing and job information. The catchword of the church, according to its pastor, is "to build the church into a family with love." The church wants those members in a new environment to rely on God, and tells them that if they believe in God, God will bless them and meet all their needs, both spiritual and material.[40]

Organizing Bible study fellowships for new immigrants has become the most popular form of Christian mission in recent decades. Besides those organized by churches, there are many large and independent Bible study groups that are very popular among new Chinese immigrants. It is interesting to note that whereas most of these groups have been organized and managed by Canadian-born Chinese or Chinese from Taiwan, Hong Kong, or other parts of Southeast Asia, most of their participants are immigrants and students from China.

The best known of these is the Overseas Chinese Bible Fellowship, which was organized in 1991 by two medical doctors' families, the Xie family from Taiwan and the Li family from Hong Kong. Located at 5889 Fremlin Street in Vancouver, it is aimed at ethnic Chinese from all over the world, but most of the participants have turned out to be immigrants from China. The fellowship organizes two gatherings each month and publishes a magazine called *Zuiqiu* (Search), most of whose articles are testaments of newly baptized Christians from China.[41]

The Chinese Christians in British Columbia have missions not only among immigrants but also among Chinese visitors to the province, such as international students, tourists, visiting scholars, businessmen, or sailors. The most important mission of this kind might be the one to Chinese sailors. Vancouver is one of the largest port cities in North America, visited by many cargo ships each year from different parts of the world. Since the early 1980s, Christians have been doing mission work among sailors from those ships. Led by Teus

Kappers, a Dutch Canadian, the mission converted an old warehouse at the Harbour Centre in downtown Vancouver into a missionary centre called Lighthouse Harbour Ministries. Those who participate in the mission offer preaching on the ships during the day and in the centre at night. Sailors can munch on free cookies in the centre's reception room, buy souvenirs in the small shop, play table tennis, or make long distance telephone calls. Although the centre is open to sailors from all over the world, sailors from China are the most frequent visitors.[42]

To overcome the language barrier between the Caucasian missionaries and the Chinese sailors, the mission to Chinese sailors was transferred to Chinese Christians in 1986. The first Chinese to participate in the work was Wang Wenquan, an independent Chinese missionary in Vancouver. He was welcomed by sailors on the Chinese cargo ships because he brought them free Bibles, but the shipboard commissars[43] did not like him at first, and sometimes even drove him off a ship. According to Wang, however, even the commissars gradually underwent a change in attitude. They no longer interfered in his mission work and sometimes sat among the sailors listening to his preaching. In some cases, they even asked him for Bibles. Chinese cargo ships are usually very large, and Wang normally preached in the dining halls. In recent years, more Chinese Christians have participated in the mission. Wang says that, of all the sailors from foreign lands, the Chinese have shown the greatest interest in their preaching, but few wanted to be baptized.[44]

Maintaining Chinese Identity

Chinese churches in British Columbia play an important role in strengthening their members' Chinese identity, but they strengthen it in such a way that all the Chinese traditions they are going to keep have to be re-evaluated or reinterpreted so that they will not be incompatible with Christian doctrine. It is very easy for Chinese Christians to identify with such Protestant values as industry, frugality, patience, perseverance, emphasis on family, and aspiration for success, because these values are similar to traditional Confucian values. Chinese Christians say that they also admire some secular values in Canadian society such as individual independence, initiative, self-confidence, and critical thinking, but they admit that these are harder to achieve. Chinese Christians strongly criticize some socially liberal views in Canadian society, especially on such matters as family or marriage, as most of the Chinese churches in British Columbia are conservative.

Highly educated Chinese Christians in North America tend to use their Christian knowledge and ideas to reinterpret Chinese history. Yuan Zhiming, one of the authors of the well-known TV program *River Elegy* (*Heshang*) and a Christian from China who now lives in the United States but frequently visits

British Columbia, argues that the ancient Chinese before Confucius were closer to God than Chinese in later dynasties because the concept of the *tian* or *tiandi* of the time actually indicated God. Dr. Liang Yancheng (In-sing Leung), director of the Culture Regeneration Research Society in Vancouver, believes that evidence in the ancient Chinese classic *Book of Songs* shows that people in ancient China had already realized the existence of God. He argues that the existence of God can be inferred from some Confucian ideas, especially Mencius' idea of compassion.[45] Some Chinese Christians are interested in talking about coded information about Christianity that they see in such Chinese characters as *chuan* (boats) and *xiang* (happiness). A book entitled *The Discovery of Genesis: How the Truths of Genesis Were Found Hidden in the Chinese Language* sells well in the Chinese Christian bookstores of Vancouver.[46]

Like Canadian-born Chinese Christians, some Chinese immigrants who were baptized in British Columbia, mostly young people with good English-language skills, identify with Western material culture. They assimilate comfortably into Western society, not necessarily because of their newfound beliefs but simply because, even before migrating to Canada, they had already accepted such facets of Western material culture as wearing jeans; eating hamburgers; drinking Coke, red wine, and coffee; listening to Western music; and watching Western TV shows and movies. Most Chinese Christians, however, still live a Chinese lifestyle – shopping in Chinese groceries, eating Chinese food at home or in restaurants, drinking tea, and watching Chinese TV channels. Their Christian identity does not seem to have an important influence on their choice of material culture and lifestyle.

There is no evidence that Chinese Christians in British Columbia are more interested than other Chinese in celebrating Western secular festivals. With regard to religious festivals, the main difference between the two groups lies in their attitudes toward the festival. For example, Christmas is a major festival for all Chinese in British Columbia, whether Christian or not; however, non-Christian Chinese view it simply as a holiday, as a time to visit friends or relax at home, whereas the Christians attach importance to its religious meaning and often complain that it has become too commercialized. They are always willing to remind people who go to church during the Christmas season that Santa Claus is not a figure in the Bible.

Like other Chinese, those who are Christians celebrate traditional Chinese festivals such as Chinese New Year, the Mid-Autumn Festival, the Dragon Boat Festival, and so on. For example, Canadian Martyrs Catholic Church in Richmond has had the celebration of Chinese New Year on its list of important events since 2001. For many years, the Regent College Bible Study Fellowship at the University of British Columbia has held a Chinese New Year *jiaozi* (dumpling) party, a Chinese tradition for the Spring Festival. Some churches and Bible study groups even put on theatrical performances such as drama or choral singing for these traditional Chinese festivals. The performances are often designed in such a way that they are related to Christian teachings and have some evangelizing effects.

Chinese languages are still the major ones used in the Chinese churches of British Columbia. At the 110 Protestant churches listed in *Truth Monthly*, Cantonese, English, and Mandarin are used for services. Some use Cantonese only, some Mandarin only; others use both Mandarin and English, both Cantonese and English, or both Mandarin and Cantonese, while still others use all three languages. None, however, uses only English in its Sunday service.[47]

Most of the Chinese churches in the province have no social service programs for the Chinese community, except Chinese-language classes, mainly for local-born Chinese children and children from other ethnic groups. Several Chinese Christian organizations have specialized in offering social services, however. One of the most important is the CCM (Chinese Christian Mission). It was founded by Reverend Thomas Wang (Wang Yongxing) in Detroit in 1961, and its Canadian branch, CCM Canada, was established in Vancouver in 1979. CCM Canada's mission statement describes its objective as "to observe the command of Jesus Christ to make disciples of all nations with the love of God by, firstly, reaching the Chinese, and then other people groups." The Chinese identity of the organization is also clearly expressed in the slogan "Reaching the Chinese to reach the world."[48]

CCM Canada has many concrete community service programs in British Columbia in the educational, spiritual, and recreational sectors. These include counselling, tutoring for high school students, scouts, art gallery displays, community theatre, chapel, cooking, music, and language classes. It also hosts practical seminars to help Chinese with their daily needs in the areas of health, marriage, family, and work. It says that it will offer service to all Chinese – men and women, Cantonese and Mandarin speaking, old and new immigrants.[49]

Although Chinese Christians maintain and reconstruct their Chinese identity, they also argue that there are some weaknesses in traditional Chinese culture. They believe that if Christian beliefs and practices could be integrated with Chinese tradition, a new Chinese culture compatible with modern society would emerge. Many believe that Christianity is closely related to modernity and democracy. For example, Yuan Zhiming wanted Chinese people to think about why most modern, developed countries are Christian countries.[50] Hong Yujian, a Christian from China now living in Vancouver, claimed in a speech that Western democracy was based on the humanist ideas in Christianity.[51]

Chinese Christians in British Columbia have been calling for a regeneration of Chinese culture for years. In 1994, a group of them founded the Culture

Regeneration Research Society, which has grown in influence in recent years in both the North American Chinese community and in China. The society's director, Dr. Liang Yancheng, a Christian from Hong Kong, obtained his PhD in Chinese philosophy at the University of Hawai'i and taught at Regent College in Vancouver for several years. Staff members come from Hong Kong, Taiwan, and China. Former British Columbia Lieutenant Governor David See-Chai Lam, also a Christian, has been one of its major financial supporters. The society publishes an academic journal, *Culture China*, with articles from Chinese scholars throughout the world, both Christians and non-Christians.[52]

Conclusion

In this chapter, we have looked at the status of Christianity in British Columbia's Chinese community and examined the driving forces behind its growth among this population in recent decades. We have seen that this popularity cannot be understood except in the context of the Chinese community's social and historical transformation over the past century and a half, a period during which Christianity in this community changed from a Western religion into a Chinese belief.

One of the most important features of Chinese Christianity in British Columbia is that, unlike other Asian religions, it was not brought here by immigrants from their places of origin. Instead, it was encouraged by the local Caucasian Christian missionaries as an instrument of assimilation into mainstream society. After the Second World War, however, the assimilating role of the churches gradually weakened as the Chinese missions of the mainstream denominational churches withdrew from the community and self-managed Chinese churches came into being. These churches took on a new role, that of solidifying the Chinese identity of their members. This fundamental shift accompanied the postwar transformation of the Chinese community into a much more complex society and is a major reason for the spread of Christianity in this community.

Christianity has re-emerged and spread rapidly in China in recent decades. The Chinese churches here, however, have little connection with churches in China, whether official "three-self churches" or "house churches." This is partly a consequence of restrictions placed by the Chinese government on outside religious influences, but also because most of the Chinese churches in British Columbia are independent churches that focus their ministry on the local Chinese community. They have no desire or interest in mission work in China, except for evangelizing Chinese students, visiting scholars, and other short-term visitors to British Columbia. Christianity practised by the Chinese in this province is a Chinese belief system with a specific context and with its own local concerns.

As the American scholar Daniel H. Bays has pointed out, on a worldwide scale, "within the past few decades Christianity in its Protestant and Catholic expressions alike has become primarily a non-western religion in terms of both numbers of adherents and local practice."[53] We have seen that this is also true in British Columbia.

NOTES

1 Statistics Canada, 2006 Census of Canada, http://www12.statcan.gc.ca/census-recensement/index-eng.cfm. The total of 365,485 from the 2001 Census of Canada is used below to calculate percentages for religious groups, since the 2006 census did not count such groups.
2 The 2006 census shows that from 2001 to 2006, 41,500 Chinese migrated from Mainland China to British Columbia. During the same period, the numbers of migrants from Taiwan and Hong Kong to British Columbia were 7,425 and 2,975, respectively. See Statistics Canada, 2006 Census.
3 Statistics Canada, 2006 Census.
4 Statistics Canada, 2001 Census.
5 This chapter is based on research reported in academic studies of the Chinese community in British Columbia, publications of the Chinese Christian institutions, and websites of the churches, as well as the author's oral interviews (both face to face and telephone) with personnel from a number Chinese Christian churches.
6 *Truth Monthly*, March 2006.
7 The second largest Chinese religion in British Columbia, Buddhism, had 53,180 believers in 2001: Statistics Canada, 2001 Census.
8 The Methodist Church of Canada merged with two thirds of the Presbyterian Church of Canada as well as some other denominations to form the United Church of Canada in 1925.
9 Interview with Wang Wenquan (an independent Chinese missionary), 20 July 2006.
10 "Vancouver Chinese Seventh-day Adventist Church," Seventh-day Adventist Church, Office of Archives and Statistics, http://www.adventistdirectory.org.
11 "Our Church's History," Burnaby Pacific Grace Chinese Church, http://www.bpgcc.bc.ca.
12 Ottawa: Dominion Bureau of Statistics, *Religious Denominations by Racial Origins*, 1931.
13 Ottawa: Dominion Bureau of Statistics, Census of Canada, 1941.
14 Phone interview with Reverend Francis X. Chang, 31 August 2006.
15 "Parish: Masses by Language," Archdiocese of Vancouver, http://www.rcav.org/parishes/languages.html.
16 "About Us," CATSO, http://www.catholic-church.org/catso. St. Mark's College is the Catholic theological college at the University of British Columbia.
17 "Background of WCCCLC," Western Canada Chinese Catholic Living Camp, http://www.catholic-church.org/wccclc.
18 S.S. Osterhout, *Orientals in Canada: The Story of the Work of the United Church of Canada with Asiatics in Canada* (Toronto: Ryerson Press, 1929), 73.
19 The United Church of Canada, *A Hundred Years of Christian Chinese Work in British Columbia 1859-1959* (Vancouver: Chinese United Church, 1959), 1, 2, 6.
20 Jiwu Wang, *"His Dominion" and the "Yellow Peril": Protestant Missions to Chinese Immigrants in Canada, 1859-1967* (Waterloo, ON: Wilfrid Laurier University Press, 2006), 38.
21 Note, however, Christianity had become a Chinese tradition in China since the sixteenth century.

22 Some Chinese Christians, such as Chang Sing Kai, Chan Yu Tan, Kwan Mou Lung, and Fung Tak Man, joined the organized missions of the Caucasian churches at the turn of the twentieth century.
23 Ottawa: Dominion Bureau of Statistics, Census of Canada, 1941.
24 See Alvyn J. Austin, *Saving China: Canadian Missionaries in the Middle Kingdom, 1888-1959* (Toronto: University of Toronto Press, 1986), 24-25, 130.
25 Ibid., 89-90, 158-59.
26 Song Jiaheng, "Jianada chuanjiaoshi zai zhongguo" (Canadian Missionaries in China), in *Jianada chuanjiaoshi zai zhongguo* (Canadian Missionaries in China), ed. Song Jiaheng and Li Wei (Beijing: Dongfang chubanshe, 1995), 1.
27 Osterhout, *Orientals in Canada*, 77.
28 Both church leaders and mainstream Canadians of the time wanted a "white BC" and supported the government policy of restriction on Chinese immigration. But church leaders, unlike ordinary Canadians, believed that the Chinese, if limited to a certain number in Canadian society, could be assimilated, and the church would take on the work of assimilating them. See Edgar Wickberg, ed., *From China to Canada: A History of the Chinese Communities in Canada* (Toronto: McLelland and Stewart, 1982), 124.
29 Ching Ma, *Chinese Pioneers: Materials Concerning the Immigration of Chinese to Canada and Sino-Canadian Relations* (Vancouver: Versatile Publishing, 1979), 91; Wang, *"His Dominion" and the "Yellow Peril,"* 66.
30 Ottawa: Dominion Bureau of Statistics, Census of Canada, 1931.
31 The total Chinese population in Canada declined from 39,587 in 1920 to 34,627 in 1941: Ma, *Chinese Pioneers*, 91, table 5.
32 Census of Canada, 1931 and 1941. But the lower ratio of Christians in British Columbia compared with that in the entire country during this period might also have resulted from the fact that more Chinese in the east were willing to become Christians because the Chinese there were discriminated against to a lesser extent, and therefore were more interested in Canadian social life, including Christianity: Wickberg, *From China to Canada*, 127-28.
33 Wang, *"His Dominion" and the "Yellow Peril,"* 84.
34 "Introduction to Vancouver Chinese Alliance Church," Vancouver Chinese Alliance, http://www.vcac.bc.ca/flc/aboutus.
35 David See-Chai Lam became the Lieutenant Governor of British Columbia in 1988.
36 "Our Church," Vancouver Chinese Baptist Church, http://www.vcbc.bc.ca/english/about/history.
37 Reverend John Sun, "God's Abundant Provision," *Evangelical Chinese Bible Church 1972-1992 Highlights,* Vancouver, BC: Evangelical Chinese Bible Church, 1992; "Brief Introduction to Evangelical Chinese Bible Church," Evangelical Chinese Bible Church, http://www.ecbc.org/chinese/home.asp.
38 "Brief Introduction to Chinese Gospel Church," Chinese Christian Gospel Church, http://ccgc-canada.org/.
39 Since it is not easy for new immigrants to find jobs in British Columbia, many Chinese immigrant families have had to be separated, with the husband going back to work in the family's place of origin while the wife and children stay in Canada to keep the family's permanent immigrant status. Such families are called *taikong* (literally "space") families, meaning that people often have to fly back and forth in the sky so that they can meet each other.
40 Interview with Zhou Xiaoan, 9 August 2005.
41 Interview with Xie Linmeilin (one of the organizers of the Overseas Chinese Bible Fellowship), 9 December 2005.

42 Interview with Wang Wenquan, 22 August 2005.
43 Representatives of the Chinese Communist Party in work units.
44 Interview with Wang Wenquan, 22 August 2005; Xu Jihua, "Fengli langli chuan fuyin" (Conducting Mission in the Wind and Waves), in *Fengsheng* (Searching for a Fulfilling Life) edited and published by *Truth Monthly*, Richmond, Vancouver, 2002, 5-10.
45 Liang Yancheng, "Kong yu qing: chuaoyue fozhi" (Empty and Feeling: Beyond Buddha's Wisdom), *Blessing* 5, 10 (2003): 7.
46 This book tries to interpret what is thought to be coded Christian information in hundreds of Chinese characters. See C.H. Kong and Ethel R. Nelson, *The Discovery of Genesis: How the Truths of Genesis Were Found Hidden in the Chinese Language* (St. Louis: Concordia Publishing House, 1979).
47 The statistics concerning languages used in services in the 110 churches are as follows: Mandarin only, 19; Cantonese only, 12; Mandarin and English, 6; Cantonese and English, 25; Mandarin and Cantonese, 16; Mandarin and Cantonese and English, 22; others, 10 (this category includes those that have no language indicated, or use Southern Fujian dialect, or use Southern Fujian dialect and another language): "Huaren jidujiaohui getang juhui," *Truth Monthly*, March 2006.
48 "Shiming xuanyan" (Mission Statement), CCM Canada, http://www.ccmcanada.org/f_mission_stmt.htm.
49 Ibid.
50 Yuan Zhiming, "Why do I believe in Jesus?," series of Yuan Zhiming Testimonies and Preachings, http://cclw.net/gospel/explore/yzmbd/index.html.
51 Hong Yujian, Speech for the 76th anniversary of the May 4th Movement at Regent College, Vancouver, 1995.
52 The Culture Regeneration Research Society is located at 201-6960 Royal Oak Avenue in Burnaby.
53 Daniel H. Bays, "Chinese Protest Christianity Today," in *Religion in China Today*, ed. Daniel L. Overmyer (The China Quarterly Special Issues New Series No. 3) (Cambridge: Cambridge University Press, 2003), 197.

12 Chinese Religions
Paul Crowe

The term "Chinese religions" should not be taken to imply a unitary "Chinese" constituency. Members of various religious groups, whether Daoist, Buddhist, or Christian (Chapter 11), have come to Canada from different countries in Asia at different times and with a variety of local customs and languages. Those who came to this country from Hong Kong in the 1950s would have faced the inequities of federal immigration policy. Desire to integrate into the new society was in tension with the necessity of cultural solidarity. Canada's Chinatowns were a vital resource for new immigrants from South China who spoke local dialects such as Toisan and Hoiping. The growth of Chinatowns was, in part, a response to the very harsh treatment Chinese labourers received during the latter half of the nineteenth and the early twentieth centuries. Today, the children of these Canadians have different expectations and perceptions of their place in Canada. Alternatively, those who left Hong Kong prior to China's reclaiming of the territory in 1997 and Taiwanese immigrants who fit the Canadian Conservative government's criteria of "investor immigrant" came to British Columbia with substantial financial resources and high levels of education.[1] They also arrived in a country that had long embraced an official policy of multiculturalism. Pressures related to integration were different, as it was less a matter of survival and more one of choice. Financial resources for the support of temple construction were more robust, and the freedom to build such obviously non-Western religious edifices could be assumed. Language is another major factor. From 1992 to 2001, nearly 70 percent of immigrants from India, China, Hong Kong, and Taiwan could not speak English.[2] This has profound implications for religious groups that may want to open their doors beyond their own cultural horizons but face the formidable barrier of language. If ceremonies in a Buddhist temple are performed in Mandarin and scriptures are written in Chinese, how do interested individuals who are unfamiliar with Chinese participate? These and other factors have a bearing on how Chinese religious groups in

British Columbia relate to broader Canadian society, and how they construct their various identities and raison d'être. The relevance of these factors to specific religious communities in the province will be addressed in the following descriptive accounts, which are divided into three sections dealing with Daoist, Popular Religious, and Buddhist groups in turn. Given the number of groups active in British Columbia, only a small representative sample could be considered. For a discussion of Chinese Christianity, see Chapter 11, which notes that 24 percent of the province's population of Chinese background is Christian.

Chinese religions arrived in British Columbia with those who crossed the Pacific in the mid-nineteenth century, after the Opium Wars between China and Britain (1839-42). The men who came to the province by way of California were drawn by tales of gold and jobs, but they left behind families and generations of ancestors buried in their home soil.[3] For over 2,000 years, the identity of individuals had been bound up with and nurtured by family traditions, roots, and connections. Thus, the first focus of Chinese religion in British Columbia was on the preservation of clan solidarity, continuing village affiliations at home. Worship of local deities and the veneration of ancestors constituted much of the religious practice.[4] Tangong Temple (Tanggong Miao 譚公廟), located in the Yen Wo clan building in Victoria's Chinatown,[5] is an example of how such local traditions were transplanted to a new cultural context. This small temple, located in the oldest Chinatown in Canada, may also be the oldest Chinese temple in the country. Tangong, or "Lord Tan," was a popular folk deity revered by members of the coastal fishing community at Huidong 惠東, east of Huizhou in Guangdong Province.[6] The emergence of Chinatowns, clan associations (*shishehui* 氏社會), and religious organizations was given impetus by the harsh reception of the Chinese in British Columbia. Their hard work was welcomed while needed, but after completion of the Canadian Pacific Rail line, it was met with resentment and hostility. Government policy disenfranchised the Chinese and limited further immigration and the ability of those already here to bring their families over from China. Ancestral veneration remains an important element in many Chinese religious sites, as we shall see in the next section.

Daoists

On a Sunday afternoon, I met George Lee outside the Lee's Benevolent Association of Canada in Vancouver's Chinatown. He took me through a ground-floor room in which elderly members chatted and played *majong* adjacent to a small family shrine altar. Upstairs, in a room measuring roughly 600 square feet, was a shrine occupying three walls, with an altar for offering incense and food to the ancestors. Side altars were divided into "halls" (*tang* 堂) that bore titles reflecting Confucian ideals such as filial piety (*xiao* 孝), humanity (*ren* 仁), and integrity (*cheng* 誠). In the centre of the rear wall was a large picture of the Lee clan's founding ancestor, Li Er 李耳, better known as Laozi 老子, a central deity[7] in Daoist pantheons and traditionally considered the composer of the *Daode jing*. Around Li Er were plaques commemorating ancestors, including Mr. Lee's grandfather, one of nine founders who established the association in 1954 in Victoria. Mr. Lee explained that, while the Lee clan acknowledges Laozi as the high ancestor, the association is not formally Daoist or even religious in orientation. Core members assume responsibility for annual banquets and coordination with other Lee associations in North America. The association also acts as a drop-in centre for the older generation living in neighbourhood seniors' residences. It has become an important part of their daily lives. The new shrine attracts many members of the Lee clan, who come to burn incense and make food offerings to their departed relatives on new and full moon days. While membership in the Lee association is robust, about 700 members, the long-term future of the association presents a challenge. The volunteer board of directors is aging and Mr. Lee's children's generation and that of their children have less motivation to maintain the organization. The social support function is no longer a daily necessity for them the way it is for many Chinese seniors. Concerns with cultural or social isolation and with language difficulties have little relevance for the younger generations. The aging board will gradually have to be replaced, but the next generation often lacks proficiency in written and spoken Chinese, which has necessitated the board's consideration of admitting new directors who have neither. Like other traditional clan associations, the Lees offer classes in Chinese, *gongfu* (*kung fu*) 功夫, and lion dancing to perpetuate an interest in Chinese culture and retain younger members. Mr. Lee noted, however, that it is becoming difficult, as children would typically rather play soccer.

The significant difficulties encountered through the 1950s and 1960s were a catalyst for the preservation of such cultural islands. Today, even the concern with social integration appears to be rapidly fading in the minds of Canadian professionals who happen to have a Chinese heritage. Perhaps large family banquets and ancestral shrines associated with Mr. Lee's generation of Chinese immigrants face an inevitable decline in the context of a lack of cultural confrontation. Michael Newton notes the occurrence of a similar generational dynamic in the case of Japanese Buddhist churches, where the social support role of the institutions is also in decline (Chapter 10).

Signs of this generational discontinuity are evident in more self-consciously religious groups such as the Evergreen Taoist Church of Canada (Qingsong Guan 青松觀) and the Po Yuen Taoist Centre Society (Daojiao Puxuan Jingshe 道教普玄精舍). Both temples are located in Chinatown a few blocks from the Lee's Family Benevolent Association of Canada. The Evergreen Taoist

Church was founded in 1993, after the visit to Vancouver of a member from the Hong Kong headquarters in 1989. Reverend Timothy Yau, who now resides in San Francisco, travels to branches, including the Vancouver site, as an "overseas missionary envoy," and ties are also maintained with the principal temple in Hong Kong. The Evergreen (Qingsong) sect was transmitted to Hong Kong from Guangzhou, with the first temple being established in Hong Kong in 1950, and through the 1990s has spread to Australia, the United States, and Singapore. Temples of this sect revere Lü Dongbin 呂洞賓, a figure with near pan-Chinese currency, as one of the famed Eight Immortals (Baxian 八仙). Lü is considered a founding patriarch in the monastic Quanzhen 全真 (Complete Perfection) sect of Daoism that originated in twelfth-century northern China. Both the Evergreen Taoist Church and Po Yuen identify themselves as Quanzhen, although they have developed as lay organizations in British Columbia.

At Po Yuen, James Lee, now in his eighties, is the Head Temple Minister and founder. Initially involved in a Hong Kong Daoist temple at Yuan Xuan Xueyuan 圓玄學院, a large and well-known Daoist temple complex in the New Territories, Hong Kong, Mr. Lee made his initial commitment to Daoism and Immortal Lü in 1959 and took the Daoist name Daomian 道勉 (strive for the Dao). After moving to Canada in 1967, he established a small temple in his basement that began to attract other Hong Kong emigrants. Subsequently the temple moved to Market Alley in Chinatown and then, in 1989, relocated to its rented space in the *Lee's Benevolent Association of Canada*. After fundraising among members, and with support from the Lee association, a building was purchased and a grand opening announced for the auspicious date of the eighth day of the eighth month, 1999.[8]

Both temples are very quiet during weekdays. The Evergreen Taoist Church is open weekdays until 4:00 p.m. and occupies three floors. An ancestral hall with ancestral plaques is on the second floor, while the third floor houses the main temple with its altar to three of the principal Quanzhen patriarchs: Lü Dongbin, Wang Chongyang 王重陽 (1113-70), and Qiu Changchun 丘長春 (1148-1227). On weekdays or weekends, there are usually a few Chinese seniors in the temple, chatting or making paper ingots for offerings. On Sunday mornings, regular chanting sessions are held, often with five to ten elderly chanters arranged at five tables.[9] Chimes, a drum, and pipes sometimes accompany the chanters. Po Yuen also holds similar sessions, although its main altar is dedicated solely to Lü Dongbin.

Regarding community relations, recruitment, and adaptation to Canadian life, the interviewee at Evergreen expressed a general satisfaction with being a representative of Chinese tradition and said that there was little interest in fostering new membership from outside the primarily Hong Kong immigrant

Chinese community. He added, though, that their door is open and visitors are always welcome. The Po Yuen temple members appear to be interested in finding ways to attract new and younger members, for example, by offering *Taiji* classes.[10] There is also interest in attracting non-Chinese members, but language was seen as a problem as temple texts are all written in Chinese and ceremonies are conducted in Cantonese. Po Yuen has regular lively meetings on Sundays, with a *zhai* 齋 (vegetarian) meal prepared by Mr. Lee's wife. In addition to regular chanting sessions, the temple conducts spirit-writing sessions that generate new scriptures.[11] These texts are shared among sister temples. The participants are energetic and supportive but the lack of younger participants may become problematic as dedicated members age.

A third Daoist group represents a departure in both its constituency and its orientation. Much like the Tibetan Buddhist organizations described in Chapter 9, it has managed to bridge the cultural gap and establish a high degree of participation by members of non-Asian origin. In 1968, the Daoist monk Moy Lin-shin (Mei Lianxian 梅連羨) and the Daoist priest Mui Ming-to (Mei Mingdao 梅明道) established Fung Loy Kok Taoist Temple (Penglai ge 蓬萊閣) on the grounds of the Yuan Xuan Xueyuan temple complex in Hong Kong, where Po Yuen leader James Lee first declared his commitment to Lü Dongbin. Moy Lin-shin also founded the Toronto Tai Chi Association in 1970, from which grew the Taoist Tai Chi Society of Canada. In 1981, Moy Lin-shin and Mui Ming-to established Fung Loy Kok's first "high shrine"[12] on Bathurst Street in Toronto, initiating both Chinese (principally Hong Kong immigrants) and non-Chinese. The Taoist Tai Chi Society, which Moy Lin-shin saw as a vehicle for Daoist cultivation, provided a natural entrée for Westerners into the more religious dimensions of Fung Loy Kok. In 1990 and 1991, small ("low") shrines to Guanyin 觀音 were established in Victoria and Vancouver. The Vancouver branch is very active, with many members of the Tai Chi Society participating in Fung Loy Kok events as non-members. During the summer of 2006, nearly a hundred people attended a workshop sponsored by Fung Loy Kok, and although most were not members, they participated in chanting and meditation as well as *Taiji* practice. Most participants were native English speakers, but the chanting was conducted in Cantonese. Efforts are being made to translate some of the key texts so that participants can better understand the content of scriptures. Workshops led by several dedicated members are held in Vancouver and Victoria and a few other sites in British Columbia, and provide opportunities for lectures, discussion, and meditation. In Vancouver, there are regular weekly chanting sessions before *Taiji* classes; they include a collection of standard Daoist chants that are also performed at Evergreen Taoist Church and Po Yuen Taoist Centre Society, as well as popular Buddhist mantras (*zhou* 咒), such as

Dabei zhou 大悲咒 and *Guanyin jing* 觀音經. Mantras are considered to have great power when chanted with sincerity, conferring fortune, averting disaster, and preventing illness, while the very act of chanting the text is a means of accruing spiritual merit.

Jim Nicholson, a national board member and leader of Fung Loy Kok, suggested that the core group of Fung Loy Kok participants consists of roughly twenty to thirty individuals in their mid-twenties to forties, most of whom are non-Chinese. The relationship of Fung Loy Kok to Daoist groups in Canada and Asia is cordial, but stronger links are not actively sought. Daoist groups in East Asia have been supportive of Fung Loy Kok: monks from the Baiyun guan 白雲觀 (White Cloud Temple) in Beijing have twice visited Fung Loy Kok in Canada and have stayed at the society's large rural *Taiji* retreat centre near Orangeville, Ontario. In 1995, Fung Loy Kok invited members of Hong Kong-based Feng Yin Seen Goon (Pengying xianguan 蓬瀛仙觀) to perform the Daoist ceremony of the Three Pure Ones at the Chinese Cultural Centre in Vancouver's Chinatown. Leaders of Fung Loy Kok regularly visit Hong Kong, maintaining informal relationships with Daoist organizations. Apart from groups of Cantonese- and Toisan-speaking Chinese seniors in the Toronto and Calgary branches, active participants are primarily non-Chinese, which means that difficulties associated with the language barrier are less of a concern. Fung Loy Kok certainly enjoys robust support from Taoist Tai Chi Society members across Canada, as evidenced by the new retreat centre near Orangeville, Ontario. The architecture reflects traditional Chinese form, with the typical curved rooflines, and yet is complemented by a relatively simple and unadorned internal space.

Except for Fung Loy Kok, with its mixed membership, Daoist groups in Vancouver consist largely of members with origins in Hong Kong, and activities are conducted in Cantonese. To some degree, this makes it difficult to move beyond their particular cultural horizon to appeal to broader Canadian society. While interviewees are aware of this, it does not evoke any sense of urgency. Contributions to Canadian society appear to hinge on maintaining a strong cultural identity that is a source of both strength and an alternate view of the human condition that remains open, to varying degrees, to newcomers.

Other Sectarian/Popular Groups

Two significant and robust popular religious groups in the Lower Mainland describe themselves variously as I-kuan Tao (Yiguan Dao 一貫道) (Way of Unity) and T'ien Tao (Tian Dao 天道 "Celestial Way"). The two groups are independent but share a common ancestry. The sect began to grow and spread throughout China in 1930, when Zhang Tianran 張天然 assumed leadership as the eighteenth patriarch. Zhang died in 1947, and his two wives, vying for leadership, split the sect.¹³ All of the myriad Lower Mainland groups are associated with the branch of one of Zhang's wives, Madame Sun 孫.

T'ien Tao patriarchs are said to have transmitted a secret dharma down through the ages to the present. Whereas in the past this dharma was transmitted mind to mind from teacher to a single worthy disciple, it is now widely available to all who have the right karmic affinity (*yuan* 緣). This teaching is believed to have been manifested in a variety of religious forms. Thus, all T'ien Tao or Yiguan Dao groups acknowledge the validity of "five religions": Islam, Christianity, Buddhism, Daoism, and Confucianism. Relinquishing religious affiliations outside of the T'ien Tao is considered unnecessary. The members I encountered during several visits to three different sites were eager to share their message of salvation; a missionary zeal is associated with efforts to establish new places of worship and practice, and the need to convert and initiate new members is essential and urgent. Urgency stems from a belief that the world, which moves through successive cycles, is now in the third phase of history and drawing close to its inevitable collapse into chaos. Only the initiated will be saved. Despite the drive to gain members, the groups are not publicly aggressive in the promotion of their Dao. Outsiders would not recognize sites visited as centres of religious practice, as members meet in locations that look like single-family homes or commercial spaces. Hence, anyone who locates such a site must do so through personal introduction.¹⁴ T'ien Tao groups have flourished in the Lower Mainland, brought both by relatively recent immigrants from Taiwan and Hong Kong and by individuals specifically charged by Asia-based centres with the founding of new sites in countries outside Asia. No overarching organizational unity exists among the various branches and sub-branches of T'ien Tao, and communication among different groups is very limited, with each group vying independently for membership. Groups of devotees gather in "public halls" (*gongtang* 公堂), buildings designated exclusively for religious activities, and in "family halls" (*jiatang* 家堂), private homes with one section reserved for religious practice while a family occupies the rest of the house.

My first visit was to a public hall named Mingde Fotang 明德佛堂 (Buddha Hall of Bright Virtue), located very near the boundary between Vancouver and Burnaby; its exterior is indistinguishable from a private home. The main floor of the house includes a small kitchen and an area for gatherings at which vegetarian food is served. The upper floor houses the main hall, with a small altar on which five figures are represented: Lü Dongbin; Living Buddha Jigong (Jigong huofo 濟公活佛), a renegade monk and popular hero; Buddha of the future, Maitreya (Mile pusa 彌勒菩薩); Bodhisattva of compassion, Guanyin 觀音; and Guan Yu 關羽, the popular red-faced martial figure seen in many of Vancouver's Chinese restaurants. The centre of the altar is occupied by a tall brass oil lamp bearing the symbol for the Venerable Mother, a circle containing the characters *wu* 無 and *ji* 極, meaning "limitless" and connoting that which is beyond human conception. Through moral discipline and religious praxis, members hope to return to the Venerable Mother, the primordial source.

The interviewees were two of three female assistants to the unmarried female leader of the Mingde Fotang, known as an "initiator" (*dianzhuan shi* 點傳師), all of whom reside at the Buddha Hall. The hall was founded in 1989 when a "Dao transmitting teacher" came to Vancouver from Hong Kong.[15] Later, the elder of the Hong Kong home branch[16] trained his daughter, and the group who accompanied her, in skills needed to establish and maintain a Buddha Hall in Canada, including vegetarian cooking, scripture study, Mandarin Chinese, and mastery of T'ien Tao doctrine. In 1992, the elder's daughter assumed leadership of the Buddha Hall.[17] The move to establish Buddha Halls outside Hong Kong was supported by a message divined through spirit writing (see note 11), which was interpreted as a suggestion that the future for T'ien Tao would be favourable in North America.[18] The Hong Kong branch elder took up residence in Canada in 2002 and now supports activities at a second Buddha Hall on East Broadway and lends support to the 1989 Buddha Hall and others in New York, Australia, England, Holland, Scotland, and San Francisco. Such efforts are all the more remarkable, given the elder's advanced age of nearly ninety.

The interviewees described a very well defined organizational structure consisting of groups with specific categories of responsibility. A diverse range of well-defined duties makes it possible for members to find a way to contribute. Clearly, the organization has been a success; with approximately 500 members, it claims to be the largest branch outside Hong Kong. At a subsequent visit to the East Broadway site on a celebration date coinciding with the full moon, this emphasis on member participation was well demonstrated. Three female members were assigned the task of greeting guests and members at a reception table. The first part of the afternoon included a brief lecture on Confucian virtues followed by several morality plays performed by men and women; these were aimed at demonstrating how basic Confucian virtues can be integrated into daily life, including the message that excessive materialism should be avoided. A dozen or so children then sang a number of songs with similar themes. The second part of the festivities included a session in which the five deities and the Venerable Mother, mentioned above, were venerated. The atmosphere was at once lively and social but focused on religious and Confucian moral education.

Participants were generally first-generation immigrants. Most spoke Cantonese, although a few members are from Taiwan and speak Mandarin. As for the group's relationship to people outside their own religious community, while there is a handful of non-Chinese participants (including Vietnamese), the group would very much like to find ways to attract more new members who are Canadian-born. It is concerned about its limited constituency, and dependence on new Chinese immigrants limits potential growth and makes it difficult to develop a profile among Canadians unfamiliar with Chinese language and traditions.

Followers of T'ien Tao claim that it is not a religion. Instead, employing the metaphor of a hand, T'ien Tao is the palm that unites the five fingers (Islam, Christianity, Buddhism, Daoism, and Confucianism). T'ien Tao embraces the five religions but is said to ultimately transcend religion. In theory, this should contribute positively to missionary activities among individuals living outside the Chinese religio-cultural complex. Practically speaking, however, the leadership is often ill-equipped linguistically to carry this message beyond the first-generation Chinese immigrant communities. Furthermore, the message presented strongly emphasizes mainstream Confucian virtues, and the principal deities that provide a focus for worship do not parallel the "five religions" and would be unrecognizable to most people who are unfamiliar with Chinese religious culture. Thus, the potential for finding an ecumenical common ground is perhaps unrealized because of the iconography and ritual performance of devotees.

Two representatives of another T'ien Tao group appear to be somewhat better placed to carry their message beyond the Chinese-speaking community. The main reason for this is that one of the local leaders came from Singapore and thus was quite proficient in English. The founder (one of the interviewees) also has a good grasp of the Western way of looking at the world and so is better positioned to explain the various doctrinal elements to individuals who have no familiarity with traditional Chinese religious symbols, iconography, and concepts. Another very committed member is non-Chinese and helps by acting as "a bridge" to those unfamiliar with Chinese religious culture. When the two interviewees were asked about the perceived needs of the group's founder and supporters to adapt to Canadian society, they noted that Westerners are difficult to approach due to a difference in worldviews and basic cultural assumptions. It was also explained that the families of Westerners have different problems, with a perceived higher rate of family instability and drug abuse. These perceived differences require those who offer the teachings of T'ien Tao to maintain an attitude of flexibility and accommodation. One illustration of this has been the removal of the five religious figures normally found on T'ien Tao altars.

Some members designate parts of their homes for T'ien Tao activities. On full-moon and new-moon days, groups of up to a dozen individuals gather in front of altars to pray and offer fruit and tea to the deities. Residents in these houses are required to offer prayers every day and to care for the altar.[19] Weekly study meetings held at the group founder's home are attended by up to twenty members. Although most participants are Mandarin speakers, primarily from

Taiwan (in their late forties and early fifties), the study sessions include translation from Mandarin to English, Cantonese, and Vietnamese. In Chapter 7, Cam Van Thi Phan includes a brief discussion of the new Vietnamese religion Cao Daiism, which also integrates ideas from Daoism, Buddhism, Confucianism, and Christianity. Translation is made possible through sons and daughters of devotees who are attending university in the Lower Mainland. Despite the willingness to make adjustments, however, it is difficult to attract non-Chinese members, who remain in the minority.

Links with T'ien Tao in Asia and the United States are ongoing and essential to the survival of Lower Mainland groups. First, any initiations must be conducted during visits by masters from Taiwan or Los Angeles. Once initiated, devotees are able to progress through participation in ongoing activities conducted in the Lower Mainland. The second essential link with centres outside British Columbia involves sacred texts. As with all T'ien Tao groups, spirit writing is an important source of sacred texts.[20] This activity, usually conducted by children who have led pure lives (including a vegetarian diet), is the principal means of generating or transmitting texts, which has proved very difficult to support in Canada. Thus, spirit-writing texts are regularly sent to the group in British Columbia from Los Angeles and Taiwan.

The group's activities revolve around two primary and connected motivations: T'ien Tao is a resource for improving and sustaining the moral fabric of Canadian society more broadly while also providing a means for self-improvement as members gradually create a path of return to the Venerable Mother. Encouragement of members to adopt a vegetarian diet is linked to a more compassionate attitude toward living things and is seen as a positive contribution to the environment. The group's identity centres on an accepting attitude toward diverse religions, which makes it possible to look more directly to a shared humanity embodied in their own Dao.

Another major group claiming a trans-religious identity is Falun Gong 法輪功. Regular practice meetings occur twice weekly in Vancouver at Queen Elizabeth Park and seven days a week in Burnaby at Civic Square (beside the Burnaby Public Library). Meetings also occur regularly in Richmond, Port Coquitlam, and Port Moody, and Falun Gong followers are active in Armstrong, Cranbrook, Whistler, Nelson, and Kelowna, and on Vancouver Island in Victoria, Nanaimo, and Duncan.[21]

Falun Gong traces its beginnings to a single living founding figure named Li Hongzhi 李洪志. The organization, which began in China in 1992, spans fifty countries, with activities in forty-five US states[22] and evolved around Li's personal vision, which takes as its central motif the Dharma Wheel (*falun* 法輪). Although the Dharma Wheel is a Buddhist symbol, Li has interpreted it in a manner that transcends Buddhism, even providing a means of gaining insight into aspects of the world usually restricted to scientific modes of inquiry. According to Li, Buddhists have only touched the tip of a vast dharmic iceberg, the immensity of which goes far beyond Buddhism and certainly beyond its misrepresentation by academic scholars of Buddhism.[23] An interviewee explained that the Dharma Wheel is related directly to the body. Each person has a wheel in their abdomen, but in most people it is still. The master is able to set this wheel in motion, even remotely for those who are not able to see him personally. Once in motion, exercises are prescribed and available on videotape or DVDs or in books, to continue the process of cultivation, a process that is both physical and spiritual. This is a practice related to salvation and not merely *qigong* 氣功 (literally, "*qi* work"), a generic term that designates a host of modern health practices, including meditation, bodily movement (*Taiji quan* 太極拳, for example), and laying on of hands. Health is central to the lives of practitioners because it is a prerequisite for spiritual advancement and the loss of their karmic burden. This link between health and religious salvation has endured in Chinese religions for centuries. Further, one of the basic assumptions in the theoretical frameworks of Chinese medical traditions has been that the individual bears responsibility for his or her own health. Health is addressed in Falun Gong by conforming to basic Confucian virtues, meditation practice, and the performance of a fixed set of slow-motion exercises, often in groups.

Activities revolve around three foci: small study groups on the founder's principal texts, group practice of the Falun exercises, and cultural events such as a large Chinese New Year gala event. Attendance at study and practice sessions varies, typically between 10 and 30. Larger sessions attract 100 to 200 people. I observed two outdoor practice sessions involving a handful of participants. A small sign in front of the practice area indicated that they were Falun Gong followers; the exercises involved a range of standing postures and seated meditation. Given the position of Falun Gong vis-à-vis the government of the People's Republic of China, group activities also involve efforts to raise public awareness of the difficulties they face in maintaining their practice. During the summer of 2006, I attended a large Falun Gong rally that took the form of a procession through downtown Vancouver, including Chinatown. The focus of the rally was the contention that practitioners in China were being systematically imprisoned so that their organs could be extracted for sale. Another example of protest is the booth set up outside the Chinese consulate on Granville Street, which is manned twenty-four hours a day. Raising public awareness of their plight and who they really are is part of being a Falun Gong practitioner. Beyond this, their contribution to society is framed in terms of being more compassionate, tolerant members of society, being good moral examples, and relieving the strain on the health care system. The social structure of the group does not include a formal hierarchy or gender-based division.

When members were asked about adaptation in Canada, the response was that, beyond adjustments concerning the necessity of translation from Chinese, changes have been minimal due to the universal nature of the teachings. Roughly half the people at meetings speak only Chinese while the rest function with varying degrees of fluency in English. Translation is routinely provided at meetings. A minority of Lower Mainland participants are non-Chinese, whereas participants at meetings in Victoria are up to 80 percent non-Chinese.

Organization of the groups occurs "naturally." Given the public nature of practice sessions, interested observers simply inquire and begin attending sessions. As this occurs, groups gradually grow and begin to cohere. When I asked about regional variations, I was told that there are no significant distinguishing characteristics. They have one teacher and one teaching, and that is the universal standard followed by all those who gather to practise. While I have not had enough exposure to various groups in the province to assess this claim, it would seem reasonable, given the absence of any formal organizational structure or leadership hierarchy (no volunteer boards, committees, or councils) and the organic nature of the group's growth.

Buddhists

In British Columbia, Chinese Buddhist groups embrace a variety of religious expressions, ranging from Pure Land rites of repentance and Chan 禪 (Zen) and *Zhiguan* 止觀 (Insight) meditation to respect for Confucian moral virtues, ancestor veneration, and divination.[24] One of the oldest Buddhist organizations is the Universal Buddhist Temple, with roots going back to a group of lay devotees who would meet in Vancouver's Chinatown during the late 1960s; it continues to conduct regular divination sessions based on the *Book of Changes* (Yijing 易經).[25] Chinese Buddhist organizations also appear in a variety of ways, as communities, societies, foundations, associations, temples, and monasteries, as is true of the Buddhist organizations originating in Thailand, Sri Lanka, and Tibet that are discussed elsewhere in this book. A description of six representative Buddhist organizations follows.

Tung Lin Kok Yuen Canada Society

The name Tung Lin Kok Yuen Canada Society (Jianada Donglian Jueyuan 加拿大東蓮覺苑) combines characters from the names of the society's two Hong Kong founders, Sir Robert Ho Tung, son of an English father and Chinese mother, and his wife, Lady Clara Lin-Kok, also of European and Asian descent. Among the Buddhist groups described here, Tung Lin Kok Yuen stands out as the only one that does not lay claim to a monastic founding figure or make specific claims concerning lineage. Robert Hung Ngai Ho, seventy-four, grandson of the Hong Kong founders and chair of the family company, immigrated to Vancouver in 1989. In 1994, he established the Tung Lin Kok Yuen Canada Society on East Broadway in Vancouver. The aim was to combine the elements of a traditional temple within the limited space of an urban site. Thus, there is a principal worship hall known as the Grand Precious Hall that can accommodate over 200 people, a Meditation Hall, a Longevity Hall with the medicine Buddha as a focal point, and a separate Ancestral Hall, with customary plaques commemorating ancestors of Tung Lin Kok Yuen attendees. In addition, there is a kitchen for preparing vegetarian food, a Multi-purpose Hall, office space, and a very good library.

The chief administrator travels regularly between Hong Kong and Canada to oversee and facilitate cooperation between the Tung Lin Kok Yuen in Hong Kong and the society in Vancouver. Visits by groups of up to seventy monastics from Asia are arranged to help with some of the larger dharma assemblies and rituals. In this cooperative relationship, each group manages its own affairs, but funding for the Vancouver group depends on support from Hong Kong.

The abbess of the temple is Venerable Sik Yin-tak, who obtained a doctoral degree in Buddhist studies while living in Japan during the 1960s. Later, in her native Hong Kong, she assisted at a private Buddhist college. She is active in leading regular ceremonies and in teaching members. Temple operations and a variety of volunteer committees are managed by a twelve-member volunteer board of directors, including Mr. Ho as permanent director. Male and female devotees do not assume distinct roles based on their gender.

Interviewees cited four defining moments in the temple's history in British Columbia. First, on 31 July 1994, shortly after construction of the new temple was completed, a grand opening was held to welcome members of the general public. Second, in 1996, the first "Sea-Land Assembly" was held. This ceremony is an act of compassion performed to assist the souls of all those who have died. Seventy monks and nuns from Hong Kong, Singapore, Malaysia, and Thailand participated. Since that first gathering, the event has been repeated and will be held at regular intervals. In 1997, the third major event, the first "Eight Precepts Assembly" retreat, led by Hong Kong dharma masters, was held. Fifty to sixty laypeople lived as monastics, beginning their days at 8:30 a.m. with chanting and meditation and following a routine during which no speaking was permitted unless absolutely necessary and monastic precepts were observed. These retreats are planned at three-year intervals. The final event mentioned was the donation of $4 million to the University of British Columbia through the Tung Lin Kok Yuen Canada Foundation, established in 2003 by Robert Hung Ngai Ho. Of this, $3 million will support a chair in Buddhism and Contemporary Society, while the remaining $1 million will be used to run a program in the Institute of Asian Research in cooperation with the Department of Asian Studies.[26] It should also be mentioned that in September 2006, the temple received a visit from the Dalai Lama, who gave a brief dharma talk on inter-Buddhist cooperation.

The motivations of those who attend the temple were described as including four general tendencies. There are those whose focus is devotional, who see the Buddha as a god to be worshipped and appealed to through petitionary prayer. Others try to learn the theory underlying Buddhist doctrine, and practise meditation primarily for its health benefits. Still others see their practice as a means of letting go of the many stresses associated with modern life. Through this they see themselves working toward inner peace. Finally, there are those who are primarily concerned with seeking wisdom and insight through meditation, chanting, and the study of sutras. Another aspect that motivates many is community service. These categories contrast with the general perceptions of approaches to Theravada Buddhism in the Myanmarese community (see Chapter 6).

Pure Land ceremonies take place every Sunday morning, led by the abbess and the nuns of the temple, and are attended by forty to fifty Chinese people. These ceremonies make it possible for participants to fully express repentance, gratitude, and faith in the Buddhas, including *Amito fo* 阿彌陀佛 (Amida Buddha), who grants entry into the Pure Land, which is separate from the sufferings of daily life and where conditions for self-cultivation are ideal. After the ceremonies, lectures conducted by the abbess and Mrs. Susan S.H. Kong, one of the directors, are often attended by over a hundred people; members also do community work such as visiting hospitals, and participate in cultural activities such as *Taiji quan* 太極拳 and calligraphy classes at the temple. The temple supports the publication of Buddhist texts and teachings, eighteen of which have been published to date. One of the main goals of Tung Lin Kok Yuen is to educate the public at large about the merits of the Buddhist way of life, so accomplished scholars and practitioners are invited to give lectures.

The temple board and Chairman Ho are concerned that the regular attendees are aging and that the future of the society will depend on bringing in new supporters and participants. Most participants appear to be elderly Hong Kong immigrants with limited facility in English. This tends to isolate the group from potential newcomers who may have an interest in Buddhism but have little familiarity with Chinese language or Buddhist rituals. These concerns parallel the experience of Japanese Buddhist churches (Chapter 10), which are also concerned with aging and declining membership and a need to move across the cultural divide between their members and broader Canadian society. A temple development committee has been convened to explore, among other things, ways of attracting students who are pursuing an academic interest in Buddhism.[27] There appears to be a great willingness to adapt if this will help develop broader participation and foster an appreciation of Buddhist teachings in a new generation.

This adaptability and accommodative approach extends to meditation practice. Individuals who may not be temple members or regular attendees and who practise different approaches to meditative training are welcome to participate in meditation at Tung Lin Kok Yuen. The willingness to accept and work with these "mobile" practitioners fits with the mission of the temple to foster exchange between traditions of Buddhism. Although Tung Lin Kok Yuen identifies itself with Pure Land teachings, dharma masters from a variety of traditions are invited to lead events and offer their teachings at the temple and at temple-sponsored events. Of course, the Pure Land traditions and others, such as Chan, have a long history of blending approaches to practice. Since the temple's founding, two distinct groups have coalesced around two teachers. One class is held upstairs and is based on a method associated with the founding of Tiantai Buddhism, known as "cessation and contemplation" (*Zhiguan* 止觀).[28] This class is attended primarily by Cantonese speakers. Downstairs, a Caucasian monk teaches Chan (Zen) meditation in English to a group that includes several non-Chinese people.[29] These groups do not interact but pursue their respective approaches within the same temple. These are perceived as diverse but equally valid approaches being passed along within a Pure Land temple.

Dharma Drum Mountain

Dharma Drum Mountain (Fagu shan 法故山), a Chan Buddhist organization, was established in British Columbia in 1994 in a rented space at the Marpole-Oakridge Community Centre in South Vancouver. This worldwide group's principal teacher was Venerable Master Sheng Yen 聖嚴 (1930-2009), a native of Jiangsu Province in China. The master combined Chan practice in the lineage of both the Linji 臨濟 (Jap.: Rinzai) and Caodong 曹洞 (Jap.: Sōtō) sects with the goal of creating a Buddhist Pure Land on Earth (*jingtu* 淨土). He began teaching in 1975 and prior to his death in January 2009 has resided half of the year at a retreat centre near New York City, in the valley of the Shawangunk Mountains of upper New York state. The other half of the year is spent at Dharma Drum Mountain, near the northern tip of the island of Taiwan, in Jinshan Township, Taipei County, where there is a cluster of four affiliated centres. Key moments have been the groundbreaking for the new centre in Richmond in May 2005, and the grand opening, which I attended in the summer of 2006. The new centre is not a temple but, rather, a practice hall. Architecturally, the structure strikes a balance between traditional Chinese forms and contemporary North American design.

The group is administered independently from the main centres in New York and Taiwan by a seven-member volunteer board whose chair is a woman.[30] Its activities have four foci:

- Chan meditation is considered the foundation and groups gather weekly in the Lower Mainland and less frequently in the BC Interior. These sessions are attended by about twenty people, with instruction available in both Mandarin and English. Less frequent three-day retreats are also held at the Richmond centre.
- Chanting and Pure Land repentance ceremonies are held regularly and are attended by Chinese practitioners.
- Sutra and text study groups meet weekly, led by meditation teachers, with about ten to twenty individuals receiving instruction.
- Social events, open to the public, are opportunities to celebrate Chinese culture and frequently include musical and other cultural performances and food for purchase.

Prior to 2003, participants were almost exclusively Chinese immigrants from Taiwan and Hong Kong, and the primary teaching language was Mandarin. By 2003, there was enough interest on the part of non-Chinese individuals to warrant a regular weekly meditation class taught in English. Increased participation by non-Chinese individuals remains a priority. The primary motivation of those following the teachings of Venerable Sheng Yen was explained as cultivating a peaceful heart (*anxin* 安心) and developing the ability to help oneself through practice. The notion of developing a Pure Land on Earth through uplifting the quality of individuals is central.

Dharma Drum's program has three components: (1) an academic education centred on the Dharma Drum Mountain's *sangha* university in Taiwan;[31] (2) the general dissemination of Chan practice as widely as possible; and (3) the active spreading of compassion through the performance of charitable deeds. All this is supported by the organization's two monthly magazines, *Humanity* and *Dharma Drum* (in Chinese), and Venerable Sheng Yen's writings of over a hundred books, including *Hoofprint of the Ox,* an overview of Chan practice.[32]

Distinctions between monastic and lay followers are generally not made, and the meditation teachers are lay practitioners. A division is made between those who have received dharma transmission from the teacher, becoming advanced teachers, and others who come to learn meditation or take part in repentance ceremonies. But the responsibility often falls on local teachers who may not yet have received full transmission. Male and female followers do not have distinct roles, although a difference between Chinese and non-Chinese members was mentioned. "Canadian" participants are more enthusiastic about learning the more abstruse teachings on subjects such as emptiness and no-self, and are considered very dedicated to meditation practice; thus, the teaching process for them was described as being more "direct." This is attributed to a lack of cultural hindrances, because everything is new to them. As with Tung Lin Kok Yuen, Chinese immigrant participants tend to favour the culturally familiar ritual dimensions of practice, whereas the "Canadian" participants are more inclined to participate in study groups and meditation classes.

As for adaptation to the Canadian context, the main obstacle is how to overcome the language barrier. Ritual chants have been produced with romanized sounds for those who cannot read Chinese, but the teaching is offered in much the same way as in Taiwan. It was conceded that further adjustments may have to be made but these are seen as "expedient means," of the sort that Buddhism has accommodated throughout its history. While there is little contact with other Buddhist groups in British Columbia, the interviewees expressed a willingness to explore this possibility when this young group becomes more established. At an international level, this is illustrated by the dialogue in 1998 between Venerable Sheng Yen and the Dalai Lama in New York. A guiding principle of Venerable Sheng Yen, a student of several major approaches to the Buddha dharma, appears to have been the gradual unification of Buddhism. Thus, there is an impetus to communicate with other groups but also formidable challenges in relations with the many organizations that wish to retain the integrity of their own approaches.

Gold Buddha Monastery

The third site, located off Main Street, a ten-minute drive from downtown Vancouver, is designated as neither a temple nor a meditation centre but a monastery. The founder of Gold Buddha Monastery was Venerable Master Hsüan Hua 宣化, who was born in 1917 in Manchuria.[33] Master Hsüan Hua "left the family" at the age of nineteen, shortly after the death of his mother, when he constructed a hut by his mother's grave and dwelt there for three years (the traditional Confucian mourning period). The master then travelled to Caoxi 曹溪, where he took up residence at Nanhua Monastery 南華寺 under the guidance of Elder Master Xu Yun 虛雲,[34] who transmitted the dharma to him. This formally established Master Hsüan Hua as the Ninth Patriarch of the Wei Yang Sect (Weiyang zong 溈仰宗).[35] As early as 1959, he began bringing the dharma to America when he established the Sino-American Buddhist Association, now known as the Dharma Realm Buddhist Association.

At the invitation of a lay Buddhist group associated with the Universal Buddhist Temple at East 49th Avenue and Fraser Street in Vancouver, the master visited Vancouver in 1984, and the old Salvation Army building at 201 East Hastings Street at Gore Avenue in Chinatown was purchased that same year. The Gold Buddha Monastery opened at that East Hastings site in the spring of 1984 and was placed under the direction of two American monks from the California headquarters. All of the monasteries are viewed as affiliates of the main centre, The City of Ten Thousand Buddhas, located in Mendocino County, California, and established by the master in 1974. The lay community of devotees provided much of the labour needed to clean and repair the building, played music for ceremonies, and provided translations for the monks' lectures from English to Cantonese. The monastery flourished with much participation from the Vancouver-area Chinese community, most of whom were Hong Kong immigrants. The current two-and-a-half-storey red brick building purchased in 2000 alternately houses resident monks or nuns (both cannot dwell at the monastery at the same time) and Chinese seniors. On the main floor there is a kitchen for the preparation of vegetarian food, an office and reception area, and the main Dharma Hall, with approximately 140 kneelers and a main altar with the figures of Sakyamuni, Manjusri Bodhisattva (Wen-shu pusa 文殊菩薩), and the Universal Worthy Bodhisattva (Puxian pusa 普賢菩薩). There is also a room with a shrine dedicated to Venerable Master Hsüan Hua, where his relics (*śarīra*) are displayed on the altar. The basement houses classrooms and a library of Buddhist texts.

The development of the initial site was supervised by the California board of directors, but the management of the monastery in Vancouver is now entirely local, with an elected volunteer board composed of laypersons and monastics. Consultation is sought with the headquarters and with a monastery in Calgary. The busy Vancouver monastery is currently in the charge of a female Caucasian dharma master who was ordained thirty-six years ago and was assigned her first posting to Vancouver by Master Hsüan Hua in 1985. It is run by monastics with lay devotees organized into various committees. There are no clear divisions between the duties of men and women, although residences for each are on separate floors in accordance with traditions of propriety. Monks and nuns have alternated as managers of the monastery throughout its history. Ceremonies of initiation ("taking refuge") and transmitting of the precepts are performed exclusively by men. Repentance rites are "hosted" and led by women. In Asia, this would normally also be done by men.

Milestones in the group's history in British Columbia include the founding of the first and second centres in 1984 and 2000, and the establishment of facilities to house Chinese seniors for some of the festivals that run for several days to a week. There is a very active translation committee that provides Buddhist texts in English translations published through the Buddhist Text Translations

Society based at The City of Ten Thousand Buddhas. In 2003, a school for children was established. Youngsters are introduced to Buddhist teachings, Chinese language and culture, and the need for good moral conduct based on eight Confucian virtues emphasized by Master Hsüan Hua: filiality (*xiao* 孝), fraternity (*ti* 悌), loyalty (*zhong* 忠), trustworthiness (*xin* 信), propriety (*li* 禮), righteousness (*yi* 義), incorruptibility (*lian* 廉), and a sense of shame (*chi* 恥). Other significant events include the 1985 visit of a Vancouver delegation to The City of Ten Thousand Buddhas, the 1997 visit of a large group of dharma masters from China, and three visits by Master Hsüan Hua, the last commemorating the tenth anniversary of the monastery.

Motivations for attending monastery activities vary, but two tendencies are evident. The older generation of Chinese participants tends to focus on rituals of repentance and chanting; I was told that this seems to give them a sense of cultural continuity with their early lives and helps affirm their cultural identity. The younger participants often appear to be more intense in their practice and study than the older Asian-born members. Their motivations are often related to questions and difficulties in their lives. Others come to question their current religious affiliations and seek answers in what is seen as a return to Buddhism. In some cases, younger people participate in the monastery's activities "despite their parents."

The Pure Land Great Compassion Repentance is held on Monday through Friday from 1:00 p.m. to 2:30 p.m. in the afternoon. Other, longer repentance ceremonies can take precedence. For example, from 12 to 18 March 2006, ceremonies commenced with the celebration of Bodhisattva Guanyin's birthday. Lectures, popular with the younger attendees, are held throughout the week on a variety of topics and, depending on the circumstances, can be translated into Cantonese, Mandarin, Vietnamese, or English. A major annual festival is held with Chinese seniors being the focal point, with a feast, prizes, and professional entertainment. This is a major though unadvertised event, and the response is great (usually 600 guests attend). Youth events include the annual Cherishing Youth Day, organized by the youth group of roughly twenty. This is an outreach event to youth in the larger community. A youth conference with guest speakers is also held each year. (Similar initiatives concerning religious education in the Vietnamese lay Buddhist community are described in Chapter 7.) Each month, a ritual known as "Seeding the Waters," a Buddhist expression of reverence for life, is performed, in which the appropriate species of fish are placed into waters around the Lower Mainland. I was told that Gold Buddha Monastery is the only Buddhist group that performs this rite, although other Buddhist groups may contribute and up to a hundred people attend. Despite the Chan origins of the founding master, practice of Chan meditation is not evident in the weekly schedule. As with Tung Lin Kok Yuen, both Chan and Pure Land figure in the identity of the monastery, but the Pure Land ceremonies hold great appeal for most of the participants.

As for its relationship with other Buddhist groups, the Gold Buddha Monastery sees itself as different because practices in the monastery lack Chinese folk or popular religious elements, and the interviewee indicated that no Daoist or popular religious influence is present. New visitors look for signs of "contamination" and are happy with what they see. Opportunities for interaction with other groups and with the broader community are welcomed. The monastery has also hosted inter-religious panels, and school groups regularly visit the monastery. Outreach is considered an important activity.

Adaptation to Canadian society has not involved adjustment to basic teachings or ceremonies, and this is related to the group's claim of orthodoxy in their religious practice. There has been a discernible shift in the tenor of the monastery in Canada compared with institutions in Asia. The interviewee suggested that Canadians are considered more laid back, with a slower pace of life that is more conducive to a contemplative life. "Canadians" are perceived as simple and good and, because they lack complex "cultural baggage," it is easier in some ways for them to be receptive to Buddhism.[36] Asians are described as very energetic, contributing much to the running of the monastery, but their cultural assumptions and expectations regarding Buddhism can be an obstacle. In general, "Canadians" are seen as both aware of and, for the most part, well disposed toward Buddhism.

Po Lam Buddhist Association

The process of adaptation in British Columbia is influenced to some extent by the location of Buddhist centres. The Po Lam Buddhist Association, a nunnery on the outskirts of Chilliwack, a solidly Christian constituency, is one example. The interviewee at Po Lam, a nun from Hong Kong, explained that they just want to fit in and be supportive of the community. The nuns are respectful of other religious traditions and simply wish to contribute to the cause of peace within individuals and in society. They do not want a "fancy" temple but prefer the simple architecture of their current centre. The focus of the nunnery is intentionally adjusted to fit with the interests of those who attend events hosted by the nuns. Meditation was contrasted with chanting, for example. The former is culturally more accessible to non-Chinese visitors, who feel awkward and unsure about chanting Buddhist sutras or participating in rites of repentance. The interviewee suggested that in the future they may look into presenting rituals in English, perhaps in combination with phonetic renderings of the Chinese texts. Outside large, culturally diverse urban centres, in locations such as Chilliwack or in the case of Yitung Buddhist Temple in Kelowna, which is located in an old church, less emphasis on the ideal of centres in Canada being exactly like those found in Taiwan or Hong Kong may have its advantages.

Tzu Chi Foundation Canada

Having looked at groups based in a temple, a practice centre, and a monastery or nunnery, we turn now to a group best described as a social service or charitable organization.[37] Gary Ho, a Taiwanese immigrant to Canada, founded the Tzu Chi Foundation Canada in British Columbia in 1992. The South Vancouver office serves as the Canadian headquarters for the larger organization, which has a presence in 300 cities in forty countries. Its roots are in Taiwan, where Master Cheng Yen 證嚴, a twenty-nine-year-old Buddhist nun, founded the organization in 1966. The organization grew out of her work with a group of thirty housewives who contributed funds to begin charitable work among the poor in Taiwan. This nun, a Nobel Peace Prize nominee, is said to have been inspired by hardship endured after the sudden death of her father and her own poor health. Her mission took shape in four areas: charity, medicine, education, and culture; the group is oriented toward a goal of transforming the world by transforming individuals.[38] Mr. Ho explained that this transformation takes place in two ways. First, there are opportunities for transformation of the recipients of charitable work. Such work includes assisting teachers in BC secondary schools and volunteering in seniors' residences, all the way up to domestic and foreign disaster relief. Second, there is the transformation experienced by those who do the work. Mr. Ho explained that this is why Tzu Chi volunteers feel a debt of gratitude for the opportunities they have to serve communities locally and globally. The projects undertaken by the foundation in British Columbia illustrate the commitment of the volunteers. Seven volunteer-run food banks have been established, with twenty volunteers at each location each week. In partnership with the Salvation Army, roughly 800 individuals are fed each day. A Chinese-language program was established in 1996 and runs in five Lower Mainland schools every week, with a total of eighty to a hundred volunteers. The foundation has also raised and donated $16 million over the past fourteen years, some of which has been allocated to educational, charitable, and cultural institutions in the province. Over $8.5 million was committed to international relief efforts.

A volunteer board of nine directors and two paid staff oversee all of this activity. Each of the five urban centres in the Lower Mainland (Burnaby, Coquitlam, Vancouver, Richmond, and Surrey) has its own leaders, who coordinate activities with volunteer teams. Altogether, 700 to 800 volunteers are active each week in British Columbia. Most are female, primarily Taiwanese immigrants who moved to Canada through the 1990s. Language difficulties are minimal because the vast majority of participants speak Mandarin. The group does not cohere around a specific body of doctrine or cultivation practices but, rather, around the general mission of social engagement with the aim of fostering a new world culture of mutual harmony and respect for each other and the Earth. This means that it is able to accommodate many approaches to the practice of Buddhism and espouses no sectarian affiliations. Like other Buddhist groups, Tzu Chi has a narrow constituency in the province. When asked about whether members of broader Canadian society understand who they are, Mr. Ho explained that this is not an issue. Over time, more people will come to understand. He views this as a natural process requiring no specific attention. Obviously, the group is interacting with Canadian society on many levels already. With its overwhelming focus on socially engaged practice, Tzu Chi Foundation Canada is a unique religious phenomenon. This is a Buddhist-inspired organization that lacks temples, monasteries, practice centres, monks, and nuns.

Vancouver International Progress Society

Another group that should be mentioned is the Vancouver International Progress Society, which has its roots in Taiwan and the huge temple complex, Foguang Shan 佛光山 (Buddha's Light Mountain), established in 1967 by Venerable Xing Yun (Xing Yun Dashi 星雲大師); institutionally, it straddles the categories of "temple" and "social service organization."[39] Located on thirty acres in Kaohsiung County, Taiwan, Foguang Shan remains a centre of monastic practice, and Venerable Xing Yun claims the title of Forty-Eighth Generation Patriarch of the Linji Chan lineage. The founder, Xing Yun, is viewed, though, as an innovator who presents his teachings in a manner that transcends sectarian and national boundaries. This approach is described as "Humanistic Buddhism" (Renjian fojiao 人間佛教), which emphasizes practice in daily life directed outward to the liberation of all. This is a basic Mahayana orientation, but, for modern Buddhist organizations, it entails social service and concern for the environment. Doctrinally, it is tied to an emphasis on the Buddha as a historical person who taught people in basic and universally accessible terms how to cultivate themselves through their ordinary engagement in social activity. Like the Tzu Chi Foundation Canada, the Vancouver International Progress Society and the other hundred chapters of the Buddha's Light International Association work on educational, health, and environmental initiatives.[40]

Ideally, the types of concern and orientation implied by "Humanistic Buddhism" mean that the founder's hope for bridging cultures is not constrained by sectarian and culture-specific practice. There can, however, be a tension between this ideal and the practical function it has for residents of the Lower Mainland. Members of the British Columbia centre located atop the Aberdeen Mall in Richmond view their place in the community as one of cultural continuity and security for those who have left their homes in Asia for a new life in British Columbia. As with many other Buddhist centres that I visited in the course of writing this chapter, my visits to the centre in Richmond made clear that this is a very lively and well-attended place of practice.[41] It was evident, though, that the participants were virtually all Mandarin speakers, many of whom hailed from Taiwan. Certainly I felt welcome and everyone was very friendly, but, as with other Buddhist groups in the province, it is a challenge to actively realize the ideal of bridging cultures envisioned by the founder and the members of the organization. Efforts are being made to actively incorporate young people into the daily activities of the centre, including assisting with ceremonies, serving food at celebrations, and taking responsibility for educational initiatives and for fundraising and donation projects for various charitable causes. Given their integration into the educational system, proficiency in English, and close familiarity with broader Canadian society, young people may well be the bridge that will take shape over the coming decades.

The variety of institutional configurations and organizational flexibility makes it difficult to generalize. Some of the Chinese who landed in Canada forty or fifty years ago had a desire for integration coupled with the need for support found in clan associations, social activities, and business associations. Perpetuation of social and cultural networks was an important part of life. Today, younger generations are not confronted by the same social dynamic. As the older generation attending Daoist or Buddhist temples for non-religious reasons declines, it is apparent that they may not be replaced by their children and grandchildren. The story is somewhat different for those groups supported, for example, by recent immigrants from Taiwan, who arrive in a country with a legacy of over thirty years of multiculturalism. The need for cultural solidarity remains, and there is considerable comfort in the familiar while adjusting to a new country. Many immigrants need a place where they can socialize freely in their first language, and religious sites often provide such opportunities. At the same time, however, there is a consciousness of the opportunities to build bridges beyond the bounds of their religious institutions, and a frank recognition of the challenges this entails. Leaders are committed to the teachings they profess and follow, and are convinced that they can enrich Canada. An impression I received from the groups I visited, both those described here and the many groups that could not be included, is that visitors are always welcome, as are opportunities for advancing the cause of mutual understanding.[42]

Notes

1 A BC Statistics report indicates that from 1990-94, 56 percent of Chinese immigrants to Canada were of the investor class, and of those, 53 percent chose to reside in British Columbia: Jennifer Hansen, *Special Feature Immigrants from India and China,* BC Stats, Management Services, March 2004, 2. See http://www.bcstats.gov.bc.ca/pubs/immig/immo34sf.pdf.
2 *Special Feature: English Language Ability of Recent Immigrants,* prepared by BC Stats, March 2004, 1. See http://www.bcstats.gov.bc.ca/pubs/immig/immo22sf.pdf.
3 The vast majority of immigrants were men, due, as Yung notes, to social mores against women leaving the home: Judy Yung, *Chinese American Voices: From the Gold Rush to the Present* (Berkeley: University of California Press, 2006), 2. A census taken in 1871 indicates that for every 1,000 Chinese, only 35 were women: Edgar Wickberg, ed., *From China to Canada: A History of the Chinese Communities in Canada* (Toronto: McLelland and Stewart, 1982), 14.
4 Discussion of this first phase of settlement and religious activity and further references are found in James Placzek and Larry DeVries, "Buddhism in British Columbia," in *Buddhism in Canada,* ed. Bruce Matthews (London: Routledge, 2006), 3-4.
5 Yen Wo Society building, 1713½ Government, Victoria, BC.
6 Tangong is said to have "attained the Dao" (*de Dao* 得道) at the age of twelve and to have had great spiritual efficacy (*shenli* 神力), with which he could summon rain and cure the illnesses of the villagers.
7 As a deity, Laozi is usually referred to as Taishang laojun 太上老君 (the most high Lord Lao).
8 The account offered here is based on a personal interview with James Lee (10 September 2006) and on an article titled "Daojiao puxuan jingshe yange" 道教普玄精舍沿革 (The Evolution of Po Yuen Daoist Temple) in a grand opening commemorative booklet provided to me during the visit.
9 The lead chanter is not a permanent designation and may be either male or female.
10 It is worth noting that the *Taiji* instructor was a member of the Taoist Tai Chi Society of Canada, which is very closely linked to its sister organization, the Fung Loy Kok Institute of Taoism. More will be said about Fung Loy Kok below.
11 Spirit writing takes place in a formal ritual context. Although procedural details may vary, it involves the "transmission" of texts through automatic writing (often in sand) performed by an individual gifted in channelling the words of various deities.
12 High shrines include paintings of the Jade Emperor, Lü Dongbin, and Guanyin on a large altar, whereas low shrines include only a painting of Guanyin on a small altar. Also, high shrines usually occupy their own building or room, whereas the smaller shrines are usually found in Taoist Tai Chi Society practice spaces.
13 Philip Clart, "Opening the Wilderness," *Journal of Chinese Religions* 28 (2000): 128-29.
14 I am grateful to Professor Emeritus Daniel Overmyer of the Department of Asian Studies and the Centre for Chinese Research at the University of British Columbia, for his introduction to members of two of the T'ien Tao sites that I visited.
15 This "Dao transmitting teacher" now resides in Toronto.
16 I was told that the Hong Kong branch was established in 1960 by the owner of a movie theatre. There are currently four branch halls in Hong Kong.
17 Sadly, the leader of this Buddha Hall passed away in 2006 during the course of my research for this chapter. Her kindness and generosity will be remembered by me and others who had the good fortune to meet her.
18 Clart, "Opening the Wilderness," 137.
19 This includes trimming wicks, adding oil to the lamps, burning incense, and changing the fruit and tea.

20 As mentioned above, this practice also figures prominently in some Daoist temples, including the Po Yuen Taoist Centre Society.
21 This list should not be taken as exhaustive, as the activities of the Falun Gong groups are subject to constant change and lack any central directing body.
22 A directory of sites is found on the main Falun Dafa website, http://falundafa.ca/contacts.htm. Elsewhere on the same site is a statement that the group is active in sixty countries.
23 These views are expressed most succinctly by Li Hongzhi in the introduction to his book titled *Zhuan falun* 專法輪 (n.p., 1996), 1, see also 12. This text is available in electronic format and contains no publication details other than the author's name and the date of publication. See http://www.falundafa.org/book/chibig5.htm.
24 See Placzek and DeVries, "Buddhism in British Columbia," for a helpful overview.
25 The Universal Buddhist Temple is now situated at 525 West 49th Avenue in Vancouver.
26 Another comparable contribution was made to the University of Toronto at Scarborough by Tung Lin Kok Yuen in Hong Kong, and assistance has been ongoing in the establishment of the Centre of Buddhist Studies at the University of Hong Kong. Funds have also been provided to support a Buddhist university in Thailand.
27 I have been working on this committee since early 2006.
28 The teacher of the *Zhiguan* meditation form is a retired gentleman who immigrated to Canada from Hong Kong to work as a project manager in the construction industry. His knowledge of meditation is based on his experiences with a Tibetan Buddhist master who resides in Toronto.
29 This monk spent thirteen years in a Japanese Sōtō Zen monastery before returning to Canada and assuming teaching duties at Tung Lin Kok Yuen.
30 Initially, in 1994, there had been two monastics from Taiwan on the board (one nun and one monk).
31 *Sangha* refers to the community of Buddhist nuns and monks who follow the Buddhist precepts and spread the dharma to humanity. The university is to be expanded with the addition of a lay university that is already under construction.
32 Venerable Sheng Yen, *Hoofprint of the Ox* (Oxford: Oxford University Press, 2002).
33 The history recounted in this opening section is taken from a personal interview with a female dharma master on 26 January 2006; a monastery publication, *Red Lotuses Abound in the Valley of a Thousand Mountains, Twenty Years of Fellowship with GBM: Commemorating the 20th Anniversary of Gold Buddha Monastery* (Vancouver: Gold Buddha Monastery, 2004); and *Xuanyan zhengfa: Wanfo cheng* 宣演正法萬佛城 (Propagating the Dharma: The City of Ten Thousand Buddhas) (Ukiah, CA: Dharma Realm Buddhist Association and the City of Ten Thousand Buddhas, 1996).
34 I encountered the name of this Chan teacher in my interviews and research at the Po Lam Buddhist Association (Baolin xuefo hui 寶林學佛會) in Chilliwack, where the abbess, Venerable Sik Yin-kit, explained that her teacher, Sing Yat (Sheng Yi 聖一), in Hong Kong had been a student of Elder Master Xu Yun. The same teacher was also revered by Lady Clara Lin-Kok and Sir Robert Ho Tung.
35 At present, I have no clear information on the origins and history of this sect.
36 The "baggage" in question seemed to have much to do with the "running around" from temple to temple, which can create a more "jaded" outlook. Westerners, on the other hand, being less knowledgeable concerning the variety of Chinese religious expression, are thought to have fewer expectations and a "simpler outlook."
37 On 9 September 2006, while attending a public photographic exhibit organized at the University of British Columbia by the Tzu Chi Foundation Canada, I was fortunate to speak with the chair of the Canadian chapter, Mr. Gary Ho, who described the foundation's activities.

38 A motto of the group is constituted by three vows of the founder: Purify minds / Harmonize society / Free the world from disasters.
39 This organization also has a centre in Victoria: Buddha's Light International Association of Victoria, 89 Somerville Road, Yarraville.
40 The main website of the association mentions that the following places have centres: the United States of America, Canada, Australia, New Zealand, France, Germany, the United Kingdom, the Netherlands, Sweden, Norway, Russia, Malaysia, Singapore, the Philippines, Japan, Hong Kong, Macao, Thailand, India, Brazil, Argentina, and Africa. See http://www.blia.org/english.
41 On the occasion of my first visit, the large and beautifully appointed Buddha Hall was filled with monastic and lay chanters.
42 Given the brevity of this chapter and the vast scope of its subject, it was not possible to consider more than a few examples of Chinese religious groups in British Columbia. Sadly, it was not possible to include several groups that had kindly consented to interviews.

Concluding Comments
Dan Overmyer

The first book to discuss some Asian religious traditions in British Columbia was *Circle of Voices: A History of Religious Communities in British Columbia*, edited by University of British Columbia scholars Charles P. Anderson, Tirthankar Bose, and Joseph I. Richardson, and published in 1983.[1] It includes chapters on Buddhism, Hinduism, Islam, the Sikh religion, the Ismaili Shia community, and Zoroastrianism. It also includes chapters on "Native Indian Spirituality," Baha'i, and Judaism, but the majority of its studies are on twelve Christian denominations.

More recently, it was the work of Larry DeVries of Langara College in Vancouver that provided the stimulus for this book – in 1999 a twenty-page list of Asian religious groups in the province, and in 2000 a proposal for a course on Asian religions in British Columbia, supported by a provincial grant. In the spring of 2000, Don Baker and Diana Lary of UBC suggested to me that we meet to "discuss a cooperative research project" in this area, so we called a meeting for 8 December of that year; the meeting was attended by DeVries, Baker, Professor Richard Menkis of the UBC Religious Studies Program, and me. We agreed to plan for a conference and publication on this project and to seek funding for these endeavours. We met again in early 2001 and put together a list of thirteen topics and scholars to write about them. The project then lost momentum for awhile because everyone was very busy with teaching and other research projects, and in 2002 I went off to teach at a university in Taiwan.

In November 2004, however, we met again to draft a formal proposal for the project and a list of research questions for its authors to consider, including such themes as the history of the ethnic groups involved and of their religious institutions, the beliefs and practices of their traditions in British Columbia, social dynamics within the group and among related groups, and their relationships to Canadian society and its multicultural policies. We also continued our efforts to recruit local scholars for the project, emphasizing that all were expected to visit a variety of sites to observe activities, interview both leaders and ordinary participants, collect written materials, and take photos. In early 2005, Pitman Potter, the director of the UBC Institute of Asian Research, told us that the Institute would provide some funding for our project. Funding was also promised by Simon Fraser University and Langara College. Once this was clear, we sought the necessary approvals for interviewing human subjects and organized a planning meeting of all involved on 23 April 2005, at which our authors discussed their preliminary ideas. That November, we met again at UBC to discuss preliminary reports by the authors, and began planning for a workshop at which all the authors would present draft book chapters on their topics, to be distributed in advance for discussion by all. This workshop was held at Langara College on 11 March 2006 and was a great success. As a result, all were asked to submit "final" drafts to me by 1 September that year, for which guidelines for content, style, and permissions were distributed to all. Our emphasis was on detailed reports of what people in the groups studied actually do, written for non-specialist readers. In the meantime, the editors prepared a detailed publication proposal for UBC Press. Then followed a long process of writing, editing, and rewriting, in the normal fashion for such publications. In the summer of 2007, DeVries compiled and re-edited all the chapters.

I have enjoyed reading and editing the detailed discussions in this book, particularly what Larry DeVries calls journeying "deep into the realm of the particular." His interview-based descriptions of the founding, activities, and rituals of Hindu groups are a fitting beginning for this book. He also discovered that the first Hindu association in British Columbia was founded by a German swami in 1957! Kamala Nayar's discussion of the gurdwara (temple) as providing the fundamental identity of the Sikh community and its social life is also beautifully done. Derryl MacLean notes that Canadian Muslims, far from moving from secular to "fundamentalist" religious life, as is commonly believed, instead absorb Canadian multiculturalism as a positive community value. This is true in part because many BC Muslims have moved here from "some part of Asia as an intermediary location, usually East Africa or Fiji," a process he calls a "double diaspora." Rastin Mehri's chapter on Zoroastrians in British Columbia provides vital background information on this less well known community, with fascinating insights into the differences between those who have come here from Iran and from the Parsi populations of India.

In their chapter on Thai and Lao Buddhism in British Columbia, James Placzek and Ian Baird note the difficulties stemming from the fact that these forms of Buddhism depend on ordained monks, who have been few and far between here. This problem has been solved in part by monks visiting from elsewhere and by ordained Caucasian monks from the Birken Forest Monastery near Princeton, British Columbia. Lay participants have also done much to keep the tradition going. In 2006, three ethnic Lao boys were ordained in a BC monastery, so a start has been made on developing local leadership. The situation has been easier for Sri Lankan Buddhist groups, because they have a larger local population to draw from, as Bandu Madanayake reports. A large vihara, or monastery, has been established in Surrey, staffed by monks from Sri Lanka, Thailand, Germany, and elsewhere in Canada. It provides a meeting place essential to community identity and activities. The author provides valuable discussions of the festivals and classes provided here, and also describes the activities of Buddhists from India and Myanmar (Burma). Cam Van Thi Phan, who is both an ordained nun and a graduate student at UBC, describes in detail the activities of Vietnamese Buddhists in the province, from both an inside and an outside perspective. She provides an interesting discussion of generational differences in attitudes toward both traditional beliefs and Canadian society in what is a valuable case study of ethnic adaptation to a multicultural milieu.

Don Baker has found that Koreans who attend Christian churches often do so not as a strategy to integrate with mainstream Canadian culture but in order to have a place of refuge where they can assemble with other Korean immigrants and speak their own language. Marc des Jardins' richly detailed study of Tibetan religions in British Columbia demonstrates the complexity of the many branches of these traditions and the heavy involvement of non-Tibetans in them, along with teachers from Tibet itself. As he comments, "[Unlike some of the other traditions discussed in this book,] Tibetan Buddhism ... has depended on non-Tibetan adherents. Religion in this fragmented community is central to its rise and establishment in the region. Tibetan lamas belonging to the community in exile from their homeland were instrumental in starting groups and centres where Tibetan Buddhism was taught and practised. In the beginning, the vast majority of members and students in these centres were Canadian- and American-born and newly converted to Buddhism." Although more people of Tibetan and Chinese origins are now involved, the tradition is still quite diverse, in part depending on whether teaching in the group is done in English or Mandarin.

Japanese Buddhist groups in our province also have difficulty recruiting and training their leaders, most of whom still come from seminaries in Japan or the Institute of Buddhist Studies in Berkeley, California. Michael Newton, the author of Chapter 10, on Japanese religions, is both an ordained Sōtō Zen priest and a faculty member of Simon Fraser University and Langara College. This dual background enables him to provide valuable introductions to Pure Land and Zen Buddhism in British Columbia and to such lay groups as the Sōka Gakkai. He also discusses the Shinto Konkōkyō and the new Institute for Research in Human Happiness, which was founded by a pious businessman in 1986. Most of the groups he discusses are open to all members of Canadian society and conduct worship services in English, with texts translated into English, so they fit more easily into the surrounding society.

The last two chapters in our book are on forms of Chinese religions in our province, by Li Yu on Chinese Christianity, and Paul Crowe on Daoist, Buddhist, and popular sectarian groups. The 2001 Census of Canada counted 365,485 people of Chinese cultural background in British Columbia, 24 percent of whom were Christians, the largest single Asia-related religious tradition in the province, so Li Yu is dealing with a quantitatively important topic. Chinese Protestantism began through the efforts of Caucasian missionaries in BC in the nineteenth century, but since the end of the Second World War, such mission work has ceased and the rapid growth in the number of Chinese Christians has been due to the efforts of Chinese immigrants and residents themselves. There has been little influence from churches in China. Li Yu comments on the important issue of cultural identity: "Although Chinese Christians maintain and reconstruct their Chinese identity, they also argue that there are some weaknesses in traditional Chinese culture. They believe that if Christian beliefs and practices could be integrated with Chinese tradition, a new Chinese culture compatible with modern society would emerge." The author concludes: "Christianity practised by the Chinese in this province is a Chinese belief system with a specific context and with its own local concerns."

The Daoist groups investigated by Crowe were founded by representatives of mother temples in Hong Kong. Their rituals are conducted in Chinese, but they attempt to reach out to people of non-Chinese background through lectures, discussions, meditation, and *Taiji* exercises. The popular sect Tian Dao (T'ien Tao "Celestial Way") attracts many laypeople through its rituals, lectures, and morality plays in Chinese, and, as I can attest, through serving excellent vegetarian meals! Meetings are held both in a chapel and in the homes of members. The well-known Falun Gong is also active in Vancouver, with lectures and meditation exercises in several locations. Crowe also discusses several Chinese Buddhist temples and lay groups, as well as local branches of international Buddhist organizations such as the Dharma Drum Mountain, the Gold Buddha Monastery, and the Tzu Chi Foundation Canada, which is best described as a social service organization with Buddhist roots that is run largely by nuns and laywomen. Its founder is a nun who has been nominated for a Nobel Peace Prize because of her successful charitable work. Chinese Buddhism is doing well in our province, as are other forms of Chinese religions.

There have been many studies of Asian religions in the United States since 1988, and three books on such traditions elsewhere in Canada were published in 2000, 2005, and 2006, but *Asian Religions in British Columbia*, the first to be published solely on this topic, is a book that we hope will lead to further study and discussion of the interactions of religions and cultures.[2]

In the introduction to their book *Asian American Religions: The Making and Remaking of Borders and Boundaries* (New York University Press, 2004), Tony Carnes and Fenggang Yang discuss what they call "Boundary Resources" provided by Asian American religions. These resources include "Spiritual Resources-Socialization with Invisible Others" such as gods and spirits, and "Symbolic-Cultural Resources for Centering, Organization, Continuity, and Control of Boundaries." These resources may include cultural centres, publications, and culture and language classes. Another resource is "Therapeutic," which refers to activities that provide affirming new identities for immigrants by "offering a network of mentors and friends that provide emotional support while empowering them to independence." A fourth resource is "Socioeconomic Services," which include "loans and gifts, job training and referrals, shelter, food and clothing." These services also include "Political-legal" aid, such as citizenship classes, voter registration, and immigration legal advice. Yet another form of aid provided by some religious groups consists of educational services, such as job training and language classes. Recreational services can include choral singing, sports, bingo, and overnight trips to places of interest.[3] Most of these resources are provided by the BC groups as well. It is this combination of resources that makes the religious groups discussed here such a vital force in the lives of those involved in them, and demonstrates their contribution to Canadian society.

This book provides much information about the history, organization, and activities of religious groups in British Columbia, but we need more detailed studies of the religious life of individuals and families in the various traditions, of the differences of belief and practice among different generations of immigrant families, of the religious situations of ethnically mixed groups, and of such topics as the development of Asian-North American forms of theology in some Christian denominations active in our province. Others can no doubt think of additional topics to investigate, but we have done our best with the resources and time available to us.

As the chapters of this book indicate, in its peaceful mix of ethnic groups and religions, British Columbia provides a positive example for the future of the world. It is a wonderfully human place, a little United Nations, with people, customs, and food from every corner of the earth. On a foundation of good, honest, and democratic government, freedom of religion, liberal immigration policies, and legally affirmed multiculturalism, people here can meet and worship as they please. Almost all the religious traditions discussed here are open to everyone, even though in practice they might appeal primarily to those of one ethnic origin. They can serve both as a refuge for recent or older immigrants and as a base for supporting and serving the community. Elsewhere in the world, some religious traditions encourage hostility and violence toward those who do not conform to them, but here, for the most part, people do their own thing and let others do theirs. Of course, there are tensions within some of these religious groups, between generations, between participants from different ethnic backgrounds and those with different interpretations of their traditions, but we are not aware of hostilities shown by one tradition toward another. In a few BC ethnic groups, old forms of coercion still exist, particularly concerning marriage and women, but on the whole, these are not supported by their religious leaders.

This book contains much information about religious traditions, but it is really intended primarily to be about British Columbia society in all its variety and complexity. For the editors, religious activities are social phenomena that deserve to be studied and understood because they tell us so much about those involved in them. As social phenomena, they are as important as ethnicity, social status, and political and economic activities. This book is written not for other scholars but for everyone who might be interested, including ordinary folk, schoolteachers, community leaders, religious groups, and those working for government and business. We hope it will be useful to all, encouraging people to rejoice in the diversity of human life in this beautiful province.

Notes

1 Lantzville, BC: Oolichan Books, 1983.
2 For examples of these earlier American studies, see Raymond Brady Williams, *Williams on South Asian Religions and Immigration: Collected Works* (Aldershot, UK, and Burlington, VT: Ashgate, 2004); David Yoo, *New Spiritual Homes: Religion and Asian Americans* (Honolulu: University of Hawai'i Press, 1999); and Pyong Gap Min and Jung Ha Kim, eds., *Religions in Asian America: Building Faith Communities* (Walnut Creek, CA: AltaMira Press, 2002). For examples of Canadian studies, see Harold G. Coward, John R. Hinnells, and Raymond Brady Williams, eds., *The South Asian Religious Diaspora in Britain, Canada, and the United States* (SUNY Series in Religious Studies) (Albany: State University of New York Press, 2000); Paul A. Bramadat and David Seljak, eds., *Religion and Ethnicity in Canada* (Toronto: Pearson Longman, 2005); Paul A. Bramadat and David Seljak, eds., *Christianity and Ethnicity in Canada* (Toronto: University of Toronto Press, 2008); and Bruce Matthews, ed., *Buddhism in Canada* (London and New York: Routledge, 2006).
3 This summary is based on Tony Carnes and Fenggang Yang, eds., *Asian American Religions: The Making and Remaking of Borders and Boundaries* (New York: New York University Press, 2004), 13-15.

Suggested Readings

Agehananda Bharati, Swami. *The Ochre Robe*. London: George Allen and Unwin, 1961.
Anderson, Charles P., Tirthankar Bose, and Joseph I. Richardson, eds. *Circle of Voices: A History of the Religious Communities in British Columbia*. Lantzville, BC: Oolichan Books, 1983.
Anderson, Kay J. *Vancouver's Chinatown: Racial Discourse in Canada, 1875-1980*. Montreal and Kingston: McGill-Queen's University Press, 1991.
Austin, Alvyn J. *Saving China: Canadian Missionaries in the Middle Kingdom, 1888-1959*. Toronto: University of Toronto Press, 1986.
Bains, Tara Singh, and Hugh Johnston. *Four Quarters of the Night: The Life Journey of an Emigrant Sikh*. Montreal and Kingston: McGill-Queen's University Press, 1995.
Basran, Gurchan Singh, and B. Singh Bolaria. *The Sikhs in Canada: Migration, Race, Class, and Gender*. New Delhi: Oxford University Press, 2003.
Bays, Daniel H. *Christianity in China: From the Eighteenth Century to the Present*. Stanford, CA: Stanford University Press, 1996.
Boyce, Mary. *A Persian Stronghold of Zoroastrianism*. Oxford: Oxford University Press, 1977.
–. *Zoroastrianism: Its Antiquity and Constant Vigour*. Costa Mesa, CA: Mazda Publishers, 1992.
–. *Zoroastrians: Their Religious Beliefs and Practices*. New York: Routledge, 2001.
Bramadat, Paul A., and David Seljak, eds. *Religion and Ethnicity in Canada*. Toronto: Pearson Longman, 2005.
–, eds. *Christianity and Ethnicity in Canada*. Toronto: University of Toronto Press, 2008.
Cadge, Wendy. *Heartwood: The First Generation of Theravada Buddhism in America*. Morality and Society Series. Chicago: University of Chicago Press, 2005.
Carnes, Tony, and Fenggang Yang, eds. *Asian American Religions: The Making and Remaking of Borders and Boundaries*. New York: New York University Press, 2004.
Chadney, James G. *The Sikhs of Vancouver*. New York: AMS Press, 1984.
Chapuis, Oscar. *A History of Vietnam: From Hong Bang to Tu Duc*. Westport, CT: Greenwood Press, 1995.
Clart, Philip. "Opening the Wilderness for the Way of Heaven: A Chinese New Religion in the Greater Vancouver Area." *Journal of Chinese Religions* 28 (2000): 127-44.
Coward, Harold G., John R. Hinnells, and Raymond Brady Williams, eds. *The South Asian Religious Diaspora in Britain, Canada, and the United States*. SUNY Series in Religious Studies. Albany: State University of New York Press, 2000.
De Silva, K.M.D. *A History of Sri Lanka*. Colombo: Vijitha Yapa Publications, 2003.

Dhillon, Mahinder Singh. *A History Book of the Sikhs in Canada and California*. Vancouver: Shiromani Akali Dal Association of Canada, 1981.
Do, Merdeka Thien-Ly Huong. *Cao Daiism: An Introduction – God-Way for the Third Universal Salvation*. Perris, CA: Cao Dai Temple Overseas, Center for Dai Dao Studies, 1994.
Dorai, Louis-Jacques. *The Cambodians, Laotians and Vietnamese in Canada*. Canada's Ethnic Group Series No. 28. Ottawa: Canadian Historical Association, 2000.
Dossa, Parin. *Racialized Bodies, Disabling Worlds: Storied Lives of Immigrant Muslim Women*. Toronto: University of Toronto Press, 2009.
Dreyfus, G.B.J. *The Sound of Two Hands Clapping: Education of a Tibetan Buddhist Monk*. Berkeley: University of California Press, 2003.
Eck, Diana. *A New Religious America: How a "Christian Country" Has Now Become the World's Most Religiously Diverse Nation*. San Francisco: HarperSanFrancisco, 2001.
Ecklund, Elaine Howard. *Korean-American Evangelicals: New Models for Civic Life*. New York: Oxford University Press, 2006.
Fields, Rick. *How the Swans Came to the Lake: A Narrative History of Buddhism in America*. Boston: Shambala, 1992.
Forsthoefel, Thomas A., and Cynthia Ann Humes, eds. *Gurus in America*. SUNY Series in Hindu Studies. Albany: State University of New York Press, 2005.
Frye, Richard N. *The Heritage of Persia*. Costa Mesa, CA: Mazda Publishers, 1993.
Guest, Kenneth J. *God in Chinatown: Religion and Survival in New York's Evolving Immigrant Community*. New York: New York University Press, 2003.
Hinnells, J. "The Modern Zoroastrian Diaspora." In *Migration: The Asian Experience*, ed. J.M. Brown and R. Foot, 56-82. Oxford: St. Martin's Press, 1994.
–. "The Zoroastrian Diaspora in Britain, Canada, and the United States." In *The South Asian Religious Diaspora in Britain, Canada, and the United States*, ed. H. Coward, J. Hinnells, and R. Williams, 35-54. Albany: State University of New York Press, 2000.
–. *Zoroastrian and Parsi Studies: Selected Works of John R. Hinnells*. Aldershot, UK: Ashgate Press, 2000.
–. *Zoroastrian Diaspora: Religion and Migration*. Oxford: Oxford University Press, 2005.
–. *Zoroastrians in Britain*. Oxford: Clarendon Press, 1996.
Hirschman, Charles. "The Role of Religion in the Origins and Adaptation of Immigrant Groups in the United States." *International Migration Review* 38, 3 (2004): 1206-33.
Israel, Milton. *In the Further Soil: A Social History of Indo-Canadians in Ontario*. Richmond Hill, ON: Organization for the Promotion of Indian Culture, 1994.
Jackson, Carl T. *Vedanta for the West: The Ramakrishna Movement in the United States*. Bloomington: Indiana University Press, 1994.
Jacobsen, Knut A., and Kumar P. Pratap. *South Asians in the Diaspora: Histories and Religious Traditions*. Leiden: E.J. Brill, 2004.
Jacobsen, Knut A., and Selva J. Raj, eds. *South Asian Christian Diaspora: Invisible Diaspora in Europe and North America*. Aldershot, UK: Ashgate Press, 2008.
Jagpal, Sarjeet Singh. *Becoming Canadians: Pioneer Sikhs in Their Own Words*. Vancouver: Harbour Publishing, 1994.
Jeung, Russell. *Faithful Generations: Race and New Asian American Churches*. New Brunswick, NJ: Rutgers University Press, 2005.
Johnston, Hugh. *The Voyage of the* Komagata Maru: *The Sikh Challenge to Canada's Colour Bar*. Delhi: Oxford University Press, 1979.
Karaka, D.F. *History of the Parsis, Including Their Manners, Customs, Religion, and Present Position*, 2 vols. London: Macmillan, 1884.
Karim, Karim H. *The Islamic Peril: Media and Global Violence*. Montreal: Black Rose Books, 2002.

Karmay, S.G. *The Great Perfection: A Philosophical and Meditative Teaching of Tibetan Buddhism*. Leiden: E.J. Brill, 1988.
Kim, Ai Ra. *Women Struggling for a New Life: The Role of Religion in the Cultural Passage from Korea to America*. Albany: State University of New York Press, 1996.
Kim, Rebecca Y. *God's New Whiz Kids: Korean-American Evangelicals on Campus*. New York: New York University Press, 2006.
Kwak, Tae-Hwan, and Seong Hyeong Lee, eds. *The Korean-American Community: Present and Future*. Seoul: Kyungnam University Press, 1991.
Kwon, Ho-Youn, Kwang Chung Kim, and R. Stephen Warner, eds. *Korean Americans and Their Religions: Pilgrims and Missionaries from a Different Shore*. University Park, PA: Pennsylvania State University Press, 2001.
Kwon, Okyun. *Buddhist and Protestant Korean Immigrants: Religious Beliefs and Socioeconomic Aspects of Life*. New York: LFB Scholarly, 2003.
Lai, David Chuenyan. *Chinatowns: Towns within Cities in Canada*. Vancouver: UBC Press, 1988.
Laquian, Aprodicio A., Eleanor R. Laquian, and T.G. McGee, eds. *The Silent Debate: Asian Immigration and Racism in Canada*. Vancouver: Institute of Asian Research, University of British Columbia, 1998.
Lawrence, Bruce B. *New Faiths, Old Fears: Muslims and Other Asian Immigrants in American Religious Life*. New York: Columbia University Press, 2002.
Lorenzen, David N., ed. *Bhakti Religion in North India: Community, Identity and Political Action*. Albany: State University of New York Press, 1995.
Ma, Ching. *Chinese Pioneers: Materials Concerning the Immigration of Chinese to Canada and Sino-Canadian Relations*. Vancouver: Versatile, 1979.
Madan, T.N., ed. *India's Religions: Perspectives from Sociology and History*. New Delhi: Oxford University Press, 2004.
Mayo, Joan. *Paldi Remembered: 50 Years in the Life of a Vancouver Island Logging Town*. Paldi, BC: Joan Mayo, 1997.
McDonough, Sheila, and Homa Hoodfar. "Muslims in Canada: From Ethnic Groups to Religious Community." In *Religion and Ethnicity in Canada*, ed. Paul Bramadat and David Seljak, 133-53. Toronto: Pearson Longman, 2005.
McLellan, Janet. *Many Petals of the Lotus: Five Asian Buddhist Communities in Toronto*. Toronto: University of Toronto Press, 1999.
Merdeka Thien-Ly Huong Do. *Cao Daiism: An Introduction*. Perris, CA: Centre for Dai Dao Studies, 1994.
Min, Pyong Gap, and Jung Ha Kim, eds. *Religions in Asian America: Building Faith Communities*. Walnut Creek, CA: AltaMira Press, 2002.
Minh Chi, Ha Van Tan, and Nguyen Tai Thu. *Buddhism in Vietnam*. Hanoi: Gioi Publishers, 1999.
Moghissi, Haideh, Saeed Rahnema, and Mark J. Goodman. *Diaspora by Design: Muslim Immigrants in Canada and Beyond*. Toronto: University of Toronto Press, 2009.
Nanji, Azim. "The Nizari Ismaili Muslim Community in North America: Background and Development." In *The Muslim Community in North America*, ed. Earle H. Waugh, Baha Abu-Laban, and Regula B. Qureshi, 149-64. Edmonton: University of Alberta Press, 1983.
Nayar, Kamala Elizabeth. *The Sikh Diaspora in Vancouver: Three Generations amid Tradition, Modernity and Multiculturalism*. Toronto: University of Toronto Press, 2004.
Nguyen Khac Vien. *Vietnam: A Long History*, rev. ed. Hanoi: Gioi Publishers, 1999.
Nigosian, S.A. *The Zoroastrian Faith: Tradition and Modern Research*. Montreal and Kingston: McGill-Queen's University Press, 1993.

Nimer, Mohamed. *The North American Muslim Resource Guide: Muslim Community Life in the United States and Canada.* New York: Routledge, 2002.
Numrich, Paul David. *Old Wisdom in the New World: Americanization in Two Immigrant Theravada Buddhist Temples.* Knoxville: University of Tennessee Press, 1996.
Osterhout, S.S. *Orientals in Canada: The Story of the Work of the United Church of Canada with Asiatics in Canada.* Toronto: Ryerson Press, 1929.
Overmyer, Daniel L., ed. *Religion in China Today.* Cambridge: Cambridge University Press, 2003.
Palsetia, J. *The Parsis of India: Preservation of Identity in Bombay City.* Leiden: E.J. Brill, 2001.
Pavri, J. *The Zoroastrian Society of British Columbia 1968-1978.* Vancouver: n.p., 1978.
Pechilis, Karen. *The Graceful Guru: Hindu Female Gurus in India and the United States.* New York: Oxford University Press, 2004.
Phan, Peter C. *Christianity with an Asian Face: Asian American Theology in the Making.* Maryknoll, NY: Orbis Books, 2003.
Placzek, James, and Larry DeVries. "Buddhism in British Columbia." In *Buddhism in Canada*, ed. Bruce Matthews, 1-29. London: Routledge, 2006.
Prebish, Charles S., and Martin Baumann, eds. *Westward Dharma: Buddhism beyond Asia.* Berkeley: University of California Press, 2002.
Rahula, Walpola. *What the Buddha Taught.* Dehiwala, Sri Lanka: Buddhist Cultural Centre, 1996. First published in 1959 by Grove Press.
Ramanujan, A.K., trans. *Speaking of Siva.* Harmondsworth, UK: Penguin, 1973.
Rochford, E. Burke. *Hare Krishna Transformed.* New and Alternative Religions Series. New York: New York University Press, 2007.
Roy, Patricia E. *A White Man's Province: British Columbia Politicians and Chinese and Japanese Immigrants, 1858-1914.* Vancouver: UBC Press, 1989.
Rukmani, T.S., ed. *Hindu Diaspora: Global Perspective.* New Delhi: Munshiram Manoharlal Publishers, 2001.
Schomer, K., and W.H. McLeod, eds. *The Sants: Studies in a Devotional Tradition of India.* Delhi: Motilal Banarsidass, 1987.
Semple, Neil. *The Lord's Domination.* Montreal and Kingston: McGill-Queen's University Press, 1996.
Sharma, Arvind. *The Concept of Universal Religion in Modern Hindu Thought.* London: Macmillan; New York: St. Martin's Press, 1998.
Smith, Jane I. *Islam in America.* New York: Columbia University Press, 1999.
Statistics Canada. *Immigrants from Vietnam in Canada.* Ottawa: Citizenship and Immigration Canada, 1996.
Suh, Sharon. *Being Buddhist in a Christian World: Gender and Community in a Korean American Temple.* Seattle: University of Washington Press, 2004.
Taylor, Charles, Amy Gutmann, et al. *Multiculturalism: Examining the Politics of Recognition.* Princeton, NJ: Princeton University Press, 1994.
Thiel-Horstmann, Monika, ed. *Images of Kabir.* New Delhi: Manohar, 2002.
Trout, Polly. *Eastern Seeds, Western Soil: Three Gurus in America.* Mountain View, CA: Mayfield, 2000.
Truth Monthly. *Searching for a Fulfilling Life: A Collection of Articles to Mark the Publication of the 100th Issue of the Truth Monthly.* Vancouver: Xuandao Press, 2001.
Verma, Archana B. *The Making of Little Punjab in Canada.* New Delhi: Sage, 2002.
Vertovec, Steven. *The Hindu Diaspora: Comparative Patterns.* London: Routledge, 2000.
Wang, Jiwu. *"His Domination" and "the Yellow Peril": Protestant Missions to Chinese Immigrants in Canada, 1859-1967.* Waterloo, ON: Wilfrid Laurier University Press, 2006.
Warder, A.K. *Indian Buddhism.* Delhi: Motilal Banarsidass, 1970.

Wickberg, Edgar, ed. *From China to Canada: A History of the Chinese Communities in Canada.* Toronto: McLelland and Stewart, 1982.
Williams, Raymond Brady. *Williams on South Asian Religions and Immigration: Collected Works.* Aldershot, UK, and Burlington, VT: Ashgate, 2004.
Yang, Fenggang. *Chinese Christians in America: Conversion, Assimilation, and Adhesive Identities.* University Park, PA: Pennsylvania State University Press, 1999.
Yao, W. "The Cult of Mahakala and a Temple in Beijing." *Journal of Chinese Religions* 22 (1994): 117-26.
Yoo, David. *New Spiritual Homes: Religion and Asian Americans.* Honolulu: University of Hawai'i Press, 1999.
Yung, Judy. *Chinese American Voices: From the Gold Rush to the Present.* Berkeley: University of California Press, 2006.
Zine, Jasmine. *Canadian Islamic Schools: Unveiling the Politics of Faith, Gender, Knowledge, and Identity.* Toronto: University of Toronto Press, 2008.

Contributors

Ian G. Baird holds a PhD in Geography from the University of British Columbia. As a mainland Southeast Asia specialist, he has lived and worked in Laos, Thailand, and Cambodia for much of the last twenty years. He is also the executive director of the nongovernmental organization Global Association for People and the Environment (GAPE), which is mainly active in southern Laos. Recently, he has developed a close relationship with the Lao community in Surrey and Abbotsford, British Columbia.

Don Baker teaches Korean civilization as a professor in the Department of Asian Studies at the University of British Columbia. He has been studying religion in Korea since 1971, when he began a three-year stay there as a Peace Corps English teacher. He earned his PhD from the University of Washington in 1983 with a dissertation on the eighteenth-century Korean Confucian confrontation with Catholicism. He has published widely on Korean religion, philosophy, traditional science, and history, including *Korean Spirituality* (University of Hawai'i Press, 2008).

Paul Crowe is director of the David Lam Centre and an assistant professor in the Department of Humanities at Simon Fraser University, where he also teaches in the Asia-Canada Program. He received his PhD in Asian Studies in 2005 from the University of British Columbia. His dissertation included partial translation and analysis of Yuan Dynasty Daoist inner alchemist Li Daochun's writings (ca. 1288). He is working on a book that expands on his graduate work. His current research combines textual translation and fieldwork in Canada and Hong Kong in order to document the history of Daoist groups in Canada.

Marc des Jardins is an assistant professor in Tibetan and East Asian Religions in the Department of Religion at Concordia University in Montreal. He has done fieldwork on Tibetan religions since 1991 and has specialized in indigenous Tibetan cults and the Bön religion. He received his PhD in 2002 from the Department of East Asian Studies at McGill University. After graduating, he pursued postdoctoral research on conflict resolution in Tibetan territories at the Institute of Asian Research at the University of British Columbia. He is currently conducting research in the Tibetan areas of Sichuan, Qinghai, and Gansu on Tibetan religious movements and the scriptural corpus of Bön. He has published several articles on the Bön religion and on an esoteric form of Chinese medieval Buddhism.

Larry DeVries obtained his MA and PhD in South Asian Studies at the University of Minnesota and is an instructor of Asian Studies and Religious Studies at Langara College in Vancouver. He has taught at the University of Minnesota, University of Washington, University of Hawai'i, and University of British Columbia, and served as co-editor on a National Endowment for the Humanities project at the University of Chicago. His interests and publications are in religion in contemporary society, myth and folklore, and language.

Derryl N. MacLean is director of the Centre for the Comparative Study of Muslim Societies and Cultures and an associate professor in the Department of History at Simon Fraser University. He is a social historian of religion with a PhD in Islamic Studies from McGill University. His work focuses on the sociology of religious contact and change, using data primarily from South and Central Asia. His current research addresses early modern Islamic millennialism, orientalism as a system, and diaspora Muslim communities in the West.

Bandu Madanayake studied Eastern and Western philosophy and received his MA and PhD in Buddhist philosophy from the University of Toronto. He has published numerous articles in various journals, most recently "Is There Consciousness in Nibbana?" "Mahabodhi Society of India," and "Mission of Arahant Mahinda to Sri Lanka." He worked for the government of Canada for over twenty years. His research focuses on Buddhist philosophy and history using Pali, Sanskrit, and Sinhalese sources.

Rastin Mehri, MA (Religious Studies, UBC), is completing his PhD in the Department of Study of Religions at the School of Oriental and African Studies in London. Since 2004, he has been the instructor for Classical Persian language at the Department of Linguistics at Simon Fraser University.

Kamala Elizabeth Nayar, PhD (1999, Asian Religions, McGill University), is lecturer in South Asian Studies at Kwantlen Polytechnic University, British Columbia. Her work on *Hayagriva in South India: Complexity and Selectivity of a Pan-Indian Hindu*

Deity (2004) is an extensive textual study of Indian religions. With *The Sikh Diaspora in Vancouver: Three Generations amid Tradition, Modernity and Multiculturalism* (2004) and several articles on the Sikh community in Western Canada, she has also branched out in South Asian diaspora studies. Her most recent work is on the Sikh spiritual tradition and is called *The Socially Involved Renunciate: Guru Nanak's Discourse to the Nath Yogis* (2007).

Michael Newton is an ordained Buddhist priest in the Sōtō Zen tradition. He obtained his MA in Japanese modern religions at Tsukuba University. He currently teaches in the Department of Humanities and the Asia-Canada Program at Simon Fraser University. His main area of interest is the mutual influences of meditative Buddhist traditions meeting in the West. He is a member of the Mountain Rain Buddhist Community and an associate member of the Soto Zen Buddhist Association of North America.

Dan Overmyer is Professor Emeritus in the Department of Asian Studies and the Centre for Chinese Research at the University of British Columbia, and Honorary Professor in the Faculty of Arts at Shanghai Normal University. He obtained his MA and PhD degrees from the University of Chicago in the History of Religions and Chinese religions, and began his teaching career at Oberlin College in 1970. He taught the history of Chinese thought and religion and the classical Chinese language at the University of British Columbia from 1973 until his retirement at the end of 2000. He has published books and articles concerning Chinese popular religious sects, Buddhism, and local community religion. He has also served as visiting professor at a number of universities in North America, Europe, and Asia, and is a Fellow of the Royal Society of Canada.

Cam Van Thi Phan (Thích nữ Trí Khả) is an ordained Buddhist nun and PhD student at the University of British Columbia. Her MA thesis focused on China Tang Dynasty (618-906 CE) Buddhism, specifically the relationship and interaction between the monastic and lay groups. Her PhD thesis will concentrate on the organization and development of the Buddhist repentance rituals during the Tang and Song (960-1279 CE) periods. She is also a member of the Vietnamese Buddhist *sangha* in British Columbia and the treasurer of the Bảo Lâm Buddhist Association.

James Placzek holds an interdisciplinary PhD in Southeast Asian Culture History from the University of British Columbia and works in that topic area, including Thai language and Thai Buddhism. He has recently retired from the Department of Asian Studies at Langara College in Vancouver and stays involved in local Thai community events.

Li Yu received his academic training in East Asian history at universities in China, Japan, and Canada. He obtained his PhD in Chinese History from the Department of History at the University of British Columbia in 1999 and is an instructor of Asian Studies at Langara College in Vancouver. He has taught at Yunnan University in China, Simon Fraser University, University College of the Fraser Valley, and the University of British Columbia. He has published articles on Chinese social history and intellectual history in major journals of Asian studies.

Index

Note: "(f)" after a number indicates a figure

'Alī-Akbar Ja'farī, 100, 101
Abbotsford (BC), 3, 11, 12, 17, 18, 46, 59, 110, 116, 117, 135, 203, 213
Abhayagiri Forest Monastery, 115
Academy for Learning Islam (ALI), 76
Afghanistan, 77, 171; Afghans, 74
Aga Khan, 75, 76, 79; Development Network, 78, 79; Foundation, 78, 79, 80; Trust for Culture, 78; University, 78
Ahir, Kamlesh, 133
Ahir, Sutey Prakash, 133
Ahmadiyya, 72, 81; movement, 72; World Religion Conference, 29
Ahmadiyya Muslim Community of British Columbia (AMCBC), 65
Akali Singh Society, 45, 46, 47, 57; in Vancouver, 45, 46; in Victoria, 45, 46
Al-Hidayah Islamic School, 72
Alberta, 112, 184, 227
Ali, Tazul Nisha, 70
Alliance Church, 235
Amazing Grace Christian Fellowship, 241
Ambedkar, B.R., 34, 35, 133
American Full Gospel Church, 168
Americans, 107, 125
Amida Buddha, 213, 215; Amitabha Buddha, 213; Amito fo, 262
Anand, Avinash, 34
ancestor, 8, 65, 145, 153, 173, 227, 250, 251, 260, 261; day for ancestors, 145
Ancestral Hall, 261
Anderson, Charles P., 275

Anglican, 235; believers, 10, 239; churches in Canada, 237; missionaries, 237
Anglican Church of Canada, 238
anti-Asian riots, 53
Aoki, Tatsuya, 214
Arabs, 9, 87, 101
Archdiocese of Vancouver, 174
Arul Migu Thurkadevi Hindu Society, 11, 25
Arya Samaj, 30, 32, 37; school, 32
Assam, 30
Assembly of Ithna-Ashari Muslim Member Associations (AIMMA), 74
Aujila, Satish, 133
Australia, 89, 114, 128, 134, 177, 202, 252, 256
Avatamsaka Monastery Meditation Centre, 12
Ayyapan (deity), 25
Az-Zahraa Islamic Centre (Az-Zahraa, ZIC), 1, 75, 78

Baha'i, 21, 275; Baha'is, 89
Bangai, Mohan, 35, 133
Bangkok, 112, 118, 120
Bangladesh, 64, 134
Bảo Lâm Buddhist Association, 146
Baptist, 235; Chinese fellowship, 239; churches in Canada, 237; Korean churches in BC, 168
Barkerville (BC), 91
Bat Nha Temple, 158

Bates, Unzan William, 223
Baumann, Martin, 19
Bays, Daniel H., 246
BC Centennial Committee, 85
BC Muslim Women's Magazine, 70
Beijing, 254
Benares, 131
Benevolent Association of Canada, 250, 252
Bengali, 28
Benson, Kōten, 222, 223
Berkeley (CA), 216, 277
Bhagavad Gita (*Bhagavadgītā*), 17, 19, 22, 23, 27, 32
Bhairava (deity), 25
Bhameshwari Mandir, 11, 25, 33
Bharat Mata (deity), 28
Bhaskarananda, Swami, 23
Bhutan, 199
Bible, 241, 242, 244
Bijak, 33
Birken Forest Monastery (Sītavana), 110, 114, 115, 120, 121, 122, 276
boat people, 144, 157
Bodhi, Chander, Venerable, 134
Bodhichitta Centre, 203
Bodhisattva of Compassion: Avalokitesvara, 148, 149, 188, 196, 198, 200, 217; Chenrezig, 190, 196; Guanyin, 21, 188, 255, 267; Kannon, 217
Bombay, 85, 89, 91, 97
Bön (*bon* or Bonpo), 204, 205; religion, 201, 204; studies, 204; traditions, 187
Bounleung Phongmany, 111
Bounmy Simmavong, 111, 119
Bowen Island, 223
Brahma Kumaris, 31
Brechin, Becky Lynn Marie, 135
Brière, Suzanne (Sooni), 97
Britain, 77, 96, 98, 114, 137, 250
British, 4, 90, 124, 125, 137, 222; Britons, 4; Commonwealth, 92; Crown, 43, 46, 54, 55, 56; Empire, 54; rule, 55, 89, 138
British Columbia Human Rights Tribunal, 36
British Columbia Interior, 3, 21, 29, 171, 214, 234, 264. *See also* Barkerville, Cranbrook, Kamloops, Kelowna, Kootenay Bay, Lytton, Nelson, Okanagan Valley, Penticton, Prince George, Prince Rupert, Princeton, Quesnel, Summerland, Terrace, Williams Creek

British Columbia Muslim Association (BCMA), 4, 65, 67, 68, 69, 70, 71, 72, 75
British Columbia Muslim School (BCMS), 69, 80
British Honduras, 53
British Indian Army, 43
British Properties, 3, 4
Browne, Geoff, 196
Buddha, 23, 34, 115, 124, 125, 126, 127, 129, 130, 131, 132, 133, 136, 137, 142, 155, 213, 217, 224, 230, 261, 262, 270; birthday, 216; Buddha Jayanti, 133, 134; Enlightenment, 216; Enlightenment Day of Shakyamuni Buddha, 217; Śākyamuni, 266
Buddha Hall of Bright Virtue (Mingde Fotang), 255, 256
Buddha's Light International Association, 270
Buddha's Light Mountain (Foguang Shan), 270
Buddhadasa Bhikkhu, 113
Buddhapanyanuntarama Buddhist Monastery (BBM), 114, 118, 120
Buddhism, 10, 19, 35, 107, 108, 110, 114, 119, 122, 124, 125, 127, 128, 133, 134, 136, 137, 141, 143, 152, 153, 156, 157, 158, 163, 175, 177, 178, 184, 185, 186, 187, 188, 190, 194, 196, 204, 205, 215, 216, 222, 223, 228, 255, 257, 258, 259, 261, 262, 263, 265, 268, 270, 275, 277; Chinese, 11, 142, 278; Korean, 176, 177; Nichiren, 212, 223; Thai, 11, 120, 276; Thai Buddhism in British Columbia, 34, 35, 108, 109, 121. *See also* Buddhist; Indian, Buddhism; Mahayana; monks; Sri Lankan, Buddhism; Theravada; Tibetan Buddhism; Vietnamese Buddhism; Won Buddhism
Buddhist, 3, 6, 19, 111, 115, 120, 121, 124, 126, 127, 131, 132, 133, 134, 137, 138, 139, 141, 142, 143, 154, 157, 158, 163, 164, 165, 178, 180, 203, 204, 205, 249, 259, 277; Chinese Buddhist groups, 250, 260, 265, 278; Chinese Buddhists, 6, 195-96, 234, 278; communities, 64; groups, 3; Japanese Buddhists, 213; Korean Buddhists, 175; mantras, 253; merit, 107, 108, 109, 111, 112, 113, 116, 132, 138, 155, 179, 254, 263; organization, 260; Path, 193; Shingon, 213; teachings, 198; temple,

271; Thai Buddhists, 132; traditions, 19; Vajrayana, 193; of West, 186, 193, 194, 207. *See also* Buddhism; Mahayana; monks; Sri Lankan, Buddhists; Theravada
Buddhist Church of Canada, 214, 216, 225, 230
Buddhist Pure Land on Earth, 263, 264
Buddhist Vihara Society, 124, 126, 127, 132, 135
Bunthaem, Ajahn, 112, 116
Burlington (ON), 134
Burma. *See* Myanmar
Burnaby (BC), 1, 2, 5, 12, 17, 21, 24, 26, 28, 29, 30, 32, 33, 35, 68, 73, 77, 79, 93, 94, 95, 96, 110, 112, 114, 120, 134, 145, 146, 163, 165, 168, 171, 172, 176, 178, 190, 215, 222, 234, 236, 240, 255, 258, 269; Asian population, 2; Korean food, 1; South Burnaby, 21
Burnaby Jamatkhana, 79
Burnaby Kidowon. *See* Holy Spirit Prayer Centre
Burnaby Pacific Grace Chinese Church, 236
Burquitlam (BC), 45
Burrard Inlet, 44, 54, 205

Cadge, Wendy, 138, 140
Caesar, Julius, 152
Cakrasamvara, 190, 200
Calgary, 28, 112, 118, 125, 158, 227, 254, 266
California, 3, 4, 18, 19, 23, 26, 32, 91, 96, 100, 101, 115, 126, 216, 222, 250, 266, 277
Calm Abiding Meditation, 190, 200
Cambodian: population, 2
Canada, Census of, 64, 109, 110, 144, 164, 233, 234, 278; Department of Canadian Heritage, 46; Eastern, 167; first Bon priest, 11; immigration policy, 53; mainstream, 121; official policy of multiculturalism, 3, 12, 48, 54, 60, 124, 249; Pacific Rim province, 6, 13; Statistics Canada, 163; Western, 43, 51, 69, 73, 99, 167, 237
Canadian Charter of Rights and Freedoms, 71
Canadian Constitution of the Ismailis, 79
Canadian Islamic Cultural Expo in Vancouver, 72

Canadian Martyrs Catholic Church, 174, 236, 243
Canadian Memorial Church, 165
Canadian Muslim Federation (CMF), 71, 80
Canadian Pacific Railway, 44, 250
Canadian Red Cross, 12, 155
Cantonese, 8, 171, 174, 196, 234, 244, 253, 254, 256, 258, 263, 266, 267
Cao Daiism, 151, 152, 258
Caodong, 263
caste, 25, 32, 35, 36, 37, 41, 42, 53, 89, 97, 133; *dalit*, 36, 37, 134
Catholicism, 163. *See also* Roman Catholic
Census of Canada: in 1960, 142; in 1999, 142; in 2001, 104, 234, 236, 245, 278; in 2006, 2, 109, 110, 144, 164, 233, 245
Central Tibet, 197, 204, 206
Central Valley (CA), 4
Chah, Ajahn, 109, 114, 115
Chamma (deity), 204
Champakhome Chanthaphasouk, 110
Chân Nguyên Temple, 147, 153
Chân Quang Temple, 145
Changling Tulku Rinpoche, 198
Cheng Yen, 269
Cherishing Youth Day, 267
Cheung, Jonathan, 239
Chicago, 19, 23, 96, 125, 135
Chiếu Văn Ngô, 152
Chhimi Kinley, Lama, 199
Chilliwack (BC), 268
China, 64, 134, 142, 163, 168, 186, 188, 193, 196, 205, 213, 218, 234, 238, 239, 241, 242, 244, 245, 249, 250, 252, 258, 259, 261, 267, 278; Greater China, 240; Han Chinese, 186, 191; immigration, 236; People's Republic, 233, 259; South China, 249; South China mission, 238. *See also* Chinese
Chinatown, 1, 2, 5, 151, 233, 238, 243, 249, 250, 251, 252, 254, 258, 260, 266, 271; Richmond, 1; Vancouver, 1; Victoria, 2, 250
Chinese: churches in Canada, 9; classes, 244; immigrants, 4, 237, 265; language, 8, 174, 205, 206, 236, 240, 243, 244, 251, 253, 257, 260, 262, 265, 267, 268, 269, 278; missionaries, 234; people, 3, 6, 8, 10, 153, 163, 180, 186, 234, 235, 236, 237, 238, 239, 240, 241, 242, 243, 244,

250, 251, 253, 254, 257, 262, 264, 278; people in Canada, 8, 233, 234, 271; population, 2; program, 269. *See also* China
Chinese Catholic Centre, 175
Chinese Catholic Society of UBC, 236
Chinese Christian Gospel Church, 240
Chinese Christian Mission (CCM), 244
Chinese Cultural Centre, 254
Chinese Exclusion Act, 239
Chinmaya Mission Advaita Vedanta Centre, 31
Chogyam Trungpa Rinpoche, 185, 193, 205
Christian: Chinese churches, 240; Chinese missions, 238; church, 214, 234; denominations, 275, 279; society, 10
Christianity, 87, 152, 164, 165, 234, 237, 238, 239, 240, 244, 245, 246, 250, 255, 257, 258; of Canada, 179; Chinese, 235, 278; of Japan, 179; of Korea, 167, 177
Christians, 89, 111, 121, 170, 171, 172, 173, 179, 180, 238, 239, 245, 249, 278; Canadian, 170; Chinese, 10, 234, 237, 239, 241, 242, 243, 244, 245, 250; Christmas, 243; Filipino, 10; Japanese, 179, 181, 182; in Korea, 172; Korean, 164, 170, 171, 172, 173, 179, 180
Church of Jesus Christ of Latter-day Saints, 12
City of Ten Thousand Buddhas, 266, 267
clan associations, 250, 251, 271
Cloverdale (BC), 50, 73
Collingwood Neighbourhood House, 150, 151
Colombo, 137, 143
Colorado, 195
community centre, 35, 36, 68, 110, 119, 205; of Hindus, 23; of Jewish, 95
Comox Valley (BC), 204; of Sōka gakkai, 224
Complete Perfection, 252
Confectioner, Sam and Villie, 91
Confucianism, 152, 255, 257, 258; Confucian ideas, 243; Confucian ideals, 250; Confucian value of Chinese Christians, 242; Confucian virtues, 256, 257, 259, 260, 267. *See* filial piety; fraternity; humanity; loyalty; propriety; righteousness; sense of shame; trustworthiness
Contemporary Tibet Research Program, 200

conversion, 31, 87, 90, 92, 96, 97, 98, 99, 101, 133
convert, 19, 38, 96, 98, 100, 228; Asians, 6; earliest Zoroastrians, 96; non-Asian, 6, 213; to Islam, 90
Coquitlam (BC), 1, 2, 5, 128, 163, 165, 168, 175, 217, 230, 234, 269; Asian population, 2; Korean food, 1
Cornell, Eishin Melody, 220
Corpus Christi Parish in Vancouver, 236
Council of Muslim Communities of Canada (CMCC), 70
Council of Shia Muslim Communities, 74
Courtenay (BC), 11
Cranbrook (BC), 258
Crystal Mountain Tibetan Buddhist group, 135
Culture China, 245
Culture Regeneration Research Society, 243, 244-45

Dahn World, 177, 178
Dalai Lama, 187, 195, 200, 201, 202, 203, 262, 265
Damdami Taksal's code of conduct, 50
dance, 21, 24, 27, 29
Daoism, 152, 234, 252, 255, 257, 258; Daoist, 249, 250, 251, 252, 253, 254, 268, 278; groups, 278; temple, 271; traditions, 19
Dar-e Mehr (Court of Mithra), 95, 97, 98, 99, 101
Das, Jagessar, 33, 37
Dashalakshana, 34
Delta (BC), 49, 73; Delta-Richmond East, 71
Denkyo Kyosan, 218
Derge Prefecture, 196, 198
Detroit, 244
Dhaliwal, Sabik Singh, 44
dhamma, 128, 129, 130, 134, 148, 149, 156, 190, 198, 205, 216, 222, 255, 265, 267
Dhammadinna, Anagarika, 126
Dhammakaya International Meditation Society, 115
Dhammika, Mirisse, Venerable, 129, 131
Dharma Drum Mountain, 263, 264, 278
Dharma Realm Buddhist Association, 265
dharma talks, 114, 141, 149, 156, 157, 222
Dharma Wheel (falun), 258, 259
Dharmadhatu, 185, 192

Dharmapala Mahakala (deity), 196
Dharmasara Satsang Society, 5
Dhyan Yoga Meditation Society, 34
diaspora, 19, 65, 74, 76, 80, 81, 82, 88, 89, 90, 97, 98, 100, 205; of Iranians, 101; of Muslims to the West, 66; Parsis in, 95. *See also* double diaspora
Dilgo Khyentse Rinpoche, 198
Disciple Methodist Church, 169
diversity, 4, 6, 12, 13, 19, 23, 45, 48, 71, 81, 181, 182, 200, 229, 280
Divine Light Society, 21
divine virtues, 131
Doctor of Divinity, 192, 204; *geshe* (degree), 204
Đời Chí Lê, 150
donations, 12, 18, 51, 76, 109, 134, 138, 155, 171, 217, 218, 230; *dana*, 126, 127, 136; "four basic necessities" offerings, 131; *mataka vastra*, 130; *trai tăng (four essentials offering)*, 155
Dorje Chang Centre, 203
Dorje Kasung Organization, 193
Dorje Shugden (deity), 203, 204, 206
double diaspora, 19, 36, 65, 67, 72, 73, 77, 81, 82, 276
Downtown Eastside (Vancouver), 20, 21
Dragon Flower Mountain, 222, 223
Drigung Kagyü Monastery, 199
Drubgen Tulku, Yizhin Norbu, 196
Duangsi Tavonesouk, 108, 119, 121
Dudjom Rinpoche, 197
Duncan (BC), 46, 202, 226, 258
Durga Devi, 25; Devi, 25, 32
Dutch, 125, 242
Dzogchen Ponlop Rinpoche, 193
Dzongsar Khyentse Rinpoche, 198

East Africa, 65, 72, 75, 76, 77, 81, 92, 94, 96, 99, 276
East Hastings Street (Vancouver), 44, 237, 266
East Indian, 54, 163; Sikh immigrants, 53
East Sooke (BC), 221
East Vancouver, 48, 111; community, 23
Eastern Tibet, 198
Edmonton, 18, 112, 113, 119
Eduljee, Eddie, 95
Eight Immortals, 252
Eight Precepts Assembly, 261
Ekanayake, Gamunu, 128

El Cantare, Lord, 228
Engineer, Hurmusji, 91
England, 21, 30, 203, 222, 256
English: language, 8, 33, 114, 120, 121, 129, 133, 138, 148, 156, 157, 165, 167, 168, 169, 173, 174, 177, 180, 181, 186, 193, 196, 205, 206, 215, 225, 228, 229, 230, 234, 236, 237, 244, 249, 253, 257, 258, 260, 262, 263, 264, 266, 267, 268, 277; people, 3; services, 166, 171, 280; skill, 77, 137, 240, 243
Esala (full-moon day of July), 131
ethnic, 2, 3, 10, 19, 26, 29, 56, 64, 67, 82, 86, 101, 135, 137; communities, 20, 23, 173, 181, 216; diversity, 23, 45; diversity of British Columbia, 6; groups, 7, 9, 10, 66, 153, 182, 191, 225, 233, 244, 275; groups in Vancouver, 1; identity, 11, 65, 94, 97, 99, 101, 144, 164; minority groups, 55; nationalism of the Muslim world, 66; organizations, 81; segregation, 4
ethnicity, 6, 7, 8, 9, 11, 12, 19, 64, 65, 66, 67, 74, 75, 77, 78, 97, 124, 138, 163, 164, 179, 230
Euro-Canadians, 45
Europe, 77, 89, 91, 114, 125, 177, 190, 228; Europeans, 3, 4
Evangelical Association, 235
Evangelical Chinese Bible Church, 239; Worship Service, 239
Evangelical Free Church, 239
Everett (WA), 93
Evergreen Taoist Church of Canada, 251-52, 253
exile communities, 88; of Vietnamese, 143

Faith Evangelical Lutheran Church, 171
False Creek (Vancouver), 44
Falun Gong, 10, 258, 259, 278
Family Benevolent Association of Canada, 251
Family Federation for World Peace and Unification, 177, 178
family halls, 255
Federation of Zoroastrian Associations of North America (FEZANA), 93, 101
Feng Yin Seen Goon, 254
festivals, 53, 70, 76, 81, 89, 95, 99, 100, 107, 108, 110, 112, 114, 120, 129, 130, 131, 135, 136, 144, 147, 148, 157, 159, 166,

Index 295

193, 243, 244, 266, 267, 277; Baisakhi (Vaisakhi), 53; of China, 244; of Chinese New Year, 243, 259; Divali (Diwali), 33, 53; Dragon Boat Festival, 243; Eid al-Adha (festival of sacrifice), 71, 76, 80; Eid al-Fitr, 71; Eid-e-Milad-un-Nabi (birthday of the Prophet Muhammad), 80; Enlightenment Day of Shakyamuni, 217; *Esala* (full-moon day of July), 131; *Hanamatsuri*, 217; Holi, 33; of Kabir's birthday, 33; *Kason* festival, 136; Lunar New Year, 145, 147, 153; Mid-Autumn Festival, 243; of New Year in Vietnam, 147; *Nōrūz* (New Year), 89, 100; *Phật Đản* (*Vesak*), 153; *segaki* (the hungry ghost festival), 217, 222; Spring Festival of China, 243; *Thaipusam*, 24; *Vesak*, 127, 130, 135, 136, 145; of Vietnamese Vu Lan (*Ullambana*), 153; Zoroastrian, 89, 100
FEZANA. *See* Federation of Zoroastrian Associations of North America
Fiji, 19, 24, 33, 65, 67, 73, 81, 276. *See also* Fijian
Fiji Canada Association, 32
Fijian: community, 23, 71; Fijian people, 24, 67, 72. *See also* Fiji
filial piety (filiality, 孝), 153, 250, 267
Filipinos, 6, 8, 10, 163; Catholics, 175; population, 2. *See also* Philippines
Five Great Treasure discoverers, 197
Foguang Shan, 270
Folk pluralism, 36
Foundation for the Preservation of the Mahayāna Tradition, 202
Fourfold Path, 228
France, 151, 177, 190, 193, 198, 202, 204
Fraser River, 165, 237
Fraser Valley, 4, 11, 12, 17; Buddhist Temple, 12, 214; Hindu Society, 11, 17, 20
fraternity (悌), 267
French, 3, 125, 171, 238
Friends of Thailand Educational Society, 111, 114
Friesone, Jacob, 180
Fujian Evangelical Church: Filipino Chinese congregation, 1
Fujinkai, 215
Fundamental Rights and Directive Principles of State Policy, 133
funerals, 156, 215, 219, 221, 222, 227

Fung Loy Kok Taoist Temple, 10, 253, 254
Fushii, Maki, 179

Gabriola Island (BC), 204
Gaden Choling Mahayana Buddhist Meditation Centre, 201
Gadr Weekly, 55
Galiano Island (BC), 135, 219
Ganesha (deity), 30
Gangteng Tulku Rinpoche, 199
Garden of Peace and Happiness, 146
Gardener, J.E., 238
gāthās (Avestan), 86, 100
gathas (*gāthā* Buddhist), 132, 215
Gelug, 184, 200; community, 204; lineage, 202; masters, 201; practice, 202; School, 187, 200, 202, 203; sect, 198, 200, 206; tradition, 202
gender, 18, 32, 70, 261; differences of gender ratios of Zoroastrians in British Columbia, 93; different garments of Sikh males and females, 48; female assistants to the unmarried female leader of the Mingde Fotang, 256 (*see also* Buddha Hall of Bright Virtue); a female Caucasian dharma master of Chinese Buddhism, 266; female members of Thai communities in British Columbia, 109; a gay, bisexual, and transgender group of SGI, 225; gender-based division of activists for Falun Gong group in BC, 259; gender groups of Hindu immigrants to British Columbia, 18; gendered uniform policy among Asian muslim diaspora, 69, 81; a Korean female pastor, 172; laymen's volunteering for Vietnamese Buddhist organization, 148; Muslim women's participation in the BCMA, 70; Swami Radha's male disciples, 21; Vietnamese Buddhist associations for women, 146; Women's Chapter of BCMA, 69; young men and women at youth services for Korean Christian churches, 170
generations, 2, 6, 8, 9, 30, 59, 66, 92, 95, 111, 119, 121, 122, 127, 133, 139, 144, 153, 154, 156, 157, 158, 159, 173, 174, 176, 178, 205, 235, 250, 251, 256, 263, 267, 270, 271, 279; of Chinese Canadians, 8; of Chinese immigrants, 251; first generation of Chinese immigrants, 256, 257;

first generation Japanese, 218; first- and second-generation Japanese Canadians, 213; next generation, 111, 119, 122, 251; second generation of Korean Canadians, 174, 176; second generation of Koreans, 173; second and third generation of Chinese immigrants, 8; second- and third- generation Japanese Canadians, 218; second- and third-generation Sri Lankans, 133; of Sikhs, 57
German, 3, 128
Germany, 177, 222, 277
Giao Châu (province in Vietnam), 142
Gifu Prefecture, 220
Gnanodbhaso, Venerable, 129
Goenka, S.N., 35
Gold Buddha Monastery, 265, 266, 267, 268, 278
Golok, 186
Gopalananda, Swami, 21
Grace Community Church, 170
Graded Path to Enlightenment, 200
Grand Precious Hall, 261
Great Perfection, 194, 197, 199, 200, 204
Great Way, 152
Green Tara, 190; ritual, 188
Guan Yu (deity), 255
Guangdong, 233, 240, 250
Guangzhou, 252
Guardian Angels Parish, 175
Guiv, Arbâb Rostam, 95, 99
Gujarat, 65, 72, 76, 93, 94, 97; Gujarati, 28, 65, 75, 77, 81
gurdwara, 1, 3, 12, 20, 35, 36, 43, 44, 45, 46, 47, 48, 49, 50, 51, 52, 53, 54, 55, 56, 57, 58, 59, 60, 276; Akali Singh Gurdwara, 48; Dasmesh Darbar Gurdwara, 49, 53, 58; Gurdwara of Amrit Prakash, 50; Gurdwara Nanaksar, 50; Guru Nanak Sikh Gurdwara, 48, 49, 50, 52, 57, 58; Khalsa Darbar Gurdwara, 50; in the Lower Mainland, 56; "mill colony" gurdwaras, 45, 46; pattern of building gurdwaras in British Columbia, 45; Shiromani Gurdwara Parbandhak Committee, 50; Vancouver Khalsa Diwan Society Gurdwara, 48, 53, 56, 57
guru, 43, 206; *Guru Granth Sahib (Ādi Granth)*, 35, 43, 44, 45, 47, 48; Guru Nanak Devji, 25; Guru Ram Dass Ashram, 19; Guru Tegh Bahadur, 53; *guruji*, 28; Shri Guru Arjan Devji, 35; Shri Guru Ravidas, 35, 36, 42, 134; Shri Guru Ravidass Sabha, 35, 134
Guru Kabir Association of Canada, 33
Guru Nanak Academy, 59
Guyana, 19, 33, 37
Guyanese, 32, 33
Gyalten Rinpoche, 196
Gyalwa Karmapa Rangjung Rigpei Dorje, 190

Hải Ấn Temple, 149
Hải Triều Âm Temple, 148
Hajj, 76
halal, 70
Halfmoon Bay (BC), 126
Halifax, 193
Hanuman (deity), 17, 25
Hashimoto, Roderick, 227, 228
Heart Sutra, 197
Heat Yoga, 191
Hellman, Sylvia, 20. See also Radha Shivananda
Highway to Heaven (Richmond), 1, 29, 168
hijab (gendered dress), 81
Hills, George, 237
Hindi, 17, 24, 28, 32
Hindu, 19, 26; communities, 89; Fijian, 24, 32; groups, 20; Hindus, 6, 20, 26, 55, 81, 121; population, 18; practice, 20; temple, 3, 17, 26; traditions, 19
Hindu Cultural Society and Community Centre, 26, 28
Hinduism, 6, 10, 20, 26, 31, 275
Hinnells J., 89, 95
Ho, Gary, 269, 270
Ho, Robert Hung Ngai, 260, 261, 262
Hoa Nghiêm Temple, 12, 146, 147
Hoiping, 249
Holiness: Korean churches in BC, 168
Holy Cross Japanese Anglican Church, 179, 180
Holy Spirit Prayer Centre, 172
homeland, 10, 43, 52, 55, 56, 57, 81, 85, 99, 100, 178, 184, 205, 277
Hong Kong, 54, 194, 233, 234, 235, 239, 240, 241, 245, 249, 252, 253, 254, 255, 256, 260, 261, 262, 264, 266, 268, 269, 278

Hong Yujian, 244
Hopkinson, W.C., 55, 56
House of Mercy (Baitur Rahman), 73
Hsuan Hua, 265, 266, 267
Htoon, Myat, 135
Hugo, Victor, 152
Huidong, 250
Huizhou, 250
hukam-nama, 49, 58
Humanistic Buddhism, 270
humanity, 250
Humphreys, Derrick, 95
Huyền Quang Vietnamese Buddhist Youth Association, 150

I-kuan Tao (Yiguan Dao, T'ien Tao), 254, 255, 256, 257, 258, 278
Iida, Shotaro, 223
Illinois, 21, 93
Imam (prayer leaders), 69, 71, 74, 75, 76, 77
Imamate, a doctrine of the, 74
immigration, 2, 3, 4, 5, 19, 36, 47, 67, 73, 91, 118, 134, 137, 138, 144, 213, 225, 230, 231; of Asians to British Columbia, 6; from China, 233, 234, 236, 237, 240, 241, 243, 244, 249, 251, 257, 264, 278; emigration, 66; from Hong Kong, 235, 249, 252, 253, 255, 264, 266; immigrants into Canada, 17, 47; from India, 17, 19, 47, 56, 249; Indian immigrant population, 20; Indian immigration into Canada, 47; from Japan, 180, 213, 230; from Korea, 165, 277; law of Canada, 3, 46, 53, 54, 91, 126, 239, 240, 249, 280; from Myanmar, 126, 138; from Pakistan, 72; Parsi immigration to North America, 89; from Philippines, 8; from Southeast Asia, 18, 38, 92, 185; from Sri Lanka, 124, 126, 138; of Sri Lankan Buddhists, 124; from Taiwan, 235, 249, 255, 264, 269, 271; from US, 235; from Vietnam, 157
incorruptibility, 267
India, 8, 19, 20, 22, 26, 29, 30, 31, 33, 34, 45, 54, 55, 64, 71, 72, 73, 74, 76, 77, 81, 85, 88, 89, 93, 94, 97, 99, 116, 124, 125, 131, 133, 134, 136, 142, 158, 184, 189, 194, 195, 196, 199, 201, 202, 205, 249, 276, 277; North India, 33, 65, 85; South India, 197; South Indian Balaji, 24. *See also* Indian

Indian: Buddhism, 34, 139; people, 8, 55, 67, 89. *See also* India
Indian Buddhist Society of Canada (IBSC), 35, 133, 134
Indo-Canadian Sikh Association, 48
Indo-Pakistanis, 74
Indonesia, 64, 65
Indonesian: mosque, 9; people, 9; population, 2
initiation: of Chinese Buddhism, 266; of Chinese T'ien Tao, 258; of Sikhs, 31; of Tibetan Buddhism, 194; of Zoroastrianism (*sedre-pūshī*), 88, 92, 95, 97, 98, 101
Insight Meditation, 260, 263
Institute of Buddhist Studies, 216, 277
Institute for Research in Human Happiness (IRH), 180, 226, 228, 229, 277
Intaranuruk, Punee, 121
integration into Canadian society, 120, 145, 249, 251, 271
integrity, 251
International Catholic Student Centre, 173
International Christian University, 179
International Sikh Youth Federation (ISYF), 57, 58
International Society for Krishna Consciousness (ISKON), 4, 29, 37, 38
internment camps, 213, 227
Iqra Islamic School, 71-72
Iran, 74, 85, 87, 89, 90, 91, 93, 95, 96, 97, 98, 100, 101, 276. *See also* Iranians
Iranian Canadian Cultural Association, 100
Iranian Studies, Drs. Fereidoun and Katharine Mirhady Lectureship in, 80
Iranians, 74, 89, 90, 93, 94, 100, 101; Muslims, 98; Zoroastrians, 6, 90, 94 *See also* Iran
Iraq, 74, 75, 76, 93, 100
Iraqis, 74
IRH Monthly, 229
Islam, 64, 65, 66, 69, 71, 72, 74, 75, 78, 79, 80, 81, 86, 87, 90, 96, 97, 101, 255, 275
Islamic Centre, 67
Islamic Heritage Association, 71
Islamic Information Centre, 72
Islamic Society of British Columbia, 72
Islamic Society of North America (ISNA), 70; Annual Conference, 70; Canada West Conference, 70
Ismaili Council of British Columbia, 77

298 Index

Ismaili Jamatkhana, 77
Ismaili Muslim Community of British Columbia (IMCBC), 65, 76, 77
Ismaili Muslim Council of British Columbia, 79
Ismaili Walk for Kids, 79
Ismailism, 77; Ismaili Shia, 72, 275; Ismailis, 75, 76, 77, 78, 79; Ismailiyah, 74; Nizari form of, 76
Italy, 177, 202
Ithna Ashari Shia, 72, 74, 75; community of British Columbia, 74; Twelver Shiism, 87

Jafar as-Sadiq, 76
Jain, Ananda K., 34
Jainism, 34; Digambara sect, 34; Svetambara sect, 34
Jama'at-i Tabligh, 71
Jamatkhana (place of assembly), 77
Jamgon Lodru Thaye, 190
Jami'a Mosque, 1
Jamyang Khyentse Wangpo, 197
Japan, 126, 158, 163, 177, 179, 212, 213, 214, 215, 216, 217, 218, 220, 221, 222, 223, 224, 226, 227, 228, 229, 261, 277; ethic segregation rule, 4; formation of BC Asian societies between late 19th and early 20th centuries, 3; relocation of Japanese Canadian in British Columbia. *See* relocation
Japanese, 8, 153, 171, 179, 180, 181; classes, 181; immigrants, 4; language, 8, 12, 165, 171, 180, 181, 215, 216, 226, 228, 229; newspapers, 230; school, 12; services, 180; people in Canada, 3, 8, 180, 181, 212, 215, 216, 217, 218, 226, 230; population, 2
Japanese Baptist Church, 180
Japanese Buddhist: churches, 262; groups, 224, 277; organizations, 226
Japanese Jōdoshū Tozenji, 5; Tozenji Buddhist Temple, 217, 218, 230
Japanese United Church, 179
Java, 134
Javeri, Maneckji F., 91
Jayawardene, J.R., 126
Jehovah's Witnesses, 235
Jesus Christ, 22, 23, 152, 244
Jetsunma Chimey Luding, 184-85, 187, 188

Jews, 3, 85, 89; Judaism, 87, 275; Judeo-Christianity, 87
Jhagra, Gurudutt, 27, 28
Jhampa Shaneman, 201, 202
Jigong, Living Buddha (Jigong huofo) 255
Jinshan Township, 263
Jiyu-Kennett, 222
Jōdo Shinshū, 12, 213, 214, 216; temples, 215, 217
Jōdoshū, 5, 213, 217
Joshu Sasaki-roshi, 219, 221; lineage of, 221

Kachhi, 75, 81
Kagyü, 189, 191, 200, 206, 207; abbot, 194; lineage, 193; masters, 192, 201; retreat centers, 190; teaching, 192
Kagyü Kunkhyab Chuling (KKC), 190, 191, 192
Kagyü Shambhala: lineage, 193
Kalu Rinpoche, 189, 190
Kalzang Gyatso, Geshe *(bsKal-bzang rgya-mtshob)*, 203
Kamalasiri, Venerable, 128, 135
Kamloops (BC), 50, 110, 115, 165, 171, 217
Kamloops Buddhist Temple, 214
Kaohsiung County, 270
Kapahi, Raj, 32
Kappers, Teus, 241-42
Karim Aga Khan, 75, 76, 77
Karma Kagyü, 193; branch, 189, 191; lineage, 195; master, 195; School, 194; tradition, 193
Karma Shri Nalanda Institute, 193
karmic affinity, 255
Kathina, 131, 135, 136
Kathok Monastery, 199
Khaki, Aziz, 94
Kefferputz, Thomas, 205
Kelowna (BC), 3, 30, 165, 171, 223, 258, 268
Kelowna Buddhist Temple, 214
Khalistan, 50, 55; movement, 56
Khalsa Diwan Society (KDS), 45, 47, 53, 54, 55, 57, 58
Kham, 192, 193, 195, 196, 197, 198, 199, 201, 204
Khantivong, Thongsouk, 119
Khenchen Thrangu Rinpoche, 195
Khenpo Tsultrim Gyamtso Rinpoche, 194
Khenrab Gajam, Geshe, 184
Khoja Shia Ithna Asharis, 75
Khön clan, 184, 187

Khyungpo Nanjor, 189
Kim, Don Tong-eun, 171
Kim, Kyŏngjin, 167-68
Komagata Maru, 54, 66
Kong, Susan S.H., 262
Konjin (deity), 226
Konkōkyō, 180, 226, 227, 228, 277; Konkō Church of Vancouver, 4; Konkō Daijin, 226, 227; Vancouver organization, 227
Kootenay Bay (BC), 21, 29
Korea, 64, 134, 163, 165, 166, 167, 168, 169, 172, 175, 176, 177, 178, 218; North Korea, 168
Korean: Christian newspaper and columns, 172, 176; churches, 9, 173; classes, 169, 174, 176; immigrants to Canada, 163, 168, 175, 178, 277; language, 163, 164, 168, 169, 171, 172, 173, 174, 176, 177, 178; people, 6, 10, 163, 164, 165, 166, 167, 168, 169, 170, 171, 172, 174, 175, 176, 177, 178, 179, 180, 205, 277; population, 2; radio stations, 172; school, 168; sign, 169(f); worship services, 165, 172, 174
Korean American Presbyterian Church, 172
Korean Baptist Church, 168
Korean Canadian Presbytery, 167
Korean Chogye Buddhist temple, 5
Korean United Church, 166
Korean Worldviews Study Program, 172
Korean Youngnak Presbyterian Church, 169
Koreatown, 170
kōshti, 88, 96; *kusti,* 88, 96
Krishna (deity), 18, 22, 23, 30, 31
Krishna janmastami, 29
Kriya Yoga: lineage, 22
Kunzang Dechen Osel Ling (KDOL), 190, 191, 192
Kuppuswami, Sevaratnakam Sadhu, 24
Kwanglim Methodist Church, 168, 169, 170
Kyi, Tin Maung, 135
Kyoto, 216, 219

Lai, David, 5
Lakshmi (deity), 27
Lakshmi Narayan Temple, 29
Lam, David See-Chai, 239, 245
Lâm Tỳ Ni (Lumbini) Temple, 148, 149

lama, 188, 192, 194, 201, 204, 205; Sakya tradition, 188; Tibetan, 191, 194, 196, 200, 202, 205, 277
Landry, Henry, 226
langar, (community dining hall), 48, 49, 51, 52, 56, 58, 59
Langara College, 275, 276, 277
Langley (BC), 5, 113, 117, 145, 172, 175, 176
language, 2, 7, 8, 9, 10, 11, 23, 26, 33, 34, 36, 37, 54, 58, 99, 100, 107, 125, 133, 137, 142, 146, 149, 151, 153, 156, 157, 171, 175, 178, 186, 196, 205, 207, 215, 227, 229, 230, 234, 251, 253, 254, 264, 265, 271, 277; Asian, 174; barrier, 153, 157, 242, 249, 265; groups, 81; Hindi, 27; Punjabi facilities, 52; Sinhalese, 132; Thai classes, 112; Tibetan, 193; Vietnamese classes, 146, 157. *See also* Chinese, language; English, language; Japanese, language; Korean, language; Mass
Lao, 107, 108, 110, 111, 122, 277. *See also* Laos
Lao Benevolent Society of British Columbia, 110, 119
Lao Buddhism, 11, 119, 276; Lao Buddhism in British Columbia, 34, 35, 108, 109, 121; Lao Buddhists, 111; Lao *sangha* (Buddhist community), 118
Lao Buddhist Cultural Society of British Columbia, 111
Lao-Canadian Buddhist Temple Association, 111, 116, 118
Laos, 107, 108, 110, 111, 116, 117, 118, 119, 134; Laotian population, 2. *See also* Lao
lay association, 150, 151
Lê Mạnh Thát, 142
Lebanon, 74
Lee, George, 250, 251
Lee, James, 252
Lee, Sang-Chul, 165
Leung, In-sing. *See* Liang, Yancheng
Levitt, Peter, 223
Lhasa, 204
Li, Hongzhi, 258, 259
Liang, Yancheng, 243, 244
Lighthouse Harbour Ministries, 242
Lin-Kok, Clara, 260
Ling Yen Mountain Temple for Chinese Buddhists, 1
Lingtrul Rinpoche, 199, 201
Linji tradition, 263, 270

lion dancing, 251
Lions Gate Buddhist Priory, 222
Lisbon, 77
Loga Rinpoche, 199
London, 77, 91, 93, 125
Longchen Nyingthig, 199
Longchen Rabjam, 198
Longevity Hall, 261
Lopez, Donald, 185
Lopon Sangngag Yeshe, 199
Los Angeles, 126, 258
Lotus Speech Canada, 198
Lotus Sutra, 223, 224, 225
Lower Mainland (BC), 2, 3, 8, 27, 29, 35, 53, 58, 60, 67, 68, 94, 107, 110, 114, 120, 124, 126, 148, 149, 163, 165, 171, 172, 174, 176, 177, 181, 190, 196, 214, 236, 254, 255, 258, 260, 264, 267, 269, 270; Asian population, 2; Asian Religious groups, 2; Asian Religious groups' location, 3; centre, 203; "fundamentalist" and "moderate" schism of Sikhs, 50; Greater Vancouver, 2, 126, 144, 145, 146, 186, 217, 228, 229, 230, 233, 234; Sikh community, 48, 49. *See also* Abbotsford, Burnaby, Burquitlam, Chilliwack, Cloverdale, Coquitlam, Delta, Fraser Valley, Langley, Mission, New Westminster, North Delta, North Vancouver, Port Coquitlam, Port Moody, Richmond, Surrey, Surrey-Delta area, Surrey-East, Vancouver, West Vancouver, Whistler
loyalty (忠), 267
Lü Dongbin, 252, 253, 255
Luang Phor Viriyang Sirintharo, 111, 112, 113, 116, 117, 120
Ludhiana (India), 134
Luding, Rinchen, 184
Luding Sey Kusho, 187
Luding Shabdrung Rinpoche, 187
Lungtok Tenpai Nyima, 205
Lutheran, 235; Korean church in BC, 168, 169
Lytton (BC), 222

Madan, T.N., 36
Magee, Jeannie Seward, 151
Magee, John, 151
Mahakarikyō, 22
Maharaj, Satyamitranand, 28
Mahasi Temple, 136
Mahayana, 193, 213; Buddhism, 142; events, 107; fellows, 107; monks, 107, 119; orientation, 270; scriptures, 213; tradition, 154, 202
Mahayoga, 197
Main Street (Vancouver), 1, 5, 26, 151, 175, 224, 265; Indian food, 1
mainstream society, 51; of Canada, 47, 48, 55, 56, 120, 122, 128, 137, 238, 245
Maitreya, 255
Makawita, Sunendra, 126
Malaysia, 19, 64, 129, 195, 222, 261
Malaysian: people, 9; population, 2
Man, Ajahn, 113
Manawmaya Theravada Buddhist Society, 135
Manchuria, 238, 265
Mandalay City, 136
Mandarin, 8, 147, 171, 174, 196, 197, 205, 207, 234, 244, 249, 256, 257, 258, 264, 267, 269, 271, 277
Manjushri Kadampa Meditation Centre, 203
Manjusri (Mañjuśrī), 196, 266
mantra, 21, 253
Market Alley, 252
Marpa Chökyi Lodro, 189
marriage, 68, 96, 97, 129, 182; ceremony of Zoroastians, 92; of gays and lesbians, 71; intermarriage for Japanese Canadians, 216; intermarriage of Zoroastrians, 96, 97, 216, 242, 244, 280; *nikah* (Islamic marriage), 68; outmarriage of Zoroastrians, 96
Martin, Eshu Karl, 221
Masjid: Al-Hidayah, 72; al-Taqwa, 69; ul-Haqq, 69; ul-Iman, 69; ur-Rahmah, 69
Mass: Asian, 174-75; English, 173; Korean attendance, 173; Roman Catholic, 8
Matsui, Fumio, 227
Maum Meditation Centres, 177, 178
Maung, Reggie Tun, 135
Mayo, Joan, 45
McDaniel, June, 39
meditation, 7, 23, 35, 115, 120, 128, 129, 130, 132, 135, 136, 137, 147, 148, 149, 151, 152, 178, 186, 189, 190, 197, 199, 200, 201, 203, 220, 221, 222, 223, 226, 228, 253, 259, 260, 261, 262, 263, 264, 268, 278; Buddhist Tantric meditation, 194;

classes, 33, 34, 156, 216, 218, 264, 265; group, 139, 222; group meeting, 22; meditation hall, 222, 261; practice, 114, 121, 259, 263, 265; rain retreat, 115; retreat, 111, 114, 115, 121, 126, 219, 220, 222; room, 219, 220; teachers, 254; training, 193; of Zen, 219, 221, 222, 263, 264, 267
Mehay, Yaspal, 133
Mehta, Sir Homi M., 91
Mennonites, 4; Brethren, 235; churches in Canada, 237; Japanese congregations in BC, 180; Korean church in BC, 168
Menri Monastery, 205
Merit, field of, 108,
messiah *(masih maw'ud)*, 72
Methodist, 235; believers, 166; Canadian churches, 170, 237; Chinese believers, 238; church in BC, 214, 238; Korean churches in BC, 168; missionaries, 237
Mewa Singh, 56
Mexico, 202
Mihirig, Ali, 72
Milad un-Nabi, 76
Mindfulness Practice Centre, 10; of Vancouver, 151
Mindroling, 197
Ming Pao Daily News, 234
Mipham Jamyang Gyatso, 198
Mission (BC), 145
Miyamae-roshi, 220, 221
Mohan, Arvinder, 29, 30
Mon (ethnic), 134
monastery, 108, 134, 136, 138, 154, 158, 186, 193, 194, 195, 198, 203, 204, 205, 206, 222, 260, 270
monks: Canadian-born, 115; of Chinese Buddhism, 255, 261, 263, 266, 270, 276, 277; of Daoism, 254; of Hinduism, 23, 33; of Japanese Buddhism, 221; of Kabir sect, 33; of Korean Buddhism, 175; of Lao and Thai Buddhism, 108, 109, 110, 111, 112, 113, 114, 115, 116, 118, 120, 276; novice, 115, 116, 119, 136, 137, 148, 154, 156, 158, 159; of Ramakrishna Order, 23; of Sri Lankan and Myanmar Buddhism, 125, 126, 127, 128, 129, 130, 131, 132, 133, 135, 136; of Tibetan Buddhism, 184, 188, 190, 194, 203, 204, 206; of Vietnamese Buddhism, 10, 142, 144, 145, 146, 147, 149, 153, 154, 155, 156, 158, 159. *See also* Mahayana, monks; Theravada, monks; *sangha*
Montreal, 37, 115, 116, 119, 166, 193; Tibetan Buddhist group, 184
Moon, Sun Myung, 177
mosque (masjid), 9, 70; *jami' masjid* (assembly mosque), 68. *See also* Shia; Sunni
Mount Tuam, 190, 191
Mountain Rain Zen Community, 11, 223
Moy, Lin-shin, 253
Muhammad (prophet), 66, 77, 80
Muharram, 75
Muharram Blood Donation Clinic, 75
Mui Ming-to (梅明道), 253
multiculturalism, 3, 5, 11, 12, 13, 35, 36, 37, 38, 56, 82, 137, 239, 271, 276; official policy of multiculturalism in 1971, 3, 12, 48, 54, 124
Mumbai, 85, 93, 94, 101
Murugan (deity), 24, 25
Muslim, 6, 9, 10, 64, 65, 66, 67, 68, 69, 70, 71, 72, 73, 74, 75, 76, 78, 79, 80, 81, 89, 90, 97, 121; Canadians, 77, 80, 276; community, 64, 74, 81, 89; Muslims in British Columbia, 64, 76, 80
Muslim Sports Association, 70
Muslim Student Association (MSA), 70
Myanmar, 108, 124, 126, 133, 134, 135, 136, 137, 138, 276; Lower Burma, 134; Myanmar Buddhism, 11, 134, 135; Myanmar Buddhists, 124, 135, 135, 137, 138

Nagpur, 133
Nalandabodhi International, 104, 193
Namdroling, 199
Namgyal, Lungrig, 200
Namo Buddha Publications, 195
Nanaimo (BC), 77, 110, 113, 145, 149, 165, 171, 204, 258
Nanak (Sikh Guru), 25
Nangzhig Monastery, 204
Nanhua Monastery, 265
Narayanan, Vasudha, 20
Naropa University, 193
Nelson (BC), 201, 258
Nepal, 194, 196, 202
Nepalis: population, 2
New Delhi, 198
New Kadampa Tradition (NKT), 203, 204, 206, 207

New Westminster, 5, 46, 165, 169, 171, 180, 237, 241
New Westminster Free Evangelical Church, 180
New York, 32, 96, 97, 256, 263, 264, 265
Nga Bích Nguyễn, 141
Ngawang Kunga, 184
Ngawang Kunga Thegchen Palbar Trinley Samphel Wanggi Gyalpo, 187
Ngor: lineage of the Sakya, 184; tradition, 187
Nhó Chùa, 141
Nichiren Buddha Hokkekyō Dharma Centre, 226
Nichiren Daishonin, 223, 225; Buddhist precepts, 226; High Priest of, 226; Nichiren-shōshū, 224, 225, 226; Nichiren-shū, 224
Nicholson, Jim, 254
Nihon Bukkyō-kai, 213
Ningbo (China), 238
Noble Eightfold Path to enlightenment, 131
Non-Sectarian School *(rigs med)*, 206
North America, 2, 70, 81, 89, 92, 93, 95, 96, 100, 101, 110, 115, 125, 177, 185, 188, 190, 191, 192, 193, 195, 218, 219, 241, 242, 251, 256
North Delta (BC), 5, 49
North Henan mission, 238
North Road (Burnaby and Coquitlam), 5, 163
North Vancouver (BC), 77, 93, 94, 99, 100, 145, 173, 175
Northern Treasure: lineage, 198; tradition, 198
Nova Scotia, 186, 195
nuns: Buddhist from Taiwan, 3; of Chinese Buddhism, 261, 262, 266, 268, 270, 278; of Korean Buddhism, 177; of Korean Catholic, 174, 175; of Thai and Lao Buddhism, 115; of Tibetan Buddhism, 189, 203, 206; of Vietnamese Buddhism, 144, 146, 148, 154, 155, 156, 158, 159, 277. *See also* monks; *sangha*
Nyingma School, 187, 194, 198, 199; lamas, 197; lineage, 193; masters, 192, 198; school, 190; sect, 200; tradition, 193, 197, 199

O'Shihan Cultural Organization, 99

Oakridge Seventh-day Adventist Church, 171
Ogyen Tulku, 197
Okanagan Valley (BC), 29, 30
Okayama Prefecture, 226
Ontario, 2, 34, 91, 112, 115, 134, 163, 184, 227, 254
Operation Bluestar, 56, 57
Order of Buddhist Contemplatives, 222
ordination, 107, 114, 115, 119, 121, 155, 216, 220
Oregon, 116
Osho, Eshin John Godfrey, 219, 220
Ottawa, 85, 112, 114
Overseas Chinese Bible Fellowship, 241

Pacific Grace Chinese Church, 235
Pacific Grace Mission Chapel, 236
Pacific Interfaith Fellowship Association, 94
Pakistan, 64, 67, 72, 73, 74, 77, 92, 94, 99, 134. *See also* Pakistani
Pakistan-Canada Association (PCA), 67
Pakistani, 67, 69; Pakistani population, 2; people, 8, 9. *See also* Pakistan
Paldi (BC), 46
Palyul, 199; lineage, 197
Pandya, Rajnikant, 92
Pannabhaso, U, 135
Parikh, Vastupal, 35
Park, Sin-il, 170
Parsis. *See* Zoroastrians
Parvati (deity), 23, 25, 30, 31
Passano, Ajahn, 115
Pavri, Jamshed K., 85, 91
Pek, Daniel Unsok, 165, 182
Penor Rinpoche, 197
Pentecostal: Korean churches in BC, 168
Pentecostal Assemblies of Canada, 168, 172
Penticton (BC), 30
Persians, 85, 86, 89
Peterson, Joseph, 97
Pha-bong-kha-pa, 201, 202
Philadelphia, 138
Philippines, 8, 64. *See also* Filipinos
Phouangphanh Mixayphon, Ajahn, 116
Phra Dhammakaya, 122
Phra Santidhammo, 114
Phra That Luang, 118
Phra Walaison, 118
Phước Long (temple), 141, 145

Phyu Win Noronha, 135
Piyadhammo, Venerable, 128
Pluralism, 38, 80; folk, 36
Po Lam Buddhist Association, 268
Po Yuen Taoist Centre Society, 251, 252, 253
Port Coquitlam (BC), 5, 72, 258
Port Moody (BC), 170, 258
Port Moody Pacific Grace Chinese Church, 236
precepts: *dasa sil* (ten precepts), 126; eight precepts, 130
Prefecture of rNga ba (Northern Sichuan), 204
Preliminary Practices (Kagyü), 190, 194, 199, 200, 204
Presbyterian, 235; believers, 166, 239; church in Canada, 167, 172, 178, 237, 238; Korean believers, 166, 167; Korean churches in BC, 168
primeval spontaneous realization, 197
Prince George (BC), 50, 203, 223
Prince Rupert (BC), 47, 48, 223
Princeton (BC), 115, 277
Prophet Muhammad Day, 76
propriety (禮), 267
proselytization, 73, 74, 230
Protestant, 236; believers, 10; Canadian churches, 238; Chinese, 234, 236, 278; Chinese churches in BC, 234, 235; churches, 235, 236, 244; Japan's Christians, 179; Korean churches in BC, 174, 175; Koreans, 166, 172; Protestant Christianity, 163, 236; Protestant Christians, 164
Punjab, 32, 43, 46, 51, 52, 55, 56, 57, 72. *See also* Punjabi
Punjab Buddhist Vihara Society, 134
Punjabi, 17, 59, 65, 134; ethnic communities, 23; immigrants, 54, 58; language, 28; population, 20; Punjabi Bazaar, 5; Punjabi Market, 5; Punjabis, 8, 48; Sikh believers, 19. *See also* Punjab
Pure Land, 213, 223, 262, 264, 268; Buddhism, 142, 213, 277; Buddhist groups, 212; rites, 260; Shin Buddhism, 214; Shin Buddhist, 213, 215; Shin Buddhist group, 214; Shin Buddhist temples, 214, 215; teachings, 263; temples, 8; tradition, 217
Pure Land Great Compassion Repentance, 267
Pure Teaching of the Pure Land. *See* Jōdo Shinshū

Qiu, Changchun, 252
Qualicum Beach (BC), 199
Quebec, 117, 238; Tibetan communities, 184
Quesnel (BC), 35
Qur'an, 64, 65

Rabten *(rab brtan)*, Lama, 194
racism, 4, 54, 94
Radha, 23, 30, 31; group, 21; lineage, 21; organization, 20; Radha House, 29; Radha Yoga and Eatery, 12, 21; Swami Radha group, 4
Radha Shivananda, 19, 20, 31, 33. *See* Radha; Swami
Rae, Shobha, 32
Raja Bear Creek Hall, 133
Ram, Khushi, 133
Ram Krishna Mandir Vedic Cultural Society, 1, 29
Ramadan, 71, 76
Ramayana, 23, 24, 27, 28
Ranchi (India), 22
Rangoon (*see* Yangon)
Ravidas, Guru. *See* guru
refugee, 72, 107, 110, 111, 116, 118, 137, 144, 177, 184, 185, 200, 240
Regina, 118
rehat maryada (code of conduct), 35, 45, 62
Reiyūkai, 226
relocation: internment camps, 213, 227; of Japanese Canadian in British Columbia, 3
repentance rites, 266
Revival Church, 171
Richardson, Joseph I., 275
Richmond (BC), 1, 2, 5, 24, 26, 29, 68, 77, 93, 94, 96, 115, 145, 165, 174, 188, 189, 194, 196, 197, 213, 214, 234, 236, 243, 258, 263, 269, 270; Asian population, 2; Richmond Chinese Evangelical Free Church, 1; Richmond Food Bank, 76; Richmond Mosque, 68, 71, 75; Richmond Muslim School, 69
righteousness (義), 267
Rimay Tsar Tsar Chokor Namgyal Ling Centre, 196
Rinzai, 218; Rinzaiji, 219

Rite of Severance, 190
Ritthi Tirajitto, Ajahn, 114
rituals, 7, 11; burial grounds, 92; burial rituals, 68, 70, 75, 114, 119, 155; Feast Offering ritual *(tshogs)* of Vajrayogini, 188, 200; Hindu fire ritual *(havan)*, 32; initiation of T'ien Tao, 257; *puja*, 18, 24, 25, 129, 130, 131, 138; ritual practices *(sgrub grwa)*, 204; Sky Burial, 88; Tibetan Buddhist initiation, 195; Zoroastrian initiation, 88, 92, 95, 97, 98, 101. *See also* initiation
River Elegy, 242
Roman Catholic, 10, 236, 246; Asian believers in British Columbia, 174-75, 181, 273; believers, 163, 237; Canadian Church, 238; Chinese believers, 234, 236, 237; Chinese organization, 236; church, 48, 174; Church in Korea, 174; churches in Canada, 173, 175, 234, 236, 238; English Canadian believers, 238; faith, 174; Filipino believers in British Columbia, 8, 175; Korean believers, 164-65, 173-74; Laotian believers in British Columbia, 111, 175; Masses, 8; parishes in British Columbia, 175; Vietnamese believers, 151
Royal Thai Consulate General, 109
Russ, A.E., 237
Russian: language, 125, 171

sacred space, 43, 44, 51, 57, 88, 97, 107, 114
Safari-bir (small, travel-sized manuscripts), 43
Sai, Ken, 136, 137
Saiva Siddhanta tradition, 26
Sakya, 184, 188, 206; lineage of, 187; monastery, 188; tradition, 188
Sakya Tsechen Thubten Ling Centre, 188
Sakyong Jamgön Mipham Rinpoche, 193
Saltspring Island (BC), 190, 191, 223
Salvation Army, 269; building, 266; church, 69; Korean congregation in BC, 168
San Francisco, 2, 5, 29, 55, 126, 127, 129, 252, 256
San Jose (CA), 101
San Juan Island (WA), 188
Sandhi, Kulwant, 133

Sangam Educational and Cultural Society of BC. *See* Then India Sanmarga Ikya Sangam Educational and Cultural Society
sangha, 135, 154, 158, 221, 264; novices: at Burmese temple, 116; of Myanmar Buddhism, 136, 137; of Thai and Lao Buddhism, 115, 119; of Vietnamese Buddhism, 148, 154, 156, 158, 159. *See also* monks, nuns
Sanskrit, 18, 24, 32, 125, 128, 196, 197, 213
Sant Nirankari Mission, 31
Santy Sisombath, Ajahn, 116, 117, 118, 119, 121
Sappakittipakorn, Manote, 109
Saranatissa, Puliyankulame, 131, 132
Sasaki, Senju, 213
Saudi Arabia, 68, 69
Savitr (deity), 18, 32
schools, 68, 76, 155, 172, 186, 187, 193, 216, 240, 269; for children in Fiji, 24; for Punjabi children, 52; religious, 1. *See also* Sunday school
Scotland, 256
Sea to Sky Retreat Centre, 198
Sea-Land Assembly, 261
Seattle, 19, 23, 25, 27, 32, 93, 113, 115, 120, 227
Second World War, 179, 213, 224, 227, 233, 234, 235, 237, 238, 240, 245, 278
Sedona (AZ), 177
Seelawimala, Madawala, Venerable, 126, 127
Seichō No Ie, 226
Seisan Jōdoshū: believers from Japan, 218; temple, 217
Self-Realization Fellowship, 22
selfless giving, 108; *seva* (selfless service), 51, 52, 59
Senaratne, Kirthi, 126, 128, 132
sense of shame (恥), 267
Seogwangsa, 5, 175, 176
Seoul, 172
Sera Monastery, 203
Sevaratnakam Sadhu Kuppuswami, 24
Seventh-day Adventist church, 168, 171, 235; North American Division, 235; Seventh-day Adventist General Conference, 235
Shahrvīnī, Mehrabān, 99

Shambhala Centre, 199
Shambhala Organization, 185, 192, 193, 194, 203, 206
Shangpa Kagyü, 189, 191; lineage, 190
Shangpa Valley branch: of the Kagyü, 189
Sharma, Darshan, 17
Sharma, Pandit Rajpal, 25
Shastri, Jagdish, 33
Shastri, Pandit Gian Chandje, 33
Shawangunk Mountains, 263
Shechen Monastery, 198
Shedra (monastic university), 193
Sheepshanks, John, 237
Sheng Yen, 263, 264, 265
Sherab Chamma Ling Tibetan Bön Buddhist Centre, 11, 204
Sherab Lodro, 194
Sherab Marwa (deity), 204
Shia, 71, 72, 74, 75, 76, 77, 81, 87, 90, 91; mosques, 9
Shia Imami Ismaili Muslims, 76; community, 77
Shia Muslim Community of British Columbia (SMCBC), 65, 75, 76, 80
Shin Araham, 134
Shinran Shōnin Memorial Service, 216
Shinto, 181
Shinzanji Heart Mountain Temple, 11, 220, 230
Shiva (deity), 17, 21, 23, 25, 26, 30, 31, 34
Shivananda: Shivananda Ashram, 31; tradition, 12
Shorinji Kempo: karate classes, 217
Shree Mahalakshmi Temple, 28, 29
Shree Sanatan Dharam Ramayana Mandali of Fiji, 4, 23
Shri Durga Bhameshwari Mandir, 26; Sichuan, 192, 197, 198, 204, 238
Siddhartha's Intent, 198
Sik Yin-tak, 261
Sikh: *Adi Granth*, 33; *ardas* (Sikh prayer), 43; believers, 3, 6, 8, 19, 43, 44, 45, 47, 48, 49, 50, 51, 52, 53, 54, 55, 56, 57, 58, 59, 60, 205, 275; groups, 3; increase of Sikh immigrants in British Columbia, 47; migrations, 4; organizations, 8; settlement of Sikh immigrants in the North Coast region of Canada, 44, 47; Sikh community, 1, 43, 45, 46, 47, 48, 49, 51, 53, 56, 60, 64, 67, 81, 276; Sikh communities in British Columbia, 46, 53, 57, 59; Sikkim, 195
Simmons, Alan B., 4
Simon Fraser University, 32, 80, 275, 277
sin, 157, 158, 239
Sindh, 72, 76, 81; Sindhis, 75, 77
Sing Tao Daily, 234
Singapore, 48, 129, 252, 261
Singh, Arjun, 55, 56
Singh, Bela, 55, 56
Singh, Giani Harnam, 44
Singh, Gurdit, 54
Singh, Harnam, 55
Singh, Mayo, 45, 46
Singh, Teja, 53
Singhai, Gyan Chand, 34
Sino-American Buddhist Association, 265
Sipa Gyalmo (deity), 204
Sirinivasa, Kumbalgoda, Venerable, 129, 130
Sito, Harreson, 151
Six Yogas of Naropa, 191
Six Yogas of Nigumas, 191
Sleep Yoga, 191
Snyder, Keith, 217, 218
social events: of Chinese community, 264; of Japanese Buddhism, 215; of Lao community, 110; of Zoroastrians, 95, 99
Sōka Gakkai, 10, 180, 224, 229, 277; Sōka Gakkai International (SGI), 224, 225, 226, 230; Vancouver Culture Centre, 224, 231
Somaratana, Venerable, 128
Sona, Ajahn, Venerable, 115, 128, 129
Sonada (West Bengal), 190
Sōtōshū, 218, 223; lineage, 218; Sōtō Zen, 277; Sōtō Zen ceremonies, 223; Sōtō Zen meditation, 222
South Asians, 64, 65, 66; ethic segregation rule, 4; formation of BC Asian societies between late 19th and early 20th centuries, 3; immigrants, 4, 18, 92; Muslims, 77; population, 2, 20; Sikhs, 52
South Korea. *See* Korea
South Okanagan Hindu Temple, 29, 30, 31
Southeast Asia, 7, 107, 134, 142, 196, 233, 240, 241; Southeast Asian population, 2
Southern Baptist Convention, 168, 172
Southwestern Qinghai, 199
Spain, 202

spirit-writing texts, 258
Squamish Nation, 205
Sri Ganesh Temple Society, 26
Sri Lanka, 11, 19, 26, 64, 124, 125, 126, 127, 128, 129, 130, 131, 132, 133, 134, 137, 138, 205, 260, 277; ethnic communities, 23; groups, 277; Hindu, 25; Sinhalese, 125, 129, 132, 133, 136, 137
Sri Lankan: Buddhism, 11, 124; Buddhists, 8, 124, 126, 129, 135, 137, 138, 139; chronicles, 125; people, 107, 133; population, 2; Tamils, 8
Sri Lankan Surrey Buddhist Vihara, 136
Sri Murugan Temple, 26, 37
Sri Sri Radha Madana-Mohan Temple, 29
Srila Prabhupada, 5
St. Andrew Kim Catholic Church, 173, 174, 175
St. Francis Xavier Church, 174, 236
St. Joseph's Parish in Vancouver, 175
St. Mark's College, 236
St. Mary's Anglican, 27, 28
St. Theresa's Parish in Burnaby, 236
status recognition, 108,
Steveston Buddhist Temple, 214, 215
Sufi, 65
Sultan Muhammad Shah Aga Khan III, 77
Sumatra, 134
Summerland (BC), 29, 31
Sun Suzhen (Madam Sun), 255
Sun, John, 239
Sunday school, 92, 131, 136, 166, 216, 240
Sunni, 70, 72, 74, 76; mosques, 9; Muslim, 67, 68, 71; *ummah*, 70
Sunshine Coast (BC), 3, 126
Surmang Monastery, 192, 193
Surrey (BC), 2, 5, 11, 18, 24, 25, 29, 30, 33, 48, 49, 50, 53, 57, 58, 59, 69, 70, 72, 77, 110, 116, 117, 127, 128, 132, 133, 135, 136, 137, 145, 147, 148, 165, 168, 171, 172, 174, 175, 176, 177, 180, 225, 234, 269
Surrey Buddhist Vihara (SBV), 35, 124, 126, 127, 128, 129, 130, 131, 133, 135, 138
Surrey-Delta area, 49, 69
Surrey-East, 69
Suzhou, 238
Swami, 29; American, 26; German, 20, 276
Syed, Itrath, 71

Taewon, Kim, 169

Tagalog, 8, 175
Taiwan, 134, 158, 195, 196, 202, 233, 234, 235, 239, 240, 241, 245, 249, 255, 256, 258, 263, 264, 265, 269, 270, 271; immigrants, 249, 269; population, 2; Taipei, 263; Taiwanese people, 196
Taiwanese/Hong Kong Pure Land Ling Yen Mountain Temple, 5
Tajikistan, 77, 89
Takshila Maha Buddhist Vihara, 133
Talent Vision, 234
Tâm Hạnh, 150, 151
Tamil: language, 24, 26, 28; people, 19, 137
Tangong Temple, 250
Tantra (Vietnamese Mật Tông), 142; Path of Tantra, 200; Tantric cycles, 194, 201; Tantric practice, 202; Tantric sādhana, 198; Tibetan, 190. *See also* Buddhism
Taoist Tai Chi Society of Canada, 253, 254
Tara (deity), 196
Tara, Lama, 191
Tata, Bella, 99
Tata, Ratanji Dadabhoy, 97
Tawatchai Keuket, 114
Tây Ninh (province),151
Taylor, Charles, 37, 38
Teacher Sang-ngag Yeshe, 199
teaching lineage, 113, 114, 120,
Temple of Divine Light, 21, 22
Tenchi Kane No Kami (deity), 227
Tenrikyō, 180, 181, 226
Tenth Avenue Alliance Church, 239
Tenzin Osel Rinpoche, Lama, 202
Terrace (BC), 50, 223
Texas, 88, 113
Thai Buddhist Society, 112
Thai Community Association of British Columbia, 109, 112
Thai Forest Tradition, 111, 114, 115
Thai people, 8, 107, 108, 109, 110, 111, 112, 113, 114, 115, 116, 117, 118, 120, 122. *See also* Thailand
Thai Wat Yan, 116, 121
Thailand, 107, 108, 109, 110, 111, 112, 113, 115, 118, 120, 128, 133, 134, 154, 195, 260, 261, 277. *See also* Thai people
Then India Sanmarga Ikya Sangam Educational and Cultural Society, 24
Theravada, 125, 193; Buddhism, 107, 116, 134, 135, 262; Buddhist, 107, 108, 132,

135; monks, 108, 117, 119, 121; Theravadins, 107
Thích Chân Hoà, 145
Thích Mãn Giác (Huyền Không), 141
Thích Nguyên Thảo, Venerable Master, 12, 146
Thích Nguyên Tịnh, 145
Thích Nguyên Trí, 145
Thích Nhất Hạnh, 151, 152, 153
Thích Nữ Tịnh Pháp, 146
Thích Nữ Trí Nghiêm, 148
Thích Pháp Ấn, 149
Thích Tâm Châu, 145
Thích Thiện Nghị, 149
Thích Tịnh Trí, 148
Thích Viên Giác, 147
Thiền Tôn Buddhist Association, 145
Thilawunta, U, 135
Thrangu Vajra Vidhya Buddhist Association, 194
Three Pure Ones, 254
Thu Văn Đặng, 152
Thubten Choling Dharma Centre, 202
Thubten Zopa Rinpoche, 202
Thunder Bay (ON), 114-15, 186
Thupten Lungtok Namgyal Thinley, 201-2
Tibet, 154, 184, 185, 187, 188, 189, 191, 194, 195, 197, 204, 206, 277; government in exile, 200, 205, 260; population, 2
Tibetan, 6, 188; groups, 81; language, 193, 194, 200, 202, 204
Tibetan Buddhism, 3, 10, 184, 185, 186, 189, 190, 191, 192, 195, 197, 202, 203, 205, 206, 277; lineages of, 186; oral lineage *(bka' rgyud)* of, 189; organizations of, 6, 253; people, 10, 184, 192; as practised by Euro-Canadians in British Columbia, 3; School of Tibetan Buddhism, 184; Tantras, 190; teacher of, 187; Way, 185
Tibetan Buddhist Clear Light Retreat Centre, 199
Tilopa Buddhist Centre, 203
Tipitaka, 125, 133
Togal, 194
Toisan, 249, 254
Tokyo, 179, 223
Toronto, 28, 93, 100, 101, 116, 119, 134, 165, 201, 253, 254
Traling Monastery, 199
Trần Nhân Tôn (king), 142

Trekchö, 194
Trí Nghiêm, 149
Tri-City Islamic Centre, 72
Trijang Rinpoche, 203
Trinley Samphel Wanggi Gyalpo, 187
Trúc Lâm (sect), 142
Trungpa Rinpoche, 192
trustworthiness (信), 267
Truth Monthly, 234, 244
Tsar Tsar Monastery, 196
Tsenjur Rinpoche, 190, 191
Tsong Khapa, 187, 200; *Treatise*, 200
Tsugphud, Geshe, 205
Tulku Karzang, 199
Tun, Mitzi, 136
Tung, Robert Ho, 260
Tung Lin Kok Yuen Canada Society, 260, 261; Tung Lin Kok Yuen, 262, 263, 265, 268
turban, 47
tutelary deities, 190
Tzu Chi Foundation Canada, 269, 270, 278

U Pannao Ba Tha, 135
U Sandha, 135
Ucluelet, 227
Uganda, 77
Ulveston (England), 203
ummah, 11, 64, 65, 66, 67, 68, 70, 71, 72, 73, 74, 76, 77, 78, 79, 80, 81, 82
Uncommon Lamdre: teachings, 188
Unification Church, 177
United Buddhist Vietnamese Association (UBVNA), 143
United Church of Canada, 165, 166, 167, 170, 172, 180, 235, 237, 239
United Church of Christ in Japan, 179-80
United Kingdom, 93, 134
United States, 3, 4, 12, 21, 24, 29, 91, 93, 94, 98, 112-13, 114, 126, 134, 143, 145, 158, 177, 204, 212, 214, 219, 222, 223, 228, 230, 235, 242, 252, 258, 278
United Vietnamese Buddhist Association, 150
Universal Buddhist Temple (世界佛教會), 260, 265; as donor for this book, ix
Universal Worthy Bodhisattva, 266
universalism, 20, 22, 26, 36
University of British Columbia, 4, 80, 182, 188, 200, 223, 236, 261, 275; Asian

Centre, 188; Department of Asian Studies, 261; first class in Buddhism in 1964, 4; Institute of Asian Research, 200, 261, 275; Medical School, 33; Museum of Anthropology, 80
University of the Fraser Valley: South Asian Studies, 11
University of Victoria, 4, 221
Upananda, Dedunupitiye, Venerable, 125
Urdu, 73, 81

Vajradhatu. *See* Shambhala Organization
Value Creation Society. *See* Sōka Gakkai
Vạn Hạnh Temple, 149, 150
Vancouver, 2, 3, 4, 5, 11, 19, 20, 21, 22, 23, 24, 26, 28, 29, 31, 32, 35, 44, 54, 55, 67, 68, 69, 77, 80, 88, 91, 93, 94, 96, 99, 100, 109, 110, 111, 112, 114, 115, 116, 126, 128, 135, 141, 144, 145, 151, 152, 163, 164, 165, 167, 170, 171, 173, 174, 175, 177, 179, 181, 186, 187, 188, 190, 191, 192, 193, 194, 195, 196, 197, 198, 199, 200, 201, 204, 205, 206, 214, 217, 218, 219, 222, 224, 225, 227, 228, 229, 233, 235, 236, 237, 239, 241, 242, 243, 244, 245, 250, 252, 253, 254, 255, 256, 258, 259, 260, 261, 265, 266, 269, 275, 278; anti-Asian riots, 53; Asian Population, 2; Asian Religious Groups and its location property, 3; East 49th Avenue, 265; Muslims, 80; South Vancouver, 48, 50, 53, 58, 263, 269; West 49th Avenue, 197
Vancouver Buddhist Church, 3, 214, 215
Vancouver Chinese Alliance Church (VCAC), 239
Vancouver Chinese Baptist Church, 239
Vancouver Chinese Seventh-day Adventist Church, 235
Vancouver Full Gospel Church, 168
Vancouver International Progress Society, 270
Vancouver Islamic Centre, 68
Vancouver Island, 3, 11, 27, 149, 173, 199, 201, 202, 204, 221, 223, 226, 227, 258; Asian Religious Groups and location, 3; settlement of Sikh immigrants in Canada, 44. *See also* Comox Valley, Duncan, Galiano Island, Halfmoon Bay, Nanaimo, Paldi, Saltspring Island, Sunshine Coast, Victoria

Vancouver Japanese Gospel Church, 180
Vancouver Khalsa Diwan Society (Vancouver KDS), 46, 57
Vancouver Korean Association, 165
Vancouver Korean Presbyterian Church, 166, 167, 168
Vancouver Korean United Church, 166, 167
Vancouver Mission House, 73
Vancouver Seventh Day Adventist Church, 169
Vancouver Zen Sangha, 223
Veda Bharati, Swami, 34
Vedanta Society, 19, 23, 37, 38
Vedas, 18, 27, 32
Vedic Cultural Society, 1, 29
vegetarian (*zhai* 齋), 253
Venerable Mother, 255, 256, 258
Vernon Buddhist Temple, 214
Vertovec, Steven, 27, 37
Victoria, 2, 3, 11, 28, 29, 35, 69, 77, 91, 110, 145, 148, 149, 150, 165, 171, 173, 174, 192, 193, 199, 203, 220, 221, 229, 230, 233, 234, 237, 250, 251, 253, 258; first wave of Asian immigration, 3
Victoria Hindu Parishad, 28, 29
Victoria Korean Church, 171
Victoria Nikkei Cultural Society, 220
Victoria Zen Centre, 221, 230
Vietnam, 134, 142, 143, 147, 149, 150, 153, 154, 155, 157, 159, 213, 218; War, 4; War resisters in the 1960s-70s, 4
Vietnamese: Catholics, 151; groups, 9; immigration to Canada, 143-44; language, 174, 258, 267; monk, 10; people, 8, 141, 145, 148, 151, 154, 156, 157, 158, 159, 256; population, 2; *thiền*, 151, 153
Vietnamese Buddhism, 11, 142, 143, 150, 152, 158, 159; Buddhist temples in Canada, 9; Buddhists, 145, 151, 277
Vietnamese Buddhist Youth Association, 151
vihara *(vihāra)*, 125, 127, 128, 129, 130, 131, 132, 133, 135, 139
Viradhammo, Ajahn, 115
Virgin Mary, 21
Vishnu (deity), 27; Narayana, 27
Vishva Hindu Parishad, 13, 23, 26, 29, 31, 32, 33, 37
Vivekananda Vedanta Society, 4, 22, 23, 32

Waddell, Augustin, 185
Wakayama, 217
Waldman, Anne, 185
Wang, Chongyang, 252
Wang, Thomas, 244
war: First World War, 43; Second World War, 179, 213, 224, 227, 233, 234, 235, 237, 238, 240, 245, 278; War Measures Act, 213
Washington, 4, 24, 37, 93, 109, 188, 235
Wat Atammayatarama, 113, 114, 120
Wat Lao, 116, 117, 118, 119, 120, 121, 122
Wat Paa Nanachaat (International Forest Monastery), 115
Wat Phra Dhammakaya, 115, 120
Wat Washington Buddhavanaram, 109, 113, 114
Wat Yanviriya, 112, 113, 116, 117, 118, 120, 122
Wei Yang Sect, 265
Wenquan, Wang, 242
West Bengal, 190
West China mission, 238
West Coast, 5, 37, 179, 213
West Sichuan, 196, 197
West Vancouver, 3, 4, 94, 95-96, 99, 100, 145, 170, 196; Buddhist group, 3;
West, Irma, 128
Western Canada, 51, 69, 73, 99
Western Canada Chinese Catholic Living Camp (WCCCLC), 237
Whistler, 258
White, Edward, 237
White Cloud Temple, 254
Williams Creek (BC), 237
Willingdon Church, 171
Willpower Institute, 113, 120, 122
Won Buddhism, 176, 177, 180, 181; Won Buddhists, 176
Woo, Jong Chul, 166
World Annual Buddhist Youth meetings, 151
World Federation of Khoja Shia Ithna Ashari Muslims, 75
World Fellowship of Buddhists (WFB), 143
World Parliament of Religions, 19, 125
World Partnership Walk, 79
World Religions Conference (Ahmadiyya), 73
World Sikh Organization (WSO), 57
World Zoroastrian Organization (WZO), 93

Xing, Yun, 270
Xu, Yun, 265

Yamantaka, 200, 202
Yamazaki, Toyomi, 228, 229
Yamazaki, Tsuneo, 228, 229
Yang, Paul, 172
Yangdak Heruka, 190
Yashodhara Ashram, 21, 34
Yau, Timothy, 252
Yazd (Iran), 87, 95
Yen Wo clan building, 250
Yeshe, Lama Thubten, 202
Yeshe Khorlo Centre, 199
Yitung Buddhist Temple, 268
Yogananda, Paramahamsa, 19, 22; Yogananda group, 37
Yoido Full Gospel Church, 172
Yoido Full Gospel Church Mission, 168
YongDong, Geshe, 204
Yuan, Zhiming, 242, 244
Yuan Xuan Xueyuan, 252, 253

Zakariya, Mohammed, 80
Zazep Tulku, 201
Zen Buddhism, 3, 218, 221, 223, 277; centre, 219, 222; Chan, 260, 267, 268; Chan Buddhist organization, 263; Chan meditation, 263, 264, 267; diffusion of Zen in British Columbia, 3; Fundamentals of Zen Practice, 221; groups, 229; meditation, 219, 221; school of Buddhism, 218; teacher, 219; *Thiền* sect, 142; Zen, 213, 218; Zen Buddhist groups, 212; Zen Buddhists, 230; Zen organizations, 221, 223, 231. *See also* Buddhism
Zen Centre of Vancouver (ZVC), 4, 218, 219, 220
Zhang, Tianran, 234
Zhao, Shichang, 239
Zoroastrian Centre, 94
Zoroastrian Society of British Columbia (ZSBC), 85, 90, 92, 93, 94, 95, 96, 98, 99, 100, 101
Zoroastrian Trust Funds of British Columbia, 91, 92

Zoroastrianism, 86, 87, 89, 90, 95, 96, 97, 98, 99, 100, 275; temple, 4

Zoroastrians, 85, 88; diaspora of Zoroastrians to British Columbia, 89; Iranian, 6, 90, 93; Parsis, 86, 87, 89, 90, 91, 92, 93, 94, 95, 96, 97, 98, 99, 100, 101, 276; temples, 4

Zuicho, Hashimoto, 217, 218

Zuru monastery, 201; Zuru Ling, 207; Zuru Ling Tibetan Buddhist Society, 201